Teachers' Unions and Education Reform in Comparative Contexts

Teachers' unions have long been controversial and divisive organizations, but criticism and distrust of them may be at an all-time high. This volume considers the prevailing assumption that unions successfully block change in education because they are primarily motivated to protect members' interests. It challenges the conceptualization of teacher union motivation and provides a more nuanced account of unions' interests, power, and impact.

Through a series of international cases from the United States, Finland, and the Canton of Zürich, this volume examines the hot-button issue of performance-related pay reform and compensation. It argues that a better understanding of the union-management relationship may be the key to securing more meaningful change and reform. It will be of use to scholars, policy-makers, union leaders, teachers, and citizens who are interested in the possibilities for the union-management relationship, rather than the limitations.

Lindsay M. Whorton received her DPhil at the University of Oxford, UK and served as Legislative Director to Colorado Senator Mike Johnston. She lives in Washington, DC.

Routledge Research in Education Policy and Politics

The Routledge Research in Education Policy and Politics series aims to enhance our understanding of key challenges and facilitate on-going academic debate within the influential and growing field of Education Policy and Politics.

Books in the series include:

Teacher Education through Active Engagement
Raising the professional voice
Edited by Lori Beckett

Health Education
Critical perspectives
Edited by Katie Fitzpatrick and Richard Tinning

US Education in a World of Migration
Implications for Policy and Practice
Edited by Jill Koyama and Mathangi Subramanian

Student Voices on Inequalities in European Higher Education
Challenges for theory, policy and practice
Edited by Fergal Finnegan, Barbara Merrill and Camilla Thunborg

Social Context Reform
A Pedagogy of Equity and Opportunity
Edited by P. L. Thomas, Brad Porfilio, Julie Gorlewski, and Paul R. Carr

Narrowing the Achievement Gap for Native American Students
Paying the Educational Debt
Edited by Peggy McCardle and Virginia Berninger

Demythologizing Educational Reforms
Responses to the Political and Corporate Takeover of Education
Edited by Arthur T. Costigan and Leslee Grey

The Politics of Compulsive Education
Racism and learner-citizenship
Karl Kitching

Educational Binds of Poverty
The lives of school children
Ceri Brown

Pedagogy, Praxis and Purpose in Education
C. M. Mulcahy, D. E. Mulcahy, and D. G. Mulcahy

Creativity and Democracy in Education
Practices and politics of education through the arts
Jeff Adams and Allan Owens

Teachers' Unions and Education Reform in Comparative Contexts
Lindsay M. Whorton

Teachers' Unions and Education Reform in Comparative Contexts

Lindsay M. Whorton

LONDON AND NEW YORK

First published 2016
by Routledge

2 Park Square, Milton Park, Abingdon, Oxon OX14 4RN
711 Third Avenue, New York, NY 10017, USA

Routledge is an imprint of the Taylor & Francis Group, an informa business

First issued in paperback 2017

Copyright © 2016 Taylor & Francis

The right of Lindsay M. Whorton to be identified as author of this work has been asserted by her in accordance with sections 77 and 78 of the Copyright, Designs and Patents Act 1988.

All rights reserved. No part of this book may be reprinted or reproduced or utilised in any form or by any electronic, mechanical, or other means, now known or hereafter invented, including photocopying and recording, or in any information storage or retrieval system, without permission in writing from the publishers.

Notice:
Product or corporate names may be trademarks or registered trademarks, and are used only for identification and explanation without intent to infringe.

Library of Congress Cataloging-in-Publication Data
CIP data has been applied for.

ISBN: 978-1-138-86018-6 (hbk)
ISBN: 978-1-138-08589-3 (pbk)

Typeset in Sabon
by Apex CoVantage, LLC

Contents

List of Tables and Figures vii
Acknowledgments ix

Introduction 1

PART I
Research Design

1 Teachers' Unions and Education Reform: A Review of the Literature 13

2 Beyond Narrow Assumptions of Interest and Power: A Conceptual Framework 47

3 Research Design, Case Selection, and Methodology 60

PART II
International Cases

4 Finland: History and Context 85

5 Quiet Compromises: Finland's New Salary System 103

6 The Canton of Zürich: History and Context 134

7 Eventually Overcoming Resistance: The MAB System 151

8 Finland and Zürich: Multiple Pathways to Reform 180

PART III
School District Cases

9 Teachers' Unions in the United States: A Sub-National Test   203

10 School District Analysis: A Series of Congruence Tests   224

PART IV
Conclusion

11 Useful Conflict?: Finding the Path to Progress   251

Glossary   267
Appendices   269
Index   287

Tables and Figures

TABLES

2.1	Attitudinal components of the relationship pattern	55
3.1	Case types: strength of union by presence of reform	64
5.1	Preferences related to the new salary system	116
5.2	Perceptions of the locally negotiated component	117
5.3	Perceptions of the performance component (HL)	118
5.4	Perceptions of the task-complexity component (TVA)	119
5.5	Perceptions of OAJ's goals according to various stakeholders	124
5.6	Relationship patterns, Finland	126
6.1	Instruments of direct democracy in Zürich through 1998	139
7.1	Perceptions and preferences of MAB	163
7.2	Relationship pattern between ZLV and policy-makers	170
9.1	School district codes	210
10.1	District.1FL and District.2FL union perceptions and preferences	228
10.2	Cooperative relationship patterns in District.1FL and District.2FL	230
10.3	School district administration preferences and perceptions	240
VI.i	Population sample statistics, Texas and Florida districts	277
VII.i	School district interviewees	280

FIGURES

4.1	OAJ organization and governance	95
4.2	Collective bargaining in the municipal sector	99
5.1	Finland's new salary system (2007)	105
5.2	Allocation of *järjestelyerä* (OVTES, % of Total)	108
5.3	Finland's new salary system reform timeline	111

5.4	OAJ strategy and tactics	115
5.5	OAJ organizational structure	122
7.1	Timeline 1: Delayed realization of a legal mandate	154
7.2	Timeline 2: MAB reform in light of economic drivers	156
7.3	Timeline 3: Early evaluation system developments	159
7.4	Delayed implementation pre- and post-1995	174
8.1	A model of reform outcomes	196
9.1	Rates of school district participation in Texas and Florida	209
9.2	School district governance in Florida and Texas	214
9.3	Multiple timelines of PRP reform	218
10.1	District.1FL timeline	225
10.2	District.2FL timeline	226
10.3	Relationships in the governance triangle in District.2FL	231
10.4	Relationships in the governance triangle in District.1FL	232
10.5	District.3FL timeline	233
10.6	Division in District.3FL (2006–2008)	235
10.7	Timeline for District.6TX's decision to participate in 'DATE II'	238
10.8	District.4TX timeline	242
10.9	District.5TX timeline	243
10.10	Revised typological theory of PRP reform	245

Acknowledgments

My deep gratitude cannot be adequately expressed to all the people who have made this book both possible and personally rewarding.

I am grateful to the Rhodes Trust and the staff at Rhodes House, who made the dreaming spires of Oxford a reality, and to The Fulbright Commission and the Centre for International Mobility (CIMO), who supported my year of research in Finland. The Lois Roth Endowment and Jesus College also generously supported field work costs. Beyond financial support, the staff at the Fulbright Center in Helsinki, along with my host institution, the University of Helsinki, provided a warm welcome into Finnish life and society.

Throughout this project, I have benefited from the mentorship of several advisers. My supervisor, Martin Seelieb-Kaiser, Auli Toom, my host at the University of Helsinki, and Jenny Ozga and Susan Moore Johnson all provided constructive feedback, advice, and encouragement.

Beyond these advisers, I benefited from the advice of countless scholars and other experts in Finland and Zürich who provided invaluable insights as I familiarized myself with the political and cultural contexts of my field sites. I am indebted to all who agreed to be interviewed, contributing their time and knowledge to make this research possible.

I am also grateful to Leslie Colwell, Stephen Danley, Mallory Dwinal, Caitlin Goss, Libby Longino, Sarah Lowe, and Kristine Milburn who read, discussed, and provided useful comments and advice on drafts of this work.

And finally, thank you to my family, whose steady support throughout this journey has been invaluable.

Introduction

"If education were a war, you would be losing it.
If it were a business, you would be driving it into bankruptcy.
If it were a patient, it would be dying."
—Bob Dole, 1996

Following the great tradition of J. Edgar Hoover's "War on Crime," Lyndon B. Johnson's "War on Poverty," and Richard M. Nixon's "War on Drugs," in which it seems that nothing is accomplished without a very public fight, a battle for public education is raging across the United States. Like all of the preceding wars that have dominated US domestic policy, the educational war is presumably focused on eradicating social ills—illiteracy, innumeracy, and educational inequality. However, the war has been framed and waged as a series of proxy battles taking place throughout the country—fights over how teachers earn and keep tenure; how teachers are hired, fired, and compensated; and how students and parents access the school of their choice. Reformers who promote these policy solutions are a diverse group—Republicans and Democrats, practitioners and philanthropists, academics and corporate icons—who believe: that great teachers in every classroom are the key to providing an excellent education to every student, that the status quo is dysfunctional, and that its defenders stand in the way of the reforms that would make the ideal possible.

In the minds of many, the battle lines are clearly drawn; this is a fight between education reformers and their fiercest adversaries—the teachers' unions. In contrast to change-demanding reformers, teachers' unions are dubbed status quo protectors, or what Minnesota Governor Tim Pawlenty called an "education cartel" that "has stood in the way of innovation, reform, and results" (Pawlenty, 2010, n.p.)—"the most formidable obstacles to meaningful and rapid educational reform" (Burns, 2011, n.p.). Many reformers publicly decry teachers' unions' pursuit of "money and power at children's expense" (Pullman, 2012, n.p.), claiming that "for all their rhetoric about 'the children'. . . [unions just want] raises, every year, for jobs they can never lose at schools that need never compete" (Pawlenty, 2010, n.p.). According to reformers, these interests—selfishness and greed—lead unions to oppose accountability; to negotiate collective bargaining agreements that provide strong protections for 'bad teachers' (Dillon, 2008, n.p.; "Unions v. Race to the Top," 2010, n.p.); and to fight for tenure, which according to reformer and former Superintendent of DC Public Schools Michelle Rhee, holds "no educational value for kids" and is the "holy grail of teachers unions" (Rhee, 2010, n.p.).

How, if the evidence for reforms is so great and the need so desperate, are teachers' unions able to block reforms that are in students' best interests? To some, the answer is simple. According to Rhee, it's all interest group politics: "powerful interests put pressure on our elected officials and government institutions to sway or stop change," which has resulted in "a bureaucracy that is focused on the adults instead of the students" (Rhee, 2010, n.p.). For many reformers, this interpretation of the facts has led them to conclude that the only way to reform the system is to remove or weaken those who oppose their vision of change.

Many believe that this is just what is happening—that the battle over education reform has turned into a war on teachers' unions, that reforms advanced with child-centered policy arguments are simply union-busting strategies in disguise:

- When Michelle Rhee took the reins of the District of Columbia Public Schools in 2007, she gained nationwide visibility both for her confrontational style—as evident in the infamous *TIME* magazine cover of broom-wielding Rhee—as well as her unapologetic efforts to weaken tenure, change the way teachers in the district were compensated, and expand school choice. *Newsweek* called her plans a "profound threat to politically powerful teachers' unions nationwide" (Thomas, 2008, n.p.). Then-union President George Parker was resistant to Rhee's reforms because he perceived that they were "just geared to busting the union" (Dillon, 2008, n.p.).
- Throughout his tenure as mayor of New York City, Michael Bloomberg was persistent in his pursuit of aggressive reforms and frequently clashed with the United Federation of Teachers (UFT)—the New York affiliate of the American Federation of Teachers (AFT)—on topics ranging from school closure to school choice to teacher evaluations. Bloomberg's response to the union's concerns was to attempt to "sidestep the union, ignore its demands and take matters into his own hands" (Santos, 2012, n.p.).
- In 2011, Wisconsin Governor Scott Walker signed a bill dramatically altering collective bargaining rights for the state's public employees and requiring them to pay more of their health insurance and pension costs. Walker's bill initiated a spate of legislation that is among the most brashly union-busting action in decades. Debates over the role of public sector unionism, including the role of collective bargaining, were initiated in 17 state capitals across the country (National Conference of State Legislatures, 2011, n.p.).

- In 2014, in *Vergara v. California*, Judge Rolf M. Treu ruled that teachers' tenure and job protections make it more difficult to fire ineffective teachers and that bad teachers "substantially undermine" a student's education and violate her right to a "basic equality of educational opportunity" (Edwards, 2014, n.p.). While Secretary of Education Arne Duncan and Michelle Rhee celebrated the decision as addressing the "broken status quo," teachers' unions "decried the ruling as part of a subversive effort to destroy labor unions" (Edwards, 2014, n.p.).

The debate over *Vergara* has been called the embodiment of the increasingly ugly "national debate over so-called education reform" (Sawchuk, 2014, n.p.). After the decision was announced, Arne Duncan opined, "Sometimes conflict is the starting point on the path to progress" (Duncan, 2014, n.p.). But are the fights that have been raging—and escalating—between reformers and unions over the last decade productive? Are these conflicts the right path to achieving anyone's—reformers' or unions'—desired outcomes?

If the public statements of prominent reformers are any indication, the reformers' view—which has gained increasing traction, visibility, and popularity over the past decade—suggests that teachers' unions, pursuing their economic self-interest, are the reason why essential reforms have gone unrealized and, implicitly, why the 'broken status quo' is so hard to fix. If this is true—if unions are intransigently opposed to reform and unwilling to be part of the solution to what ails the system—then, reformers argue, the only response is to remove the obstacle to change. This view mirrors the account advanced by Terry Moe in *Special Interests: Teachers Unions and America's Schools* (2011). His account joins others in portraying teachers' unions as immovable objects—powerful organizations with fixed, stable, and predictable interests. Moe argues that the immovable object has consistently bested the irresistible force of education reform in the United States. In this paradigm, the only way to reform public education in the United States is to "weaken or eliminate union power over the schools" (Moe, 2006, p. 230).

But what if this paradigm doesn't accurately describe teachers' unions' preferences and power? What if unions don't unequivocally oppose all reform at all times? What if 'non-reform' is explained by something other than union opposition? Any of these scenarios would suggest that there might be different strategies and tactics to accomplish reformers expressed short-term[1] and long-term objectives.[2] It might even be possible that the fighting and name-calling between unions and reformers is actually a distraction from, rather than a solution to, the most pressing problems of public education in the US.

Although there are significant disputes in the literature on teachers' unionism, scholars can agree on one thing—that the existing research is limited, generally inconclusive, and lacks specificity (Goldhaber, 2006; Johnson & Kardos, 2000; Koppich, 2007; Koppich & Callahan, 2009; Malen, 2001; Moe, 2006). Further, they agree that research on teachers' unions is more often shaped by rhetoric and ideology than by inquiry, which has both contributed to and been fuelled by, a dearth of empirical work (Eberts & Stone, 1984; Hoxby, 1996; Johnson & Kardos, 2000; Koppich, 2007; Koppich & Callahan, 2009; Kurth, 1987; Nelson & Gould, 1988). In the absence of empiricism, 'theorizing' often takes an ideologically self-confirming path in which grounding assumptions are not subjected to empirical scrutiny.

The 'unions-block-reform' account—reflected in some academic work, littering the press, and even gracing the silver screen in 2010 with the release of the documentary *Waiting for Superman*—is a great example of this kind of explanation. First, the account posits, but does not test, that teachers' unions are primarily self-interested, and that this self-interest leads them to oppose reforms that threaten their economic security, or those that have been popularly dubbed 'bread-and-butter issues.' Second, it claims that unions are powerful enough to block policies that they oppose. Then, given these assumptions, one can only conclude that unions always oppose and block certain reforms: like changes to how teachers are hired, fired, and compensated. However, predictive rather than explanatory, this account is correlational, not causal. It observes that strong unions and non-reform are often correlated and assumes that union influence is the mitigating factor; it does not attend to the particular causal mechanisms that produce the predicted effects (George & Bennett, 2005; Salmon, 2006). It doesn't explain *how* unions block reform, nor what is happening in the growing number of cases where reform occurs.

Explanations based on correlation are not helpful for choosing a course of action, when one needs to understand what is *actually* happening in a particular case or set of cases. In order to make effective decisions, policy-makers need diagnostic theories—explanations that can actually explain what is happening and how the effect is produced (George & Bennett, 2005). A closer look at the 'irresistible force paradox'[3]—cases in which reform movements and strong teachers' unions have collided—reveals a more complex picture.

Although teachers' unions' reaction to reform could be measured against any number of particular policies, this book will focus on one—performance-related pay (PRP). The decision to focus exclusively on one reform was guided by Geddes' (2003) admonishment that:

> The work that best succeeds in meeting social scientific criteria of evidence and falsifiability, the work that can be used as a solid building block rather than a sand castle, is work that precisely models a set of causal mechanisms and clearly delimits their domain of operation. Scholars can still ask big questions, but only certain kinds of big questions. (as cited in Levi, 2008, p. 122)

Thus, the focus is on a detailed exposition of the particular process of PRP reform across cases. PRP has been implemented in many cases in spite of the presumed opposition of powerful teachers' unions. These 'exceptions' prompt two types of questions, which will guide this research:

- When do such results—performance-related pay reform—occur? Why don't they always? And what role do teachers' unions play in the performance-related pay reform process?
- How do the answers to these problem-oriented questions inform theories of teachers' unions—their preferences and impact on policy-making?

Substantive, problem-driven questions—what is happening here and why?—are often divorced from theory-driven questions—what is the nature of teachers' unionism? However, this inquiry is motivated by both problem-driven and theory-driven questions. Rather than conflicting, these aims are mutually reinforcing.

Chapter 1 will review the literature relevant to this inquiry, focusing on two themes—the immovable object, teachers' unions, and the irresistible force of reform. PRP reform in education will be traced to broader reform dynamics that have characterized both public sector and education reform and restructuring over the past three decades. Namely, the global dynamics of neoliberalism (Harvey, 2007) and New Public Management (NPM) (Hood, 1991) are significant, as efforts to connect teachers' pay more closely to their performance can be linked to these more general reform movements. Then, the second half of Chapter 1 will turn to a closer examination of teachers' unions' preferences and power. Although the research on teachers' unions—their preferences, strength, and power—is limited in important ways, it sits at the nexus of several disciplines. Weaving together cross-disciplinary accounts from industrial relations, political science, and sociology of preferences, strength and power will provide a broader foundation for this inquiry.

Chapter 2 will outline the theoretical framework that guides the inquiry. It draws on Richard E. Walton and Robert B. McKersie's *A Behavioral Theory of Labor Negotiations* (1991) as well as components of F. W. Scharpf's actor-centered institutionalism (ACI) (Scharpf, 1997, 2000). In contrast to the rational choice assumptions—of stable and predictable preferences guided by self-interest—that are foundational to the unions-block-reform account, these resources provide a framework that remains open to the ways in which actors' interests may deviate from the stylized assumptions of perfect information and complete self-interest.

The methodological approach and research design is outlined in Chapter 3. Although the research problem emerges from the US policy-making context and US-based theories of teachers' unionism, this research employs an iterative comparative design to test and probe prominent theoretical assertions in two stages—first looking outside of US borders to probe conventional assumptions, and then returning to the US to test new theoretical insights at the school district level. This twofold approach is based on the premise that comparative understanding is iterative; we understand the particular case better as we develop our understanding of the general, and we understand the general in light of the particular.

The first stage will examine two crucial cases, Finland and the Canton of Zürich, where PRP has been implemented in spite of strong unions (Eckstein, 1975; Lijphart, 1971). Crucial cases provide the best opportunity to test a theory and the inductive case study approach maximizes opportunities to produce new theoretical insights and to uncover new causal pathways (Dogan & Pelassy, 1990; Eckstein, 1975; George & Bennett, 2005). As outlined in Chapter 3, the cases were inductively explored using interviews supplemented with document analysis in order to understand the reform processes, the relevant causal mechanisms, and the role and responses of teachers' unions. In Finland, the research investigated the development and implementation of a new salary system from 2001–2007, which included a PRP component. In Zürich, the research focused on the implementation in 1999 of a new evaluation system linked to teachers' pay, called the *Mitarbeiterbeurteilung für Schulleitende (*MAB) system. These case studies—guided by the theoretical framework—focused explicitly on the problem-oriented questions: When do such results (PRP) occur? Why don't they always? And what role do teachers' unions play in the PRP reform process? The analysis and within-case findings are presented in Chapters 4–7.

Several significant findings emerge from these cases, outlined in Chapter 8. Both case studies confirm the complexity of union preferences—that the goals of teachers and their unions are numerous, diverse, and competing. Furthermore, they confirm the contingency of union power, which varies over time, space, and issue. Finally, Finland and Zürich illuminate the significance of union-management relationship patterns (Walton & McKersie, 1991), and point to two different pathways through which reform occurs. In Finland, the new salary system was a product of compromise that occurred in the context of long-term, stable, and trust-based cooperative relationships—the cooperative-compromise path. In Zürich, reform was eventually powered-through, when a series of shifts neutralized union opposition. These findings challenge many dominant assumptions about teachers' unions' preferences and power and provide new insights into why and when reform occurs. They create a far more complex causal picture, confirming causal complexity and equifinality: they provide a typological theory with multiple causal paths to replace existing correlational accounts (George & Bennett, 2005; Ragin, 2000, 2008).

However, these new causal pathways and theoretical insights must be tested in order to determine if they are generalizable beyond the contexts in which they were observed. Particularly important given Moe's exclusive focus on US teachers' unions, and the emphasis of the second phase of research, is the degree to which these theories apply in the US. The typological theory produced from the crucial case studies will be operationalized and tested using the deductive congruence method (George & Bennett, 2005) at the school district level in the United States (Chapters 9–10). The US case studies include a sample of districts from Texas and Florida, where districts had the opportunity to design PRP systems funded by state dollars. Despite the strong financial incentives to do so, the majority of districts in both states declined to participate in the state-funded program. Comparing participating districts to non-participating districts in a state where unions have notably different opportunities for influence[4] provided pseudo-experimental conditions in which to test the findings from the international cases.

To adherents of American Exceptionalism, the findings of the US cases will be surprising. It is not hard to hypothesize why cooperation may not be salient in the US context: its size and diversity produces a different political culture than 'small nations' like Switzerland and Finland, and its majoritarian, two-party political system fuels conflict and disincentivizes compromise. These are reasonable hypotheses based on solid scholarship and reinforced by a deep archive of anecdotes. However, the US case studies reveal that the *tendency* toward competition is not an inescapable fate or destiny—especially at the school district level. Even if they are common or prominent, gridlocked, conflict-ridden union/policy-maker relationships are not inevitable; productive, collaborative problem solving is possible.

This research raises significant questions about the validity of both dominant assumptions about unions and beliefs about the inevitability of conflict. Sometimes conflict is a part of progress, but it isn't always. Because many policy-makers believe that the *only* way to reform and improve the system is by powering-through, they seem willing to tolerate very high levels of conflict for very little short-term 'progress'—with little consideration of long-term impacts. However, if more collaborative, trust-based relationships are possible, the threshold for the productivity of conflict—both in the short- and long-term—should be much higher.

NOTES

1. Particular policy changes
2. Improved educational outcomes for all students
3. What happens when an irresistible force meets an immovable object?
4. Unions in Texas are very weak; collective bargaining is illegal and union density is low. Unions in Florida are strong relative to their Texas counterparts.

SOURCES

Burns, A. (2011, June 21). Tim Pawlenty blames teachers' unions for 'vicious cycle.' *Politico*. Retrieved from http://www.politico.com/news/stories/0611/57479.html

Dillon, S. (2008, November 12). A school chief takes on tenure, stirring a fight. *The New York Times*. Retrieved from http://www.nytimes.com/2008/11/13/education/13tenure.html?pagewanted=all

Dogan, M., & Pelassy, D. (1990). *How to compare nations: Strategies in comparative politics*. Chatham, NJ: Chatham House.

Duncan, A. (2014, June 16). *Drawing the right lessons from Vergara* [Web log post]. Retrieved from http://www.ed.gov/blog/2014/06/drawing-the-right-lessons-from-vergara/

Eberts, R. W., & Stone, J. A. (1984). *Unions and public schools: The effect of collective bargaining on American education*. Lexington, MA: Lexingtion Books.

Eckstein, H. (1975). Case studies and theory in political science. In F. I. Greenstein & N. W. Polsby (Eds.), *Handbook of political science. Political Science: Scope and theory* (Vol. 7). Reading, MA: Addison-Wesley, 94–137.

Edwards, H. S. (2014, October 30). The war on teacher tenure. *TIME*. Retrieved from http://time.com/3533556/the-war-on-teacher-tenure/

George, A. L., & Bennett, A. (2005). *Case studies and theory development in the social sciences*. Cambridge, MA: MIT Press.

Goldhaber, D. (2006). Are teachers unions good for students? In J. Hannaway & A. Rotherman (Eds.), *Collective bargaining in education: Negotiating change in today's schools*. Cambridge, MA: Harvard Education, 141–159.

Harvey, D. (2007). Neoliberalism as creative destruction. *The ANNALS of the American Academy of Political and Social Science, 610*(1), 21–44.

Hood, C. (1991). A public management for all seasons? *Public Administration, 69*(1), 3–19.

Hoxby, C. M. (1996). How teachers' unions affect education production. *The Quarterly Journal of Economics, 111*(3), 671–717.

Johnson, S. M., & Kardos, S. (2000). Reform bargaining and its promise for school improvement. In T. Loveless (Ed.), *Conflicting missions? Teachers unions and educational reform*. Washington, DC: The Brookings Institution, 7–46.

Koppich, J. E. (2007). *Resource allocation in traditional and reform-oriented collective bargaining agreeents*. Seattle, WA: School Finance Redesign Project, Center on Reinventing Public Education.

Koppich, J. E., & Callahan, M. (2009). Teacher collective bargaining: What we know and what we need to know. In G. Sykes, B. Schneider, & D. Plank (Eds.), *Handbook of education policy research*. New York: Routledge, 296–306.

Kurth, M. M. (1987). Teachers' unions and excellence in education: An analysis of the decline in SAT scores. *Journal of Labor Research, 8*(4), 351–367.

Levi, M. (2008). Reconsiderations of rational choice in comparative and historical analysis. In M. I. Lichbach & A. S. Zuckerman (Eds.), *Comparative politics: Rationality, culture, and structure* (2nd ed.). Cambridge: Cambridge University Press, 117–133.

Lijphart, A. (1971). Comparative politics and the comparative method. *The American Political Science Review, 65*(3), 682–692.

Malen, B. (2001). Generating interest in interest groups. *Educational Policy, 15*(1), 168–185.

Moe, T. (2006). Union power and the education of children. In J. Hannaway & A. Rotherman (Eds.), *Collective bargaining in education: Negotiating change in today's schools*. Cambridge, MA: Harvard Education Press, 229–256.

Moe, T. (2011). *Special interests: Teachers unions and America's public schools*. Washington, DC: Brookings Institution.

National Conference of State Legislatures. (2011, February 15). *2011 legislation on unions and collective bargaining*. Retrieved from: http://www.ncsl.org/documents/employ/Unions2-15-11.pdf

Nelson, F. H., & Gould, J. C. (1988). Teachers' unions and excellence in education: Comment. *Journal of Labor Research, 9*(4), 379–386.

Pawlenty, T. (2010, September 7). America wants school reform. *The National Review*. Retrieved from http://www.nationalreview.com/articles/245742/america-wants-school-reform-tim-pawlenty

Pullman, J. (2012, December 14). Teachers unions steer clear of race to the top. *Washington Times*. Retrieved from http://www.washingtontimes.com/news/2012/dec/14/teachers-unions-steer-clear-of-race-to-the-top/

Ragin, C. C. (2000). *Fuzzy-set social science*. Chicago: University of Chicago Press.

Ragin, C. C. (2008). *Redesigning social inquiry: Fuzzy sets and beyond*. Chicago: University of Chicago Press.

Rhee, M. (2010, December 6). Why Michelle Rhee isn't done with school reform. *Newsweek*. Retrieved from http://www.newsweek.com/why-michelle-rhee-isnt-done-school-reform-68975

Salmon, W. C. (2006). *Four decades of scientific explanation* (2nd ed.). Pittsburgh: University of Pittsburg Press.

Santos, F. (2012, January 13). Bloomberg focuses his legacy on education reform. *The New York Times*. Retrieved from http://www.nytimes.com/2012/01/14/nyregion/bloomberg-focuses-his-legacy-on-education-reform.html

Sawchuk, S. (2014, July 7). For *Vergara* ruling on teachers, big questions loom. *Education Week*. Retrieved from: http://www.edweek.org/ew/articles/2014/07/09/36vergara-update.h33.html?tkn=SQUFBlq64d2KyqKpPxy%2BbwzcYgdMOijQ%2FIsz&print=1

Scharpf, F. W. (1997). *Games real actors play*. Boulder, CO: Westview Press.

Scharpf, F. W. (2000). Institutions in comparative policy research. *Comparative Political Studies, 33*(6–7), 762–790.

Thomas, E. (2008, August 22). Can Michelle Rhee save D.C.'s schools? *Newsweek*. Retrieved from http://www.newsweek.com/can-michelle-rhee-save-dcs-schools-88041

Unions v. race to the top. (2010, January 7). *The Wall Street Journal*. Retrieved from http://www.wsj.com/articles/SB10001424052748703483604574630423614312770

Walton, R. E., & McKersie, R. B. (1991). *A behavioral theory of labor negotiations* (2nd ed.). New York: McGraw Hill.

Part I
Research Design

1 Teachers' Unions and Education Reform
A Review of the Literature

The debate over the impact of teachers' unions on reform echoes the irresistible force paradox—what happens when an irresistible force (reform) meets an unmovable object (unions)? Union critics imply that the unmovable objects always best the irresistible force—that strong unions always impede reform. However, although plenty of anecdotal evidence has been marshaled to support this view, even a cursory glance across school districts, states, and countries confirms that the empirical reality is far more complex. Reforms that are unpopular with unions have quickly advanced both within and beyond US borders, complicating any straightforward solutions to the irresistible force paradox.

Understanding the union reform conflict requires a closer examination of a series of questions. Do teachers' unions always oppose reform? If not, why not? When unions oppose reform, are they always successful in blocking its implementation? Or, put another way, are teachers' unions as powerful as their critics often imply? These questions cannot be approached without a thorough examination of their component parts. This chapter reviews cross-disciplinary literature, illuminating a number of significant gaps in the existing literature which must be carefully considered and addressed in the theoretical framework (Chapter 2) and research design (Chapter 3).

This chapter first explores international education reform. Although the orienting questions of this research are focused on education policy and change, particularly changing approaches to teachers' compensation vis-à-vis performance-related pay (PRP), the specific reforms investigated in the case studies are part of broader public sector restructuring and reform and the ideas and ideologies that have informed them. Specifically, these shifts must be read in the context of public sector restructuring, neoliberalism, and New Public Management (NPM), factors that emerged from the 1980s crisis of the welfare state. Failing to understand the general context within which these reforms occur is to misread the particular changes—their practical meaning and theoretical significance.

The second half of this chapter reviews the literature on teachers' unions, drawing on interdisciplinary resources that can inform theorizing about teachers' unions' preferences, strength, and influence. Allegations that teachers' unions use their power in service of their self-interest to block education reform, and that this blocking is bad for students and against the public interest (Moe, 2006, 2011), prompt a number of questions, both theoretical and empirical:

- On one hand, to what do 'power' and 'self-interest' refer?
- And, are teachers' unions (empirically) powerful and acting solely in line with a narrowly defined self-interest?
- With what frequency are teachers' unions blocking reforms?
- And, is this blocking bad for public education, as union critics claim?

These questions, and the answers provided by the existing literature, will be considered in the second half of this chapter. However, before turning to considerations of union interests, power, and impact, we must first interrogate the essential question—what is 'education reform'?

THE IRRESISTIBLE FORCE: EDUCATION REFORM

Unpacking education reform requires attention to the interplay between the particular and the general. The case studies examined in the second half of this book focus on teachers' unions' response to and impact on PRP reforms. A single reform was selected because it aids comparability and conceptual clarity. PRP was selected, rather than any of the other eligible candidates, both because of its commonality—it has a long history and a relatively wide, global reach—and because of the way that it maps onto perceived union interests: it is *the* classic 'bread-and-butter issue,' the space where teachers' unions' self-interest should be the most evident. However, a variety of approaches to compensation reform sit under the PRP label. Thus, it is essential to define PRP and briefly discuss its history and evidence base. However, PRP reform cannot be treated in a vacuum. Its particular shape in the education sector is formed by the global education reform movement as well as broader public sector reform and restructuring over the past four decades and the ideologies that have animated it. This section will first frame education reform in its global and local contexts, then it will turn to the interrelationships between education reform and broader reform ideologies. Finally, PRP will be outlined with these two influences in mind.

Education Reform: The Local and the Global

Since *A Nation at Risk* was published in 1983 (National Commission on Excellence in Education, 1983), frenetic reform in the US has been fuelled by a sense that "school systems have failed to deliver what is required, and that the failure is especially lamentable in view of the high level of spending on education" (Levin, 1997, p. 48). Driven by this perception of underperformance, the 'accountability movement,' which emphasizes the use of incentives or sanctions to reward or assign consequences for school performance, has become a dominant force in US education policy, manifested in and complimented by competition, markets, choice, performance objectives, and targets (Apple, 2001; O'Day, 2002; Ravitch, 2010). An emphasis on "indirect steering from a distance which replaces intervention and prescription with target setting, accountability, and comparison" (Ball, 1998, p. 123) has been attributed to the new emphasis on targets and incentives, an ideological preference for markets rather than bureaucracies, and the resulting emphasis on 'performativity' (Ball, 2001, 2003). In addition to incentivizing performance at the district or school level, many have advocated for expanded choice for students and families vis-à-vis the charter and voucher movements and have proposed new approaches for driving accountability measures to the level of the individual, including new approaches to teachers' compensation that would link their pay more closely to their performance.

Although many of these reforms have Anglo-American origins, they are not unique to the United States; they are a part of a larger "global education reform movement (GERM)" (Sahlberg, 2011, p. 99). According to Ball (1998), these forces have spread via three transmission mechanisms: social and political networks, policy entrepreneurs, and the sponsorship and enforcement of multinational organizations like the World Bank and the Organization for Economic Co-operation and Development (OECD). In the developed west, the OECD has received significant attention as a reform conduit—especially since the establishment of the Programme of International Student Assessment (PISA) exams in 2000. Rizvi and Lingaard (2009) link the global movement to the OECD and its promotion of a "particular notion of 'good governance'" (p. 119), which they locate within the OECD's New Public Management (NPM) ideology[1] and its emphasis on steering at a distance through competitive performance measures (OECD, 1995). The speed and scope of proliferation have led some to conclude that "it is now increasingly difficult to understand education in any context without reference to the global forces that influence policy and practice" (Crossley, 2000, p. 324).

GERM significantly impacts teachers and their work through its emphasis on management and regulation over pedagogy and classroom practice. Maroy (2009) describes the reform movement as a shift in governance models—the way that good steering or governance is defined. The emphasis has shifted away from the bureaucratic-professional model—regulation based on standardized rules and where the teaching profession has significant influence over its work and working conditions—to a series of post-bureaucratic governance models (Maroy, 2009). Examples of post-bureaucratic governance include evaluative approaches—goals, external evaluation, and incentives and sanctions—and quasi-market mechanisms—centrally defined objectives, autonomy, and school choice. These strategies are united by a shift toward monitoring, incentivizing, and outcome management (Maroy, 2009). The new managerialism challenges the authority, control, and, ultimately, professional autonomy of teachers as it pivots away from horizontal and internal professional control and toward top-down accountability measures (Mattei, 2007).

Hargreaves (2000) distinguishes between professionalism—'being professional' in terms of the quality of what teachers do—and professionalization—how teachers are viewed by others. The shift in governance models impacts both. First, shifts in governance—a move from self-monitoring and enforcement to monitoring and accountability—can result in a deskilling of teaching, as "the structure of accountability imposed on schools by current political trends demeans teachers and undermines their occupational integrity" (Apple & Teitelbaum, 1986; Burbules & Densmore, 1991, p. 48). Second, accountability reforms often criticize—either implicitly or explicitly—teachers' work, contributing to deprofessionalizing:

> recent reports, the best known being *A Nation at Risk*, that criticize the mediocrity of schooling in the United States, implicitly and often explicitly [attribute] this decline to teacher mediocrity or incompetence.... [These reports] have undermined the public appreciation and status accorded to teaching. (Burbules & Densmore, 1991, p. 47)

Although Burbules and Densmore focus on the deprofessionalization of teaching in the United States, Compton and Weiner (2008a)—citing examples from around the world—argue that "though the titles and acronyms of policies differ from one country to another, the basics of the assault are the same: undercut the publicly supported, publicly controlled system of education, teachers' professionalism, and teacher unions as organizations" (p. 4). Thus, although the reform mechanisms associated with new approaches to education governance are wide-ranging—increasing school autonomy; tinkering with the centralization/decentralization balance; and increasing emphasis on external evaluation, parental choice, and diversification of educational offerings—they have had a common and cumulative effect on teachers' work. They have been perceived as efforts to control teaching: "a tendency to erode teachers' individual professional autonomy" (Maroy, 2009, p. 75).

Education Reform in Context: Neoliberalism and NPM

Although education reform has its distinctions and particularities, it has also been occurring in a common historical period of restructuring, and must be situated in this broader context of what many would label neoliberalism. Neoliberalism has been defined as "a theory of economic practices proposing that human well-being can best be advanced by the maximization of entrepreneurial freedoms within an institutional framework characterised by private property rights, individual liberty, unencumbered markets, and free trade" (Harvey, 2007, p. 22), which emphasizes a limited state role and promotes the creation of markets in education, health, and other policy arenas.

After a period of growth and expansion from the end of World War II through the mid-1970s, which has been dubbed the golden age of welfare capitalism, neoliberalism emerged alongside the 'new politics' of permanent austerity in the 1980s (Pierson, 2001). The post-1973 stagnation and the shifting labor market structure vis-à-vis post-industrialization and demographic change created public sector deficits which combined with globalization to create the perfect storm of massive strains on welfare states (Pierson, 1998; Swank, 2001). Neoliberalism is often linked to the policies of Ronald Reagan and Margaret Thatcher and its progenitors Friedrich Hayek and Milton Friedman, who preached the power of markets and the need for limiting the role of the state in economic, social, and political decisions (Harvey, 2005; Pierson, 1994). However, the widespread welfare state reforms associated with this era—reduced generosity of benefits, tightened program eligibility, mechanisms for cost control, the privatization of some social services, and increased targeting—was not confined to the neoliberal ideological leaders or even to the Anglo American welfare states (Krejsler, 2005; Mudge 2008; Stephens, 1986; Swank, 2001).

One particular brand of reforms commonly associated with neoliberalism, which has informed the restructuring of public employment across countries and sectors since the 1980s, is New Public Management (NPM) (Peters, 2012). NPM has been defined as "hands-on professional management that allows for active, visible, discretionary control of an organization by persons who are free to manage; explicit standards of performance; greater emphasis on output control; increased competition; contracts devolution; disaggregation of units; and private sector management techniques" (Christensen & Laegreid, 2001, p. 19). Under the market-oriented neoliberal umbrella, NPM is a broadly encompassing term that includes a diverse set of strategies and reforms ranging from accountability mechanisms, greater consumer choice, and many others, which remake the public sector in the private sector's image (Bordogna, 2008).[2] NPM has been prominent across sectors, including in public education where an education "policy epidemic" (Levin, 1998, p. 131) has been associated with neoliberal thinking—marked by its decentralization, goal steering, accountability, managerialism, evaluation, choice, compensation reform (i.e., PRP), competition, and privatization (Ball, 2001; Compton & Weiner, 2008a; Halpin & Troyna, 1995; Levin, 1997, 1998; Maroy, 2009; Rinne, Kivirauma, & Simola, 2002; Whitty & Edwards, 1998).

Despite their prominence, both neoliberalism and NPM have been deployed in broad, sweeping, and unspecific ways. As a construct, neoliberalism lacks a consistent or unifying doctrine and has been employed in vague and undefined ways, usually in the context of sinister attempts to dismantle the welfare state (Hudson, 2007; Krejsler, 2005; Mudge, 2008; Robertson, 2008). The common theme across the strategies and reforms to which it has been applied is a perceived link to markets, or, in more extreme cases, privatization (Hudson, 2007).

Two important distinctions increase clarity around the terms' meaning and use in this book. First, the perceived ideology of neoliberalism and NPM must be distinguished from the specific policies and reforms that have been commonly associated with the terms. In the context of the era of retrenchment, neoliberalism has been employed as a catch-all term for all efforts, either overt or more covert, to dismantle, shrink, or beat back the state—to abdicate its commitments to equality and citizenship rights (Hudson, 2007; Krejsler, 2005). However, the perspective of Ozga and colleagues on decentralization—often identified as a neoliberal strategy—in education provides an alternative view:

> Rather than interpreting these developments as evidence of the dismembering of the state, we suggest . . . that we must open up approaches to understanding the state that explore its reconfiguration, its new roles and its governing practices. (Ozga, Simola, Varjo, Segerholm, & Pitkanen, 2010, p. 108)

This book emphasizes the common mechanisms of reforms rather than the ideological orientation or goals of reforms. Yes, restructuring approaches labeled neoliberalism may be used to shrink the state, but the same approaches or mechanisms may be used to attempt to fulfill the state's existing goals and responsibilities more efficiently or effectively. After all, any attempts to claim that neoliberalism or NPM is based on a uniform set of goals or intentions is further complicated by the history and emergence of the term as an academic construct: NPM was coined by Hood (1990) to *retrospectively* describe changes that had taken place across OECD countries in the 1980s (Christensen & Laegreid, 2001).

In addition to delineating ideology from mechanisms, the second critical distinction relates to the degree of diversity within these common mechanisms (Sahlin-Andersson, 2001). The proliferation of reform mechanisms should not necessarily be read as policy convergence, as the doctrines of NPM are transformed by historical-institutional traditions and policy style differences (Christensen & Laegreid, 2001). Instead, NPM reforms should be understood as a group of ideas (Hood, 1991); "variations on a theme" (Hood, 1995, p. 93); or "a cluster of ideas" (Sahlin-Andersson, 2001, p. 8).

A study of Scandinavian states,[3] for example, finds that all the states have adopted NPM-inspired reforms without dismantling welfare services and while maintaining strong traditions of collective bargaining in the public sector—commonly perceived to be under threat from NPM (Bach & Kessler, 2007). In all the Scandinavian states under investigation, "NPM (was) filtered, modified, and translated to each national context in a pragmatic and corporatist manner in which unions are partners rather than adversaries" (Ibsen, Larsen, Madsen, & Due, 2011, p. 2308). So NPM, a subset of neoliberalism, is best conceptualized as a loosely coupled set of reforms that have been employed in a variety of contexts.

Thus, reform in an increasingly interconnected policy world may best be understood as what Ball (1998) calls "bricolage"—a process of borrowing reforms from elsewhere but reworking, adapting, and recreating them within the new context. One must recognize the global—to identify the common themes that have emerged—while also still attending to the local—the particular nuances and reinterpretations within a given context. Although PRP, GERM, and NPM may be global phenomena to a certain degree, the tensions between global similarity and local particularity lie, at least in part, in the complex ways that policy travels, is borrowed, or is imitated—a process that is highly contingent (Ball, 1998; Bowe & Ball, 1992). Rather than creating a false dichotomy between *either* global convergence *or* local difference, it is important to hold the two in tension, examining what others have called commonality within difference or paradigm convergence (Ball, 1998, 2001).

Therefore, identifying these common global trends should not be confused with a claim of convergence around neoliberal ideals, either in the countries investigated or more generally. Reform is situated between global pressures and local vernacular interpretations and responses which produce variability, and this interplay between global and local—the nature of institutional structures as well as ideological receptivity to global reform ideas—significantly informs the nature and effectiveness of union responses to reform proposals (Levin, 1998; Ozga & Lingard, 2007). Discursive and ideological contexts may significantly impact a country's receptivity to neoliberal reforms, as the 'new' global trends are entangled with and rearticulated through the 'old'—"the deep-seated historical traditions, structures, practices, and institutional cultures specific to each nation" (Green, 1997, p. 23). Aasen (2003) found that the neoliberal emphasis in education was significantly mediated in countries with stronger or more extensive social democratic policies or visions. Similarly, Martens and colleagues (2010) argued that national veto players may influence the extent to which international organizations or reform trends impact national policy.

Performance-Related Pay

PRP sits in the cross hairs of these pressures and shifts. Robertson (2008) identifies the global restructuring of education as a comprehensive change that affects the mandate of education, the work of teachers, the level and types of financing, and the basis of teachers' salaries. She also frames GERM within public sector austerity and restructuring, arguing that "teacher unions have been placed under enormous pressure to yield to performance-based or 'merit' pay," due, at least in part, to the fact that "internationally teachers' salaries were seriously affected by austerity measures during the 1980s" (Robertson, 2008, p. 20).

Although problem-oriented analysis—determining whether a given policy is the best response to a problem (see Chapter 3 for further discussion)—is not the central aim of this research, there are several reasons to briefly survey the evidence in the existing research. First, PRP must be clearly defined in order to provide analytic clarity to a broad concept with multiple policy implications and manifestations. Second, it is important to frame the problem(s) which PRP is purported to solve and the theoretical and empirical evidence regarding its effectiveness or limitations. This evidence base, and the disputes surrounding it, will inform both the design of PRP and objections and resistance to it.

Performance-Related Pay Defined

Historically, the research on differentiated compensation in education often distinguishes between three types of compensation reforms (Podgursky & Springer, 2007; Prentice, Burgess, & Propper, 2007):

- *Merit Pay*: individual incentives based on subjective assessments of teaching effectiveness, a common civil service reform in the 1980s.
- *Performance-Related Pay*: individual incentives based on objective measures like test scores or other quantifiable indicators.
- *School-Level or Group Incentives*: incentives awarded to groups of teachers on the bases of either subjective or objective measures.

However, these categories—merit pay, performance-related pay, and school-level incentives—are often used interchangeably by practitioners, and even if they were applied in a more systematic way, they would still obscure important nuances (Gratz, 2005). Many contemporary approaches to differentiated compensation are hybrid types, combining group and individual rewards, inputs and outputs, as well as subjective and objective measures of inputs. And there can be wide and important variation in terms of the size of the reward, whether it is a one time or annual award, and whether it is a bonus or contingent[4] pay scheme, which all greatly impact the (in)effectiveness of the incentive (Armstrong, 2010). As a result, there may be as much variation within the existing definitions as between them (Prentice et al., 2007).

In this book, PRP will refer to all approaches that link teacher compensation—either in terms of teachers' base pay or through bonuses—to outputs,[5] whether subjectively or objectively measured.[6] All proposals under the PRP banner share an emphasis on paying teachers on the basis of outputs rather than the inputs which have traditionally defined teachers' and many civil servants' salary schedules: years of experience and levels of education, among others. However, within this commonality there is significant diversity in the way performance is measured and the design and distribution of the rewards.

Johnson and Papay (2009) provide a framework for PRP in education which further differentiates strategies on three dimensions: how performance is measured—student achievement, professional evaluations, or some combination of the two; whether awards are standards-based or relative; and whether awards go to groups or individuals. Performance measurement can be further differentiated by how student achievement is measured: objective measures can include standardized assessments or teacher-designed assessments, and subjective evaluations can be conducted by principals, peers, or others. Although all of the reforms investigated in Finland, Zürich, and the United States meet this definition, they also reflect a diversity of approaches and strategies.

As much as PRP and teachers' unions' responses to it may be united by common tensions and questions about the nature of linking teachers' pay to various outputs, the particularities of systems' design—the measure of performance, the size of the reward, whether it is a bonus or added to base salaries, and whether it is awarded to groups or individuals—will inform the debate about systems' proposed effectiveness and teachers' unions' responses to these systems. Although the particular policies and the debates they generated will be outlined within the case studies, a brief review of the evidence for and against PRP is provided here.

The Evidence For and Against PRP

At the most general level, PRP is proposed as a solution for two problems. First, the public sector—including education—needs to be able to attract and retain the highest quality workforce in the most cost-effective way. Public-private wage gaps, anticipated teacher shortages, and retention challenges are all components of this problem. Hypothetically, significant across-the-board raises could address this problem, but PRP is often proposed as a more targeted and cost-effective solution. Second, PRP is thought to provide a targeted incentive that encourages better workforce performance. This effect could occur in two ways: either through working as a 'sorting device' which attracts and retains the best teachers or by motivating teachers to work harder or more effectively (Dohmen & Falk, 2010; Hoxby & Leigh, 2004; Lazear, 2000, 2003; Podgursky & Springer, 2007; Woessman, 2010). Proponents of PRP point to its use in non-sectarian private schools and charter schools to demonstrate that it is possible in education but blocked by teachers' unions (Ballou, 2001; Podgursky, 2007; West & Mykerezi, 2011).

Although PRP in education is often presented as extending widespread best practices from the private to public sector, Adams and Heywood (2009) argue that the pervasiveness of PRP in the private sector is overstated. Furthermore, critics argue that PRP is inappropriate in education for a variety of reasons: the difficulty of measuring outputs in education, the potential for incentives to distort 'multitasking,' and the potentially corrosive effects of introducing competition and undermining collaboration (Dixit, 2002;

Hannaway, 1992; Murnane & Cohen, 1986; Prendergast, 1999; Rothstein, 2009). Furthermore, in the private sector, PRP systems have been criticized for being time-consuming to administer and for creating dissatisfaction (Pfeffer 1998).

Empirically, the evidence on PRP in education is mixed. Experimental studies of incentives have found positive effects on measured outcomes in India and Israel, with mixed effects in Kenya (Glewwe, Ilias, & Kremer, 2010; Lavy, 2007; Muralidharan & Sundararman, 2008). Similarly, an evaluation of a PRP scheme in Little Rock, Arkansas found a positive effect on student achievement (Winters, Greene, Ritter, & Marsh, 2008). In the case of mixed or negative findings proponents of PRP emphasize the importance of *well-designed* incentives. Even advocates call PRP promising but unclear and emphasize the need for further research on the role of measurement, the size of the bonus, and the locus of decision-making (Lazear, 2003; Woessman, 2010).

PRP conclusions remain tentative. It *may* motivate teachers, but questions remain as to whether they will be motivated in ways that are ultimately productive. Will incentivizing outputs lead to multitasking or other moral hazards? Is linking pay to quantitative indicators problematic? Are those indicators valid? Are they subject to inflation or distortion that would render them useless in measuring educational outputs? Will extrinsic motivators undermine intrinsic motivations, eroding professionalism and the service ethos of teaching? Even if all these questions can be favorably resolved, the degree of motivation or sorting will depend on the specific way that incentives are designed; even proponents acknowledge that further research is required and that effective design will require significant experimentation (Podgursky & Springer, 2007).

Despite ongoing debates about the usefulness of PRP and the specifics of its design, there has been widespread interest in public sector compensation reforms. PRP as a broad construct must be understood in the larger context of education policy-making and reform and the broader dynamics of public sector restructuring and welfare state change, particularly NPM. This contextualization confirms that, despite their particularities and contingencies, the reforms explored in each case study are linked to common models and frameworks.

Conclusion: The Irresistible Force?

The shift toward austerity in the public sector—demands to do more with less—provide one significant context within which education reform must be understood. The other important movements—fundamentally related to the first—are broader shifts in conceptions of the teaching profession and teachers' work (Compton & Weiner, 2008a,b). The teaching profession sits in the cross hairs of competing pressures. On one hand, the quality of the teaching force is deemed to be the single most important school-level determinant of the quality of education that students receive (Hanushek & Rivkin, 2006). But on the other hand, staffing is the biggest line item within education budgets, which means that governments are faced with the paradox of trying to contain expenditure while maintaining and improving the quality of its teachers and schools (OECD, 2012). Both neoliberalism and NPM are a significant part of the story of efforts to restructure teachers' compensation; in both international cases, reforming teachers' compensation was approached as a part of broader reforms of public sector employment.[7] These are the reforms to which teachers' unions must respond. What should we expect in terms of the nature and result of teachers' unions' reactions to these reforms? These expectations are framed by our understanding of teachers' unions' preferences, power, and impact—the subject of the rest of this chapter.

THE IMMOVABLE OBJECT: TEACHERS' UNIONS

What impact do teachers' unions have on public education? The empirical measurement of union influence on the organization of schooling is complex and findings have been mixed. Even if it is accepted that teachers' unions increase overall spending and teachers' salaries as well as influence the appropriation of funds and the rules that govern the organization of schooling, the empirical challenges only increase when researchers attempt to measure the effect of unionism on student achievement (Argys & Reese, 1995; Carini, Powell, & Steelman, 2000; Eberts, 2007; Eberts, Hollenbeck, & Stone, 2004; Eberts & Stone, 1984, 1986; Hoxby, 1996). Findings have varied in part due to differences in research design and operationalization of union strength, union power, and union impact (Argys & Reese, 1995; Baugh & Stone, 1982; Eberts, 2007; Eberts et al., 2004; Eberts & Stone, 1984, 1986, 1987; Gallagher, 1978; Hall & Carroll, 1973; Hoxby, 1996).

In the absence of definitive empirical evidence, two 'union stories'[8] dominate research in the United States,[9] where widespread consensus has determined that unions are one of the most powerful organizations in education politics (Bascia, 1990; Cooper & Sureau, 2008a; Hess & West, 2006; Kahlenberg, 2006; Koppich, 2005; Koppich & Callahan, 2009; Moe, 2006). In one account, often labeled 'professional unionism,' unions are—or at least can be—either partly or entirely interested in defending what is best for students *and* teachers,[10] promoting professionalism, preserving flexibility, and attending to issues beyond salaries and working conditions (Cooper & Sureau, 2008b; Crouch, 2005; Johnson & Kardos, 2000; Johnson & Donaldson, 2006; Kerchner & Koppich, 1993; Koppich & Callahan, 2009).

In contrast, in the second account, teachers' unions and education reform—two nuanced and theoretically complex entities, often loosely defined and poorly specified in popular debates—are fundamentally antithetical to one another. Teachers' unions are self-interested actors who slow, impede, or block educational progress (Chubb & Moe, 1990; Lieberman 2000; Moe, 2006, 2011). Terry Moe's *Special Interests: Teachers Unions and America's Public Schools* (2011) provides the most systematic explication of this perspective in which teachers' unions and education reform are on a collision course and only one can survive. Moe's account suggests that powerful teachers' unions consistently and systematically best education reforms. According to Moe, the strength of teachers' unions in the United States—their unique position among interest groups as an unrivalled influence on education policy—is mobilized to achieve the preferences of teachers' unions; this power is bad for public education and disadvantages students (Moe 2006, 2011).

He argues that the teachers' unions use their strength—via collective bargaining and political influence—to promote their interests, which has institutionalized these 'inefficient work rules' in collective bargaining contracts and state laws (Chubb & Moe, 1990; Moe, 2006, 2011). Furthermore, teachers' unions exercise their political power to engage in the "politics of blocking" (Moe, 2011, p. 275)—preventing reforms that would address these inefficiencies and organize schools in the best interests of students. In short, according to Moe, teachers' unions are powerful organizations that, because of their fundamental self-interests, stand against the public good and must be eliminated:

> the problems associated with union power are inherent to the organizations, are very much to be expected, and cannot be eliminated by some sort of 'reform unionism' that relies on the unions themselves to adopt a more enlightened, public-spirited approach. It follows that, if public education is to escape the stultifying drag of the unions' grip on the system—and if the system, therefore, is to evolve into a new form that is better suited to providing a quality education to children—it will happen only through reforms that weaken or eliminate union power over the schools. (Moe, 2006, p. 230)

Ultimately, accounts of and disputes over what unions do involve three key concepts: teachers' unions' interests, strength, and influence or power:

- *Union Interests*: Although rational choice assumptions—a presumption of rationality and self-interest—are pervasive in interest group and union theories, as exemplified by Moe's (2011) work, individualism is not the only possible conception of union preferences, as evident in a review of interdisciplinary literature.
- *Union Strength and Union Power*: Although the two terms are often used interchangeably, they must be kept conceptually distinct; union strength refers to static assessments of resources and union power refers to the dynamic process through which unions impact outcomes.

Teachers' Unions' Preferences: Moving Beyond Simple Self-Interest

The two teachers' union stories are founded on very different assumptions of unions' interests. In professional unionism, unions are, or at least can be, interested in defending public education on the basis of what is best for students and teachers. In the second account—the unions-block-reform story—teachers' unions are self-interested actors who slow, impede, or block educational progress. The interests that drive unions are critical to understanding what teachers' unions do, both in terms of the action they take and the impact they have.

Given the fragmentary nature of the existing literature on teachers' unions, zooming out to examine what resources other disciplines might contribute is essential. Although labor economists generally agree with the unions-block-reform account of unions' interests—that the objectives of unions are to advance the preferences of their members by pressuring employers and governments for improved terms and conditions[11] (Bennett & Kaufman, 2004; Taft, 1950)—there is some debate in the field about union behavior and impact. In their seminal work, Richard Freeman and James Medoff (1984) challenged traditional conceptions of 'what unions do,' and what impact they have on firm performance, suggesting that unions have two faces—a monopoly and voice face. These two faces provide a useful framework for considering the ways in which union preferences—and impact—may vary.

The Monopoly Face

The monopoly face mirrors the dominant view that unions function as a special interest group using economic and political action to improve the material well-being of their members at the expense of the welfare of the larger community (Bennett & Kaufman, 2004; Olson, 1982). If one adopts an exclusively economic conception of union preferences—what Freeman and Medoff call the 'monopoly face' of unions, in which their goal is to protect and raise wages and benefits for their workers—then the *effect* of this exclusive promotion of members' material interest is to raise wages above competitive levels and to introduce a number of distortions and inefficiencies, including allocative inefficiency, technical inefficiency, inflationary bias, and cyclical instability (Booth, 1995; Hirsch & Addison, 1986; Kaufman, 2004).

In terms of the two union stories, Terry Moe (2011) provides the prototypical monopoly face account of teachers' unions. Although he is not alone in his self-interest-based account of teachers' unions (Chubb & Moe, 1990; Hanushek, 1994; Hess & West, 2006; Hill, 2006; Lieberman, 2000), Moe is the leading voice. For the leaders of teachers' unions, Moe argues, the primary concern is pleasing their members. He uses a nationally representative survey of 3,328 teachers conducted in 2003 to measure the interests of teachers and finds that they want unions to "protect their jobs, to get them higher wages and better benefits, to push for teacher-friendly work rules, to oppose threatening changes, and in general to fight for their basic job-related interests" (Moe, 2011, pp. 21, 67). These demands require unions to promote specific policies. In short, union leaders must satisfy members and are therefore constrained by members' interests (McDonnell & Pascal, 1988; Moe, 2011).

Thus, the goals and strategies of teachers' unions are derived from the preferences of their membership, which Moe identifies as a common occupational interest shared by all teachers (2011). The next postulate of Moe's argument is that what is in the best interests of teachers is often not in the best interest of children, quality education, or effective schools. Furthermore, according to Moe, any claims to the contrary—that unions *are* primarily concerned about children and quality education—are simply strategic branding to gain democratic support, critical to union political success. As a result, Moe argues that the organization of schooling—class sizes, school hours, tenure, and teacher compensation—is currently driven by what is best for teachers, and that it should be driven, instead, by what is best for students.[12]

This unions-block-reform account is a monopoly view in which unions work to secure maximum benefits for their members with no consideration for success or quality for the organization as a whole. This view of teachers' and their unions' preferences closely mirrors a particular understanding of group representation drawn from interest group theory (Garceau, 1958), and is based on a narrow conception of preferences—exclusive self-interest or individualism.

Interest Group Theory

Interest Group Theory (IGT) is concerned with several basic questions: Why do groups form? How do they overcome the collective action[13] problem? How are groups maintained? And how are internal divisions resolved? Until Mancur Olson's groundbreaking work in 1965, the pluralist theory of interest groups dominated the field. It argued that groups are an aggregation of individuals' common preferences—that individuals work together because they want similar things and can achieve more together than they can alone. Within the pluralist model, groups provide an accurate representation of politically relevant preferences (Bentley, 1907/1978; Truman, 1971).

But in 1965, Olson argued that groups are unlikely to form around 'common interests' due to free-rider incentives, or what he labeled the collective action problem. In short, it may be true that individuals want the same thing, but if everyone would benefit from the action of a few, then everyone's incentives are to do nothing and to be 'free-riders'—to wait to benefit from others' action without incurring any of the costs of action. Olson argued that the collective action problem is overcome through selective incentives—discrete benefits or perks provided to members that incentivize their membership, like providing insurance and publications. Thus, Olson argued that groups are not an accurate indicator of society's preferences, as they distort and misrepresent the preferences of organized individuals:

members join *not* because they agree with the union's goals, or due to purposive incentives, but in order to gain access to selective incentives. In *The Rise and Decline of Nations* (1982), Olson ultimately concludes that the inevitable accumulation of interest groups causes the eventual decline of democratic societies as interest organizations reduce the efficiency and aggregate income of societies in which they operate because "there is for practical purposes no constraint on the social cost such an organization will find expedient to impose on the society in the course of obtaining a larger share of the social output for itself" (Olson 1982, p. 44).

"Interest group" has become a dirty word in American politics, and on the playground of education politics, it is the label of choice deployed by critics of teachers' unions. When teachers' unions are called an interest group, it comes loaded with connotations of a corrosive self-interest. One can see how this conclusion finds support in some of Olson's work and the theorizing of IGT. However, although IGT is premised on rational choice assumptions—that actors act strategically to maximize their goal attainment—it also provides resources for considering the complexity of union action and impact.

- First, teachers' unions clearly provide both selective incentives like insurance, newsletters, and other benefits, and purposive incentives, or unity around the attainment of common goals. Those who argue that unions *must* behave in a particular way because of the interests of their membership presume that membership is exclusively based on purposive incentives and ignore the complexities introduced by selective incentives.
- Second, in terms of purposive incentives, although members *may* be united—a significant assumption that requires empirical support—in their opinions about accountability, the use of standardized tests, compensation, and teacher tenure, the relative weight of their preferences for those things remains unknown. For example, is higher compensation more important than long-term job security? It is likely that the answer to that question varies across teachers, significantly complicating any efforts to describe union preferences as monolithic and straightforward.
- Third, despite teachers' presumed unity about issues like accountability, compensation, and tenure, these preferences may be outweighed by their preferences for other things—for example, to be respected and perceived as professionals. Said differently, the purposive incentives that most strongly unite teachers may or may not be opposition to, or support for, particular policies. IGT assumes that individuals are rational actors attempting to maximize their self-interests. Although it is generally presumed that these interests are economic, non-economic motives—like benevolence—could provide the foundation for group formation.

These alternative explanations and complexities remain largely unexplored. Like Freeman and Medoff's monopoly face, IGT predominantly emphasizes individualism. However, a variety of alternative conceptions exist.

Challenges to an Exclusively Economically Self-Interested Monopoly Face

Although narrowly conceived economic self-interest receives significant theoretical attention in cross-disciplinary literature, the straightforward conception of union goals as the exercise of self-interest within a monopoly has been challenged in several ways. First, some have challenged whether the goals of the union are as universal and uniform as they appear within this view, as workers are interested in a full range of terms and conditions, the profits of which are not necessarily shared equally between the workers (Kaufman, 2002). So even if unions *are* always promoting the material interests of their members—are showing their 'monopoly face'—those preferences and goals are likely to be diverse, competing, and unclear in practice.

Second, unions' individualism may be limited by external constraints. For example, extracting rents beyond competitively sustainable levels would be antithetical to the union's long-term economic interests.[14] Even within an exclusively economic and self-interested framework, the union is not immune to consideration of firm performance; in fact, there may be good reasons for the union to balance maximizing both firm performance and their individual preferences, or what Freeman and Medoff call unions' voice face.

The Voice Face

Freeman and Medoff (1984) argue that unions have a voice face which may offset some of the costs associated with the monopoly face—negative impacts on resource allocation, productivity, and social welfare via strikes; restricting workplace practice; and raising wages above the competitive norm—by boosting morale, loyalty, and commitment; reducing turnover; and providing information. The voice face may be efficiency-enhancing, especially in light of market imperfections like information asymmetry and mobility costs—a possibility neglected in most economics literature by the a priori assumption of perfect markets. Implicit in the voice face is the idea that unions may be motivated to help the firm—that a gain for one isn't necessarily a loss for the other—and that they may have information and knowledge that could improve firm decision-making.

The positive contribution of the voice face has resonances with what Richard E. Walton and Robert B. McKersie call distributive versus integrative bargaining in their seminal text *A Behavioral Theory of Labor Negotiations* (1965/1991). The majority of the literature on teachers' unions and their impact on public education is united by a common conceptualization of collective bargaining, what Walton and McKersie label distributive bargaining: a zero-sum conflict over a problem in which the parties' interests are diametrically opposed. However, although distributive bargaining is the most common conceptualization of the union-management relationship, it is not the only possible arrangement. An alternative model is provided by integrative bargaining, in which solutions exist that could benefit both parties—increasing the size of the pie rather than exclusively determining its division.

However, integrative solutions are not self-evident—they are discovered through joint problem solving, which is only possible under particular circumstances and contexts (Walton & McKersie, 1965/1991). Bennett and Kaufman (2004) argue that the benefits of voice can only be realized when management takes a constructive approach to collective bargaining and the parties deal with one another in a "spirit of mutual cooperation and gain" (p. 342). Similarly, Walton and McKersie (1965/1991) emphasize the importance of trust and transparent communication—relational factors absent from many theories of union behavior and which are incorporated into the theoretical framework of this research (Chapter 2).

The discussion thus far has focused on private sector unions. Public sector unions may provide both constructive, efficiency-enhancing voice as well as monopoly-based constraints (Freeman & Medoff, 1984). But how might these concepts differ in the public sector? Although public sector unions may behave like private sector unions—their actions are driven by similar goals, i.e., scarcity consciousness—the institutional opportunity structure for exercising their power is thought to be unique (Freeman, 2005).

Three major differences between public and private sector unions exist. First, the public sector may face lower fiscal constraints. Because the public sector cannot 'go out of business,'[15] public sector management may have fewer incentives to resist union demands. Thus, public sector unions' individualism may operate unchecked by fiscal discipline that would otherwise force them to work cooperatively with management—at least on some issues. This may be exacerbated by the second key difference—the fact that public sector unions get to elect their negotiating partners, providing unions with an additional avenue for advocating for public spending increases and altering the nature of bargaining (Freeman, 2005). The third difference is that cooperation and compromise in the public sector may not be efficiency-enhancing, as compromises may maximize the welfare of negotiating parties at the expense of non-represented parties—the public (Moe, 1995).

The differences in the institutional environments of public and private sector unionism—lack of fiscal constraints, ability to elect bargaining opponents and lobby them politically—are significant. However, there are a number of ways in which unions' voice face may actually be enhanced in the public sector. A narrow, monopolistic conception of teachers' unions' preferences, emphasizing economic self-interest, is not self-evident. Theories of professionalism and corporatism bolster Freeman and Medoff's voice face and provide alternative conceptions of organizational preferences, including, and possibly especially, in the public sector.

Professionalism: Beyond Self-interest?

Gunderson (2005) applies Freeman and Medoff's (1984) two faces framework and argues that in the public sector, voice is relatively more important than in the private sector because of the highly educated and professional character of the public workforce, in contrast to their predominantly blue-collar private sector counterparts. Gunderson suggests that part of what professional public sector unions do is to bring the workers' expertise to bear on workplace issues. This voice may improve the working conditions for employees, but may also have significant benefits for the successful execution of the work—benefiting both management and students, in the case of education.

The distinct challenges of the public sector environment and the unique characteristics of public employees meet in discourses of professionalism. States' ability to act unilaterally in the development and implementation of policy—for example in education—is limited; they depend on producers to inform their decision-making and will rely on them to implement policies after they are formulated (Williamson, 1988). Furthermore, the fact that producers in the welfare fields are often considered professionals or 'semi-professionals' imbues these occupations with a special status and credibility in the policy-making process (Gunderson, 2005; Krejsler, 2005). Thus, their involvement is viewed as more "legitimate because of their public-regarding ethos than the inclusion of economic producers whose motives are seen as obviously centered on their material self-interest" (Williamson, 1988, p. 178).

Parsons (1954) defined a profession—a highly contested term—as an occupation that maintains a monopoly position, has secured the rights of self-regulation, is organized to defend its position of power, and acts, or is thought to act, in an altruistic and public-regarding manner. The degree to which professionals and the organizations that represent them are motivated by an altruistic or public-regarding manner is the subject of great debate both theoretically and empirically (Brante, 1988; Friedson, 1988, 1994; Gross, 1978; Larson, 1977; Marshall, 1939). However, the key distinction is that it is possible that public sector workers are motivated by altruism or solidarity extending beyond their material self-interest.[16] This assumption has significant implications for teachers' unions' behavior and impact.

Choosing Voice Over Monopoly through Patterns of Cooperation: Corporatism and Consociationalism

Although a pluralist approach to unions—with its emphasis on conflict and distributive bargaining—is ideologically dominant in the United States, it is not the only available framework. European labor relations—particularly Germany, Northern Europe, and Scandinavia—approach unions quite differently, guided by an emphasis on social partnership and codetermination which is rooted in a history of corporatism (Jurgens, Berthon, Papania, &

Shabbir, 2010; Tucker, 2011). In contrast to the pluralist conception, in Northern Europe, corporations include employees in decision-making and are "a coalition of various participants . . . striving for continuity of the firm as a whole" (Lenssen & Verobey, 20051, as cited in Jurgens et al., 2010, p. 771). Without this representation, the voice might be expressed in a more threatening way. As Cawson (1985) argues:

> not all interest organizations are simply aggregate containers into which preferences are poured. Certain kinds of organizations have developed a semi-compulsory character; they constrain and discipline their members. (p. 4)

Even Olson (1982), who suggests that competition between rent-seeking interest groups undermines economic efficiency and growth and associates interest group proliferation with the decline of nations, portrays encompassing organizations as a solution to the interest group problem. Because of their exclusivity and homogeneity, narrow distributional coalitions promote their members' preferences at the expense of benefits to non-members. However, the inclusivity of membership in encompassing organizations[17]—or peak organizations—disciplines their interests and advocacy; they have "some incentive to make the society in which they operate more prosperous" (p. 74).

The theoretical alternative to pluralist policy-making is concertation or corporatism (Schmitter, 1982). Corporatism is a contested term,[18] but is generally used to refer to particular institutional arrangements that formalize negotiation, including encompassing organizations or peak associations that participate in centralized or tripartite negotiations (1982). Despite institutional changes in the formal representation of labor market organizations—what some have identified as the decline of corporatism—the process of compromise and negotiation with organized labor and interest groups remains central to the policy-making *process* in many nations (Molina & Rhodes, 2002; Rhodes, 2001). Rather than disappearing, corporatism has been updated in the form of concertation (Schmitter, 1982).

The subtle shift in the discussion from institution-centric corporatism to process-focused concertation reflects an emphasis on policy style—the standard operating procedures for handling issues which arrive on the political agenda, which include both the government's approach to problem solving and its relationship with other actors (Richardson, 1982; Bacarro, 2003). In contrast to pluralism, in which parties battle for influence, the effect of policy concertation is to align the incentives of all bargaining parties. Theoretically, with voice in the decision-making process comes accountability for the effective provision of the public good: with influence come incentives to behave responsibly.[19] This influence-for-responsibility exchange may be particularly salient in the provision of public services, particularly when the central state is dependent on others for the successful realization and implementation of services (Williamson, 1988). It also may be closely linked to, and justified by, the public-serving ethos of professionalism, as outlined in the previous section (Cawson, 1982).

Compston (2003) identifies concertation as the product of three factors: policy problems that are solvable with cooperation, the degree of preexisting shared frameworks for the goals of economic policy, and the degree to which all sides can be expected to fulfill their commitments. Although Compston focuses on national-level agreements and public policy broadly defined, the shift from institution-focused corporatism to process-focused concertation is significant for two reasons.

First, it extends the potential influence of compromise and negotiation *beyond* the coordinated market economies with the formal institutional arrangements that mark corporatism (Hall & Soskice, 2001). Research on concertation has demonstrated that what Culpepper (2002) calls 'social pacts' are being implemented in countries without the institutional prerequisites—organized, centralized, internally coordinated and encompassing unions and employers with authority over their constituencies (Rhodes, 2001). So, concertation is not restricted to small corporatist nations or coordinated market economies (Hall & Soskice, 2001; Katzenstein, 1985). And, it is possible that patterns of policy-concertation may be observed at the sectoral level even when they are not observed at the state level. For example, in Scandinavia, which is known for high levels of formal and informal policy coordination, "there have been marked differences between policy areas with respect to the extent of routine pressure group involvement" (Arter, 1999, p. 163). A similar diversity of interest group involvement is feasible in education politics in the United States, given its strong history of local educational governance in school districts as well as highly differentiated laws on unionization and collective bargaining (Berkman & Plutzer, 2005; Johnson & Donaldson, 2006).

Second, whether policy-making is viewed through a pluralist or corporatist/concertation lens has important implications for conceptions of the role of interest groups in policy-making and reform—including the role of public sector unions in public sector restructuring and reform. Although pluralist policy-making assumes a power-oriented approach to policy-making, concertation provides a theoretical mechanism through which interest groups may be incentivized to behave as co-producers, or to utilize their voice face. The resilience of concertation suggests that a relatively collaborative approach to union preferences, goals, and demands is both theoretically and empirically possible.

Collaborative approaches should not be misconstrued with the absence of conflict. Katzenstein is clear that the "ideology of social partnership" (1985, p. 88) is not rooted in an individual predisposition toward compromise, but that the 'culture of compromise' is an institutional pattern or a shared commitment—in spite of disagreement. Similarly, in their writing about US teachers' unions, Koppich and Kerchner (2000) argue that collaboration is not synonymous with 'consistent civility' or an absence of conflict. This distinction—that parties can collaborate in spite of disagreement—is crucial.

The contribution of theories of concertation to this research is twofold. First, the research must be sensitive to the structures that may enhance unions' voice face, that "manage to couple narrowly conceived group interests with shared interpretations of the public good" (Katzenstein, 1985, p. 32). Second, this research will remain open to the way that actors' first-order preferences may be disciplined or modified by relationship patterns rooted in both formal and informal institutions.

Union Preferences, Interests, and Goals: Remaining Open to Complexity

It is important to remain open to the ways in which union preferences may be more complex and variant. Scharpf (1997, pp. 85–87)[20] provides an overview of relational preferences that includes but extends beyond self-interest:

- **Individualism:**[21] Self-interest maximization ($U^x = X$)[22]
- **Solidarity:** Unrestrained cooperation ($U^x = X + Y$)
- **Competition:** Need to win, envy ($U^x = X - Y$)
- **Altruism:** 'Helping professions;' the good of the other ($U^x = Y$)
- **Hostility:** Hate ($U^x = -Y$)

Although these are ideal-typical configurations and they refer to relational preferences rather than specific policy preferences—for higher salaries or better working conditions, for example—they provide a helpful framework for approaching the various perspectives on union preferences. Although rational choice theory-based individualistic preferences dominate the theoretical landscape, alternatives exist. This section has traced the ways the literature on unions remains open to the contribution of non-economic motivations. Interest groups may be united by solidarity rather than individualism. Professionalism may promote solidarity or altruism, providing an important check against unions' economic interests—particularly amongst public sector unions. Finally, theories of corporatism suggest that institutions can be arranged in such a way that actors are incentivized to cooperate—to maximize their joint gain. Thus, the individualism of unions is subjected to pressures to promote the public good (Cawson, 1985).

Furthermore, research that explicitly focuses on teachers' and union leaders' preferences supports a view of preference complexity, suggesting that self-interests and other interests are "always present and that the union's emphasis cycles back and forth, depending on the contextual conditions that vary across time" (Poole, 2000, p. 98). Furthermore, the relative weight assigned to various goals varied across individuals (Poole, 2000). Any investigation of teachers' unions must remain open to the ways in which non-economic interests may inform union preferences, strategies, or actions. The theoretical framework provides a structured but open approach to union preferences, incorporating both short- and long-term interests and both economic and non-economic goals and preferences (Chapter 2).

Union Strength and Union Power: Synonymous or Distinct?

When teachers' unions are identified as powerful,[23] what does that mean? In the field of labor relations, union strength is often synonymous with density—the ratio of unionized versus non-unionized workers in a given industry. However, union strength, power, and influence are often used interchangeably, with confusing results. For example, although acknowledging that as a whole, union strength in the US, as measured by union density, was declining in the 1980s, Fiorito and Maranto (1987) went on to suggest that "in certain industries, occupations, and areas of the United States, unions are strong *in the sense that they continue to achieve favorable bargaining settlements and or legislation* that would not have been obtained but for unionism" (p. 12, emphasis added). Fiorito and Maranto's multiple definitions of union strength—one that is quantifiable and objective and another that is subjective and unquantifiable—illustrate the challenge of achieving conceptual clarity around strength and power.

Measuring strength as 'successful influence'[24] is untenable for theory building as it creates an unfalsifiable hypothesis. Stating that "strong unions block reform" is more akin to a self-fulfilling prophecy than a prediction or hypothesis. If reform occurs, the prediction isn't wrong, we are just left to conclude that the union must have been weak. On the other hand, if legislation or bargaining settlements are—or appear to be—influenced by unions, then their blocking-power is confirmed. However, there is no insight into when or why union influence varies, nor is it possible to consider situations in which the outcome—whether the presence of absence of reform—may not have been primarily or exclusively due to union influence. In order to be able to test, and possibly challenge, refine, or falsify the hypothesis that strong unions shape outcomes in suboptimal ways, conceptual clarity about union strength, as distinct from the *effect* of union strength, is required. The following sections distinguish between union strength and union power.

Defining Union Strength

What is union strength and how should it be measured? Traditionally, density has been a proxy for strength; especially in international comparison, the two terms are often used interchangeably (Blanchflower & Freeman, 1992; Kahn, 1979; Oskarsson, 2003). Examining international trends in union density provides the opportunity to make three important distinctions:

- First, although a secular decline in union density across the OECD area has been observed since the 1960s, marked differences between countries persist with significant differences between the Nordic countries and the United States, for example (Visser, 2013). So it is important to be cautious in speaking about a decline in union strength, and the relative decline should not be perceived as convergence or universal weakening of unions.

- Second, focus on the secular decline in aggregate union density ignores significant differences between trends in public and private sector membership in many countries. For example, although total union density in the United States has fallen from 20.1% in 1983 to 6.6% in 2011, public sector unionization was 35.9% in 2011 (Bureau of Labor Statistics, 2013), suggesting that general conceptions of union strength may obscure important differences between sectors and industries within a country.
- Third, when union strength is examined in comparative context, it confirms the importance of keeping static measures of union strength distinct from union power or influence. The relationship between strength (resources) and power (influence) seems to vary cross-nationally. For example, despite their weakness according to density,[25] French unions are generally regarded as influential or powerful (Goetschy, 1998), suggesting that power and strength are not identical.

Therefore, 'union strength'—as measured by density alone or in combination with other contributing variables like union competition or financial and political resources like assets, net worth, revenues, and political action committees (Bennett, 1991; Ebbinghaus & Visser, 1999; Masters & Atkins, 1996; Mitchell, 1996; Willman, 1990)—refers to unions' static, measurable resources.

Defining Union Power

Ultimately, unlike strength, which is static and measurable, power is dynamic and contingent—realized through the influence process—and more difficult to define (Immergut, 1992; Laswell & Kaplan, 1950). Some distinguish between coercive and consensus-based power: Laswell and Kaplan (1950) identify power as coercive action motivated by sanctions as distinct from influence,[26] and Parsons (1963) refers to positive influence—inducement or persuasion—and negative sanctions—coercion or activation of commitments or obligations. Moe (2005) argues that cooperative and mutually beneficial relationships *between* insiders should not be taken as a sign of power-free, neutral institutions. Instead, to the extent that cooperation occurs, it should be seen as a manifestation of power as only some of the players in part of the story are included in cooperative processes and these players use cooperation to "impose institutions on political losers" (Moe, 2005, p. 228).

In this research, power is defined as "the ability of one party to fix or alter the conditions of exchange in its favor" (Armstrong, Bowers, & Burkitt, 1977, p. 91), which rests on political, social, and economic factors.[27] Furthermore, this research adopts Immergut's (1992) view of the contingency of power. She argues that "power is not an essential or invariant characteristic of particular interest groups," but instead is "contingent on strategic opportunities stemming from the logic of political decision processes" (Immergut, 1992, p. 8). Thus, power is a "circulating medium, analogous to money" (Parsons, 1963, p. 236). These definitions are consistent with the ways teachers' unions' power has been observed in the literature. In his review of teachers' unions' power in the US, Urban (2004) argues that while union membership and other strength resources from 1980–2000 were steady, the mobilization of those resources—the currency conversion into power—was highly variable. Furthermore, the purchasing power of strength resources can vary across domains—national, state, or local politics versus bargaining (Streshly & DeMitchell, 1994).

Theoretically and methodologically, emphasizing the contingency of power places the focus on the *process* through which strength resources are translated into power. The question is not who is powerful in the abstract, but which actors were influential on *this issue* at *this time?* Tracing the impact of unions on public policy-making is difficult because no single process by which policies are formed exists—behavior and frameworks vary from issue to issue. Educational policy-making is hard to model due to the proliferation of forms: how do problems develop? Who is involved in their formation? On what issues? Under what conditions? In what ways? (Bent & Reeves, 1978). For example, in the United States, is the policy primarily a federal, state, or local decision? Furthermore, is the policy determined through bargaining or politics? The contingency of power makes the identification of the theoretically significant activities of public sector unions—their conversion of strength into power—more complex. Perhaps this complexity explains the curious opacity of union activity in the theoretical literature (Pocock, 1999). Thus, despite the inherent challenges, explicating the contingent process through which strength resources are translated into power will address a significant gap in the existing literature.

CONCLUSION

Theories of teachers' unions and common assumptions of their interests, strength, and power are plagued by two major limitations. First, the dominant assumptions about teachers' unions' interests are overly narrow, excluding real alternatives. Despite sweeping generalizations about union interests and influence, there is great—and documented—local variation in union interest and responses as well as policy outcomes (Bascia, 1990; Johnson & Donaldson 2006; Johnson & Kardos 2000; Murray, 2004). Intraorganizational demands and the requirements of political legitimacy are context dependent, critical to organizational survival, and may vary over time and space (Bascia, 2009; McDonnell & Pascal, 1988; Urban, 2004). The way that leaders manage the tension between internal and external demands—when they are in conflict—may lead to different union strategies and policy outcomes. Second, union strength[28] is poorly conceptualized and operationalized in teachers' union research. Policy-making influence may fluctuate by issue, arena, political culture, institutional arrangement, strength of contending groups, and the degree of cohesion or fragmentation within the union itself (Malen, 2001).

As a result of these limitations, empirical research cannot adequately explain "why some union-district negotiations are more peaceful than others or why conflict may surge and fall from one contract negotiation to the next within a given district" (Hess & Kelly, 2006, p. 61). Nor can it produce reliable generalizations about the influence of teachers' unions on policy outcomes. If a union fails to achieve its assumed policy goal—for example, to increase teachers' salaries or to obtain stronger tenure protections—is that because the union was weak? Or could it have been because the union's interests deviated from theoretical predictions?

These gaps are exacerbated by a systematic neglect of the *process* through which teachers' unions impact education policy. Virtually all empirical research attempts to measure the correlation between unionism[29] and some measureable outcome.[30] However, the relationship between independent and dependent variable—the variable process through which unionization or union strength is employed to influence policy—is ignored (Goldhaber, 2006). The process-oriented focus of this research—when does PRP reform occur; why doesn't it always; and what is the role of teachers' unions in these processes.

NOTES

1. Discussed below.
2. Bordogna (2008) identifies decentralized collective bargaining, the elimination of automatic salary increases, and the introduction of performance-related pay as three NPM-based ideas.
3. Denmark, Sweden, and Norway
4. Going into teachers' base pay.
5. Proposals to pay teachers on the basis of knowledge and skills or for additional work/responsibilities that do *not* include any link to outputs will be referred to under the more general label of differentiated compensation.
6. For teachers, subjective measures typically refer to evaluations and objective measures include a variety of quantitative measures of student learning.
7. Interviewees and informants explicitly referred to neoliberalism in Finland and NPM in Switzerland.
8. These stories typically emerge from theorizing about unions' goals and then imputing their effects on student achievement.
9. Due to the disproportionate amount of research on teachers' unions that is conducted in the US, these stories about teachers' unions are often 'locally focused,' however, they have global reach.
10. The two are inseparable, either because teachers are altruistically motivated to sacrifice their economic self-interest; because there is a symbiotic relationship between professionalism and economic self-interest; or because there is no tension between teachers' best interests and students' best interests (Bascia & Rottmann, 2011; Johnson & Donaldson, 2006; Kahlenberg, 2006).
11. Selig Perlman (as cited in Taft, 1950) suggests that this self-interest is rooted in a 'consciousness of scarcity,' which was a significant departure from ideological, class-based consciousness conceptions of the labor movement.
12. This view of 'working conditions' as 'what's best for teachers' and antithetical to 'what's best for students' has been challenged (Bascia & Rottmann, 2011).
13. Collective action problems refer to situations in which the action of a few individuals would benefit a large group of people, but because the entire group

benefits from the action of a few, individuals are incentivized to do nothing and to 'free ride' on others' work.
14. This is consistent with the Coase Theorem (Moe, 1995), which suggests that voluntary agreements among rational and self-interested actors can produce welfare gains.
15. Which imposes a constraint on union demands because they too will suffer—in terms of job losses—if the firm cannot maintain economic competitiveness.
16. Professionalism will be further explored in Chapter 2.
17. Encompassing organizations are defined as "large heterogeneous interest organizations" that through corporatist arrangements are encouraged "to accept public responsibility for their demands and actions" (Micheletti, 1990, pp. 255–256).
18. Korpi (1983) distinguishes between state corporatism—a tool for state control and coercion—and what he labels 'societal bargaining,' which Cawson (1985) calls neo-corporatism.
19. More cynical interpretations suggest that corporatism was motivated by the state's need for control and legitimacy, i.e., the appearance of democracy (Lehmbruch, 1977).
20. Walton and McKersie (1965/1991) also identify individualism, solidarity, and competition.
21. 'Individualism' when applied to the union—a 'composite actor' (Scharpf, 1997)—refers to the individualistic orientation of the organization relative to other actors, not necessarily to the preferences of individual teachers.
22. Preferences (Ux) of Ego (X) relative to Alter (Y)
23. For example, in Bascia (1990), Cooper & Sureau (2008b), Hess & West (2006), Kahlenberg (2006), Koppich (2005), Koppich & Callahan (2009), and Moe (2006).
24. Or, "achiev(ing) favorable bargaining settlements and or legislation that would not have been obtained but for unionism" (Fiorito & Maranto, 1987).
25. 7.6% in 2009 (Visser, 2013).
26. They also identify a third category, 'authority,' which enables acceptance to be motivated by attitudes toward legitimacy.
27. This is also similar to Hobbes' definition of power as the capacity to attain ends or goals in social relations.
28. Similarly, unionization is poorly understood. When does an organization of teachers go from an association to a union? When their memberships include more than 50% of teachers within their district; when teachers' organizations are legally given the right to collectively bargain at the state level; when they actively engage in a contractual agreement with the school district; or some combination of the three?
29. However defined.
30. Organization of schooling as reflected in collective bargaining agreements or spending or student achievement.

REFERENCES

Aasen, P. (2003). What happened to social democratic progressivism in Scandinavia? Restructuring education in Sweden and Norway in the 1990s. In M. W. Apple & P. Aasen (Eds.), *The state and the politics of knowledge*. London: Routledge, 109–147.

Adams, S. J., & Heywood, J. S. (2009). The perils of quantitative accountability. In S. J. Adams, J. S. Heywood, & R. Rothstein (Eds.), *Teachers, performance pay, and accountability: What education should learn from other sectors.* Washington, DC: Economic Policy Institute, 13–64.

Apple, M. W. (2001). Comparing neo-liberal projects and inequality in education. *Comparative Education, 37*(4), 409–423.

Apple, M. W., & Teitelbaum, K. (1986). Are teachers losing control of their skills and curriculum? *Journal of Curriculum Studies, 18*(2), 177–184.

Argys, L. M., & Reese, D. I. (1995). Unionization and school productivity: A reexamination. *Research in Labor Economics, 14*, 49–67.

Armstrong, K. J., & Bowers, D., & Burkitt, B. (1977). The measurement of trade union bargaining power. *British Journal of Industrial Relations, 15*(1), 91–100.

Armstrong, M. (2010). *Armstrong's handbook of reward management practice: Improving performance through reward.* London: Kogan Page Publishers.

Arter, D. (1999). *Scandinavian politics today.* Manchester: Manchester University Press.

Bacarro, L. (2003). What is alive and what is dead in the theory of corporatism. *British Journal of Industrial Relations, 41*(4), 683–706.

Bach, S., & Kessler, I. (2007). Human resource management and the new public management. In P. Boxall, J. Purcell, & P. Wright (Eds.), *The Oxford Handbook of Human Resource Management.* Oxford: Oxford University Press, 469–488.

Ball, S. J. (1998). Big policies/small world: An introduction to international perspectives in education policy. *Comparative Education, 34*(2), 119–130.

Ball, S. J. (2001). Global policies and vernacular politics in education. *Curriculo sem Fronteiras, 1*(2), 27–43.

Ball, S. J. (2003). The teacher's soul and the terrors of performativity. *Journal of Education Policy, 18*(2), 215–228.

Ballou, D. (2001). Pay for performance in public and private schools. *Economics of Education Review, 20*(1), 51–61.

Bascia, N. (1990). Teachers evaluations of unions. *Journal of Education Policy, 5*(4), 301–312.

Bascia, N. (2009). Pushing on the paradigm: Research on teachers organizations as policy actors. In G. Sykes, B. Schneider, & D. Plank (Eds.), *Handbook of education policy research.* New York: Routledge, 785–792.

Bascia, N., & Rottmann, C. (2011). What's so important about teachers' working conditions? The fatal flaw in education reform. *Journal of Education Policy, 26*(6), 787–802.

Baugh, W. H., & Stone, J. A. (1982). Teachers, unions, and wages in the 1970s: Unionism now pays. *Industrial and Labor Relations Review, 35*(3), 368–376.

Bennett, J. T. (1991). Private sector unions: The myth of decline. *Journal of Labor Research, 12*(1), 1–12.

Bennett, J. T., & Kaufman, B. E. (2004). What do unions do? A twenty-year perspective. *Journal of Labor Research, 25*(3), 339–349.

Bent, A. E., & Reeves, T. Z. (1978). *Collective bargaining in the public sector: Labor-management relations and public policy.* Menlo Park, CA: Benjamin/Cummings Publishing Co.

Bentley, A. F. (1978). *The process of government.* Chicago: University of Chicago Press. Original work published 1908.

Berkman, M. B., & Plutzer, E. (2005). *Ten thousand democracies: Politics and public opinion in America's school districts.* Washington, DC: Georgetown University Press.

Blanchflower, D. G., & Freeman, R. B. (1992). Unionism in the United States and other advanced OECD countries. *Industrial Relations: A Journal of Economy and Society, 31*(1), 56–79.

Booth, A. L. (1995). *The economics of the trade union.* New York: Cambridge University Press.

Bordogna, L. (2008). Moral hazard, transaction costs, and the reform of public service employment relations. *European Journal of Industrial Relations, 14*(4), 381–400.

Bowe, R., & Ball, S.J. (1992). *Reforming education and changing schools: Case studies in policy sociology.* London: Routledge.

Brante, T. (1988). Sociological approaches to the professions. *Acta Sociologica, 31*(2), 119–142.

Burbules, N.C., & Densmore, K. (1991). The limits of making teaching a profession. *Educational Policy, 5*(1), 44–63.

Bureau of Labor Statistics. (2013). *Union Members—2012* (U.S. Department of Labor. USDL-13-0105). Retrieved from September 4, 2013, from http://www.bls.gov/news.release/pdf/union2.pdf

Carini, R.M., Powell, B., & Steelman, L.C. (2000). Do teacher unions hinder educational performance? Lessons learned from state SAT and ACT scores. *Harvard Educational Review, 70*(4), 437–467.

Cawson, A. (1982). *Corporatism and welfare.* London: Heinemann.

Cawson, A. (Ed.). (1985). *Organized interests and the state: Studies in meso-corporatism.* London: Sage.

Christensen, T., & Laegreid, P. (2001). New public management: The effects of contractualism and devolution on political control. *Public Management Review, 3*(1), 73–93.

Chubb, J.E., & Moe, T.M. (1990). *Politics, markets, and America's schools.* Washington, DC: Brookings Institution.

Compston, H. (2003). Beyond corporatism: A configurational theory of policy concertation. *European Journal of Political Research, 42*(6), 787–809.

Compton, M., & Weiner, L. (2008a). The global assault on teaching, teachers, and teacher unions. In M. Compton & L. Weiner (Eds.), *The global assault on teaching, teachers, and their unions: Stories for resistance.* New York: Palgrave Macmillan, 3–10.

Compton, M., & Weiner, L. (Eds.). (2008b). *The global assault on teaching, teachers, and their unions: Stories for resistance.* New York: Palgrave Macmillan.

Cooper, B.S., & Sureau, J. (2008a). The collective politics of teacher unionism. In B. Cooper, J.G. Cibulka, & L. Fusarelli (Eds.), *Handbook of education politics and policy.* New York: Routledge, 263–282.

Cooper, B.S., & Sureau, J. (2008b). Teacher unions and the politics of fear in labor relations. *Educational Policy, 22*(1), 86–104.

Crossley, M. (2000). Bridging cultures and traditions in the reconceptualisation of comparative and international education. *Comparative Education, 36*(3), 319–332.

Crouch, L. (2005). Political economy, incentives and teachers unions: Case studies in Chile and Peru. In E. Vegas (Ed.), *Incentives to improve teaching.* Washington, DC: World Bank, 389–424.

Culpepper, P.D. (2002). Powering, puzzling, and 'pacting': The informational logic of negotiated reforms. *Journal of European Public Policy, 9*(5), 774–790.

Dixit, A. (2002). Incentives and organizations in the public sector: An interpretative review. *The Journal of Human Resources, 37*(4), 696–727.

Dohmen, T., & Falk, A. (2010). You get what you pay for: Incentives and selection in the education system. *The Economic Journal, 120*(546), 256–271.

Ebbinghaus, E., & Visser, J. (1999). When institutions matter: Union growth and decline in Western Europe, 1950–1995. *European Sociological Review, 15*(2), 135–148.

Eberts, R.W. (2007). Teachers unions and student performance: Help or hindrance? *The Future of Children, 17*(1), 175–199.

Eberts, R.W., Hollenbeck, K., & Stone, J.A. (2004). Teachers unions: Outcomes and reform initiatives. In R.D. Henderson, W.J. Urban, & P. Wolman (Eds.), *Teachers unions and education policy: Retrenchment or reform?* Oxford: Elesevier, 51–80.

Eberts, R. W., & Stone, J. A. (1984). *Unions and public schools: The effect of collective bargaining on American education.* Lexington, MA: Lexingtion Books.
Eberts, R. W., & Stone, J. A. (1986). Teacher unions and the cost of public education. *Economic Inquiry,* 24(4), 631–643.
Eberts, R. W., & Stone, J. A. (1987). Teachers' unions and the productivity of public schools. *Economic Inquiry,* 24, 631–644.
Fiorito, J., & Maranto, C. (1987). The contemporary decline of union strength. *Contemporary Policy Issues,* 5(4), 12–24.
Freeman, R. B. (2005). What do unions do? The 2004 m-brane stringtwister. *Journal of Labor Research,* 26(4), 641–668.
Freeman, R. B., & Medoff, J. L. (1984). *What do unions do?* New York: Basic Books.
Freidson, E. (1988). *Professional powers: A study of the institutionalization of knowledge.* Chicago, IL: University of Chicago Press.
Freidson, E. (1994). *Professionalism reborn: Theory, prophecy, and policy.* Cambridge: Polity.
Gallagher, D. G. (1978). Teacher bargaining and school district expenditures. *Industrial Relations: A Journal of Economy and Society,* 17(2), 231–237.
Garceau, O. (1958). Interest group theory in political research. *Annals of the American Academy of Political and Social Science,* 319, 104–112.
Glewwe, P., Ilias, N., & Kremer, M. (2010). Teacher incentives. *American Economic Journal: Applied Economics,* 2(3), 205–227.
Goetschy, J. (1998). France: The limits of reform. *Changing Industrial Relations in Europe,* 2, 357–394.
Goldhaber, D. (2006). Are teachers unions good for students? In J. Hannaway & A. Rotherman (Eds.), *Collective bargaining in education: Negotiating change in today's schools.* Cambridge, MA: Harvard Education, 141–159.
Gratz, D. B. (2005). Lessons from Denver: The pay for performance pilot. *Phi Delta Kappan,* 86(8), 569–581.
Green, A. (1997). *Education, globalization, and the nation state.* London: Macmillan.
Gross, S. J. (1978). The myth of professional licensing. *American Psychologist,* 33(11), 1009.
Gunderson, M. (2005). Two faces of union voice in the public sector. *Journal of Labor Research,* 26(3), 3939–3958.
Hall, P. A., & Soskice, D. (2001). *Varieties of capitalism: The institutional foundations of the comparative advantage.* Oxford: Oxford University Press.
Hall, W. C., & Carroll, N. (1973). The effect of teachers organizations on salaries and class size. *Industrial and Labor Relations Review,* 26, 834–841.
Halpin, D., & Troyna, B. (1995). The politics of education policy borrowing. *Comparative Education,* 31(3), 303–310.
Hannaway, J. (1992). Higher order skills, job design, and incentives: An analysis and proposal. *American Educational Research Journal,* 29(1), 3–21.
Hanushek, E. (1994). *Making schools work: Improving performance and controlling costs.* Washington, DC: The Brookings Institute.
Hanushek, E., & Rivkin, S. G. (2006). Teacher quality. In E. Hanushek & F. Welch (Eds.), *Handbook of the economics of education.* Oxford: Elsevier, 1051–1078.
Hargreaves, A. (2000). Four ages of professionalism and professional learning. *Teachers and teaching: Theory and practice,* 6(2), 151–182.
Harvey, D. (2005). *A brief history of neoliberalism.* Oxford: Oxford University Press.
Harvey, D. (2007). Neoliberalism as creative destruction. *The ANNALS of the American Academy of Political and Social Science,* 610(1), 21–44.
Hess, F. M., & Kelly, A. P. (2006). Scapegoat, albatross, or what? In J. Hannaway & A. Rotherham (Eds.), *Collective bargaining in education: Negotiating change in today's schools.* Cambridge, MA: Harvard Education Press, 53–87.

Hess, F. M., & West, M. R. (2006). *A better bargain: Overhauling teacher collective bargaining for the 21st century.* Cambridge, MA: Program on Education Policy and Governance, Harvard University.

Hill, P. (2006). The costs of collective bargaining agreements and related district policies. In J. Hannaway & A. Rotherman (Eds.), *Collective bargaining in education: Negotiating change in today's schools.* Cambridge, MA: Harvard Education Press, 89–110.

Hirsch, B. T., & Addison, J. T. (1986). *The economic analysis of unions: New approaches and evidence.* Boston: Allen & Unwin.

Hood, C. (1990). De-Sir Humphreyfying the Westminster model of bureaucracy: A new style of governance? *Governance, 3*(2), 205–214.

Hood, C. (1991). A public management for all seasons? *Public Administration, 69*(1), 3–19.

Hood, C. (1995). The new public management in the 1980s: Variations on a theme. *Accounting, Organizations and Society, 20*(2), 93–99.

Hoxby, C. M. (1996). How teachers' unions affect education production. *The Quarterly Journal of Economics, 111*(3), 671–717.

Hoxby, C. M., & Leigh, A. (2004). Pulled away or pushed out? Explaining the decline of teacher aptitude in the United States. *American Economic Review, 93*(2), 236–240.

Hudson, C. (2007). Governing the governance of education: The state strikes back? *European Educational Research Journal, 6*(3), 262–282.

Ibsen, C. L., Larsen, T. P., Madsen, J. S., & Due, J. (2011). Challenging Scandinavian employment relations: The effects of new public management reforms. *The International Journal of Human Resource Management, 22*(11), 2295–2310.

Immergut, E. (1992). *Health politics.* Cambridge: Cambridge University Press.

Johnson, S. M., & Donaldson, M. (2006). The effects of collective bargaining on teacher quality. In J. Hannaway, & A. Rotherman (Eds.), *Collective bargaining in education: Negotiating change in today's schools.* Cambridge, MA: Harvard Education Press, 111–140.

Johnson, S. M., & Kardos, S. (2000). Reform bargaining and its promise for school improvement. In T. Loveless (Ed.), *Conflicting missions? Teachers unions and educational reform.* Washington, DC: Brookings Institution, 7–46.

Johnson, S. M., & Papay, J. P. (2009). *Redesigning teacher pay: A system for the next generation of educators.* Washington, DC: Economic Policy Institute.

Jurgens, M., Berthon, P., Papania, L., & Shabbir, H. A. (2010). Stakeholder theory and practice in Europe and North America: The key to success lies in the marketing approach. *Industrial Marketing Management, 39,* 769–775.

Kahlenberg, R. D. (2006). The history of collective bargaining among teachers. In J. Hannaway & A. Rotherman (Eds.), *Collective bargaining in education: Negotiating change in today's schools.* Cambridge, MA: Harvard Education Press, 7–26.

Kahn, L. M. (1979). Union strength and wage inflation. *Industrial Relations, 18*(2), 144–154.

Katzenstein, P. J. (1985). *Small states in world markets: Industrial policy in Europe.* Ithaca, NY: Cornell University Press.

Kaufman, B. E. (2002). Models of union wage determination: What have we learned since Dunlop and Ross? *Industrial Relations, 41*(1), 303–316.

Kaufman, B. E. (2004). What unions do: Insights from economic theory. *Journal of Labor Research, 25*(3), 341–372.

Kerchner, C. T., & Koppich, J. E. (1993). *A union of professionals: Labor relations and educational reform.* New York: Teachers College Press.

Koppich, J. E. (2005). Addressing teacher quality through induction, professional compensation, and evaluation: Effects on labor-management relations. *Educational Policy, 19*(1), 90–110.

Koppich, J. E., & Callahan, M. (2009). Teacher collective bargaining: What we know and what we need to know. In G. Sykes, B. Schneider, & D. Plank (Eds.), *Handbook of education policy research*. New York: Routledge, 296–306.

Koppich, J. E., & Kerchner, C. T. (2000, April 24–28). *Rethinking labor-management relations: It's a matter of trust, or is it?* Paper presented at the Annual Meeting of the American Educational Research Association, New Orleans, LA.

Korpi, W. (1983). *The democratic class struggle*. London: Routledge & Kegan Paul Books.

Krejsler, J. (2005). Professions and their identities: How to explore professional development among (semi-)professions. *Scandinavian Journal of Educational Research*, 49(4), 335–356.

Larson, M. S. (1977). *The rise of professionalism: A sociological analysis*. Berkeley: University of California Press.

Laswell, H., & Kaplan, A. (1950). *Power and Society*. New Haven: Yale.

Lavy, V. (2007). Using performance-based pay to improve the quality of teachers. *The future of children*, 17(1), 87–109.

Lazear, E. P. (2000). The power of incentives. *American Economic Review (Paper and Proceedings)*, 90(2), 410–414.

Lazear, E. P. (2003). Teacher incentives. *Swedish Economic Policy Review*, 10(2), 179–214.

Lehmbruch, G. (1977). Liberal corporatism and party government. *Comparative Political Studies*, 10(1), 91–126.

Levin, B. (1997). The lessons of international education reform. *Journal of Education Policy*, 12(4), 253–266.

Levin, B. (1998). An epidemic of education policy: (What) can we learn from each other? *Comparative Education*, 34(2), 131–141.

Lieberman, M. (2000). *The teachers unions: How the NEA and AFT sabotage reform and hold students, parents, teachers, and taxpayers hostage to bureaucracy*. New York, NY: Free Press.

Malen, B. (2001). Generating interest in interest groups. *Educational Policy*, 15(1), 168–185.

Maroy, C. (2009). Convergences and hybridization of educational policies around "post-bureaucratic" models of regulation. *Compare*, 39(1), 71–84.

Marshall, T. H. (1939). The recent history of professionalism in relation to social structure and social policy. *The Canadian Journal of Economics and Political Science*, 5(3), 325–340.

Martens, K., Nagel, A. K., & Windzio, M. (Eds.). (2010). *Transformation of education policy*. New York, NY: Palgrave Macmillan.

Masters, M. E., & Atkin, R. S. (1996). Financial and political resources of nine major public sector unions in the 1980s. *Journal of Labor Research*, 17(1), 183–198.

Mattei, P. (2007). Managerial and political accountability: The widening gap in the organization of welfare. *International Review of Administrative Sciences*, 73(3), 365–387.

McDonnell, L. M., & Pascal, A. (1988). *Teacher unions and educational reform*. Santa Monica, CA: The Rand Corporation.

Micheletti, M. (1990). Toward interest inarticulation: A major consequence of corporatism for interest organizations. *Scandinavian Political Studies*, 13(3), 255–276.

Mitchell, N. J. (1996). Theoretical and empirical issues in the comparative measurement of union power and corporatism. *British Journal of Political Science*, 26(3), 419–438.

Moe, T. (1995). The politics of structural choice: Toward a theory of public bureaucracy. In O. E. Williamson (Ed.), *Organizational theory from Chester Barnard to the present and beyond*. Oxford: Oxford University Press.

Moe, T. (2005). Power and political institutions. *Perspectives and Politics*, 3(2), 215–232.

Moe, T. (2006). Union power and the education of children. In J. Hannaway & A. Rotherman (Eds.), *Collective bargaining in education: Negotiating change in today's schools*. Cambridge, MA: Harvard Education Press, 229–256.

Moe, T. (2011). *Special interests: Teachers unions and America's public schools*. Washington, DC: Brookings Institution.

Molina, O., & Rhodes, M. (2002). Corporatism: The past, present, and future of a concept. *Annual Review of Political Science, 5*(1), 305–331.

Mudge, S. L. (2008). What is neo-liberalism? *Socio-economic review, 6*(4), 703–731.

Muralidharan, K., & Sundararman, V. (2008). *Teacher incentives in developing countries: Experiemental evidence from India* (Working paper 2008-13). Nashville, TN: National Center for Performance Incentives.

Murnane, R. J., & Cohen, D. K. (1986). Merit pay and the evaluation problem: Why most merit pay plans fail and few survive. *Harvard Educational Review, 56*(1), 1–17.

Murray, C. E. (2004). Innovative local teachers unions: What have they accomplished? In R. D. Henderson, W.J. Urban, & P. Wolman (Eds.), *Teacher unions and education policy: Retrenchment and reform*. Oxford: Elesevier, 149–166.

National Commission on Excellence in Education. (1983). A nation at risk: The imperative for educational reform. *The Elementary School Journal, 84*(2), 112–139.

O'Day, J. (2002). Complexity, accountability, and school improvement. *Harvard Educational Review, 72*(3), 293–329.

Organization for Economic Co-operation and Development. (1995). *Governance in transition: Public management reforms in OECD countries*. Paris: OECD Publishing.

Organization for Economic Co-operation and Development. (2012). *Education at a Glance 2012*. Paris: OECD.

Olson, M. (1965). *The logic of collective action*. Cambridge, MA: Harvard University Press.

Olson, M. (1982). *The rise and decline of nations: Economic growth, stagflation, and social rigidities*. New Haven: Yale University Press.

Oskarsson, S. (2003). Insitutional explanations of union strength: An assessment. *Politics & Society, 31*(4), 609–635.

Ozga, J., & Lingard, B. (2007). Globalisation, education policy and politics. In B. Lingard & J. Ozga (Eds.), *The RoutledgeFalmer reader in education policy and politics*. Abingdon: Routledge, 65–82.

Ozga, J., Simola, H., Varjo, J., Segerholm, C., & Pitkanen, H. (2010). Central-local relations of governance. In J. Ozga, P. Dahler-Larsen, & H. Simola (Eds.), *Fabricating quality in education: Data and governance in Europe*. London: Routledge, 107–126.

Parsons, T. (1954). *Essays in sociological theory*. London: Free Press.

Parsons, T. (1963). On the concept of political power. *Proceedings of the American Philosophical Society, 107*(3), 232–262.

Peters, J. (2012). Neoliberal convergence in North America and Western Europe: Fiscal austerity, privatization, and public sector reform. *Review of International Political Economy, 19*(2), 208–235.

Pfeffer, J. (1998). Six dangerous myths about pay. *Harvard Business Review, 7*(3), 109–119.

Pierson, P. (1994). *Dismantling the welfare state? Reagan, Thatcher, and the politics of retrenchment*. Cambridge, MA: Cambridge University Press.

Pierson, P. (1998). Irresistible forces, immovable objects: Post-industrial welfare states confront permanent austerity. *Journal of European Public Policy, 5*(4), 539–560.

Pierson, P. (2001). *The new politics of the welfare state*. Oxford: Oxford University Press.

Pocock, B. (1999, February 8). *A tale of two unions: The theory and practice of Australian union strategy now*. Paper presented at The Future of Solidarity Conference, Adelaide, Australia.

Podgursky, M. (2007). Teams versus bureaucracies: Personnel policy, wage-setting and teacher quality in traditional public, charter, and private schools. In M. Berends, M. Springer, & H. Walberg (Eds.), *School outcomes*. Mahwah, NJ: Lawrence Erlbaum Associates, 61–84.

Podgursky, M., & Springer, M. G. (2007). Teacher performance pay: A review. *Journal of Policy Analysis and Management, 26*(4), 909–948.

Poole, W. (2000). The construction of teachers' paradoxical interests by teacher union leaders. *American Educational Research Journal, 37*(1), 93–108.

Predergast, C. (1999). The provision of incentives in firms. *Journal of economic literature, 37*(1), 7–63.

Prentice, G., Burgess, S., & Propper, C. (2007). Performance pay in the public sector: A review of the issues and evidence. *Office of Manpower Economics*, Retrieved on June 2, 2015 from http://citeseerx.ist.psu.edu/viewdoc/download?doi=10.1.1.232.7993&rep=rep1&type=pdf

Ravitch, D. (2010). *The death and life of the great American school system*. New York: Basic Books.

Rhodes, M. (2001). The political economy of social pacts: Competitive corporatism and European welfare reform. In P. Pierson (Ed.), (2001). *The new politics of the welfare state*. Oxford: Oxford University Press, 165–196.

Richardson, J. (1982). *Policy styles in Western Europe*. London: Allen & Unwin.

Rinne, R., Kivirauma, J., & Simola, H. (2002). Shoots of revisionist education policy or just slow readjustment? The Finnish case of educational reconstruction. *Journal of Education Policy, 17*(6), 653–658.

Rizvi, F., & Lingard, B. (2009). The OECD: Global shifts in education policy. In F. Rizvi & B. Lingard (Eds.), *International Handbook of Comparative Education*. Dordrecht, Netherlands: Springer Verlag, 437–453.

Robertson, S.L. (2008). 'Remaking the world': Neoliberalism and the transformation of education and teachers' labor. In M. Compton & L. Weiner (Eds.), *The global assault on teaching, teachers, and their unions*. New York: Palgrave Macmillan, 11–30.

Rothstein, R. (2009). The perils of quantitative accountability. In Adams, S. J., Heywood, J. S., & Rothstein, R. (Eds.), *Teachers, performance pay, and accountability: What education should learn from other sectors*. Washington, DC: Economic Policy Institute, 69-107.

Sahlberg, P. (2011). *Finnish lessons: What can the world learn from educational change in Finland?* New York, NY: Teachers College Press.

Sahlin-Andersson, K. (2001). *National, international and transnational constructions of new public management*. Stockholm: SCORE (Stockholm Center for Organizational Research).

Scharpf, F.W. (1997). *Games real actors play*. Boulder, CO: Westview Press.

Schmitter, P. (1982). Reflections on where the theory of neo-corporatism has gone and where the praxis of neo-corporatism may be going. In G. Lehmbruch & P. Schmitter (Eds.), *Patterns of corporatist policy making*. London: Sage, 259–279.

Stephens, J.D. (1986). *The transition from capitalism to socialism*. Urbana: University of Illinois Press.

Streshly, W.A., & DeMitchell, T.A. (1994). *Teacher unions and TQE: Building quality labor relations*. A Thousand Oaks: Corwin Press.

Swank, D. (2001). Political institutions and welfare state restructuring: The impact of institutions on social policy change in developed democracies. In P. Pierson (Ed.), *The new politics of the welfare state*. Oxford: Oxford University Press, 197–237.

Taft, P. (1950). A rereading of Selig Perlman's 'A theory of the labor movement.' *Industrial and Labor Relations Review, 4*(1), 70–77.

Truman, D. B. (1971). *The governmental process* (2nd ed.). New York: Knopf.

Tucker, M. S. (2011). *Teachers, their unions, and the American education reform agenda.* Retrieved from the National Center on Education and the Economy http://www.ncee.org/wp-content/uploads/2011/03/Teachers-and-Their-Unions-NCEE-March-2011-FinalDRM.pdf

Urban, W. J. (2004). Teacher politics. In R. D. Henderson, W. J. Urban, & P. Wolman (Eds.), *Teachers unions and education policy: Retrenchment or reform?* Amsterdam: Elesevier, 51–80.

Visser, J. (2013). *ICTWSS: Database on institutional characteristics of trade unions and wage setting, state intervention and social pacts in 34 countries between 1960 and 2012* [Data set]. Retrieved from http://www.uva-aias.net/208

Walton, R. E., & McKersie, R. B. (1965/1991). *A behavioral theory of labor negotiations* (2nd ed.). New York: McGraw Hill.

West, K. L., & Mykerezi, E. (2011). Teachers' unions and compensation: The impact of collective bargaining on salary schedules and performance pay schedules. *Economics of Education Review, 30*(10), 99–108.

Whitty, G., & Edwards, T. (1998). School choice policies in England and the United States: An exploration of their origins and significance. *Comparative Education, 34*(2), 221–237.

Williamson, P. J. (1988). *Corporatism in perspective.* London: Sage.

Willman, P. (1990). The financial performance of British trade unions. *British Journal of Industrial Relations, 28*(3), 313–328.

Winters, M., Greene, J. P., Ritter, G., & Marsh, R. (2008). *The effect of performance-pay in Little Rock, Arkansas on student achievement* (Working Paper No. 2008–02). Nashville, TN: National Center on Performance Incentives, Peabody College of Vanderbilt University.

Woessman, L. (2010). *Cross-country evidence on teacher performance pay* (Discussion Paper No. 5101). Retrieved from the Institute for the Study of Labor http://ftp.iza.org/dp5101.pdf

2 Beyond Narrow Assumptions of Interest and Power
A Conceptual Framework

The unions-block-reform account—its claims about what unions oppose and why they oppose it—is implicitly grounded in rational-choice assumptions: that teachers' unions have fixed, uniform, predictable, and standardized interests and that they exclusively attempt to maximize their preference-attainment through strategic interactions with other fixed-preference, utility-maximizing actors (Hall & Taylor, 1996). Crucial cases, where reform occurs in spite of strong unions, challenge the rational-choice foundations for theorizing about unions' power—the predictability of their preferences. They suggest that, perhaps, actors are neither always nor exclusively perfectly informed and acting on the basis of their individual or organizational self-interest. They may not be acting on the best available information because of lack of access, idiosyncratic interpretations, or ignorance; they may be motivated by preferences or interests other than exclusive short-term self-interest, including interaction orientations;[1] or their ability to act in exclusively rational and self-interested ways may be complicated by internal diversity and evaluative capacities.

These crucial cases provide insights into teachers' unions' preferences toward and impact on reform. However, to uncover their lessons, we must know where to look. Successful analytic explanations—accounting for what is happening and why—critically depend on the theoretical framework, which, in its organization of key variables, "must be adequate to capture and record the essentials of a causal account of the outcome in the case" (George & Bennett, 2005, p. 93).

This chapter outlines the theoretical framework that guides this research, an approach that Scharpf (1997, 2000) calls "actor-centered." The literature review revealed a number of significant gaps in the existing literature, and the theoretical resources gathered in this chapter have been selected for their ability to bridge some of those gaps. Specifically, an actor-centered approach remains open to the ways that actors' preferences may vary; the ways that actors' preferences may ignore, include, or extend beyond economic self-interest; and the ways that actors' environments influence their perceptions, preferences, and strategies. Walton and McKersie's *A Behavioral Theory of Labor Negotiations* (1965/1991) provides the central framework

THE PROBLEM WITH NARROWLY CONCEIVING ACTORS' INTERESTS

The problem with many existing explanations of teachers' unions' activity and impact is the same thing that Brennan (1990) critiques in RC theories—they lack predictive value. The first objection to the predictive value of RC theories is that actors *cannot* actually behave in the way the model describes—that no real person is like *homo economicus*. Defenders of RC models brush this criticism off as irrelevant to theorizing, stating:

> Truly important and significant hypotheses will be found to have 'assumptions' that are wildly inaccurate assumptions of reality ... the relevant question to ask about the 'assumptions' of a theory is not whether they are descriptively 'realistic,' for they never are, but whether they are sufficiently good approximations for the purpose in hand. And this question can be answered only by seeing whether the theory works, which means whether it yields sufficiently accurate predictions. (Friedman, 1966, p. 14)

In short, they argue, the specific causal mechanisms[2] through which teachers' unions wield their influence are unimportant and can remain ambiguous, as long as the theory seems to get the outcome right most of the time. So, it doesn't matter if unions' interests and impact are as stable and predictable as the covering law suggests, as long as the outcome the model predicts occurs.

However, this response is problematic. It reflects a blatant neglect of causal mechanisms; even if a theory predicts an outcome with a high degree of accuracy, it is not a causal explanation unless it can demonstrate that the implied causal mechanisms were operative in the particular case (George & Bennett, 2005). If actors are not *always* nor *exclusively* acting on the basis of their self-interest—especially if they are often not doing so—RC lacks a micro-level consistency which requires "that individuals must have the capacity to behave as the macro-level theory states, and that they did in fact behave the way they did because of the explicit or implicit micro-level assumptions embedded in the macro-level theory" (George & Bennett, 2005, p. 142).

Furthermore, Brennan argues that in order for rational choice assumptions to accurately predict outcomes, in addition to positing agents' rationality, the researcher would also need "knowledge of what the agent's ends or purposes *actually are*" (1990, p. 53, emphasis added). Put another way, and applied to dominant theories of teachers' unions, it is not enough to argue that teachers' unions are self-interested; in order for the assumption of self-interest to have predictive power, one needs to understand how the union—or its members—understands its self-interest. Filling the vacuum created by vague statements about rationality or self-interest with the researchers' beliefs about what a rational or self-interested actor would do overlooks the inherent complexity in actors' purposes and preferences:

> Agents' purposes are surely among the most complex and obscure aspects of the social landscape. Moreover, even apparently simple psychologically plausible purposes—the desire for affection, or for prestige, or for survival, say—are hardly sufficiently concrete to permit anything except extremely rough and coarse-grained predictions. . . . Once one allows for even minimal psychological complexity, any suggestion that specific actions can be deduced from the assumption of rationality alone seems hopelessly farfetched. The sorts of ends relevant to immediate action can be expected to vary widely across persons and to be differentially weighted across persons, times, and places. They cannot be taken as self-evident. (Brennan, 1990, p. 53)

The predictive value of any theory will rest on correspondence between theoretical assumptions of actors' motivations and reality; RC theories will fail to predict outcomes in situations where actors' goals are broader than the ex ante assumptions (Levi & Cook, 1990). This might point to why the unions-block-reform account fails to explain crucial cases, states and districts that advance reforms in spite of teachers' unions who would be expected to block them: because the theoretical assumptions about actors' motivations, goals, and purposes are inaccurate.

Furthermore, by failing to sufficiently account for non-egoistic goals, interests, or purposes—like altruism or fairness—in their models, RC theorists are consistently able to predict certain types of outcomes but not others: they are able to account for why people do not vote, but not why they do; why people do not contribute, but not why they do (Levi, 1997). And perhaps these models are better able to account for why teachers do not support reform than why and when they do. Levi argues that "the aim must be to specify the conditions under which more instrumental motivations are triggered [versus when] more ethical considerations dominate" (Levi, 1997, p. 34). If the goal is to understand how reform could be possible—the situations in which it is likely to occur and why—then developing a particular explanation of those cases, rather than a covering law that explains why reform does not happen *most* of the time, is essential. Although remaining open to the variability and complexity of actors' preferences may come at the cost of theoretical parsimony, it has the advantage of more closely approximating reality and of explaining why PRP is possible in some cases but not others—of utmost importance in problem-driven research (Levi, 1997).

MOVING BEYOND NARROW CONCEPTIONS OF INTERESTS

Throughout the case studies, this research will remain open to the variability of actors'—both unions and policy-makers—preferences and perceptions. This is a critical component of the theoretical framework and will be a key focus of data collection and analysis. However, before turning to the framework, actors' preferences, interests, and strategies must be carefully defined.

In this research, *preferences* denote an actor's goals or interests, which are defined independently of other actors, threats, and incentives (Moravcsik, 1997). Preferences can be long- or short-term; they can be general, referring to organizational aims or purposes without reference to a particular policy, or specific, in relation to a particular policy problem or outcome. *Interests* reflect relative preferences for policy options which are "defined across intermediate political [or bargaining] aims" (Moravcsik, 1997, p. 519), which are subjectively calculated based on preferences and perceptions of reality and presumed cause and effect—what is preferable and what is possible (Scharpf, 2000). These interests are then translated into *courses of action*, or *strategies* and *tactics* (Kochan, McKersie, & Cappelli, 1984; Moravcsik, 1997; Scharpf, 2000). Thus, the key distinction between preferences and interests is not their particularity or time horizon but the fact that preferences are defined independently of other actors while interests take context into account.

From Fixed Preferences to Purposive Action

Research on teachers' unions has confirmed the significance of multiple goals: in addition to promoting members' interests in terms of wages and working conditions, unions are also concerned with status enhancement[3] and increasing the sphere of their influence, or what Scharpf (1997) calls system-maintenance and goal-attainment (Loyo, 2001, as cited in Vaillant, 2005; Poole, 2000). As discussed in Chapter 1, in research on teachers' unions, goal-attainment preferences informed by norms and identity are often associated with conceptions of professionalism, while system maintenance preferences are usually linked with traditional unionism, or 'industrial bargaining' (Kerchner & Koppich, 1993; Kerchner & Mitchell, 1988).

Given the existing evidence for the diversity and variability of union goals, it is essential to avoid adopting an overly deterministic approach to union preferences—either that unions are exclusively self-interested or benevolent, are motivated by system-maintenance or goal-attainment, or show a monopoly or voice face. Scharpf argues that one can neither assume "that [actors] merely follow cultural norms or institutional rules," nor that "the goals pursued and the interests defended are invariant across actors and across time" (Scharpf, 1997, p. 36). Instead, he emphasizes "purposive action"[4] in which "actors select their best available course of action under the circumstances given their preferences and perceptions" (Scharpf, 1997, p. 31).

This mirrors what Immergut calls "alternative rationalities," allowing that "individuals and collectivities may develop interpretations of their interests and goals—worldviews—that deviate from those predicted by means-ends rationality" (1998, p. 18). This view of preferences and its conception of actors' capacities and orientations provides the starting point for considering the ways in which, rather than assuming they are fixed, actors' interests may vary; and the way those varying interests inform strategies, tactics, and ultimately, policy outcomes. Purposive action is based on a series of subjective phenomena:

- Perceptions of reality,
- resulting valuations and interests,
- and "normative convictions [of what is] right, good or appropriate" (Scharpf, 1997, p. 19).

Union preferences may deviate from simple conceptions of economic self-interest in several ways. First, actors' perceptions of a given policy issue may vary. Perceptions refer to known empirical facts and hypotheses, which will be shaped largely through shared knowledge or ignorance of the policy issue and the way in which those perceptions deviate from the best available knowledge about a given policy problem, either because of imperfect or incomplete knowledge of the available policy options or because idiosyncrasies, institutional norms, or conventions cause an actor to ignore or reject components of prevailing theories or empirical facts (Scharpf, 1997, 2000).

Second, these perceptions interact with unions' complex preferences to inform their conclusions about which policies are in their best interest—as they define it based on their goals. This framework does not deny the possibility of exclusive self-interest, it simply allows a more complex picture of actor preferences—one in which individual or organizational self-interest may compete with preferences shaped by normative obligations and aspirations and by identity constructs. In terms of system-maintenance, unions may have a long-term view of their economic self-interests which leads them to sacrifice short-term 'losses' in favor of perceived long-term gains related to organizational preservation, autonomy, or growth. Or, identity constructs, like 'professionalism' or 'social partnership,' as discussed in Chapter 1, may influence the way organizations define priorities and competing interests and norms, in order to "selectively emphasize certain aspects of self-interests as well as certain rules and normative purposes" (Scharpf, 1997, p. 65).

To be clear, deep and protracted debate runs through the discourse of professionalism regarding its impact on the goals and interests of teachers and their unions and settling these debates—Are teachers professionals? Are teachers' unions professional organizations? If so, does that change anything about their interests?—is beyond the scope of this book. However, all of the literature reviewed in Chapter 1, from IGT to the two faces of unionism to theories of professionalism and concertation, suggested that non-pecuniary interests are theoretically possible (Bennett & Kauffman, 2004; Compston, 2003; Freeman & Medoff, 1984; Katzenstein, 1985; Lehmbruch, 1977; Molina & Rhodes, 2002; Olson, 1965, 1982; Schmitter, 1982; Williamson, 1988). With this in mind, this research does not take an a priori view of teachers' unions' preferences. Unions *may* be entirely and exclusively self-interested. However, they may be driven by a number of other motivations and goals. These goals may be linked to professionalism or to some other, unanticipated, source. There are no shortcuts; attention must be paid to what unions' preferences and perceptions actually are.

From Preferences in a Vacuum to Strategic Interactions

In their seminal text, *A Behavioral Theory of Labor Negotiations* (1965/1991), Walton and McKersie conceptualize bargaining as four simultaneous, iterative, and mutually reinforcing processes:

- *distributive bargaining*, which is focused on resolving conflicts of interests;
- *integrative bargaining*, which identifies common interests and focuses on solving shared problems;
- *intraorganizational bargaining*, or the ways in which organizations achieve internal consensus;
- and *attitudinal bargaining*, or the way in which discrete negotiations impact long-term attitudes and bonds.

Distributive and integrative bargaining, which are also presented in Fisher and Ury's (1981) *Getting to Yes*, were discussed in Chapter 1 in the context of unions' monopoly (distributive) and voice (integrative) faces. However, whether bargaining takes a distributive versus integrative form significantly depends on intraorganizational and attitudinal bargaining. These processes also illuminate the interactions that may contribute to the complexity of union preference- and interest-formation.

Internal Interactions: Intraorganizational Bargaining
What Walton and McKersie call intraorganizational bargaining refers to the process of group preference-formation. The complexities of predicting an individual's preferences are exponentially magnified when considering group preference-formation. It is easy to anthropomorphize representative organizations, to wrongly apply all assumptions of individuals to unions without attending to the significant differences and added complexities of representative organizations. Walton and McKersie observe that, in contrast to the assumption that:

> each organization acted with single purpose in a manner that was generally acceptable internally and with perfect coordination. . . . The

organizations participating in labor negotiations usually lack internal consensus about the objectives they will attempt to obtain from negotiations, and this is especially true for labor organizations. Different elements of the organization may have different ideas about the priorities assigned to various objectives being pursued. (1965/1992, p. 281)

Chapter 1 outlined IGT and the ways it accounts for the relationship between the sum of individuals' preferences and the expressed preferences of the interest group. IGT research on selective versus purposive incentives documents the ways in which group goals may differ wildly from the mean or modal preferences of individual members. However, rather than a static formula in which the sum of members' preferences are mediated by some set of factors—like the incentives for membership—to produce a more or less democratic group preference, intraorganizational bargaining emphasizes the dynamism of the interest aggregation process.

It presumes that members may have different views of the purpose of the organization, different preferences or perceptions of particular issues, and assign different weight to the significance of these issues. To add to the complexity, all of these views may vary over time. As a result, figuring out what 'the group wants' is a constant negotiation. Although the process can vary in its representativeness, effectiveness, and efficiency, all groups conduct internal negotiations.

Scharpf (1997) labels intraorganizational bargaining 'internal capacity' and says that it is a function of two things:

- *cognitive capacity*, or the diversity of views within an organization, and
- *evaluative capacity*, defined as an organization's ability to overcome diverse and competing views in order to reach a unified view.

Intraorganizational bargaining points to the first way in which union preference-formation does not occur within a vacuum. You could think of cognitive capacity as the 'level of difficulty' of reaching a unified view within a union, and its evaluative capacity as the resources—charisma, organizational sophistication, etc.—available to do so. A union's effectiveness and the degree to which it represents its members' interests is a function of its capacity and adroitness in these internal interactions and negotiations.

External Interactions: Attitudinal Bargaining

Attitudinal bargaining points to the second way in which preference-formation is defined by interactions—in this case, external interactions—and refers to two interrelated phenomena: actors' relationship pattern and their interaction orientation. The *relationship pattern*, "a set of reciprocal attitudes salient to the parties in their interaction" (Walton & McKersie, 1965/1991, p. 185), is the aggregate picture of four attitude dimensions: motivation orientations, beliefs about legitimacy, feelings of trust, and feelings of friendliness versus hostility (Table 2.1). It is a snapshot of the relational modus operandi. An actors' *interaction orientation* is related to, but distinct from, the relationship pattern: it refers to an actors' desire to maintain or change the relationship pattern—the relative cooperation or conflict—in the future.

Walton and McKersie identify five relationship patterns based on four dimensions (Table 2.1). The first dimension includes motivational orientation and action tendencies—competitive, cooperative, or individualistic tendencies. The second dimension is an actor's beliefs about the other's legitimacy. The third and fourth dimensions include an actor's feelings of trust and friendliness or hostility toward the other. These four dimensions can be used to infer an actor's relationship pattern: conflict, containment-aggression, accommodation, cooperation, or collusion.

Regardless of the current state of the relationship pattern, interaction orientations refer to actors' relational aspirations—to increase, maintain, or decrease the relative level of conflict or cooperation in the relationship. Two questions help build a better understanding of interaction orientations. First, what factors seem to influence or determine an actor's interaction orientation toward another actor? And second, what might cause actors to value one form of interaction over another? What would cause an actor to want to move from a relatively hostile relationship to a relatively cooperative one and vice versa? Answering the first question is important because it identifies the discrete factors that might suggest an actor's interaction orientation. Walton and McKersie suggest that interaction orientations are likely informed by several factors: the context of interaction, i.e., institutions; the personality dispositions of key individuals; the social beliefs systems of individuals and their respective organizations; and the history of bargaining experiences.

In terms of the second question, organizational interaction orientations may be motivated by a variety of factors (Walton & McKersie, 1965/1991). First, they may be valued in their own right either as a result of personal preferences or ideological convictions. Second, certain orientations may be preferred as a means to more effective implementation. Specifically, the nature of the relationship may determine how subsequent problems are handled—either through power, legal mechanisms, or informal social relations. And thirdly, the nature of interactions may have a long-term impact on the possibilities for and outcomes of future negotiations and decisions. However, the *cause* of various interaction orientations is tangential to the aims of this study. Of central importance to this research is the idea that relationship patterns and interaction orientations—goals to maintain or change the relationship pattern—could vary and that they may have important impacts on the policy process and outcomes. Thus, actors' interaction orientations could have a significant impact on the process through which teachers' strength is translated into power.

Table 2.1 Attitudinal components of the relationship pattern (Walton & McKersie, 1965/1991, p. 189)

Pattern of Relationship

Attitudinal Dimensions	Conflict	Containment-Aggression	Accommodation	Cooperation	Collusion
Motivational orientation and action tendencies toward other	Competitive tendencies to destroy or weaken	Competitive tendencies to destroy or weaken	Individualistic policy of hands off	Cooperative tendencies to preserve	Cooperative tendencies to assist or preserve
Beliefs about legitimacy of other	Denial of legitimacy	Grudging acknowledgment	Acceptance of status quo	Complete legitimacy	Not applicable
Level of trust in conducting affairs	Extreme distrust	Distrust	Limited trust	Extended trust	Trust based on mutual blackmail potential
Degree of friendliness	Hate	Antagonism	Neutralism-Courteousness	Friendliness	Intimacy—"Sweetheart relationship"

Note: Reprinted from *A Behavioral Theory of Labor Negotiations: An Analysis of a Social Interaction System, Second Edition*, by Richard E. Walton and Robert B. McKersie. Copyright © 1965 by Richard E. Walton and Robert B. McKersie. Used by permission of the publisher, Cornell University Press.

Institutions: Environments Informing Actors' Interactions

Although the mutually informing bargaining processes outlined by Walton and McKersie are 'behavioral'—influenced by attitudes, beliefs, and habits—they also occur in a particular context and are informed by patterns and structures, or institutional arrangements. There is significant disagreement[5] and a "clear lack of conceptualization of what institutions are or how they can be defined" (Keman, 1997, p. 1). But in this research, institutions will be defined as both "rules [and] conventions promulgated by formal organization" as well as "formal or informal procedures, routines, norms and conventions embedded into organizational structure" (Hall & Taylor, 1996, p. 938).

Institutional arrangements are significant to the theoretical framework—defining 'where to look' and 'what to look for'—in several ways. First, they determine the constellation of actors involved in a given policy-making process and also shape the modes of interaction—unilateral action, negotiated agreement, majority vote, or hierarchical agreement—of those actors (Scharpf, 1997).[6] For example, in Finland, the decision to implement PRP components occurred exclusively within the bargaining domain, and in Zürich, it was a political decision influenced by formal legislation and referendum as well as informal consultation processes. The particular institutional arrangements of each case determined who was at the table, as well as constraining or enabling their influence within that process. For example, laws determining teachers' right to organize, including stipulations regarding collecting dues, strikes, and collective bargaining, influence the strength resources available to unions. This frames the context of union activity and basic conceptions of union power. Because they are often inherited from the private sector, in the case studies, the institutions that delimit teachers' organizing will be traced from the private sector in both Finland and Zürich.

Second, the 'rules of the game' may be as important as 'who gets to play.' In addition to formal rules—like the significance of the referendum in Switzerland—it is also important to attend to "informal procedures, routines, norms and conventions embedded into organizational structure" (Hall & Taylor, 1996, p. 938), such as norms related to consensus or cooperation, which have a significant impact on the existing relationship pattern as well as actors' interaction orientation. What is important when it comes to these institutions will be context and domain specific.

It is worth noting that interests and institutional arrangements should not be conflated. In the debate about the professionalism of teachers' organizations some have argued that, in contrast to non-bargaining professional associations, unions are organizations who bargain, which is—by definition—exclusively concerned with the distribution of zero-sum economic benefits. These are false distinctions. Assuming that bargaining is either inherently zero-sum or exclusively concerned with economic questions, or, on the other hand, that the political advocacy of non-bargaining associations is somehow inherently more altruistic, is not justifiable (Fisher & Ury,

1981; Gunderson, 2005; Walton & McKersie, 1965/1991). Furthermore, the preferences of teachers' organizations—the degree to which they are selfish or altruistic, among a host of other motivational factors—is not inherently linked to, nor can they be imputed from, their institutional function as a bargaining or non-bargaining organization. The institutional context and mode of interaction are important because they identify the relevant actors and focus attention on the types of interactions most significantly impacting policy outcomes, not because they are a proxy for actors' preferences.

CONCLUSION

One criticism of RC theory has been that it is "theory-driven rather than problem driven" and aimed at saving or vindicating "some variant of rational choice theory, rather than accounting for . . . political phenomena" (Green & Shapiro, 1994, p. 6). In contrast, this research—particularly in terms of its conceptualization of actors' preferences—takes a middle way between deductive and inductive approaches, using existing theories and hypotheses to structure the inquiry while remaining open to other explanations (Layder, 1998).[7] Perhaps the unions-block-reform account is correct, but it is also possible that crucial cases might point in a different direction.

It is possible that teachers' unions may pursue interests, strategies, and tactics that are inconsistent with their individualistic self-interests, in which case, Scharpf argues that "the explanation must be found in actor orientations that differ from the stylized assumptions underlying our predictions" (2000, p. 784). Specifically, attention must turn to the perceptions that deviate from the information and policy analysis generally held to be true and to the actor preferences that deviate from a priori expectations.

Or, actors may have relationally defined preferences that impact their decision-making. That is to say, teachers' unions might be *able* to block the policy and hypothetically *prefer* to do so, in terms of their policy-outcome preferences, but they may *choose* not to. One major reason why an actor may choose not to act in accordance with its interests—whether motivated by self-interest or normative aims—when it is powerful enough to impact the outcome may be explained by its relational preferences.

These hypotheses are tested in international cases in Chapters 4–7. Chapter 3 outlines the methodology of these case studies.

NOTES

1. Actors' relational preferences
2. "An unobservable entity that—when activated—generates an outcome of interest" (Mahoney, 2001, p. 580).
3. Professional image

4. Although this emphasis is also reflected by other HI approaches, which have been dubbed the 'calculus approach' (e.g., Immergut, 1992).
5. RC institutionalism defines institutions as "sets of rules (and sanctions) that structure social interactions and whose existence and applicability are commonly known within the relevant community" (Levi, 1997, p. 25), and sociological institutionalism identifies them as a "collection of interrelated rules and routines that define appropriate actions in terms of relations between roles and situations. The process involves determining what the situation is, what role is being fulfilled, and what the obligation of that role in that situation is" (March & Olsen, 1989, p. 160).
6. For example, differences in collective bargaining laws across states and school districts result in modes of interaction that range from complete unilateral action by the school district to a negotiated agreement.
7. This will be discussed further in Chapter 3.

REFERENCES

Brennan, G. (1990). Comment: What might rationality fail to do? In K. S. Cook & M. Levi (Eds.), *The limits of rationality*. Chicago: The University of Chicago Press, 51–59.

Compston, H. (2003). Beyond corporatism: A configurational theory of policy concertation. *European Journal of Political Research, 42*(6), 787–809.

Fisher, R., & Ury, W. (1981). *Getting to yes: Negotiating agreement without giving in*. New York: Penguin Group.

Freeman, R. B., & Medoff, J. L. (1984). *What do unions do?* New York: Basic Books.

Friedman, M. (1966). The methodology of positive economics. In M. Friedman (Ed.), *Essays in positive economics* (2nd ed.). Chicago: University of Chicago Press, 3–16.

George, A. L., & Bennett, A. (2005). *Case studies and theory development in the social sciences*. Cambridge, MA: MIT Press.

Green, D. P., & Shapiro, I. (1994). *Pathologies of rational choice theory: A critique of applications in political science*. New Haven, CT: Yale University Press.

Gunderson, M. (2005). Two faces of union voice in the public sector. *Journal of Labor Research, 26*(3), 3939–3958.

Hall, P. A., & Taylor, R. C. (1996). Political science and the three new institutionalisms. *Political Studies, 44*(5), 936–957.

Immergut, E. (1992). *Health politics*. Cambridge: Cambridge University Press.

Immergut, E. (1998). The theoretical core of the new institutionalism. *Politics Society, 26*(5), 5–34.

Katzenstein, P. J. (1985). *Small states in world markets: Industrial policy in Europe*. Ithaca, NY: Cornell University Press.

Keman, H. (1997). Approaches to the analysis of institutions. In B. Steunenberg & F. Van Vught (Eds.), *Political institutions and public policy: Perspectives on European decision-making*. Dordrecht: Kluwer, 1–27.

Kerchner, C. T., & Koppich, J. E. (1993). *A union of professionals: Labor relations and educational reform*. New York: Teachers College Press.

Kerchner, C. T., & Mitchell, D. E. (1988). *The changing idea of a teachers' union*. New York: Falmer Press.

Kochan, T. A., McKersie, R. B., & Cappelli, P. (1984). Strategic choice and industrial relations theory. *Industrial Relations, 23*(1), 16–39.

Layder, D. (1998). *Sociological practice: Linking theory and social research*. London: Sage.

Lehmbruch, G. (1977). Liberal corporatism and party government. *Comparative Political Studies*, 10(1), 91–126.

Levi, M. (1997). A model, a method, and a map: Rational choice in comparative and historical analysis. In M.I. Lichbach & A.S. Zuckerman (Eds.), *Comparative politics: Rationality, culture, and structure*. Cambridge: Cambridge University Press, 19–41.

Levi, M., & Cook, K.S. (1990). *The limits of rationality*. Chicago: University of Chicago Press.

Mahoney, J. (2001). Beyond correlation analysis: Recent innovations in theory and method, *Sociological Forum*, 16(3), 575–593.

March, J.G. & Olsen, J.P. (1989). *Rediscovering institutions: The organizational basis of politics*. New York, NY: The Free Press.

Moe, T. (2011). *Special interests: Teachers unions and America's public schools*. Washington, DC: Brookings Institution.

Molina, O., & Rhodes, M. (2002). Corporatism: The past, present, and future of a concept. *Annual Review of Political Science*, 5(1), 305–331.

Moravcsik, A. (1997). Taking preferences seriously: A liberal theory of international politics. *International Organization*, 51(4), 513–553.

Poole, W. (2000). The construction of teachers' paradoxical interests by teacher union leaders. *American Educational Research Journal*, 37(1), 93–108.

Scharpf, F.W. (1997). *Games real actors play*. Boulder, CO: Westview Press.

Scharpf, F.W. (2000). Institutions in comparative policy research. *Comparative Political Studies*, 33(6–7), 762–790.

Schmitter, P. (1982). Reflections on where the theory of neo-corporatism has gone and where the praxis of neo-corporatism may be going. In G. Lehmbruch, & P. Schmitter (Eds.), *Patterns of corporatist policy making*. London: Sage, 259–279.

Walton, R.E., & McKersie, R.B. (1991). *A behavioral theory of labor negotiations* (2nd ed.). New York: McGraw Hill.

Williamson, P.J. (1988). *Corporatism in perspective*. London: Sage.

Vaillant, D. (2005). Education reforms and teachers' unions: Avenues for action. *Fundamentals of educational planning*. Paris: UNESCO International Institute for Educational Planning.

3 Research Design, Case Selection, and Methodology

Although the unions-block-reform account suggests that strong teachers' unions always block policies that they oppose, like PRP, there are a number of cases that appear to defy these theoretical expectations. How do these cases inform theories of teachers' unions—their preferences and impact on policy-making?

The nature of the research questions—their emphasis on the *process* through which unions influence policy—requires description of the policy-making process. Because this research aims to uncover the causal mechanisms through which union preferences are converted into policy influence, or not, case studies are especially well suited to this inquiry. Case studies proceed in two phases. In the first, the focus is on international cases where reform has been implemented in spite of strong unions. These cases provide paradigmatic value and may serve to refine and improve theories of teachers' unions' interests, power, and impact (Collier, 1993; Immergut, 1992; Kocka, 2003). In the second phase, the revisions and new theoretical insights—what George and Bennett (2005) call the revised typological theory from the international cases—are tested within the US context in a study of six school districts' experiences with PRP reform.

This chapter outlines the methodological choices guiding this research. Although the majority of this chapter is relevant to both phases of the investigation, the methodological choices regarding case selection, data collection, and analysis are particularly focused on the first phase of research—the international case studies.[1] However, before turning to these issues, this chapter will first provide a brief discussion of case study research, given its wide-ranging uses.

DEFINING SOCIAL SCIENTIFIC CASE STUDIES

'Case study' is an encompassing label, defined in wide-ranging ways. Van Wynsberghe and Khan (2007) argue that although scholars have referenced a case study approach as a method, a methodology, *and* a research design, a case study is neither a method, because researchers employ various methods to uncover many different types of cases, nor a research design, as case studies do not guide the research from questions to conclusions including data collection, analysis, and interpretation. Thus, a case study is not a methodological choice about *how* to do research but a choice of *what* is to be studied, which is guided by a research process (Gerring, 2004; Meyer, 2001; Stake, 2005).

This research adopts George and Bennett's (2005) definition of a case as a class of events, "a well-defined aspect of a historical episode" (p. 18). In terms of the research process, given the emphasis on causality in this research, comparative case studies must extend beyond description to produce analytic explanations (Ragin, 2000). They must "examine similarities and differences across many cases while preserving the integrity of cases as complex configurations" (Ragin, 2000, p. 38). Thus, a theoretical rather than chronological focus distinguishes social scientific case studies from their historical counterparts (George & Bennett, 2005). Successful analytic explanations critically depend on the theoretical framework, which, in its organization of key variables, "must be adequate to capture and record the essentials of a causal account of the outcome in the case" (George & Bennett, 2005, p. 93). Thus, case studies in this research are guided by a diversity- or case-oriented approach that: has an outcome-orientation, views cases as configurations, and views causation as conjunctural and complex (Ragin, 2000).

CASE SELECTION: THEORY DEVELOPMENT VIA CRUCIAL CASES

George and Bennett suggest that "case selection is arguably the most difficult step in developing a case study research design. It is an opportunistic process of seeking . . . the kind of cases and comparisons that are likely to best test or develop theories" (2005, p. 234). Which cases are most appropriate in light of the research objectives? According to George and Bennett (2005), new or untested research programs are likely to benefit from inductive studies of apparently deviant cases: inductive studies can identify overlooked variables, clarify interactions, and refine theories. Furthermore, the analysis of crucial cases—those that "*must closely fit* a theory if one is to have confidence in the theory's validity, or conversely, *must not fit* equally well any rule contrary to that proposed" (Eckstein, 1975, p. 118)—is a useful theory-building approach as it may help disclose new causes and reformulate a particular theory in a more generally valid way (Dogan & Pelassy, 1990). Vis-à-vis the unions-block-reform account, crucial cases are defined as those where reform (PRP) has been implemented in spite of strong unions. However, before turning to the way these cases were selected, the decision to focus on PRP deserves further comment.

Selection of Performance-Related Pay

Some may object to the decision to study the incidence of PRP, arguing that it is bad policy without an evidence base to support it. Proponents of this view might suggest that PRP does not solve any of the problems for which it is proposed as a solution (see Chapter 1), and may even create deleterious unintended consequences. They might argue that rather than documenting the when, where, and why of PRP reform, the pages of this book could be better utilized convincing reformers to give up on PRP altogether.

However, the evidence regarding the effects and effectiveness of PRP, although 'clear' to both its proponents and detractors, is completely contradictory and, on the whole, indeterminate. So rather than settling the arguments about PRP's effectiveness, explaining differential reform outcomes in light of this indeterminate evidence is the central aim of this research. In Scharpf's terms, this research is "interaction-oriented" rather than "problem-oriented" (1997, pp. 7–10). Problem-oriented research is interested in the nature and causes of problems that policy could or should solve, and the effectiveness—potential or empirical—of various solutions (Scharpf, 1997). Interaction-oriented research, on the other hand, is concerned with the conditions that enable or constrain the adoption or implementation of policy responses that problem-oriented analyses have identified as potentially effective (Scharpf, 1997, 2000).

While the former asks questions about 'the what'—understanding the problem and evaluating potential responses or solutions, the latter explores 'the how'—the political process through which proposed solutions are adopted and implemented. Why are solutions to public problems successfully implemented in some countries but not others? Why can a set of actors, in the face of a common policy problem, block—or alternatively, successfully agitate for—a particular reform in one country but not the next?

This research adopts a consequential interaction-oriented perspective,[2] investigating how institutions and actors shape the process through which policy solutions—in this case, PRP for teachers—are successfully adopted and implemented. The distinction between interaction-oriented and problem-oriented research is significant. Within the education literature—where problem-oriented research on the impact of tenure, transfer and dismissal, and teacher compensation policies is conducted—ongoing debate and exploration continue and the evidence on PRP is inconclusive (Adams, Heywood, & Rothstein, 2009). However, because this inquiry focuses on questions that are interaction-oriented and consequential in nature, boundaries must be drawn around problem-oriented debates. Ultimately, determining the key policy problem and identifying the optimal solution to it is within the domain of problem-oriented research.

Despite the ongoing debate about the effectiveness of various education reforms, including PRP, in order to test and refine existing theoretical claims about teachers' unions and their role in the reform process, this research accepts the popular policy solution—that differentiating teachers' salaries and linking their pay to their performance is a better compensation strategy than lock-step salary schedules—in order to more closely examine teachers' unions' influence on policy-making. Even if the critics of PRP are right, adopting this assumption is defensible for several reasons. First, although one *could* criticize reformers' arguments on the grounds that they are wrong about education policy and the reform they promote, this would be a problem-oriented objection. Adopting a problem-oriented perspective would lead the research away from questions about teachers' unions and their preferences, strategies, and impact on education policy. It should be noted that, borrowing a term effectively employed elsewhere, this is a "narrow look" (Immergut, 1992, p. 67) at education policy and politics. 'Narrow' is employed because, rather than taking a comprehensive view of education policy or an education system within a given country or set of countries, this research focuses on a specific issue—teachers' compensation and the use of performance to inform pay levels.[3]

Second, empirically, liberal democracies increasingly display trends toward differentiating compensation for public sector employees, including teachers, as part of broader NPM reforms (discussed in Chapter 2). Even if these policies are not actually preferable to other compensation strategies—from a problem-oriented perspective—they *are* being promoted and pursued by governments in many nations. Therefore, this research does not need to make normative claims about whether these reforms are optimal policy solutions. Instead, it simply acknowledges that PRP has been identified as a solution in many countries and explores the role of teachers' unions in the differing reform outcomes. The outlined approach mirrors Immergut's (1992) investigation of countries' efforts to implement national health insurance. Rather than take a position on whether comprehensive national insurance was the 'right' solution, Immergut simply acknowledged that France, Switzerland, and Sweden had all proposed the same health programs with different outcomes. The variation in outcomes—not the evidence behind these reforms—was the focus of the research.

Finally, any problem-oriented challenges are minimized because crucial cases are selected on the dependent variable (discussed below). Growing consensus toward a particular reform certainly does not indicate uniformity of opinion across countries. So, even though many countries appear to be interested in PRP in the public sector, some may be entirely disinterested in doing so on problem-oriented grounds. Any research design that assumed consensus would be inherently problematic, but selecting on the dependent variable avoids these problems.

Identifying and Selecting Crucial Cases[4]

Table 3.1 maps the criteria of crucial case selection—union strength and presence of reform. The unions-block-reform account predicts that the effect of strong unions would be to block PRP (cell two, Table 3.1). By implication, the assumption is that cell four would be empty. Therefore, crucial cases are those in cell four—where PRP has been implemented in spite of strong unions. Thus, selecting crucial cases requires selecting on the dependent

Table 3.1 Case types: strength of union by presence of reform

		REFORM OUTCOME	
		NO PRP	PRP
UNION STRENGTH	WEAK	(1) WEAK UNION + LOCK-STEP SALARY SCHEDULE (NO PRP)	(3) WEAK UNION + PRP
	STRONG	(2) STRONG UNION + LOCK-STEP SALARY SCHEDULE (NO PRP)	(4) STRONG UNION + PRP

variable. Although doing so can be controversial, within a case-oriented paradigm, selecting on the dependent variable is encouraged (Berg-Schlosser, De Meur, Rihoux, & Ragin, 2009; King, Keohane, & Verba, 1994; Ragin, 1987, 2000; Robinson, 1951). The disagreement about selecting on the dependent variable is linked to differing assumptions about causality—symmetric and correlational versus asymmetric and set-theoretic (Ragin, 2008).

This book adopts Ragin's (1987, 2000, 2008) view that causality is best captured using set-theoretic rather than symmetric correlational arguments. Set-theoretic logic assumes two things. First, it posits that causality is complex or characterized by equifinality: that an outcome can follow from several combinations of causal conditions or recipes (George & Bennett, 2005; Ragin, 1987, 2000, 2008). Causal complexity focuses attention on causal necessity—does the effect always include the cause?—and sufficiency—does the cause always produce the outcome? Second, it assumes that causation is often asymmetric—that the explanation of a positive instance is not necessarily a complete explanation of *all* instances, nor can the absence of that cause explain the absence of instances. Together, these tenets suggest that several causal pathways exist and that avoiding these pathways *may not* provide much protection against the outcome. Based on the assumption of causal complexity, the absence of the cause (weak union) is not assumed to produce the inverse outcome (PRP) (cell 3). Thus, finding cases in cells one or three would not be incompatible with the proposed effect of strong unions on reform. Only cell four contains the cases with the greatest potential for theoretical falsification and also new theoretical insights.

In addition to holding the greatest theoretical value, these cases also hold the greatest practical value if, as George and Bennett (2005) argue, one aim of political science is to equip policy-makers with general knowledge that helps them form effective strategies. For this purpose:

> Highly general and abstract theories ('covering laws' in Carl Hempel's term), which set aside intervening processes and focus on correlations

between the 'start' and 'finish' of a phenomenon are too general to make sharp theoretical predictions or to guide policy. (George & Bennett, 2005, p. 7)

If the goal is to escape the "politics of blocking" (Moe, 2011, p. 275), instead of covering laws, what is needed are contingent generalizations, which describe the conditions under which the norm—successful opposition from powerful unions—is actualized or overridden (George, 1993; George & Bennett, 2005; Immergut, 2005). If the goal is to understand how a given policy can be successfully implemented, then cell four cases will provide the greatest insights.

The Difficulty of Identifying Crucial Cases within US Borders

Thus, crucial cases have two features: First, they are cases where PRP has been implemented, and second, they are cases with 'strong unions.' Although identifying PRP is relatively straightforward—defined as compensation schemes that link teachers' pay to outcomes—identifying strong unions is less straightforward due to the ambiguities of union strength and power, particularly in the United States.

US teachers' unions are widely considered to be powerful; they have considerable resources at their disposal and benefit from a number of institutional advantages. Compared to the labor movement as a whole—the Bureau of Labor Statistics (2013) reported that in 2011, 6.6% of the US workforce was unionized—teachers are considerably better organized. In 2010, the combined membership of the two main teachers' unions in the United States—the National Education Association (NEA) and the American Federation of Teachers (AFT)—was 4.6 million teachers, which makes up 25% of *all* US union members (Brill, 2010). US teachers' unions also have considerable advantages in terms of their opportunity to influence policy—their money, manpower, legions of activists, and superb organization (Moe, 2011). Unlike their private sector counterparts, teachers' unions can influence outcomes of interest through both collective bargaining and politics. And politically, they have considerable advantages as they are unrivalled in the education sector and often target small, low-turnout school district elections (Berkman & Plutzer, 2005; Heidenheimer, 1973; Moe, 2011).

Many accounts of US teachers' unionism treat it as a relatively monolithic and invariant whole. However, in spite of general consensus that US teachers' unions are powerful, they are not uniformly strong everywhere, on every issue, all the time. In 2007–2008,[5] in Type I states[6] where collective bargaining is required,[7] 88%[8] of teachers are members of a teachers' union or association; in Type II states where collective bargaining is optional,[9] the number is closer to 66%; and in Type III states where collective bargaining is illegal,[10] only 55% of teachers are members of a teachers' organization (U.S. Department of Education, National Center for Education Statistics, 2009). The marked differences in membership and coverage levels and financial resources across types of states suggest that the 'American system' of education policy, and the role of teachers' unions in that system, may be quite varied. But in addition to variation between state-types, meaningful differences *within* state-types[11] must be acknowledged, as important differences between states are not captured by differences in the type of collective bargaining laws alone. For example, in New Mexico, where collective bargaining is required, only 41% of teachers are members of a union or association and in Arkansas, where bargaining is allowed, the number is closer to 35%. Both figures are far below the average rate in states where collective bargaining is illegal (55%).

In addition to meaningful differences between states—which may be partly, although not completely, captured by differences in collective bargaining laws—there may also be important differences in the strength of unions *within* states, at the local level. Broadly, at the state level, teachers' unions in Type I states may be more powerful than those in Type III states due to the significant difference in both membership levels and coverage levels.[12] And in states where virtually all teachers are union members and covered by a collective agreement, district-level differences will likely be negligible and unimportant. But, in Type II states where the majority of teachers are *not* covered by a collective bargaining agreement, the teachers' unions in districts where teachers *have* secured the right to bargain for their members will be meaningfully different from the 'typical' teachers' union within that state. For example, in Missouri, only 8% of teachers are covered by a collective bargaining agreement (Moe, 2011, pp. 54–55), so teachers' unions in Missouri would likely be described as weak relative to their Type I counterparts. However, teachers' unions in both Kansas City and St. Louis—the state's two largest cities—have secured the right to collectively bargain. So at the local level, these unions are likely much different, and potentially stronger, than their Missouri counterparts.

The potential for local variation may be especially true in Type III states where collective bargaining is not permitted. These states are all southern states with notably conservative political cultures. However, even in these 'right to work' states where collective bargaining is not permitted, important variation may exist at the local level. Some districts in these states will engage in 'meet-and-confer' agreements—an informal consultation process that functions almost identically to collective bargaining. In a state like Texas where fewer than 15% of teachers are covered by meet-and-confer agreements, unions may be notably more influential in districts that meet-and-confer than those who do not. These districts likely have notably higher membership levels than other districts within the state, and would be expected to have increased financial and political resources. Similar results would be expected if data were available to disaggregate union membership and resources at a district level.

Although variation of teachers' unions and their effects across states and school districts is well documented, there are few systematic explanations of why policy-making processes and outcomes differ across the US and what role differences in unions' power or preferences play in those processes and outcomes, significantly complicating the selection of crucial cases within the US (Bascia, 1990; Johnson & Donaldson, 2006; Johnson & Kardos, 2000; Murray, 2004; McDonnell & Pascal, 1988). In terms of selecting crucial cases, existing research lacks an adequate theoretical account for the variability of unions' strength resources as it relates to their local influence. Absent this account, positing that strong teachers' unions block reform amounts to little more than a covering law with no explanatory power regarding the particular causal mechanisms through which that influence occurs or does not occur.

The lack of an adequate theoretical account of the variability of unions' strength resources and power—particularly as it relates to their local influence—makes it difficult to select crucial cases within the US. The problem isn't identifying cases where reform has occurred; even prior to Race to the Top, when PRP was relatively rare across the US, a variety of cases defied the prediction that strong unions will use their influence to block policies (i.e., PRP) they oppose. Even Moe (2011) identifies three states—Texas, Florida, and Minnesota—that implemented 'innovative' programs that provided money to districts who designed PRP plans which linked student test score gains to teachers' pay. Although the majority of school districts opted out of these programs, a few districts in each state chose to participate.[13] There were also a number of districts who participated in the Department of Education's Teacher Incentive Fund (TIF) (United States Department of Education, 2010). These cases, both the states that passed the legislation and the districts that designed their own systems or participated in state programs in spite of union opposition, meet the first criteria of crucial cases. However, in order to challenge existing theoretical expectations, that strong unions block unpopular reforms, they must be cases where reforms have been implemented *in spite of strong unions*.

That is the problem—that existing research does not provide sufficient tools for evaluating the relative strength of unions across states or across districts in a theoretically or methodologically robust way. Is a school district in a Type III state that engages in meet-and-confer negotiations stronger than its counterpart in a Type II state where the district does not consult the union at all? Without the conceptual tools to deal with relative union strength at the local level—a priori conceptions of when unions are more or less strong independent of their effect on policy outcomes—it is impossible to engage in fruitful subnational generalization with confidence. The conditions under which teachers' unions are more or less powerful across the United States, as well as how these variations might be linked to different policy outcomes and what they might contribute to theories of teachers' unionism, are currently unknown, making the selection of crucial cases within the United States inherently difficult.

International–Subnational Comparative Research Design
Many accounts of teachers' unions are US-centric, which might lead some—particularly those who subscribe to views of 'American

Exceptionalism'—to question the appropriateness of international comparison. However, there were a number of advantages, beyond the inherent difficulty of selecting crucial cases within the US, to beginning with an international comparative test. Kocka (2003) describes four functions of comparison—heuristic, analytical, descriptive, and paradigmatic—and although all are relevant to this inquiry, the latter objective deserves special mention in terms of the international–subnational comparative research design.

Paradigmatically, international cases serve to distance the researcher "from the case [he or she] knows best" (Kocka, 2003, p. 41). But they also can expand the diversity of an observed phenomenon. For example, a study of the relationship between unionization and variable pay schemes in Germany's private sector found that cooperative union–management relationships increased the likelihood of pay-related innovations (Heywood, Hübler, & Jirjahn, 1998). Although the correlation between cooperation and variable pay had been hypothesized and tested in the United Kingdom and Australia, there was no empirical relationship in those contexts. Based strictly on the Anglo-Saxon cases, researchers could have concluded that cooperation was either impossible or irrelevant to decision-making. However, the German case pointed to different conclusions and prompted different questions: What is distinct about the labor relations systems and contexts? What does cooperation mean in the German context? Can the concept travel? Why or why not? Thus, international comparison had a "de-provincializing, a liberating, an eye-opening effect" (Kocka, 2003, p. 41), particularly useful given the fierce and seemingly intractable debate about teachers' unions in the United States.

International comparison may cause the researcher to see the 'original' case differently—to be more sensitive to theoretically important but previously ignored variables. For example, perhaps observing cooperative labor-management relationships in Germany prompts the researcher to reexamine labor relations in the UK context, enabling her to see nuanced differences that were always there but previously overlooked. Or, the researcher may conclude that the two cases are fundamentally different—that the cooperative relationships observed in Germany are impossible in the UK due to institutional structures or other explanations. In the latter case, "the discovery of the extraordinary urges the observer to explain why the rule that exists here is absent there and vice versa" (Dogan & Pelassy, 1990, p. 9). The international cases may confirm the unions-block-reform argument, greatly strengthening it. However, if they challenge this hypothesis, they provide opportunities for theory building. The international cases may reveal new insights—evidence of limitations within existing theoretical models—that could explain 'exceptional' cases within the US. Alternatively, perhaps this particular argument *is* explaining something unique or extraordinary that is not, in fact, generalizable outside of US borders. In that case, "the observer [must] explain why the rule that exists here is absent there, and vice versa" (Dogan & Pelassy, 1990, p. 9). Such an explanation would need to be able to identify the unique conditions that define the particularity of union preferences and influence in the US. The process of constructing such an explanation—contingent generalization (George & Bennett, 2005)—would strengthen existing theories.

Consistent with the view that comparative understanding is iterative—that the particular is understood in light of the general and vice versa—international comparison moves between the particular and the general to check the soundness of the theory. Understanding particular cases is important, but building general hypotheses sharpens perceptions of the particular. Thus, this research utilizes two comparative lenses, first applying an internationally comparative lens, and then, testing the theoretical insights within the US. This iterative comparative approach may serve to produce a more finely differentiated set of contingent generalizations—attending to the particular causes and delimiting conditions of a causal theory (Ragin, 2000).

International Case Selection: Identifying 'Cell 4' Cases

International crucial case selection proceeded through several steps. First, the class of cases was determined, establishing the relevant subset of the population. Dogan and Pelassy (1990) argue that the quality of a comparative study will depend on the accuracy of conceptual tools and the consistency of the field—the part of the system being studied and the kind of units compared. Thus, the search for international crucial cases was limited to western liberal democracies—the original OECD 20. The decision to focus on one particular type of reform (PRP), instead of comparing a variety of reform processes, was also motivated by an effort to maintain maximum consistency of the field. Although the specific PRP reforms across cases differ, they are all of the same type of reform and are responses to similar policy problems (Chapter 1).

From the population of western liberal democracies, cases where PRP for teachers had been implemented were identified based on data reported by the OECD (2006, 2007, 2008, 2009, 2010, 2011, 2012). Three countries were highlighted on the basis of notable reform in the area of teacher compensation—Finland, Sweden, and the Cantons of Zürich and St. Gallen in Switzerland. In addition, based on reports of approaches to teacher compensation displayed for all countries included in *Education at a Glance* (OECD, 2011), Denmark and the Netherlands were also identified as compensating teachers in ways that deviated significantly from traditional approaches.

Although the potential sample of cases was selected to feature crucial cases, selection within the sample was guided by an effort to maximize the diversity of cases in terms of institutional arrangements. For example, due to some similar institutional arrangements in Sweden and Finland, only one of these cases was selected. Although the relative similarity of potential cases is a limitation in terms of case diversity—they are all small European states (Katzenstein, 1985) and consensus democracies (Lijphart, 1999)—the researcher attempted to maximize the diversity of cases from within the sample. On the basis of this logic, two cases were selected—Finland[14] and the Swiss canton of Zürich.[15] Methodologically, the decision to examine different policy-making units—a nation, a region (canton), and, later, school districts in the United States—is an important component of conceptual validity: measuring the indicators that best represent the theoretical concepts the researcher intends to measure (George & Bennett, 2005). Conceptual validity is achieved through contextualized comparison, which "self-consciously seeks to address the issue of equivalence by searching for an *analytically equivalent* phenomenon—even if expressed in substantively different forms—across different contexts" (Locke & Thelen, 1998, p. 11).

If the contestation of the US-Finland comparison of education systems is any indication, many will argue that Finland and Zürich are ill suited to be compared to the United States. In addition to the significant descriptive differences—size and diversity, for example—the political cultures stand far apart. However, the differences in political culture may be an asset, rather than a limitation, of the comparative design. Katzenstein argues that "normally, comparative analysis explores objects that, to the uninitiated, look similar on the surface . . . or it points to continuities in objects that appear very dissimilar at first glance" (1987, p. 32).

The second selection consideration, or perhaps more aptly, a criteria for potential exclusion—presence of a strong union—presented a greater challenge in terms of the "accuracy of conceptual tools" (Dogan & Pelassy, 1990, p. 161). Cases could not be selected as a priori models of the most powerful unions—due to the emphasis on the contingency of power outlined in Chapter 1. However, in order to attempt to select cell 4 cases (Table 3.1), it was important to ensure that the selected cases were not 'weak'—that they had the requisite strength resources to hypothetically impact policy outcomes. Thus, the criterion for selection was *strength*, not power (see Chapter 1). Therefore, it was possible to rely on strength resources while remaining open to the contingency of power—whether or not these strength resources were translated into influence in the cases under investigation. Thus, unions were labeled 'strong' if they had the potential to impact policy outcomes—taking basic institutional arrangements into account.

Although considerable attention is paid to unions' strength resources and the opportunity structure for participation and influence in the case studies, an overview of the cases will suffice here. Finland's teachers' union's strength resources are considerable; the Trade Union of Education (OAJ) organizes over 95% of Finland's teachers and is included in the country's extensive tripartite bargaining system (OAJ, n.d.). Although evaluating union strength resources in Switzerland, including the Canton of Zürich, was less straightforward, as union density levels are considerably lower, unions and special interest groups in Switzerland are often thought to have unique opportunities for political influence through referenda and institutions of direct democracy (Aubert, 1989; Immergut, 1992; Ladner & Brändle, 1999; Wagner, Santiago, Thieme, & Zay, 2004).

DATA COLLECTION METHODS

Miles and Huberman (1994) argue that the methodological emphasis—rather than arguing for 'one best method'—should be on orderliness, or a methodological thoroughness and explicitness which facilitates clear, verifiable, and replicable findings. As Popper (1959) said, "There is no such thing as a logical method of having new ideas. . . . Discovery contains an irrational element, or a 'creative intuition'" (as cited in King et al., 1994, p. 14). However, sound methodological choices can discipline the inquiry and ensure the scientific reliability of the findings. With this in mind, this section outlines methodological choices regarding "focusing and bounding the collection of data" (Miles & Huberman 1994, p. 16) and the development and refinement of instrumentation.

Focusing and Bounding the Collection of Data

The collection of data was first bounded through case definition. As discussed in the previous section, in this research, the relevant cases—the class of events—were attempts to reform teachers' salaries and compensation, specifically attempts to implement PRP. Furthermore, analysis focused on recent[16] reform efforts in western liberal democracies. Thus, the unit of analysis was not necessarily the nation-state, but the institutions and actors within a given nation-state that determine education policy and reform. Thus, in Finland, where education policy institutions are relatively centralized, the nation-state was the appropriate unit of analysis. In Switzerland, on the other hand, the canton was the appropriate unit of analysis. Furthermore, because this research takes what Immergut (1992) calls a "narrow" view of education policy, examining a specific issue (PRP) rather than the entire education system, the focus was on the specific events, interactions, or conflicts that contributed to the policy outcome of interest (p. 67). Ultimately, determining the scope of events or interactions constituting the case was a methodological choice about "focusing and bounding the collection of data" (Miles & Huberman, 1994, p. 16).

On the spectrum of qualitative research design—ranging from pre-structured design to a loose, emergent design—this study is closer to the pre-structured paradigm, a degree of structure necessitated by comparative demands (Miles & Huberman, 1994). The case studies were conducted according to what George and Bennett label "structured focused comparison" (2005, p. 67). Cases were focused because they only dealt with certain aspects of cases—in this case reforms of teacher compensation—and they were structured in the sense that interview schedules across cases were oriented around the same general areas of inquiry. In Finland, a new salary system, implemented in 2007, was the focus of the case study. In Zürich, the case study examined the process of designing and implementing a new teacher evaluation system linked to teachers' pay, initiated in the late 1990s and implemented in 2000. In both cases, the emphasis was on the institutions and the actors' preferences and perceptions, which produced the policy outcome. The focus was both descriptive—what happened?—and analytic—why did it happen and what role did the unions play in the process?

Data Collection

In terms of choices of data collection, case studies can involve a number of types of data, including archives, interviews, questionnaires, and observations (Layder, 1998; Yin, 1989). The case studies in this book relied primarily on elite interviews supplemented both by information available through secondary source materials and documents as well as that provided by informants (Dexter, 1970/2006).

The central research strategy was to rely on semistructured interviews with 'elites'[17] supplemented by knowledgeable informants (Dexter, 1970/2006; Kvale & Brinkman, 2009; Paul, 1954).[18] Informants provided historical and institutional context and access to elites. The following sections describe the elite interviewing process and the role of informants as well as the construction and use of semistructured interview schedules and the execution of interviews.

Elite Interviewing and Informants

This research adopts Dexter's definition of elite interviewing, provided in *Elite and Special Interviewing* (1970/2006): an interview approach that allows the interviewee to teach the investigator what the problem, question, and situation are. Elite interviewing—approaching interviews with a briefer, semistructured interview schedule that uses more open questions as opposed to a more structured approach to interviewing—is most appropriate for this inquiry for two reasons (Peabody et al., 1990).

First, it is more efficient in determining what is important. It seems best to operate under the assumption that attempting to interview policy-makers, union leaders, and other stakeholders will likely be met with "limited cooperation" (Gordon, 1987, p. 100), and that those who agree to be interviewed may place significant limits on the length of the interview (Peabody et al., 1990). A more structured schedule that probed into each of the numerous mechanisms that *may* be important would be extensive, requiring more than an hour to complete. Due to time limitations, the interview schedule was designed to be completed in 20–30 minutes, if necessary, with questions prepared for further elaboration if time allowed (Peabody et al., 1990). Second, elite interviewing was a preferred methodological approach because of the dispositions of interviewees and the nature of their knowledge. Elites may resist structured approaches to interviewing because they are accustomed to defining what is important. Preventing them from telling their stories could cause elites to disengage from the interview process (Dexter 1970/2006).

The utilization of informants was critical to the elite interviewing approach. Informants were a helpful avenue to access to elites, providing advice about the most effective and appropriate strategies for contacting elites within each context (Dexter, 1970/2006). In both contexts, informants suggested that it was appropriate to contact potential interviewees via e-mail followed by a phone call, if necessary. In all introductory contacts, the researcher explained the nature of the research project, the purpose of the interviews, and the way that data would be stored, protected, and used. Additionally, informants were sometimes willing and able to endorse the researcher or connect her directly to potential interviewees.

Informants were also valuable because of their ability to verify information collected through secondary literature about institutional arrangements and their influence on the policy-making process as well as providing more detailed information about the sequence of events and relevant actor constellations not available in the secondary literature prior to interviews. Conversations with informants were focused on the first five questions of the analytic framework—those related to the policy process and institutions (see Appendix I). This information was important for two reasons. First, it allowed elite interviews to focus on the nature of the interactions that produce policy, including actors' orientations, perceptions, and preferences. By using informants to build a robust understanding of the facts—institutional arrangements, historical context, and relevant events—interviews could be focused on the *meaning* of events (Dexter, 1970/2006).

The contribution of informants was also important because of the pre-information that it provided to the researcher—critical in eventually securing the trust and confidence of the interviewee (Meyer, 2001). Adequate pre-knowledge allowed the researcher to establish competence and credibility and it also allowed questions to be framed with enough specificity to uncover new information and to engage knowledgeable elites and experts. However, the researcher was careful in the use of pre-knowledge so as not to reveal the research hypotheses. Furthermore, the researcher could not allow the goal of appearing knowledgeable and credible to interfere with framing open-ended questions that allowed the interviewee to explain what was important (Dexter, 1970/2006; Kvale & Brinkman, 2009).

Developing and Refining Interview Schedules
Miles and Huberman (1994) describe field research as having both a descriptive and an explanatory function in which the aim is "to depict the local context and what happens within it *and* to disclose the rules and reasons that determine why things happen the way they do" (1984, p. 132). Consistent with this approach—and with the problem-oriented research questions guiding this research—the interview schedules had both descriptive and explanatory functions—uncovering *what* happened and *why* it happened.

The interviews were relatively brief—approximately 20 questions and lasting from 40–90 minutes—and questions were posed in general terms, consistent with the methodology of elite interviewing that aims to discover. Although the wording of questions was tailored to the details of each case and the role of the interviewee and instruments[19] were revised throughout the research process,[20] they were guided by the theoretical framework and, ultimately, the research questions (Miles & Humberman, 1994). Furthermore, questions were worded carefully in order to avoid projecting definitions with which the interviewee may be uncomfortable or resistant:

> In most political interviews, certainly, and I think in most interviews where the important thing is the discovery of a social pattern or value of any sort, it is important to start off with comments or ask questions where the key words are quite vague and ambiguous, so the interviewee can interpret them in his own 'terms.' (Dexter, 1970/2006, p. 53)

This is strategically important, according to Dexter, because "a question which sharply defines a particular area . . . is far more likely to result in omission of some vital data which you, the interviewer, have not thought of" (1970/2006, p. 54). An appropriate vocabulary is that which facilitates clear understanding, establishes an optimal relationship between researcher and interviewee, provides a vocabulary for response without violating etiquette, and avoids emotional or 'loaded' words (Gordon, 1987).

In terms of this research, attention to appropriate vocabulary was critical. Many interviewees were sensitive to language about education 'reform'—particularly because of the researcher's American accent and assumptions about what reform means in the American lexicon. Therefore, the researcher avoided use of the term 'reform' and instead referred to 'policy changes,' 'legislative changes,' or 'the new system.' Similarly, the researcher avoided referring explicitly to 'PRP' or 'merit pay' and instead attempted to always refer to the policy changes by their local title.

Furthermore, the researcher avoided stressing particular themes until the interviewee raised them, at least until the end of the interview (Dexter, 1970/2006; Peabody et al., 1990). However, as a part of the interview schedule, the researcher had instructions about issues on which the interviewee would have been expected to respond—as defined by the theoretical framework (1970/2006). Then, at the end of the interview, or as appropriate, the researcher probed further with specific questions in areas where general questions failed to produce a response (1970/2006).

Methodologically, this was important because perhaps the omission—for example, if the interviewee did not discuss an actor that the interviewer expected to be significant—was the product of the omitted actor being unimportant to the policy-making process and outcome in question. In this case, the unimportance of the actor in question could be confirmed in targeted follow-up questions. At the same time, if the omitted actor *was* in fact important, the interviewee had an opportunity to clarify that in response to more targeted probing. Although elite interviews allow the interviewee to define 'what is important,' the researcher ensured that interviews were similar in their coverage by including detailed instructions about anticipated responses within the schedule.

Although elite interviewing presents advantages over more structured approaches (Dexter, 1970/2006), it also poses challenges. Specifically, information gathered across interviewees—both within one country and also in the common themes that are generated between countries—tends to be less standardized than information gathered through a more structured process. Can the researcher be sure that the elite accounts of what is important in the reform process do not neglect other important—although potentially unobserved or underestimated—mechanisms? Standardization was accommodated by using similarly structured guides informed by the analytic framework and by using strategic probes into theoretically important but neglected areas. Secondary sources were also used to corroborate and supplement details provided in elite accounts.

Execution of Interviews

Four criteria, based on Pettigrew's (1990) pluralist view[21] and modeled in other research (Meyer, 2001), guided the sampling of interviewees. First, interviewees were selected from multiple perspectives, constituencies, or stakeholder groups. Second, the researcher sought multiple interviewees within a given perspective or constituency. Third, interviewees needed to be knowledgeable about the reform process. Finally, interviewees with a range of involvements[22] were selected (Pettigrew, 1990). In practice, this meant that in addition to interviewing individuals—within the teachers' union for example—who were *directly* involved in negotiations or consultations about the reforms in question, other staff members[23] who may have been less involved were also consulted. Consistent with Layder's (1998) recommendations, the sample was not predetermined, as key questions about which events were relevant and which individuals were knowledgeable could not be answered prior to the research.

In Finland, before conducting interviews, the researcher met with over 15 informants—these individuals ranged from academic researchers to those working at the National Board of Education, the municipal employer organization (KT), the central teachers' union (OAJ), or at the local education level. Then, 14 individuals were interviewed.[24] Interviews ranged in length from 47 to 108 minutes, averaging approximately 73 minutes. In addition to the individuals who were interviewed, three provided written responses. Follow-ups were conducted primarily via e-mail, although the researcher met with three individuals a second time (see Appendix IV).

In Zürich, prior to conducting interviews, the researcher spoke with 13 informants—primarily researchers. The researcher also visited a school and talked with a teacher in the city. Then, six individuals were interviewed or provided written responses. Interviews ranged from 34 to 103 minutes and averaged approximately 57 minutes. Follow-ups were conducted via e-mail (see Appendix V).

Interviews were conducted in English. Interviewees were given a choice to conduct the interview in their mother-tongue using a translator or to provide written responses to questions in their mother-tongue either in addition to or instead of an oral interview. Two individuals in Finland provided written responses in Finnish and declined to be interviewed, and it is possible that some individuals may have been unresponsive to requests for interviews due to language-related ambivalence. However, the interviews conducted in both cases reflect a good cross sampling of individuals and organizations. Interviews were recorded in order to ensure accuracy unless interviewees objected to the use of a recorder—none did. In all interviews, the researcher took notes, which were typed up promptly after the interview in order to reconstruct content and to capture nuances and impressions that may not be captured in the notes or recording (Miles & Huberman, 1994). Initially, the interviews were not transcribed but were stored. The researcher listened to all the interviews in order to verify accuracy, check for omissions, and to add any quotes or details to interview notes. After initial analysis, the researcher decided to produce transcripts, which were then used in further analysis.

Documentary Sources

Three major types of documents were used in this research: documents provided by interviewees, newspaper articles and other secondary sources, and publically available documentation about collective bargaining or legislative changes. The latter two types of documents were exclusively in Finnish or German; some versions of documents provided by interviewees were available in English.

Because the researcher is not fluent in German or Finnish, there were real, but not insurmountable, language challenges. Upon receiving documents, the researcher worked to produce provisional translations of documents and to work with interviewees and informants to identify critical documents. Then, the researcher used hired translators to translate critical documents. The researcher's work in producing provisional translations was essential because it allowed the researcher to identify and recognize key vocabulary—critical to identifying other sources and also for use in interviews. Originals and translations of documents were kept and stored together. Although these sources were not the primary data source, they were helpful for validating and supplementing information provided by interviewees (see Appendix I).

DATA ANALYSIS METHODS

Data analysis proceeded through four stages: a preliminary phase, a period coterminous with data collection, within-site analysis, and comparative analysis and analytic generalization (Miles & Huberman, 1994). Exclusively focusing on within-site analysis—constructing descriptive accounts, themes and related matrices, and unpacking causal mechanisms—before turning to comparative analysis was a strategic choice, in order to ensure that each case's unique patterns were not lost in an effort to construct generalizations (Eisenhardt, 1989).

Preliminary Phase

Before conducting interviews, in the preliminary stage, the researcher used secondary sources and informants to understand the institutional structure—the legal determinants of policy-making and change, the interactions that produce policy, and the way that these arrangements constrained or enabled the involvement of teachers' unions. Then, data gathered through secondary sources, informants, and interviews was used to construct a preliminary chronology of relevant events (Miles & Huberman, 1994). This chronology—the descriptive component of the research—was revised and clarified throughout the research process (Miles & Huberman, 1994).[25]

Analysis Throughout Data Collection

The second phase of data analysis was coterminous with data collection, as write-ups, memoing, and intermediary case analyses were used to generate strategies for the collection of new data on the basis of emerging hypotheses (Layder, 1998; Miles & Huberman, 1994). These records—particularly interview write-ups—were then used in later analyses.[26] The researcher, following Miles and Huberman's (1994) recommendations, used field notes, contact summary forms, and periodic interim site summaries throughout the data collection process.

Within-Site Analysis

After all interviews had been conducted, the researcher used field notes and contact summary sheets—which were checked against interview recordings for comprehensiveness—as well as supplementary documentary evidence to begin conducting within-site analysis. Within-site analysis involved two major components, which are linked to the guiding research questions. First, analysis attempted to explain 'what happened,' developing a sound chronology of events and tracing causal pathways through those events. Second, analysis focused on 'why it happened'—with particular attention to actors' orientations and the institutions that constrained or enabled their participation.

The field notes were first analyzed through repeated rereading or "soaking and poking" (George & Bennett, 2005, p. 96), which allowed the researcher to become familiar with the interview accounts and their interrelationships. Then the researcher coded the field notes using descriptive codes based on the analytic framework's three key factors—institutions, actors' orientations, and policy process. The process of applying these descriptive codes produced many new pattern codes, as new themes emerged (Miles & Huberman, 1994).

Though there were some basic codes related to institutional arrangements, interview materials were primarily used to confirm, validate, and supplement secondary information. It was primarily used to confirm, validate, and supplement secondary source material. In contrast, the event-based codes were almost entirely pattern codes—based on refinements of the provisional chronologies produced in the first and second phases of data analysis (Miles & Huberman, 1994).

Pattern coding was particularly important regarding actors' orientations—the preferences, perceptions, and relationship patterns and orientations. The process was extensive and iterative. Although the preferences and capacities of both government decision-makers and unions were collected, the majority of the analysis focused on the preferences, perceptions, and capacities of the union. In both cases, the general subcategories—the union's preferences, perceptions, and capacities—were further disaggregated based on both general distinctions that applied to each case and particular themes that emerged from each respectively. For example, preferences were disaggregated according to general goals or preferences as well as to particular reform-related preferences or perceptions articulated in each context. The pattern coding process was iterative, moving between theory and data (Layder, 1998; Miles & Huberman, 1994).

After multiple readings, and as coding became more extensive and interpretative, emerging themes related to actors' perceptions, preferences, and relationships required greater precision than available through interview notes and summaries (Miles & Huberman, 1994). As a result, the researcher transcribed the majority of interview data—excluding sections like career background or irrelevant historical context that clearly fell outside of the codes. Then, based on the applied descriptive and pattern codes, interview data was combined into a spreadsheet where all data could be viewed together. Each interviewee was assigned a row and each code a column. All excerpts relevant to each code were pasted into individual cells; when a section applied to multiple codes, it was included in multiple cells. This process also aided in the production of new codes and refinement of existing codes.

Comparative Analysis

Only after careful within-case analysis did between-case comparison and analytic generalization—comparison with existing theories—begin (Meyer, 2001; Miles & Huberman, 1994). The extensive focus on within-case analysis before turning to comparison was important to ensure "the integrity of cases as complex configurations" (Ragin, 2000, p. 38), and reflects the case-oriented assumptions that guide this research. Parts II and III provide both descriptive accounts of each case as well as explanatory hypotheses derived from comparative analysis. On the basis of the comparison between cases, the researcher then moved to analytic generalization in the fifth phase (Yin, 1989) (Part IV).

NOTES

1. The specific methodological choices employed in the US cases will be outlined in Chapter 8.
2. This perspective focuses on the process through which policy solutions are successfully adopted or implemented (Scharpf, 1997, 2000).
3. This 'narrow' view doesn't mean that context will be ignored. Chapter 2 emphasized the importance of attending to the broader reform dynamics that animate PRP reforms, and there will be careful methodological attention to institutional and historical context in Chapter 4.
4. Sometimes called 'critical cases' (Flyvbjerg, 2006; Gerring, 2007; Miles & Huberman, 1994).
5. The latest year for which data was available, at the time of research.
6. Alaska, California, Connecticut, Delaware, District of Columbia, Florida, Hawaii, Illinois, Indiana, Iowa, Kansas, Maine, Maryland, Massachusetts, Michigan, Minnesota, Montana, Nebraska, Nevada, New Hampshire, New Jersey, New Mexico, New York, Oklahoma, Oregon, Pennsylvania, Rhode Island, South Dakota, Vermont, Washington, Wisconsin
7. Classification of state laws is based on reports by the National Council for Teacher Quality (CITE).
8. Percentages are weighted averages (percentage of teachers unionized in each state times the total number of teachers in the state).
9. Alabama, Arizona, Arkansas, Colorado, Idaho, Kentucky, Louisiana, Mississippi, Missouri, North Dakota, Ohio, Tennessee, Utah, West Virginia, Wyoming
10. Georgia, North Carolina, South Carolina, Texas, Virginia
11. As defined by collective bargaining laws.
12. Whether measured by collective bargaining coverage or meet-and-confer agreement coverage.
13. This will be the focus of Chapter 9.
14. Finland has been the focus of significant international attention since the 'miracle of PISA' in 2000. However, it should be noted that this research does not, in its inclusion of Finland, make any attempts to provide explanations for Finland's success on the PISA exams nor to promote an argument that Finland's approach to teacher compensation, or its teachers' union (OAJ), is a cause of the performance of Finnish 15-year-olds on the PISA exams.
15. The Netherlands was also originally selected but was eliminated after preliminary research and conversations with informants confirmed that it could not be classified as a case of 'successful' reform.
16. 'Recent' will be defined as reforms since 1990, which will all fall within the 'era of permanent austerity.'
17. Any interviewee in important or exposed positions who is given 'special treatment:' letting the interview define the situation, structure the account, and define relevance and irrelevance (Dexter, 1970/2006).
18. This research adopts Paul's (1954) definition of informants: "individuals who have not only proved themselves well informed and well-connected but have demonstrated a capacity to adopt the standpoint of the investigator. Informing him of rumors and coming events, suggesting secondary informants, preparing the way, advising on tactics and tact, securing additional data on their own, and assisting in numerous other ways" (p. 44).
19. Interview guides are reproduced in Appendices II and III.
20. Process or descriptive questions were somewhat basic at the beginning of the research process. As the research process developed, these questions were

able to get more specific or move toward more detailed questions. Follow-up contacts were also used where appropriate.
21. Analyzing competing versions of reality as seen by actors.
22. This was truer in Finland than Zürich. In Zürich, the reform process was relatively 'closed,' which meant that only a small circle had knowledge of the events in question.
23. But who were also knowledgeable—consistent with the third principle.
24. 12 interviews were conducted—two interviews included two individuals.
25. The preliminary chronology was more complete in Zürich than Finland; therefore, interviews in Finland had a substantial chronological/descriptive component.
26. Recordings were stored and used to verify information in write-ups, notes, and summaries.

REFERENCES

Adams, S. J., Heywood, J. S., & Rothstein, R. (Eds.). (2009). *Teachers, performance pay, and accountability: What education should learn from other sectors.* Washington, DC: Economic Policy Institute, 13–64.

Aubert, G. (1989). Collective agreements and industrial peace in Switzerland. *International Labour Review, 128*(3), 373–388.

Bascia, N. (1990). Teachers' evaluations of unions. *Journal of Education Policy, 5*(4), 301–312.

Berg-Schlosser, D., De Meur, G., Rihoux, B., & Ragin, C. C. (2009). Qualitative comparative analysis (QCA) as an approach. In B. Rihoux & C. C. Ragin (Eds.), *Configurational comparative methods: Qualitative comparative analysis (QCA) and related techniques.* Los Angeles: Sage, 1–18.

Berkman, M. B., & Plutzer, E. (2005). *Ten thousand democracies: Politics and public opinion in America's school districts.* Washington, DC: Georgetown University Press.

Brill, S. (2010). *Class warfare: Inside the fight to fix America's schools.* New York: Simon & Schuster.

Bureau of Labor Statistics. (2013). *Union Members—2012* (U.S. Department of Labor. USDL-13-0105). Retrieved September 4, 2013, from http://www.bls.gov/news.release/pdf/union2.pdf

Collier, D. (1993). The comparative method. In A. W. Finifter (Ed.), *Political science: The state of discipline II.* Alrington, VA: American Political Science Association, 105–119.

Dexter, L. A. (1970/2006). *Elite and specialized interviewing* (2nd ed.). Colchester: ECPR Press Classics.

Dogan, M., & Pelassy, D. (1990). *How to compare nations: Strategies in comparative politics.* Chatham, NJ: Chatham House.

Eckstein, H. (1975). Case studies and theory in political science. In F. I. Greenstein & N. W. Polsby (Eds.), *Handbook of political science. Political Science: Scope and theory* (Vol. 7). Reading, MA: Addison-Wesley, 94–137.

Eisenhardt, K. M. (1989). Building theories from case study research. *Academy of Management Review, 14,* 532–550.

Flyvbjerg, B. (2006). Five misunderstandings about case-study research. *Qualitative Inquiry, 12*(2), 219–245.

George, A. L. (1993). *Bridging the gap: Theory and practice in foreign policy.* Washington, DC: United States Institute of Peace.

George, A. L., & Bennett, A. (2005). *Case studies and theory development in the social sciences.* Cambridge, MA: MIT Press.

Gerring, J. (2004). What is a case study and what is it good for? *American Political Science Review, 98*(2), 341–354.

Gerring, J. (2007). Is there a (viable) crucial-case method? *Comparative political studies, 40*(3), 231–253.

Gordon, R. L. (1987). *Interviewing: Strategy, techniques, and tactics.* Chicago: Dorsey Press.

Heidenheimer, A. J. (1973). The politics of public education, health and welfare in the USA and Western Europe: How growth and reform potentials have differed. *British Journal of Political Science, 3*(3), 315–340.

Heywood, J. S., Hübler, O., & Jirjahn, U. (1998). Variable payment schemes and industrial relations: Evidence from Germany. *Kyklos, 51*(2), 237–257.

Immergut, E. (1992). *Health politics.* Cambridge, MA: Cambridge University Press.

Immergut, E. (2005). Historical-institutionalism in political science and the problem of change. In A. Wimmer & R. Koessler (Eds.), *Understanding change: Models, methodologies, and metaphors.* Basingstoke: Palgrave, 237–259.

Johnson, S. M., & Donaldson, M. (2006). The effects of collective bargaining on teacher quality. In J. Hannaway & A. Rotherman (Eds.), *Collective bargaining in education: Negotiating change in today's schools.* Cambridge, MA: Harvard Education Press, 111–140.

Johnson, S. M., & Kardos, S. (2000). Reform bargaining and its promise for school improvement. In T. Loveless (Ed.), *Conflicting missions? Teachers unions and educational reform.* Washington, DC: The Brookings Institution, 7–46.

Katzenstein, P. J. (1985). *Small states in world markets: Industrial policy in Europe.* Ithaca, NY: Cornell University Press.

Katzenstein, P. J. (1987). *Corporatism and change: Austria, Switzerland, and the politics of industry.* Ithaca, NY: Cornell University Press.

King, G., Keohane, R. O., & Verba, S. (1994). *Desiging social inquiry: Scientific inference in qualitative research.* Princeton, NJ: Princeton Unviersity Press.

Kocka, J. (2003). Comparison and beyond. *History and Theory, 42*(1), 39–44.

Kvale, S., & Brinkmann, S. (2009). *Interviews: Learning the craft of qualtitative research interviewing.* Los Angeles, CA: Sage.

Ladner, A., & Brändle, M. (1999). Does direct democracy matter for political parties? An empirical test in the Swiss cantons. *Party Politics, 5*(3), 283–302.

Layder, D. (1998). *Sociological practice: Linking theory and social research.* London: Sage.

Lijphart, A. (1999). *Patterns of democracy: Government forms and performance in thirty-six countries.* New Haven, CT: Yale University Press.

Locke, R., & Thelen, K. (1998). Problems of equivalence in comparative politics: Apples and oranges, again. *Newsletter of the APSA Organized Section in Comparative Politics, 9*(1), 9–12.

McDonnell, L. M., & Pascal, A. (1988). *Teacher unions and educational reform.* Santa Monica, CA: The Rand Corporation.

Meyer, C. B. (2001). A case study in case study methodology. *Field Methods, 13*(4), 329–351.

Miles, M. B., & Huberman, A. M. (1994). *Qualitative data analysis: An expanded sourcebook.* London: Sage Publications.

Moe, T. (2011). *Special interests: Teachers unions and America's public schools.* Washington, DC: Brookings Institution.

Murray, C. E. (2004). Innovative local teacher unions: What have they accomplished. In R. D. Henderson, W. J. Urban, & P. Wolman (Eds.), *Teacher unions and education policy: Retrenchment and reform.* Oxford: Elesevier, 149–166.

Opetusalan Ammattijärjestö. (n.d.). *OAJ: The trade union of education in Finland* [brochure]. Helsinki, Finland: OAJ.

Organization for Economic Co-operation and Development. (2006). *Education at a glance 2006.* Paris: OECD.

Organization for Economic Co-operation and Development. (2007). *Education at a glance 2007.* Paris: OECD.
Organization for Economic Co-operation and Development. (2008). *Education at a glance 2008.* Paris: OECD.
Organization for Economic Co-operation and Development. (2009). *Education at a glance 2009.* Paris: OECD.
Organization for Economic Co-operation and Development. (2010). *Government at a glance 2010.* Paris: OECD.
Organization for Economic Co-operation and Development. (2011). *Education at a glance 2011.* Paris: OECD.
Organization for Economic Co-operation and Development. (2012). *Education at a Glance 2012.* Paris: OECD.
Paul, B. (1954). Interview techniques and field relationships. In A. L. Kroeber (Ed.), *Anthropology today.* Chicago: Unviersity of Chicago Press, 430–451.
Peabody, R. L., Hammond, S. W., Torcom, J., Brown, L. P., Thompson, C., & Kolodny, R. (1990). Interviewing political elites. *PS. Political science and politics, 23*(3), 451–455.
Pettigrew, A. M. (1990). Longitudinal field research on change: Theory and practice. *Organization science, 1*(3), 267–292.
Ragin, C. C. (1987). *The comparative method: Moving beyond qualitative and quantitative strategies.* Berkeley: University of California Press.
Ragin, C. C. (2000). *Fuzzy-set social science.* Chicago: University of Chicago Press.
Ragin, C. C. (2008). *Redesigning social inquiry: Fuzzy sets and beyond.* Chicago: University of Chicago Press.
Robinson, W. S. (1951). The logical structure of analytic induction. *American Sociological Review, 16*(6), 812–817.
Scharpf, F. W. (1997). *Games real actors play.* Boulder, CO: Westview Press.
Scharpf, F. W. (2000). Institutions in comparative policy research. *Comparative Political Studies, 33*(6–7), 762–790.
Stake, R. (2005). Qualitative case studies. In N. K. Denzin & Y. S. Lincoln (Eds.), *The Sage handbook of qualitative research* (3rd ed.). Thousand Oaks, CA: Sage, 433–466.
U.S. Department of Education. (2010). *Teacher incentive fund: Frequently asked questions for the 2010 competition and grant awards.* Retrieved from http://www2.ed.gov/programs/teacherincentive/faq.html
U.S. Department of Education, National Center for Education Statistics. (2009). *Schools and staffing survey (SAS), "Public school teacher data files," 1999–2000, 2003–04, and 2007–08; and "Charter school teacher data file" 1999–2000.* Retrieved from http://nces.ed.gov/surveys/sass/dataproducts.asp
Van Wynsberghe, R., & Khan, S. (2007). Redefining case study. *International Journal of Qualitative Methods, 6*(2), 80–94.
Wagner, A., Santiago, P., Thieme, C., & Zay, D. (2004). *Country note: Switzerland.* Retrieved from OECD, Education and Training Policy Division http://www.oecd.org/switzerland/33684152.pdf
Yin, R. K. (1989). *Case study research: Design and methods.* Applied Social Research Series, 5. London: Sage.

Part II
International Cases

4 Finland
History and Context

Finland is currently one of the most unionized countries in the world, with around 70% of workers belonging to unions and nearly 90% covered by collective bargaining agreements (Jokivuori, 2011). Finland's teachers' union, The OAJ, is equally strong. In the United States, where teachers' unions are lauded as some of the most powerful organizations in public education, 4.6 million are members of either the American Federation of Teachers (AFT) or the National Education Association (NEA), roughly 40% of the teaching workforce (Winkler, Scull, & Zeehandelaar, 2012). The OAJ represents over 95% of Finland's teachers—an eye-popping statistic and nearly double the percentage of organized teachers in the United States.

The OAJ is a dominant force in Finnish public education. However, the story goes deeper than the sheer number of teachers it represents. Unions in Finland are extensively incorporated into both formal and informal decision-making processes. All unions are involved in Finland's extensive collective bargaining agreements. The *tripartite agreements*—involving a prescribed set of actors: organized labor, employer organizations, and the government—are multilevel and cover a wide range of terms and conditions. But beyond these formal negotiations, unions consistently have a seat at the table; they are frequently involved in decision- and policy-making processes through Finland's extensive consultation processes. Together with the high professional status of teachers in Finland, these features combine to produce a very powerful teachers' union.

According to one OAJ official, if the teachers' union opposes something, it will not happen. This sounds a bit like the narrative that often dominates discussions about teachers' unions in the United States. However, in 2007, by all accounts, a puzzling event occurred in Finland. The teachers' salary system was modernized, updating a system that had been in place for decades and introducing changes that the OAJ opposed. Historically, Finnish teachers had been paid on the basis of a number of factors—grade level, years of experience, and number of lesson hours.[1] In many respects, it was the Finnish equivalent of the step-and-lane salary schedule, with two differences: teachers were not compensated for additional degrees because they all had master's degrees and the historical inequities between the pay of class (elementary) and subject teachers (secondary) had never been equalized. But, like the step-and-lane system, the factors that defined the old system were consistent and predictable. In the old system, any changes or raises to the salary structure were negotiated at the national level with *Kunnallinen Työmarkkinalaitos* (KT), the representative of the municipal employers in Finland.

The new salary system introduced a series of changes. The first change was that a percentage of the nationally negotiated annual increase, called *järjestelyerä*, could be negotiated locally between individual municipalities and local union association shop stewards. The second change was that the OAJ agreed that locally negotiated money could be allocated in one of three ways: it could be applied to teachers' base salaries without deviating from the centrally negotiated contract and raises, it could be applied to particular jobs based on locally agreed definitions of 'task-complexity' (*TVA-osuus*, TVA), or it could be distributed to individual teachers on the basis of their superior effort or performance (*henkilokohtainen lisä*, HL).

According to interviews with union officials and negotiators, the OAJ opposed—to varying degrees—all three of these changes. And at the same time, one of these officials claimed that whatever the OAJ opposes cannot happen—yet these changes occurred. How can this apparent contradiction be explained? Examining the reform process and the pivotal role that the OAJ played in it will be the focus of Chapter 5. As will become increasingly clear, the teachers' union was a key actor in the introduction of the 'new salary system' in 2007.

However, in order to be able to understand what happened, why it happened, and how that process might inform our understanding of teachers' unions' interests, power, and impact on reform outcomes, this chapter delves into Finland's history and institutional context. Reforms are not one-off events that can be studied in isolation. The drivers for reform and change emerge within the particularities of historical context, and the strength of various actors and their strategic calculations are informed by the cultural and institutional patterns that constrain and enable their participation in the decision-making process.

First, this chapter provides some historical context. Although the reforms occurred in the 21st century, some understanding of Finland's history is essential. The preceding historical periods—nation-building from the late 19th century through the 1940s, the development of the welfare state from the end of World War II through the 1980s, and the recession of the 1990s—provide important context for understanding the reforms that occurred from 2000 to 2007. Second, this chapter outlines the institutional arrangements, the structures and rules that govern *who* participates in decision-making and *how* they are able to influence decisions. A few of these features—collective bargaining agreements and consultation processes—have already been mentioned, but greater depth is required. This chapter provides the historical and institutional context that is required in order to unpack the story behind how the teachers' salary system was reformed.

FINLAND: A BRIEF NATIONAL HISTORY

Finland is a small Nordic country of 6.1 million people whose story has been defined by its location—the gateway to Russia on the periphery of Europe. Finland's most dominant historical narrative is of a small nation struggling against various external and internal threats, first to claim its independence and then to maintain its security and promote its flourishing. The narrative of struggle is woven throughout Finland's independence movements, the military conflicts of the first half of the 20th century, and its industrialization and modernization in the postwar era. The 'struggle narrative' is essential for understanding the development of Finnish unity and emphasis on consensus. Although the salary reform process is the focus of Chapter 5, the reform should be understood within its historical context.

- **Nation-Building (1917–1960s):** The process of nation-building, beginning with Finland's struggle for independence from Sweden and then Russia, but particularly the rapid industrialization, modernization, and state-building of the 1950s and 1960s, defined Finland's state structure and shaped its public policies—including public education.
- **Public Policy Expansion (1960s–1970s):** Finland's rapid postwar development established its welfare state—particularly in terms of education policy and Finland's commitment to educational equality. A number of significant education reforms, including comprehensive education reform, were undertaken in the 1970s and continue to define Finnish education policy and shape the development of the teachers' union, the OAJ (discussed below).
- **Decentralization (1980s):** Welfare and education systems were further refined by the decentralization of the 1980s, as Finland moved away from the highly centralized 'planning state' of the 1950s–1970s. Thus, modern Finnish institutions must be understood in light of a 'strong central state,' but also one that has delegated responsibility to regional governments and municipalities.
- **Responding to Recession (1990):** The changes to the teachers' salary system were significantly informed and impacted by the economic difficulties that Finland experienced in the 1990s. Although economic recovery was underway by 2000, the effects of the recession could still be felt, including in public sector compensation, which lagged behind other sectors.

Nation-Building (1917–1960s)

A young nation that didn't gain independence until 1917 after centuries of Swedish and Russian rule, due to the turmoil of a series of wars from the Finnish Civil War in 1918 to the end of World II, Finland did not begin state-building until the 1950s and 1960s. Following World War II, Finland's predominantly agrarian economy was saddled with significant war debt as well as the task of resettling 12% of its population, who had been displaced when it lost 10% of its land, 13% of its wealth, and 20% of its rail system when it ceded Karelia[2] to the USSR. Finland also faced heavy war reparations; in 1945, reparations accounted for 61% of exports and 6.4% of GDP (Pesonen & Riihinen, 2002). However, by the 1950s, Finland had paid off its reparations—the only country to do so. In 1952, the Summer Olympics were hosted in Helsinki, a celebration and a dawning period of optimism for a country that had experienced so much adversity.

Finland spent the majority of the 20th century attempting to catch up to more established democracies; industrialization happened later and faster in Finland than in the rest of Europe. As late as the 1960s, Finland lagged behind the rest of Europe in terms of industrialization as well as economic growth, but the number of Finns working in agriculture declined from 50% to 15% in 26 years (1946–1972) compared with 50 years in Sweden (1909–1959) and 80 years in Norway (1882–1963) (Pesonen & Riihinen, 2002). The 1950s through the 1970s was a period of rapid growth and change in Finland both politically and economically, as Finland transitioned from an agrarian to a modern, industrial economy. From 1950–1970, one third of the population moved to the cities and experienced a marked increase in the material standard of living (Ahonen, 2002).

Public Policy Expansion (1960s–1970s)

The significant challenges and changes of the postwar era also promoted the rapid development and institutionalization of the Finnish welfare state. As the structure of the Finnish economy was changing, so was the Finnish state: the postwar era saw Finland establish a "Nordic Model" of welfare, marked by a view of the welfare state and social rights as inherent to citizenship and the regulation of working life issues through autonomous collective agreements (Kettunen, 2001). Pekka Kussi, in his visionary text that shaped the formation of the welfare state, *Social Policy for the Sixties* (1964), argued that if Finland wanted to survive between Sweden and the USSR—a tension of two political systems as well as two dynamic economies—then it was doomed to grow.

Alongside welfare state expansion, Finland's comprehensive school system was established in the 1970s, prompted by the tectonic shifts that occurred in Finnish society in the 1950s and 1960s. The idea of the comprehensive school was promoted by a coalition of the national union of elementary teachers, the political left, and the Centre party.[3] The elementary teachers' union created a proposal for comprehensive reform in 1955. The Centre party and the political left promoted the comprehensive reform vision as a strategy for accessing Finland's 'vast educational reserve'—the human potential which was not realized within the current educational system. After parliament unanimously approved the recommendation of a committee for comprehensive education in 1967, comprehensive reform was initiated in Lapland in 1972 and completed in 1979, only one year behind schedule (Sahlberg, 2011).

The development of the welfare state, and its promise of comprehensive and equal services for all citizens, including public education, fuelled a massive growth of the state and central planning. The 1970s has been called the height of the planning society as well as the decade of consensus—all oriented at the achievement of a socially just society. The 1970s marked the beginning of Finland's Golden Age of stability, economic growth, and low unemployment, which lasted through the end of the 1980s (Ahonen, 2002).

Decentralization and Recession (1980s–1990s)

The relationship between the state and municipalities in Finland has been a dynamic one, with the relative authority of the central state and autonomy of municipalities varying over time (Finnish Work Environment Fund, 2008; Pesonen & Riihinen, 2002). From the late 1980s, there was a marked turn toward giving more autonomy and responsibilities to municipalities (Finnish Work Environment Fund, 2008; Niemi, 2012; Pesonen & Riihinen, 2002). Finland must be understood as a country that has preserved a role for local decision-making in the context of a strong central state (Salminen, 2008). Understanding the nature of municipal authority is significant to this inquiry, as partial decentralization of negotiations was a significant component of the reform. These broader shifts created pressure, or at least a precedent, for the salary reforms. The shift of decision-making authority as well as financial responsibility to municipalities through the 1990s created pressures for municipal employers to have greater influence over teachers' salaries.

Although Finland is often labelled a 'planning state,' the planning state was a modern phenomenon—a response to the demands of welfare state development in the 1960s. Historically, from the period of Swedish rule, local government in Finland had significant autonomy and authority, which was vested first in churches and then in local councils. However, the municipalities sometimes chose to ignore central mandates, which resulted in uneven policy implementation (Pesonen & Riihinen, 2002; Pulma, 1999; Salminen, 2008). So, when the welfare state was being developed, the central state expanded its powers (Rainio-Niemi, 2010; Waris, 1964). By the 1970s, comprehensive planning in Finland had produced a "jungle of central government subsidies;" although there were some efforts to give municipalities more flexibility, far-reaching control mechanisms remained through the 1980s in order to ensure uniform implementation of social policy throughout the country (Pulma, 1999).

However, the strengthening of the central 'planning state' was not permanent and began to reverse course in the 1990s, in the face of the severe economic recession (Niemi, 2012; Pesonen & Riihinen, 2002). In 1986, a committee report on the decentralization of administration was published which framed the restructuring of Finland's large public sector (Ahonen, 2002; CR 1986, as cited in Kivirauma, Rinne, & Seppännen, 2003). The committee report eventually produced a series of legislative changes. The Free Municipality Experiment Law (1988) abandoned the highly detailed and focused steering regulations, which were seen as too slow, too bureaucratic, and too tightly regulated (Rinne, Kivirauma, & Simola, 2002; Simola, Rinne, & Kivirauma, 2002).

Furthermore, the 1990s was a pivotal decade for Finland, as it was plunged into a severe recession, which lasted from 1991 to 1994. Finland's economic struggles were even more severe than the rest of the world, as its recession was exacerbated by the fall of the USSR, a significant market for Finnish goods. The financial challenges combined with political movements that had begun in the late 1980s resulted in significant decentralization, as some of the control of the central planning state, which was necessary to build comprehensive welfare services, was returned to municipalities. Municipalities were given greater control of their budgets in 1993 and the autonomy of municipalities was established in the Municipal Administration Act of 1995 (Pulma, 1999). According to Salminen (2008), the reforms gave municipalities more freedom and fewer resources.

In education, decentralization has been identified with the 'culture of trust' (Aho, Pitkänen, & Sahlberg, 2006), and was a product of three types of changes: legislation, budgeting, and curriculum. Legislation in 1991 linked school funding to the number of pupils who attended, and in 1992 the law that regulated the maximum distance between a student's school and home was abolished.[4] The final piece of legislation that formalized the decentralization of educational decision-making was the Basic Education Act of 1999, which shifted the authority for the provision of the comprehensive system to municipalities and increased their decision-making power; for example, it abolished any central regulations on class sizes (Ahonen, 2002). The law also required accountability of individual schools and information to be provided to parents about the schools' performance (Aho et al., 2006; Ahonen, 2002).

The move to link school funding to the number of pupils, which was legislated in 1991, was a part of a larger movement toward 'lump sum budgeting' (Ahonen, 2002). Prior to the 1990s, municipal funding had come with specific earmarks; beyond determining how much of the budget would be spent on education versus healthcare, the earmarks often specified how much funding should go to school lunches, how much to books, and how much to building maintenance (Rinne et al., 2002; Ahonen, 2002).

The final component, alongside legislation and budgeting, of the decentralization of education was the change in national curriculum. In 1994 a new curriculum was adopted which, rather than being a detailed, prescriptive guide to what should be taught in schools, was a framework of the goals of education, which were then specified at the municipal and school level (Ahonen, 2002). Furthermore, the framework curriculum allocated fewer hours to compulsory subjects and more hours to optional subjects, which gave schools and municipalities more space to create 'distinct profiles' in terms of what they would offer within those optional hours.

A common explanation for decentralization—given its correlation across Europe with the economically turbulent 1980s and 1990s—has been shifting the responsibility for difficult decisions and cuts away from the central state. Evidence in Finland in the 1990s lends support to this explanation. Shrinking education budgets prompted difficult decisions—like closing small, economically unsustainable, schools—that were more politically legitimate when made at the local level (Rinne et al., 2002; Simola et al., 2002).

However, regardless of the goals or effects—in terms of the provision of public education—two significant points on local authority are significant to the salary system reforms from 2002–2007. First, local authority and autonomy and a belief in the competence of local bureaucracy have a long and established history in Finland. Second, the significant devolution of responsibilities—including education—to municipalities that occurred in the 1990s stood in sharp contrast to the way that teachers' compensation continued to be highly centrally determined. Local authorities were responsible for administering schools and appointing teachers—either through municipal boards, school boards, or principals—and were also primarily responsible for funding public education with local tax revenues, financing, on average, 58% of all pre-tertiary education (Sahlberg, 2011). But through 2007 the salaries and conditions of teachers were almost exclusively determined by the centrally negotiated agreements. Although implemented in 2007, the system was the culmination of a series of agreements, called the KUNPAS agreements, that trace their roots back to 2002. However, before we can unpack these reforms, their implications, and significance in Chapter 5, we must first understand the educational policy-making and labor relations context in Finland.

THE OAJ: FINLAND'S TRADE UNION OF EDUCATION

The teachers' union in Finland has played a significant role in Finnish education policy throughout the 20th and 21st centuries. Today, over 95% of teachers are represented by The Trade Union of Education (OAJ). With over 118,000 members in 2009, OAJ is the sixth biggest trade union in the country (OAJ, n.d.). Beyond mere 'strength in numbers,' the power and strategy of OAJ is linked to four factors: the professional standing of teachers, the structure of the union, Finland's extensive consultative practices, and the structure of collective bargaining. This section will address each factor in turn.

Professional Standing of Teachers

The teaching profession is highly regarded in Finland. Finland's recent PISA success has been attributed to the high quality of the teaching corps and the rigorous training they receive (Rautalin & Alasuutari, 2007). However, the respect for teaching in Finland precedes its international acclaim. Finnish teachers' professional prestige springs from three roots. First, professionalism is rooted in the high societal value placed on education. Second, teachers' prestige has historical roots as the position was linked to significant civic leadership and a public-serving ethos since the 19th century. Third, teaching in Finland has been successfully established as a formal profession with high standards for training and high barriers to entry.

Public education emerged in the 1860s, and from its first days it was closely connected to Finland's national aspirations—a kind of 'hidden politics' through which Finns could prepare for independence from Russia, according to J. V. Snellman. Through the 19th century, despite low salaries and a lack of formal training in small villages with farming traditions, even elementary teachers were 'highly educated.' Because of this, teachers were often leaders with significant 'social capital' in rural communities, serving as civic leaders involved in local government and the cooperative movement (Niemi, 2012).

Cygnaeus, the founder of elementary education, promoted a view of teachers as "candles of the nation"—bringing the light of the state and nation-building to rural children. In this vein, Cygnaeus promoted an idea of teachers' 'model citizenship.' One element of this idea was that teachers did the work because of a sense of vocation, *not* because of salaries; teachers were paid an intentionally low salary to reinforce this idea of vocation and to ensure that teachers were connected to the people they served (Niemi, 2012).

With industrialization and other societal shifts, teachers began to demand conditions that were consistent with a more 'formal profession.' As teachers moved from rural areas to cities, they began to think of themselves less as the 'nation's candles' and more as civil servants. Thus, they began to demand to be treated—and compensated—accordingly. The fact that men were paid 10% more than their female counterparts was no longer acceptable to teachers. The shift in teachers' professional ideology—from Cygnaeus's 'model citizenship' vocation to a civil servant conception—can also be seen in the development and evolution of teachers' associations in Finland. Although the Teachers' Association in Finland represented around 50% of the nation's teachers in 1919, by the 1950s, around 80% of teachers were organized, and in 1958, teachers began to demand equal pay for equal work.

The second big shift in the advancement of teachers' professionalism was in reforming teacher training and qualifications. Despite the fact that teachers began demanding better salaries in the 1960s, primary teachers (class teachers) were still only given two to three years of training in teachers' education seminaries. Lower and upper secondary (subject) teachers, on the other hand, were trained in their respective subject departments at universities. The 1979 Act on Teacher Education moved all teacher education programs to universities and established a master's degree as the basic qualification to teach in Finnish schools (Sahlberg, 2011). However, while comprehensive school reform facilitated OAJ's organization building, the establishment of Finnish teacher education as an academic discipline was a significant boon to teachers' professionalism.[5]

Pasi Sahlberg, who was a subject teacher and worked at the Ministry of Education before joining the World Bank as an expert on Finnish education, argues that raising the minimum requirement for permanent employment to a master's degree and affirming teacher education as a scientific discipline established teaching as a profession—in contrast to the semiprofessional status it holds in many other nations: "The seeds were sown for believing that the teaching profession is based on scholarly research" (Sahlberg, 2011, p. 78). Teacher education reform also facilitated the unification of primary teachers and lower and upper secondary teachers. It also continues to serve as the foundational justification for teachers' demands for higher salaries.

However, despite the fact that teachers in Finland now all have master's degrees, Finnish classroom teachers still earn less than subject teachers[6]—differences rooted in the historical development of the school system and evolution of the teaching profession. But class teachers' lower pay should not be interpreted as a lower social standing or prestige for these teachers. Teachers in Finland enjoy a high level of respect; each year the university teacher training departments receive eight times more applicants for the class teacher program than available slots (Niemi, 2012; Sahlberg, 2011). The prestige of the teaching profession is a significant component of their influence in Finnish society; teachers are regarded as an independent profession, which is driven "mainly by moral purpose, rather than by material interests or rewards," and is therefore on equal footing with doctors, lawyers, or economists (Sahlberg, 2012, pp. 2–6). However, these compensation differences are interlinked with the history and development of the salary system.

The professional standing of teachers in Finnish society critically informs their potential influence in policy-making processes—reflecting both a resource as well as a potential restraint on the teachers' unions' influence. Because teachers are respected, the union may have more influence here than in other societies. However, the union's strategies, tactics, and 'policy style' may also be informed by efforts to maintain that level of respect.

OAJ Organizational Structure

The OAJ's history and growth is intertwined with the development of Finland's comprehensive school system, which was established in the 1970s. Its origins and development were a fundamental part of the tectonic shifts that occurred in Finnish society from 1950–1970. The idea of the comprehensive school was promoted by a coalition of the national union of elementary teachers,[7] the political left, and the Centre party.[8] After parliament unanimously approved the recommendation of a committee for comprehensive education in 1967 (CR 1966, as cited in Kivirauma et al., 2003), comprehensive reform was initiated in Lapland in 1972 and completed in 1979 (Sahlberg, 2011). One significant effect of comprehensive education was that teachers who had previously worked in different schools—and often with students with different abilities—found themselves working in the same school.

This move from a segmented to a unified system mirrored the changes in the teachers' union organizational landscape. One year after comprehensive education reform was initiated, in 1973, the primary teachers' organization and secondary teachers' organization merged to form a joint organization—the OAJ. In 1984, after a strike by the primary and secondary teachers demonstrated the OAJ's influence, the consolidation of existing teacher organizations accelerated. Although there were over a dozen organizations in 1984, the next 10 years featured rapid mergers, and by 1995 OAJ became the representative union for the whole field of education. Although the organizations merged, the original organizations and their unique identities were not dissolved by the merger. Each group maintains its own organization under the OAJ umbrella, which will be significant for understanding intraorganizational bargaining in Chapter 5.

Centrally, each member-group has a voice in union governance (Figure 4.1). All of these associations are represented on both the OAJ's 150-member Council as well as the 21-member Executive Board. Both elected representative bodies are also selected to reflect regional and organizational diversity. In practice, this means that the central union organization is responsible for representing a diverse set of preferences in national-level negotiations with KT. The OAJ is extensively included in decision-making processes in Finland through both negotiation and consultation.

Figure 4.1 illustrates the structure of the OAJ. Although the President of the OAJ is ultimately responsible for conducting negotiations, the goals for negotiations are set by the Executive Board—particularly the salary committee based on the recommendations of the Council. The Council meets twice a year and representatives typically meet with their member-group association in order to represent the concerns of its constituents to the council. According to a member of the Executive Board, the Council produces a general strategy and then it is the Executive Board's responsibility to establish the exact goals:

> "Our council has 150 members—too many in my opinion, but that is the price for democracy—from all our member-groups as well as from different [regions] of Finland. . . . That means that our council doesn't make very exact decisions. Usually, they are on a quite [general] level. . . . Our Executive Board's duty is to find our exact goals." (Local_A.Union)

Although the Executive Board member identified the size of the group as resulting in imprecise goals, a point of some frustration, one of OAJ's negotiators saw advantages in the general negotiating goals—at least in terms of his job:

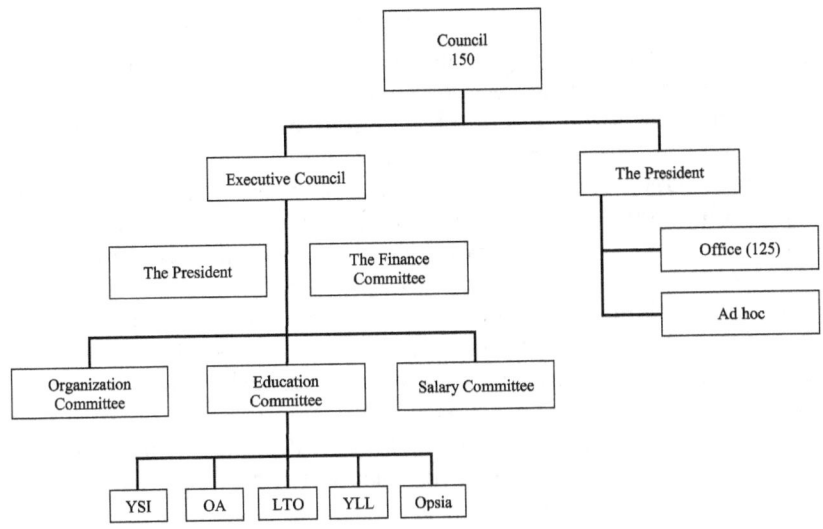

Figure 4.1 OAJ organization and governance

Note: Author's translation produced in consultation with OAJ staff.

"There is a quite good system with OAJ. Members can give input to OAJ and then there were a lot of goals—so many goals that 'we always win.' . . . You could [always] say 'Hey, that was something that we wanted.'" (OAJ.Negotiator.2)

The major reasons why the goals are so general is because of the diversity of interests that are represented by the 150-member council. According to another OAJ negotiator, because of historical differences in teachers' contracts, which cause teachers to get paid different amounts due to their grade level and subject, "We have problems because there are different kinds of teachers and they all want salary raises for their exact group. Our job is to try to get them changes that are tactically clever" (OAJ.Negotiator.1). The OAJ's structure and the complex process of interest representation will be a significant contributor to the OAJ's strategy for negotiating salary reform, which will become evident in Chapter 4.

Consultation in a Consensus Democracy

The OAJ operates in a political context that has often been described as a consensual democracy—characterized by broad coalitions, executive-legislative balance, a multiparty system, proportional representation, and a coordinated or corporatist interest group system which is aimed at compromise and concertation (Lijphart, 1999). In addition to extensive consultation, the Finnish polity is characterized by broad governing coalitions and interest representation. Broad governing coalitions, which have been typical since the 1970s, lend stability to the collective bargaining process, as these coalitions have ensured that the government can deliver legislatively what they have promised in negotiations—preserving trust in and the legitimacy of collective bargaining (Arter, 1987). Interest group alliances are often similarly broad. Unlike some contexts where unions are closely aligned with one party, unions in Finland—especially the OAJ and other professional unions—are nonpartisan groups that work closely with all major parties. According to the OAJ, they work with any party who 'supports public education.' This nonpartisan commitment is reflected not just in OAJ's organizational work and efforts, but in its membership distribution. In Finnish municipal elections that occurred in the autumn of 2012, nationwide, 4.23% of candidates for municipal council were current or former teachers (Finnish Ministry of Justice, 2012). Although there was variation across political parties, there were teacher candidates across all major political parties.[9] This trend likely has at least two contributing explanations. First, the OAJ represents over 90% of teachers. But second, there appears to be genuine nonpartisanship when it comes to educational issues. OAJ's broad political engagement has significant implications for the particular character of teachers' unionization in Finland, illuminating the norms and informal rules of participation.

The nature of the political structure and culture has significant implications for the strength and strategy of unions. Due to the importance of broad representation and alliances, interest groups are frequently and extensively consulted. In Finland, decision-making across policy sectors has been identified as "broadly inclusive and based on extensive consultation with key interest groups" (Raunio, 2004, p. 147). Tripartite negotiations are one way that interest groups are incorporated in state decision-making processes (Bruun, 2005). But they are not the only channel for influence. Several arenas are available for interest group participation in Finland, but one of the most significant is the committee system, which includes both permanent groups[10] and temporary or ad hoc groups[11] (Numminen, 1999). Although its roots trace to state committees established under Swedish rule in the 17th century, the committee system has evolved over time, its rapid expansion fuelled by the growth of the welfare state in the 1960s and 1970s—particularly in the Ministry of Education and the Ministry of Social Affairs and Health (Helander, 1979; Numminen, 1999; Rainio-Niemi, 2010). The development of tripartite negotiation in the 1960s further institutionalized the incorporation of interest groups; the two arenas—committees and income policy agreements—became closely interlinked, giving labor market actors a significant voice in policy making (Arter, 1987; Helander, 1979; Rainio-Niemi, 2010). The committees serve a number of functions: producing reports, policies, and legislation; providing a platform for the exchange of knowledge and expertise; anticipating and resolving resistance in order to ensure smooth policy implementation; and providing a channel of participation, and potentially influence, to interest groups (Numminen, 1999; Rainio-Niemi, 2010).

Despite some decline in state committees, and a decline in formal, systemic consultation, according to Rainio-Niemi, "the most powerful associations ... have not lost much of their influence" (2010, p. 262). The evidence in the education sector bears out Rainio-Niemi's argument. According to the OAJ's records for ongoing committees, commissions, or councils, or those that have concluded their work within the last calendar year, the OAJ is currently represented in over 150 consultative groups.[12]

Although none of these features—broad governing coalitions, the resulting broad alliances, nor consultative bodies—have a direct bearing on the reforms under investigation in this case study, they provide important context that should not be overlooked. Consultation defines both the general patterns of education decision-making and the particular character of the OAJ. The fact that various actors—employer associations, employee associations, and government representatives—are in regular contact means that negotiating parties know one another well and work together frequently. But it also means that discrete interactions are part of a broader set of interactions and occur within a long-term relationship. These institutionalized relationships create incentives for cooperation that inform the bargaining process in important ways. These routines and procedures are a significant piece of the actors' interaction orientations and provide the underlying context that informs the negotiation of the new salary system.

Collective Bargaining in Finland

Although the first trade union was founded in 1907, unions were marginal players—particularly relative to their importance in contemporary Finland—through the 1940s (Bruun, 2005; Rinne, 1964). The weakness of unions throughout industrialization may be linked to the legacy of the Civil War of 1918 and the lingering divisions between social democrats and communists that affected union organizations for decades (Arter, 1987; Ornston & Rehn, 2006). Although late-emerging, trade unions in Finland have become a significant and stable part of the Finnish policy-making landscape (Böckerman & Uusitalo, 2006).

The first general agreement was signed in 1944, and the labor movement strengthened considerably in the late 1960s and early 1970s, fuelled by the establishment of tripartite negotiation, or the 'TUPO' system, in 1968. In 1970, the right to collective bargaining was also officially extended to the public sector, which was a significant boon to AKAVA, the peak association that represents all 'professional' workers. Finland's 70 trade unions are organized into three central confederations—The Central Organization of Finnish Trade Unions (SAK), the Finnish Confederation of Salaried Employees (STTK), and the Confederation of Unions for Academic Professionals in Finland (AKAVA). SAK organizes around one million workers; STTK is the organization of white collar workers and has 643,000 members; and AKAVA represents 424,000 professionals and academically educated workers including teachers, doctors, and engineers (Böckerman & Uusitalo, 2006). Although there has been some decline for the membership of SAK and STTK post-1990,[13] membership in AKAVA—the peak association of which the OAJ is a member—has held steady or increased (Komsi, 2010).

Although unions in Finland were relatively weak through the end of World War II, their growth has been significant since the establishment of tripartite negotiation in the late 1960s—a significant strategy of the 'planning state' that built the Finnish welfare state (Alaja, 2011). Tripartite negotiations were seen as a way to regulate the labor market but also to develop social policy and protection (2011). Although tripartite negotiations were the cornerstone of union development in the era of the planning state, collective bargaining in Finland has evolved since the 1970s. Consistent with both international trends as well as Finland's shift away from strong central-planning, collective bargaining in Finland has become more decentralized and multilayered (Bruun, 2005; Nomden, Farnham, & Oonnee-Abbruciati, 2003).

Today, collective bargaining in Finland is multilevel and is also notable for its extensive scope. Both features are significant to understanding the patterns of decision-making, the character of unions, and the reform process. Turning first to the scope of bargaining, the previous discussion of consultation and consensus orientation is insightful. At its peak, the line between negotiation, legislation, and policy-making was blurry (Bruun, 2005). The legacy of this comprehensive and interrelated view of policy-making and negotiation has resulted in a relatively broad view of the scope of bargaining. Negotiation, rather than being isolated and exclusively concerned with zero-sum distributional issues, is—according to several interviewees—fundamentally linked to curriculum, legislative, and policy changes.

Second, collective bargaining in Finland's TUPO system[14] occurs at multiple levels; the relative significance of each type of agreement—central framework agreements, nationwide sectoral agreements, and 'firm-based' agreements—have changed over time. The general trend in Finland from the 1990s onwards—mirroring patterns across Europe (Nomden et al., 2003)—has been toward greater decentralization and more firm-level autonomy and decision-making in the private sector. In the public sector, the best way to describe decentralization trends is delegation within a framework; the dominant bargaining level has not necessarily changed, but more elaboration and interpretation occurs at local levels (Karlson & Lindberg, 2011).

Before turning to the way delegation within a framework has evolved in Finland's municipal sector, the details of municipal sector bargaining require further elaboration (Figure 4.2). In the municipal sector, the situation is complex because the municipal sector agreement is not one agreement, but five. *Kunnallinen Työmarkkinalaitos* (KT) represents municipal employers and negotiates five major sectoral agreements with the various organizations that represent municipal employees. The General Collective Agreement (KVTES) covers a wide range of municipal employees, including teachers, doctors, the technical sector, and hourly employees, who each negotiate their own

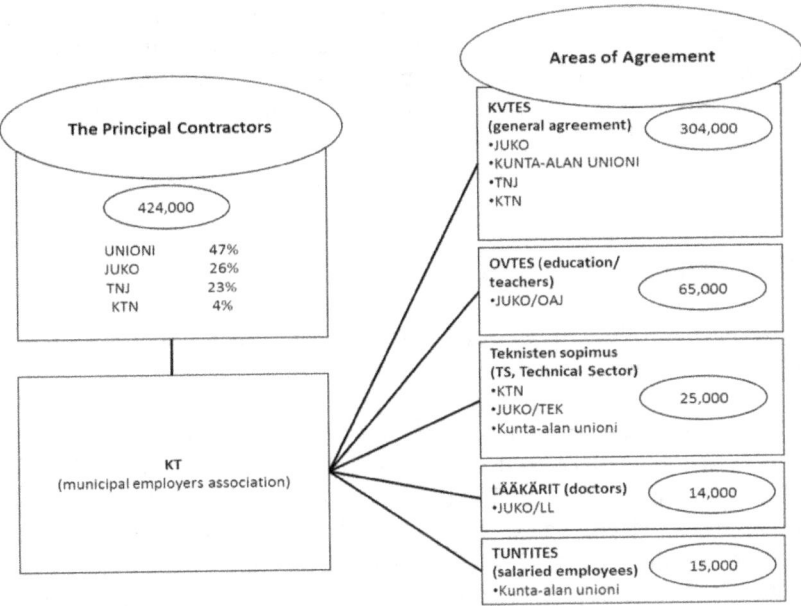

Figure 4.2 Collective bargaining in the municipal sector

Note: Author's translation produced in consultation with OAJ staff.

agreement with KT[15] (KT.Social_Scientist; OAJ.Negotiator.2). However, although teachers have their own agreement, many aspects of the KVTES agreement still apply to teachers. So the KVTES agreement provides the general working conditions for all municipal employees unless specifically negotiated within the other agreements (OVTES, TS, LS) (OAJ.Negotiator.2).

Prior to 2007, delegation to the municipal sector—in terms of the OVTES contract—was relatively limited. The centrally determined raises were negotiated for teachers (OVTES), allocating the wage increases based on seniority, types of work, or other criteria.

However, although this system describes OVTES negotiations until 2007, the rest of the municipal sector was far more decentralized by the early 2000's, mirroring decentralization in the private sector and broader reforms of local governance. After legislation in 1993 expanded municipal bargaining rights (Bruun, 2005; Finnish Ministry of Labor, 2003), the technical sector agreement (TS) introduced more local bargaining as well as a new evaluation and reward system in 1995. The general KVTES agreement and the doctors' agreement followed suit in 2001 and 2002 respectively. However, despite changes in other municipal sector agreements and despite policy changes that gave municipalities more autonomy and responsibility, the OVTES agreements were not decentralized. Local negotiation and new evaluation and reward systems that had been in place in other municipal agreements since the mid-1990s were not realized until the new salary system was implemented in 2007.

100 *International Cases*

Thus the effect of the KUNPAS agreement in education was to further delegate decision-making in the education agreement to individual municipalities, bringing it in line with the practices across the other agreements. The centrally negotiated raise was subdivided into two components—one that was assigned at the municipal sector level, just like the old system, and a second, which was locally determined.

CONCLUSION

According to all three measures of strength resources—political, organizational, and professional—the OAJ appears strong. Together, these features provide a composite picture of the OAJ's internal and external capacities. But how were these resources deployed in the 2007 reforms? Was the OAJ opposed to the changes, and if so, why did it not block them? Why was reform possible in Finland? What might it suggest about why PRP reform has not occurred elsewhere? Answering these questions requires specific attention to the process through which the changes were designed and implemented. The historical and institutional context of Finland provides the clues essential to contextualizing and understanding what happened.

NOTES

1. There were also some adjustments for subject areas and some adjustments based on where teachers lived.
2. Land on Finland's eastern border.
3. Finland's rural or agrarian party.
4. Together, these laws made it economically necessary and legally possible to close small schools (Ahonen, 2002).
5. It is worth noting that OAJ played a significant role in the negotiation of both comprehensive and teacher education reforms (Rautalin & Alasuutari, 2007).
6. The starting salaries for primary, lower secondary, and upper secondary teachers (PPP) are $32,692, $34,707, and $35,743 respectively; while salaries at the top of the scale are $50,461 for primary, and $54,181 and $61,089 for lower and upper secondary teachers (OECD, 2011).
7. Primary and secondary teachers maintained their own unions in large part due to their disagreement over comprehensive education.
8. Finland's rural or agrarian party.
9. Including the National Coalition, Centre Party, Communist Workers' Party, True Finns, Communist Party, Christian Democrats, Swedish People's Party, Social Democratic Party, Left Alliance, and Green Party.
10. Boards, councils, and delegations.
11. Established by government, committees, and ministries.
12. Internal communication with OAJ.
13. This decline has been attributed to a shift away from the ghent-system and the establishment of an independent 'general unemployment fund' (*Yleinen työttömyyskassa YTK*) created in 1992 (Böckerman & Uusitalo, 2006).

14. Although there are contemporary questions about the future of the TUPO system, through 2007, the period of interest in this case, the TUPO system was firmly in place (Alaja, 2011).
15. Teachers got their own agreement in 1984 after a strike; other employee groups followed their lead and demanded their own contracts as well.

REFERENCES

Aho, E., Pitkänen, K., & Sahlberg, P. (2006). Policy development and reform principles of basic and secondary education in Finland since 1968 (Working Paper No. 2). Retrieved from World Bank http://siteresources.worldbank.org/EDUCATION/Resources/278200-1099079877269/547664-1099079967208/Education_in_Finland_May06.pdf

Ahonen, S. (2002). From an industrial to a post-industrial society: Changing conceptions of equality in education. *Educational Review*, 54(2), 173–182.

Alaja, A. (2011). Tripartite political exchange and the Finnish social model. In V. Sorsa (Ed.), *Rethinking social risk in the Nordics*, 147–168.

Arter, D. (1987). *Politics and policy-making in Finland*. New York: Wheatsheaf Books.

Böckerman, P., & Uusitalo, R. (2006). Erosion of the ghent system and union membership decline: Lessons from Finland. *British Journal of Industrial Relations*, 44(2), 283–313.

Bruun, N. (2005). *The evolving structure of collective bargaining in Europe 1990-2004: National report Finland*. Retrieved from the European Commission and the University of Florence http://eprints.unifi.it/archive/00001158/01/Finlandia.pdf

Finnish Ministry of Justice. (2012). *Municipal elections 28/10/2012: List of candidates*. Retrieved November 1, 2012, from http://192.49.229.35/K2012/e/ehd_listat/kokomaa.htm

Finnish Ministry of Labour. (2003). *Industrial relations and labour legislation in Finland*.

Finnish Work Environment Fund. (2008). *Local bargaining: A matter of necessity and trust—studies of actual practice*. Retrieved from https://www.vm.fi/vm/en/04_publications_and_documents/01_publications/06_state_employers_office/20081110Localb/paikallinen_eng-B_5_11_08.pdf

Helander, V. (1979). Interest representation in the Finnish committee system in the post-war era. *Scandinavian Political Studies*, 2(3), 221–238.

Jokivuori, P. (2011). *Finland: Industrial relations profile*. Retrieved from https://eurofound.europa.eu/sites/default/files/ef_files/eiro/country/finland.pdf

Karlson, N., & Lindberg, H. (2011). *The decentralization of wage bargaining: Four cases*. Retrieved from http://ratio.se/media/95338/nk_hl_wage%20bargaining_178.pdf

Kettunen, P. (2001). The Nordic welfare state in Finland. *Scandinavian Journal of History*, 26(3), 222–247.

Kivirauma, J., Rinne, R., & Seppänen, P. (2003). Neo-liberal education policy approaching the Finnish shoreline? *Journal for Critical Education Policy Studies*, 1(1), 513–531.

Komsi, V. (2010). *Determinants of trade union membership in Finland 1975–2008* (Master's thesis). Aalto University, 47. Retrieved from http://epub.lib.aalto.fi/fi/ethesis/pdf/12397/hse_ethesis_12397.pdf

Kussi, P. (1964). *Social policy for the sixties: A plan for Finland*. Helsinki: Finnish Social Policy Association.

Lijphart, A. (1999). *Patterns of democracy: Government forms and performance in thirty-six countries*. New Haven, CT: Yale University Press.

Niemi, H. (2012). The societal factors contributing to education and schools in Finland. In H. Niemi, A. Toom, & A. Kallioniemi (Eds.), *Miracle of education*. Rotterdam: Sense Publishers, 19–38.

Nomden, K., Farnham, D., & Oonnee-Abbruciati, M. (2003). Collective bargaining in public services: Some European comparisons. *International Journal of Public Sector Management, 16*, 412–423.

Numminen, J. (1999). The council of the state. In J. Selovuori (Ed.), *Power and bureaucracy in Finland 1809–1998*. Helsinki, Edita LTD.

Opetusalan Ammattijärjestö. (n.d.). *OAJ: The trade union of education in Finland*. [brochure]. Helsinki, Finland: OAJ.

Organization for Economic Co-operation and Development (2011). *Education at a glance 2011*. Paris: OECD.

Ornston, D., & Rehn, O. (2006). An old consensus in the "new" economy? Institutional adaptation, technological innovation and economic restructuring in Finland. In J. Zysman & A. Newman (Eds.), *How revolutionary was the digital revolution?* Stanford: Stanford Business Books, 78–100.

Pesonen, P., & Riihinen, O. (2002). *Dynamic Finland: The political system and the welfare state*. Helsinki: Finnish Literature Society.

Pulma, P. (1999). Municipal autonomy, local democracy and the state. In J. Seluovori (Ed.), *Power and bureaucracy in Finland 1809–1998*. Helsinki: Edita LTD.

Rainio-Niemi, J. (2010). State committees in Finland in historical comparative perspective. In R. Alapuro & H. Stenius (Eds.), *Nordic associations in a European perspective*. Nomos: Baden-Baden, Ch. 8.

Raunio, T. (2004). The changing Finnish democracy: Stronger parliamentary accountability, coalescing political parties and weaker external constraints. *Scandinavian Political Studies, 27*(2), 133–152.

Rautalin, M., & Alasuutari, P. (2007). The curse of success: The impact of the OECD's programme for international student assessment on the discourses of the teaching profession in Finland. *European Educational Research Journal, 7*(4), 349–364.

Rinne, R. (1964). Industrial relations in post-war Finland. *International Labour Review, 89*(1), 461–481.

Rinne, R., Kivirauma, J., & Simola, H. (2002). Shoots of revisionist education policy or just slow readjustment? The Finnish case of educational reconstruction. *Journal of education Policy, 17*(6), 653–658.

Sahlberg, P. (2011). *Finnish Lessons: What can the world learn from educational change in Finland?* New York: Teachers College Press.

Sahlberg, P. (2012). The most wanted: Teachers and teacher education in Finland. In L. Darling-Hammond & A. Lieberman (Eds.), *Teacher education around the world: Changing policies and practices*. New York: Routledge, 1–21.

Salminen, A. (2008). Evaluating the new governance of the welfare state in Finland. *International Journal of Public Administration, 31*(10–11), 1242–1258.

Simola, H., Rinne, R., & Kivirauma, J. (2002). Abdication of the education state or just shifting responsibilities? The appearance of a new system of reason in constructing educational governance and social exclusion/inclusion in Finland. *Scandinavian Journal of Educational Research, 46*(3), 247–264.

Waris, H. (1964). Introduction. In P. Kussi (Ed.), *Social policy for the sixties: A plan for Finland*. Helsinki: Finnish Social Policy Association, 13–27.

Winkler, A. M., Scull, D. Z., & Zeehandelaar, D. (2012). *How strong are U.S. teacher unions? A state-by-state comparison*. Washington, DC: Thomas Fordham Institute. Retrieved from ERIC database; (ED537563)

5 Quiet Compromises
Finland's New Salary System

In 2007, a new salary system, often called the KUNPAS system, which allowed municipalities to differentiate teachers' compensation on the basis of their task complexity as well as their professional performance, was introduced for teachers in Finland. The reform was a marked shift from the status quo. It occurred in spite of resistance from the OAJ—considered a formidable player in Finnish education policy. In order to understand this apparent paradox and how it reveals the union's interests, strength, and impact, this chapter will explore three questions:

1. What was the change and is it important?
2. How or why did the change occur?
3. What was the role of the OAJ in this process?

THE KUNPAS REFORMS: WERE THEY SIGNIFICANT?

In order to understand what was new and why it was significant, one must understand the 21st century salary system that had been in place, with few modifications, for decades. *Kunnallinen Työmarkkinalaitos* (KT), the municipal employers' association, argued that the reforms were essential to 'modernize' the Finnish teachers' salary system. What did modernization look like in the Finnish context?

The Salary System Pre-2007

Entering the 21st century, teachers' salaries in Finland were determined by a number of factors. The building block for all teachers' salaries was the base salary, or *peruspalkka*. The base salary was linked to a prescribed number of lesson hours that a teacher had to teach in order to receive his or her full salary. Then, any additional lessons earned the teacher supplemental compensation, or *ylituntipalkkioperusteiset*. Teachers also received raises based on their years of experience, or *työkokemus*. Because all teachers in Finland now receive a master's degree in order to be certified, education level was not a differentiating factor for most teachers.[1] However, the definition of the base varied according to the type of teacher—whether class teacher or subject teacher—and then, according to the *type* of class or subject teacher—grade-level or subject. The system was and is highly technical and complex, but the basic formula would look like this:

$$\text{Total Salary} = \text{Base Salary}*(\text{Level} * \text{Subject}) + \text{Supplemental}*(\text{Total Hours} - X) + \text{Experience}$$

In the formula, 'X' is the number of lesson hours a teacher must teach in order to earn her base salary. While classroom teachers' base salary was linked to 24 lesson hours per week, subject teachers' base ranged from 18 to 24 hours. In practice, the difference between class and subject teachers meant that class teachers had to teach more lessons in order to receive the same compensation as their secondary peers. Many in Finland—particularly the union—see this as a historical remnant of the division between primary and secondary education that is unfair now that all teachers receive the same level of training.

Under the old system, in addition to supplements for extra hours and years of experience, the OAJ and KT could also agree centrally to attach additional compensation to particular jobs that were deemed more challenging. However, in the old system, all decisions were based on a principle of uniformity—that the "same kinds" of teachers should have the same salaries. So, all salaries were negotiated and determined at the national level, which meant that a Finnish class 1 teacher in small town in northern Finland received the same salary as a Finnish class 1 teacher in Helsinki. The centralization of teachers' salaries had persisted even as municipalities were being given more autonomy and responsibilities through the decentralization reforms of the 1990s.

Given the significant portion of education budgets that are allocated to teachers' salaries, this was a significant imposition on local freedom and flexibility. Further, it seemed that definitions of 'complexity' or 'challenge' might vary across municipalities. As municipalities were becoming more autonomous and also more responsible for the provision of education, in the view of KT, it was harder to justify their inability to make the choices about how to allocate their resources locally. Thus, modernization in the view of KT involved both greater local freedom and decision-making and also the introduction of new approaches to compensating teachers:

> The outcome of [the old system] was that all teachers got the exact same. We saw that this was not the modern way because the employer should have the decision about who he or she rewarded. (KT.Social_Scientist)

The 'New' Salary System

The new salary system, or the KUNPAS agreement, could be seen as a bargain in which higher wages were given in exchange for restructuring (Kunnallinen Työmarkkinalaitos, 2002a,b). The agreement promised a 3–4%

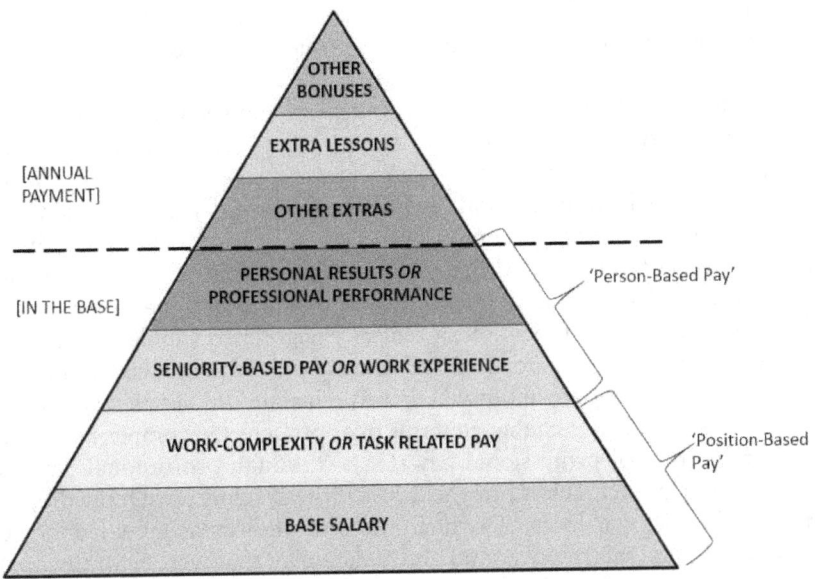

Figure 5.1 Finland's new salary system (2007)

Note: Opetusalan Ammattijärjestö (2012). Author's translation produced in collaboration with OAJ staff.

raise over the course of the four years of the contract in exchange for a series of restructuring changes. But what *exactly* changed with the shift from the old to the new salary system in 2007? Was this an important shift in teachers' compensation or a reform in name only? Figure 5.1 illustrates the new salary system. Relative to the pre-2007 system, several differences emerge. But first, three common elements deserve attention. First, the base salary is unchanged from the old to new system. Then, also like the pre-2007 system, any additional lessons earn a teacher additional compensation. The final common component is seniority-based pay.[2]

There were three major changes associated with KUNPAS. First, teachers' wages had to be transferred to the Euro system, which was a significant undertaking. Second, some of the decisions regarding wages had to be left to municipalities to decide. Prior to 2007, all of teachers' wages were negotiated centrally. After 2007, a percentage of the total increase would still be negotiated centrally, but the remaining increase would be left to municipalities.[3] Third, the locally negotiated component of teachers' salaries could be allocated in one of three general ways:

1. It could be applied to the base salary, or in other words, it could be distributed proportionally, according to the centrally negotiated priorities;
2. it could be distributed on the basis of locally determined 'task complexity' criteria (*TVA-osuus*, TVA);

3. or it could be distributed as a 'personal wage' or on the basis of teachers' 'professional performance' (*henkilokohtainen lisä*, HL).

Locally negotiated TVA—additional compensation dispensed on the basis of 'task-complexity'—was both a point of overlap between the old and new system and also an important change. TVA was not a new idea in 2007. The old system also provided differential rewards for complexity of teachers' work. However, as previously discussed, those rewards were determined exclusively at the central level. Although 'centrally negotiated TVA' still exists, many of these distinctions were reevaluated with decision-making moved to the municipal level. For example, a centrally negotiated supplement for first class teachers was eliminated in 2007, leaving individual municipalities and local unions to negotiate about whether to reinstate this supplement.[4]

The most significant change in terms of approaches to compensation was the introduction of professional pay (HL). Although professional pay was used in some municipalities prior to 2007, those systems were funded by the municipalities' 'own money'—which refers to additional money allocated toward teachers' salaries over and above the raises that were centrally negotiated. So, the change in 2007 made it possible for municipalities, who may or may not have already used HL, to use the locally negotiated money that was a part of the centrally negotiated raises toward HL bonuses.

In addition to capturing the types of compensation available in the new system, Figure 5.1 draws attention to several other important distinctions. First, one-off annual payments must be delineated from those that go into teachers' base salary. Annual payments—like extra lessons, other extras, and other bonuses[5]—are one-off 'bonus payments,' which means that they do not impact teachers' compensation beyond that year. These payments take two forms. They may be determined by the *rules*—distinct and independent from the centrally negotiated annual raises—of the centrally negotiated agreement, like defining extra lessons. Or, these payments may be above and beyond the negotiated raises and paid at the discretion of a municipality using its 'own money.'[6]

Salary components that go into teachers' base—including TVA and HL as well as seniority-based raises—are payments that become a permanent part of teachers' salaries. Because HL is a contingent payment, a teacher who receives it—for example a €100 per month increase—will continue to receive an additional €1,200 a year for the duration of the time that he or she teaches at that school or municipality.[7] As seen in Figure 5.1, contingent pay can be further broken down into position-based pay and person-based pay. Although the distinction—position-based payments are linked to particular jobs rather than individuals—is fairly self-evident, it significantly informs OAJ's preferences and the reform dynamics. Position-based payments are viewed as more 'permanent' and thus are typically preferred by the union.

However, setting aside these technical details about the size of rewards and how they are distributed, the changes represent a marked shift in how teachers earn more money in Finland. According to an OAJ negotiator, in the old system, "Teachers [thought that] if you want[ed] more money, then you just worked more hours instead of working harder or better" (OAJ. Negotiator.1). The new system embodied a sense that teachers were compensated on the basis of the quality and complexity of their work—a view that the OAJ casts as professionalism enhancing.

Are These Changes Significant?

The previous section identified three major changes introduced by the KUN-PAS Agreement: the transition to euro-denominated wages, the introduction of the locally negotiated component, and the opportunity for locally designed task-complexity (TVA) and professional performance (HL) pay. Were these significant changes?

The transition from paying teachers' salaries in euros instead of the Finnish markka was a significant undertaking, but one that was inevitable due to the larger politics of joining the European Monetary Unit—it was simply a question of when and how. So, the question of the significance of the reform should be focused on the other two shifts: the decentralization of some bargaining to the local level (*järjestelyerä*), and the resulting opportunity for locally designed TVA and HL. Consistently, when a member of the OAJ—irrespective of whether the individual worked at the national or municipal level—was asked about the new components of the salary system (TVA or HL), one of the first responses was usually that these components make up a very small percentage of teachers' total salaries (Local_B.President; Local_C.Shop_Steward; Local_C.Union_Leader; OAJ.Negotiator.2). However, the shift is both theoretically and practically important.

Like the total raises negotiated in collective agreements, the size of the locally negotiated component is described relative to the total amount of money allocated toward teachers' salaries in the previous year. As a result, the raises *sound* insignificant—they have always been less than a 1% raise—relative to all of the money that goes to teachers' salaries. However, because not all teachers receive these raises—they are targeted by nature—discussing the size of the raises as a percentage of total teachers' salaries is misleading.

The percentage of teachers who received raises from locally negotiated money from 2007–2011 ranged from 16–44% (Kunnallinen Työmarkkinalaitos, 2008, 2009, 2011). Although recalculating these raises as a percentage of an individual teachers' base salary is impossible—because recipient teachers' base salaries would differ on the basis of the complex salary system—it is certainly a more significant raise for these teachers than the size of the raise relative to the total base would reflect. Furthermore, because these raises go into recipient teachers' *base salaries*, the impact on a teacher's lifetime earnings is not insignificant. Furthermore, the locally negotiated component is not an insignificant portion of the total money that has come into the teachers' salary system each year since 2007.[8]

In addition to the size and significance of the locally negotiated portion, the allocation of the money between TVA or HL is also significant. Due to the OAJ's preference for 'position-based' rather than 'person-based' pay, the OAJ preferred and continues to prefer position-based TVA to person-based HL. However, when the salary development contract was originally negotiated, HL was not a major concern, in part because it was a *very* small part of the locally negotiated funds—less than 5% of the locally negotiated component in 2007 (KT.Social_Scientist). Because there was so little money going toward HL at the time, the union did not perceive it to be a significant problem: communities could put money toward HL, but they were not (KT.Social_Scientist). As a result, the union's primary concern was ensuring that the money that went into the system via TVA stayed in the system. To the extent that HL was being used, it was more like a trial or experiment.

But as Figure 5.2 demonstrates, the relative percentage of the locally negotiated component allocated toward HL has increased since 2007. According to both KT and OAJ, getting the local money to HL is increasingly the employers' policy (KT.Social_Scientist; OAJ.Negotiator.1). The explanation provided by KT is that there is "nothing left to pay" with TVA; municipalities have targeted increases to all of the positions where they think such increases are necessary and so their attention is turning, increasingly, toward the use of HL (OAJ.Negotiator.1).

The apparent shift in employers' priorities for the locally negotiated component and the marked increase in the allocation of local funds to HL versus

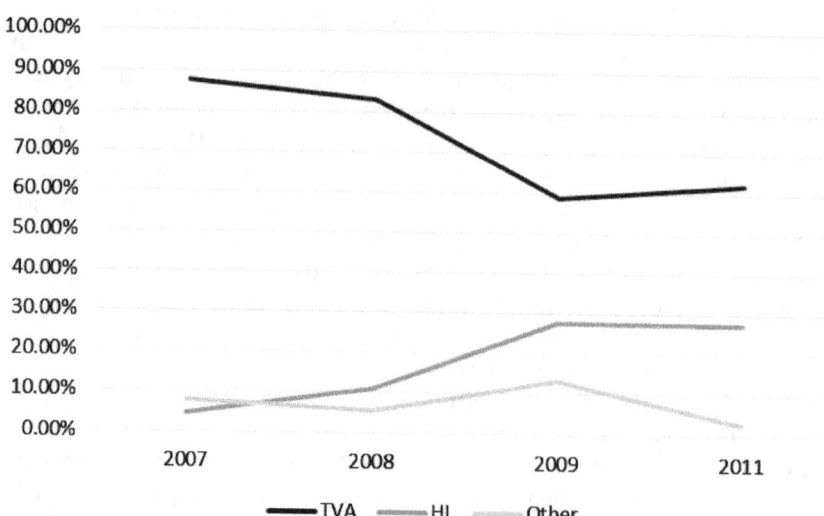

Figure 5.2 Allocation of *järjestelyerä* (OVTES, % of Total)
Source: Kunnallinen Työmarkkinalaitos 2008, 2009, 2011

TVA points to the third reason why the shift to the new system in 2007 was both theoretically and practically significant. While the process for negotiating collective agreements—including sectoral agreements like OVTES and KVTES as well as the TUPO system—are governed by laws that protect the right of the unions not to sign an unfavorable agreement, including processes for mediation and, potentially, industrial action, local 'negotiations' are notably different. The locally determined money is discussed by the local union and the municipal authority but, unlike the collective agreements, if the two sides do not agree, the employer has the legal authority to decide unilaterally (Kunnallinen Työmarkkinalaitos, 2004; KT.Social_Scientist; Local_A.Employer; Local_A.Shop_Steward; Local_B.Employer; Local_B. President; Local_B.Shop_Steward; Local_C.Shop_Steward; Local_C. Union_Leader; OAJ.Negotiator.1; OAJ.Negotiator.2). According to a summary of the 2003–2007 Wage Development Contract:

> The allocation of local elements shall be negotiated with the trade unions or their representatives in accordance with § 14 of the main contract, trying to reach a consensus. Should consensus not be reached, the employer is free to choose how the local element is allocated for task-specific and personal bonuses. (Kunnallinen Työmarkkinalaitos, 2002a)

Many individuals—from both the union and employer perspective—indicated that it would be inappropriate to even call the local conversations 'negotiations.' One local superintendent described the process this way:

> In negotiation, you listen, because the employer thinks it is good to hear them. And then [the employer does] what is best. For the unions, they try and try, and then they accept it because if they don't accept it, the employer dictates. The feeling is much better when we agree. Still, they don't like it all, but . . . whoever has the money decides. (Local_A.Employer)

According to data provided by KT, in 2011, 1.6% of respondents reported that the employer made a unilateral decision when it came to determining the locally negotiated money within the OVTES agreement. However, based on conversations with local union leaders, it seems possible, if not likely, that many of the 98.4% of respondents who indicated decisions based on employer-union agreement simply reflect a formality of agreement. According to local shop stewards:

> The problem is that if the city doesn't like the deal, then they decide, so the local union has little leverage. . . . Too many times, they have already decided. So, we can change small details, but the big lines are already decided—that's what I feel. (Local_A.Shop_Steward)
>
> It is not in our best interest to disagree too much. We try to find some common ground and agree so that there is room to negotiate next year. (Local_B.President)

Thus, local unions have limited scope to influence the allocation of this locally negotiated money.

Partly as a result of the variability of local decision-making processes, despite the trends evidenced in Figure 5.2, the effect of the 2007 changes—decentralization of bargaining and giving municipalities the option to pay teachers based on their professional performance (HL)—are far from uniform across Finnish municipalities. Although KT surveys municipalities on the outcomes of their local consultations, only the national averages are publically available. As a result, speaking about how, exactly, municipalities have differed in their utilization of the changes made possible by the new salary system is difficult. Ultimately, the extent to which municipalities choose to utilize the freedom to pay teachers based on their professional performance is a question of the preferences, goals, and administrative capacity of the municipality. It does not speak to a question of union strength.

THE STORY OF THE KUNPAS NEGOTIATIONS (2000–2007)

The question of how the salary system was reformed can be approached from a number of angles. Historically, it is a question of the sequence of events that led to the changes. This section will outline that series of events. But behind the superficial narrative of the steps that were taken to arrive at the outcome is a deeper narrative of the driving forces that influenced and constrained those events. Two underlying factors appear to animate the reform process:

- *First, PRP in Finland was facilitated by a series of economic factors.* The reforms occurred immediately after a recession and at a time when there were 'spoils to divide.' Although there were things that the union disliked about the reform, accepting the reforms was perceived to be in their best short- and long-term economic interests.
- *Second, PRP in Finland occurred as part of broader reform movements*—the decentralization of decision-making to local authorities and the restructuring of salary systems throughout the municipal sector to include local decision-making and an emphasis on outputs and employees' performance. In addition to the financial inducements, many of the unpopular reform components—local decision-making and PRP—had already been introduced throughout the rest of the municipal sector. This may have strengthened the employers' bargaining position or convinced the union that reforms were inevitable.

These themes—economics and broader public sector reform—can be traced throughout the sequence of events that culminated in the new salary system. However, to fully see these dynamics at play, we cannot begin in 2007 or even a few years prior—we must rewind over a decade.

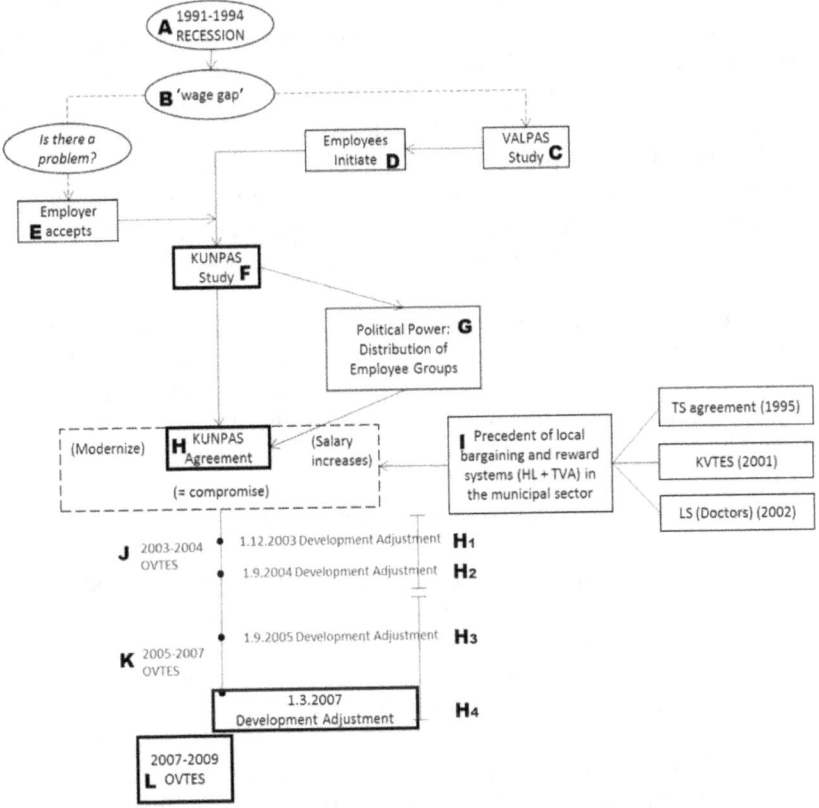

Figure 5.3 Finland's new salary system reform timeline

At the beginning of the 21st century—on the heels of the 1991–1994 economic recession and decentralization—many perceived that the wages of public sector workers had fallen behind private sector wages (Figure 5.3, A) (Local_C.Union_Leader; OAJ.Negotiator.2). The municipal employees[9] wanted to undertake a study to determine the severity of the wage gap between private sector employees and public sector workers who were employed by municipalities (D) (KT.Social_Scientist). The employee associations' idea for the study was likely prompted by a similar study that had been conducted in the state sector (KT.Social_Scientist; OAJ.Social_Scientist). The 1987 collective agreement in the state sector created a working group[10] to investigate salary levels in the state sector compared to the private and municipal sectors. Two years later, this group produced the 'VALPAS study' (C) (Holm, Tossavainen, Tuomala, & Valppu, 1999).

At the initiative of the employee associations in the municipal sector, a similar working group was part of the municipal sector's collective agreement in 2000 (Heiskanen et al., 2001). The employees argued that public sector wages lagged behind the private sector, which would create challenges to attracting and retaining employees. In education, a significant portion of the workforce was projected to retire which could produce a teacher shortage, the OAJ argued, if salaries were not improved (OAJ.Negotiator.1). According to KT.Social_Scientist, "As an employer organization, we knew that this would create pressure for us (to increase salaries), but we also wanted to know what the situation was—maybe there was something that needed to be done." The KT knew that a significant wage gap *could* produce shortages of qualified employees or create other problems (**B, E**).

> In the years to come, the municipalities and the communities will have to compete for workforce in the labor market. . . . The staff policies of the municipalities need to focus on preparing for future challenges . . . the profitability of the organization and the ability to present the municipality as an interesting and inspiring employer. (Kunnallinen Työmarkkinalaitos, 2001)
>
> During the negotiations for collective agreements, the parties acknowledged that they share the objective of securing the competitiveness of the municipal jobs and the availability of competent employees in the coming years. The parties were to start a statistical survey on the wage levels as well as the terms and conditions of employment in the municipal sector, and compare the results with the rest of the labor market. (Kunnallinen Työmarkkalaitos, 2002a)

The employers and the unions worked together on the study with Statistics Finland—who functioned as the neutral party responsible for the research (**F**). The resulting 'KUNPAS' study, published in December of 2001 (Kouvonen & Suoperä, 2001), found that there was, on average, a 7–8% wage gap (Kouvonen & Suoperä, 2001; Kunnallinen Työmarkkinalaitos, 2002a).

The response to the 'wage gap problem' identified by the KUNPAS study was the 2003–2007 Salary Development Agreement (**H**) for Municipal Employees between KT and its negotiating partners—UNIONI, JUKO (the official bargaining agent of AKAVA), TNJ, and KTN—giving municipal employees about a 3–4% raise over the course of the four years[11] (Kunnallinen Työmarkkinalaitos, 2002ab; KT.Negotiator.1; KT.Social_Scientist). These raises were over and above the TUPO raises centrally negotiated in tripartite negotiations; because these raises applied to all sectors, public employees would never catch up based on TUPO raises alone (KT.Social_Scientist; OAJ.Negotiator.1; OAJ.Negotiator.2).

The KUNPAS study strengthened the position of employees to demand raises. However, the Salary Development Agreement also provided an opportunity for employers to accomplish one of their long-standing objectives—to 'modernize' the salary system (KT.Social_Scientist). In 2001, KT published a report on staffing strategies and human resource management (HRM), which included an emphasis on 'motivational reward systems:'

> The aim of rewards and incentive bonuses is to encourage the development of versatile professional skills, collaboration and the improvement of work. . . . Both individuals and working communities must be encouraged to improve their results, service quality and initiative.
>
> Municipal collective agreements are adapted locally so that one's wage is based on the demands of the task, the office-holder's or employee's work experience, individual results, and the profitability of the working unit in question. (Kunnallinen Työmarkkinalaitos, 2001)

KT's underlying belief was that "you should leave it to communities to decide what is difficult and who is performing well" (KT.Social_Scientist). The perceived need for this modernization was especially acute in terms of teachers' salaries. KT "knew there would be wage costs, but we wanted to get our wage systems more modern—especially for teachers. The system was from like 100 years ago, and it was really out of this world and we knew we needed to do something about it" (KT.Social_Scientist). According to one local superintendent, changes in teachers' compensation system had not caught up with changes in teachers' work:

> Teachers are no longer planning by themselves, teaching by themselves, evaluating by themselves, and then going home. That was the 1930s. Now the law has changed, the goal has changed—to support [growth and development] and after that to teach the skills they need in life. (Local_A.Employer)

Although some changes had been made to the general municipal agreement, KVTES for example, teachers (OVTES) had resisted these changes. However, in the employer's view, as a general principle, you need money to restructure wages "because there is always this principal that, in practice, you can't start by lowering anyone's salary" (KT.Social_Scientist). So KUNPAS provided a strategic opportunity for the employers to 'buy' the changes (Local_A.Shop_Steward).

FROM DESCRIPTION TO ANALYSIS: WHY WAS KUNPAS POSSIBLE?

Economic conditions and the reform context were clearly factors in the reform process. However, they cannot answer the key paradox that was presented in Chapter 4. How can the competing claims—that nothing that the OAJ opposes can occur and that the OAJ opposed the changes to the salary system—be explained? Yes, the economy and historical context may tell us something about what was going on, but in addition to the contextual factors that contributed to reform, a significant part of the story is contained in the behavior and activity of the OAJ itself.

There are two actor-centric factors that inform the reform process: OAJ's orientation and the interaction orientation between OAJ and KT.

First, OAJ's orientation refers to its short- and long-term preferences, its perceptions of the reforms, and its internal capacity or intraorganizational bargaining. In contrast to many oversimplified accounts of union behavior (see Chapter 1), the OAJ's preferences were complex and competing rather than fixed and predictable. In the end, the union did not strictly oppose reform—its role in the reform process was far more complicated. Instead, it was a collaborator, and even played a role in initiating the reforms. A closer look at the union's goals, policy-related preferences, and the demands of diverse interest representation—intraorganizational bargaining in Walton and McKersie's framework—reveals that these significantly informed the OAJ's strategies and tactics. These factors will be outlined in the first part of this section.

However, they were not the only factors at play. The second key factor was the interaction orientation between OAJ and KT. An established cooperative relational pattern systematically informed the union's decision-making and bargaining strategies, including the KUNPAS agreement. The relationship pattern is rooted in the contextual factors that were outlined in Chapter 4—extensive negotiation and consultation—and can be traced throughout the narratives of both union and school leaders. The collaborative relationship between the OAJ and the municipal employers (KT) is a significant part of the reform story in Finland, as any union opposition was overcome, not by power, but by compromise.

Actor Orientation: The Preferences, Perceptions, and Capacity of the OAJ

If the OAJ—and especially teachers—were opposed to the KUNPAS reforms, why would the union accept this unpopular reform against the self-reported preferences of its membership? Answering this question requires an understanding of several concepts, which are derived from Walton and McKersie's framework (Chapter 2) and explored in this section with supporting evidence from interview data (Figure 5.4).

The OAJ's strategies and tactics—both generally and in terms of the 2007 system in particular—must be understood in terms of the diversity of members' preferences (cognitive diversity [Figure 5.4, A]), and the evaluative processes (B) through which consensus around preferences—both in terms of general and particular goals (C)—are generated. Two themes emerge when it comes to negotiating strategies and tactics (D). First, the union attempts to find solutions that are 'tactically clever' (F)—a strategy that sits at the nexus of the OAJ's preferences and its capacities. Second, compromise (G) is an essential part of the union's strategic calculation. The perceived necessity of compromise must be understood through the lens of the OAJ's interaction orientation (E), which can only be understood within Finland's institutional context, outlined in Chapter 4. Both strategic considerations—tactically clever changes and compromise—are mutually reinforcing, as compromise informs the union's conception of what is possible. These strategic considerations

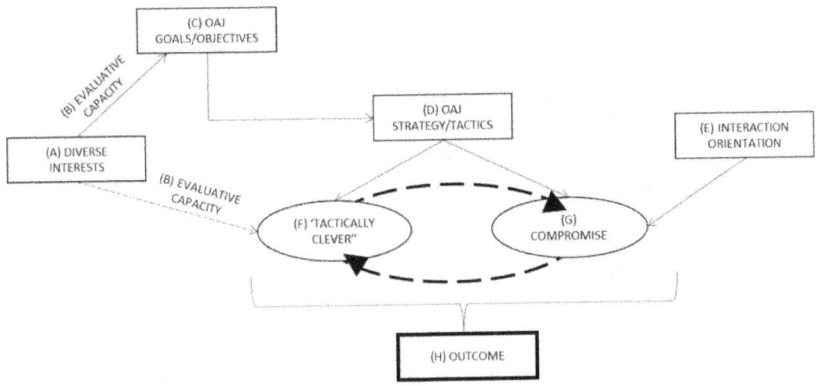

Figure 5.4 OAJ strategy and tactics

become evident through a close examination of OAJ's policy-specific perceptions and preferences, its internal capacity or intraorganizational bargaining, and its broad, long-term goals.

OAJ's KUNPAS-Specific Perceptions and Preferences

According to one negotiator with KT, neither locally negotiated TVA nor HL were priorities or preferences of the OAJ (KT.Negotiator.1). As a general rule, although the union generally accepts some local negotiation and pay for task-complexity in particular, reservations about the locally negotiated component as well as ambivalence about the PRP component (HL) remained (Table 5.1).

The preferences for TVA and the locally negotiated component (JAR, as displayed in Table 5.2) are fairly straightforward. First, there was widespread support of TVA; this support reflects both contemporary and historical preferences. When the 'new system' was implemented in 2007, the idea of task-complexity was not new, but the locus of decision-making was different. So there was a general acceptance that the complexity of teachers' work was different and should be rewarded appropriately, however, there were concerns about decentralizing decision-making to the local level.

Table 5.2 displays contemporary perceptions of the locally negotiated component. Unpacking the data on perceptions (Table 5.2, as well as Tables 5.3 and 5.4, below) requires one methodological note. Although effort was taken to ask interviewees about historic preferences, many interviewees discussed contemporary perceptions or preferences. The consensus was that all parties—teachers as well as the organization and its leadership—had moved from a position of resistance to *relative* acceptance, although not necessarily endorsement, of the locally negotiated component and HL.

Table 5.2 reflects the union ambivalence about the locally negotiated component. Although there were concerns due to its novelty, there was consensus, despite the fact that some municipalities thought local negotiation would be too much work, that local differences exist and that the locally

Table 5.1 Preferences related to the new salary system

		JAR	HL	TVA
PRESIDENT	OAJ.President	Important decisions can be made locally; can't be all local; strategic opportunity	Good and necessary part of the system; requires careful implementation	Good; work is not the same
CENTRAL UNION	OAJ.Negotiator.1	Can be good; hard when new; local shop stewards don't want it	Acceptance; questions about measurement	Good; differences between jobs exist
	OAJ.Negotiator.2	Strategic opportunity	Mixed view	Good
	Local_A.Union_Leader	Good; hard when new	Good	Good
LOCAL UNION	Local_C.Shop_Steward	Good; deal with local differences	Good (personally); teachers dislike	Good
	Local_C.Union_Leader	n/a	Dislikes	Good
	Local_B.President	Sometimes good; hard work	Teachers dislike	Good
	Local_B.Shop_Steward	Good; hard when new	Acceptance; hard when new	Good
	Local_A.Shop_Steward	Good	Unsure	Good

Table 5.2 Perceptions of the locally negotiated component

		Local Differences Exist	Too Much Work	Way to Get More Money	'Hard when New'
PRESIDENT	OAJ.President	X		X	
CENTRAL UNION	OAJ.Negotiator.1	X	X	X	X
	OAJ.Negotiator.2			X	
LOCAL UNION	Local_A.Union_Leader	X		X	X
	Local_C.Shop_Steward	X		X	X
	Local_C.Union_Leader			X	
	Local_B.President	X	X	X	

negotiated component provided an opportunity to address those differences. The view of one local union president is representative of these tensions:

> [We] would be happy to have it done centrally [because] . . . everyone is replicating the same work—it's kind of like reinventing the wheel. . . . It's more responsibility and more work without resources. But, there are some pieces where you get better results this way. (Local_B.President)

Several respondents identified the locally negotiated component as a change that was difficult and unwelcome when first implemented, but has gotten easier with time. The ability to address local differences was part of the appeal of accepting the locally negotiated component, but the overwhelming motivation—articulated by every respondent—was that accepting local negotiation was a way to get more money from municipalities. According to an executive board member:

> In other municipal professions, local salary items have played [a] significant role for a long time. They haven't been big parts of [the total raise], but after many years other professions have got something locally that we haven't. (Local_A.Leader)

The KUNPAS agreement and the additional raises it provided guaranteed a short-term boost in teachers' salaries, but the union also hoped it might provide long-term opportunities as well. The idea was that if each municipality developed its own wage system, outlining the groups of teachers and

Table 5.3 Perceptions of the performance component (HL)

		Performance Differences Exist	Immeasurable	Biased (Not Objective)	Unfair	Good in Theory; Challenging in Practice	'Getting Used to it'
PRESIDENT	OAJ.President	X	X			X	
CENTRAL UNION	OAJ.Negotiator.1	X	X	X		X	X
	OAJ.Negotiator.2	X (t)	X (t)	X (t)	X (t)	X	
	Local_A.Union_Leader					X	
LOCAL UNION	Local_C.Shop_Steward	No		(t)	(t)	X	
	Local_C.Union_Leader	X (t)		(t)	(t)		
	Local_B.Union_President	X	(t)		(t)		X
	Local_B.Shop_Steward	X		(t)	(t)	X	X
	Local_A.Shop_Steward			X (t)	X (t)	X*	

Table 5.4 Perceptions of the task-complexity component (TVA)

		Job Differences Exist	Measurable	Objective	Fair
PRESIDENT	OAJ.President	n/a	n/a	n/a	n/a
CENTRAL UNION	OAJ.Negotiator.1	X	X		
	OAJ.Negotiator.2	X	X	X	X
LOCAL UNION	Local_A.Union_Leader	X			
	Local_C.Shop_Steward	X	X	X	X
	Local_C.Union_Leader	X			X
	Local_B.Union_President	X		X	X
	Local_B.Shop_Steward	X			(t)
	Local_A.Shop_Steward	X			

types of performances that deserved higher salaries, then the municipality would be encouraged to allocate its 'own money' toward teachers' salaries. The chief shop steward at OAJ said that the union is attempting to convince municipalities "that even if there are economic difficulties ... the most important thing is the salary system" and that "even if they put small shares to the salary system there are still possibilities that they will have good results. So they can spare some money because the results will be good and it will, in a sense, cost less" (OAJ.Negotiator.1). However, it has been difficult to convince municipalities of this 'investment opportunity.' A local union leader called this strategy "wishful thinking" and said that municipalities would only raise salaries using their 'own money' "maybe if [they] are 'nice'" (Local_B.President).

However, despite the general support for the locally negotiated component as a way to address local differences and the importance of local negotiation as a strategic opportunity, the union only supports locally negotiated monies *within limits* as evidenced by the responses included in Table 5.1. As OAJ.President made clear, if all of the money were negotiated locally, it would threaten the union's existence. Exclusively local negotiation would challenge the need for a strong central organization. Furthermore, with exclusively local negotiations, many members could go several years without receiving raises, creating discord and dissatisfaction within the union.

In terms of preferences, HL was and remains controversial. However, as Table 5.2 makes clear, the fervor of the controversy—and cleavages within the union—has changed over time and must be unpacked. First, like with the locally negotiated monies, there is a historical dimension to the OAJ's perceptions and preferences related to HL that reflects a move from relative resistance to acceptance. As OAJ.President said about HL:

> I can't say that they (teachers) are happy . . . but they understand . . . if teachers don't want it, we can't do it . . . they are not happy, but they agree.

In addition to the temporal dimension—that there has been growing acceptance over time as teachers 'get used to the system' (OAJ.Negotiator.1, Local_B.President, Local_B.Shop_Steward)—OAJ.President's comment also points to another important dimension when considering the preferences and perceptions of the teachers' union: the role of *teachers'* preferences and perceptions.

This distinction can be seen more clearly in Table 5.3, which provides a more detailed display of interviewees' perceptions of HL. Table 5.4 displays perceptions of TVA, which provides a useful contrast to the perceptions of HL. While teachers' perceptions (marked (t)) were rarely distinguished from the views of interviewees' or the OAJ more generally, in terms of TVA, interviewees were frequently distinguishing their personal views—or the views of 'union leadership' generally—from the views of teachers when it came to HL.

If any general 'union view' of HL emerged it is this: that although the *leadership* understands that not all teachers work equally hard or as effectively, *teachers* perceive HL to be difficult to measure and as a result prone to bias and unfairness. Local_C.Union_Leader was the only interviewee to personally object to HL categorically. The rest expressed personal views ranging from openness—there are questions, but it can be good—to acceptance, to support:

> In my opinion, it's a good part of our system—we need that part. All 100,000 teachers are not working at the same style or level. (OAJ_President)
>
> In my opinion, we need both [TVA] and [HL] . . . I think that sometimes it's useful to pay for personal skills, if there [is a] clear basis for that. (Local_A.Union_Leader)

Union leaders were consistently careful to point out that they were sharing "*their opinion.*" Their general support for HL tended to come with two caveats. First, they argued, explicitly or implicitly, that PRP is theoretically possible and valuable but difficult to execute in practice. So they support the *idea* of PRP—that some teachers work harder or better than others and should be rewarded—without supporting all forms or systems of HL:

> No matter your profession, there are always better performers—it's just a fact. How you measure it is another question. (Local_B.Union_President)

> We (the OAJ) have a common opinion about how you can prove you are good. Maybe this is a bit idealistic, but we are not aiming for teachers to be competing. (OAJ_President)

Second, they acknowledged that although they supported the idea of HL *personally*, that this was not the view of all, or most, teachers. When they distinguished the view of teachers from their own view, teachers' views of HL were universally negative (Table 5.2). One local shop steward described how she balanced her own opinions with teachers' perceptions and beliefs about fairness:

> [I think personal bonuses are] not so bad . . . it's a question of what is more fair—personal bonuses for good workers or for more experience? Well, I don't know. When you are more experienced, maybe you are a better teacher—I know I am. But do you work hard or not? That seems to matter too. I don't have the answer, and that is why we have the local association. They decide and then tell me the goals. (Local_A.Shop_Steward)

The dissention, among teachers in particular, over HL's measurability, fairness, and objectivity can be contrasted with perceptions of the reliability and validity of TVA. There was universal recognition that job differences exist—a contested claim when it comes to teachers' performance—and consensus[12] that these differences are measurable, objective, and a fair basis for compensation differences. At best, teachers' reaction to HL has been characterized as a kind of grudging 'acceptance.'

OAJ's Capacity: Internal Pressures Incentivizing Compromise

As previously discussed, the OAJ is comprised of a variety of smaller units reflecting both regional and job-function diversity. Basic education teachers (YSI) are the largest sub-organization, with 90 of the 150 Council seats, in addition to organizations representing secondary, vocational, university teachers, and others. However, these organizational lines may not always reflect the only or most important intraorganizational disagreements. *Within* basic education,[13] important differences exist both in the preferences of class versus secondary teachers as well as within those groups as contract details—number of lesson hours and related working conditions that qualify for the 'full' salary—vary across subject areas. According to a local shop steward, "There are so many groups, so interests are not shared. If you ask [primary] education, you will get one answer, and high school, another. The question is how to make everyone happy." These struggles and tensions are not a secret outside of the union; a local superintendent highlighted the challenges of internal struggles between teachers:

> And now [all teachers have] master's degrees [but] the salaries are [still] not the same for class teachers and subject teachers. Subject teachers' [salaries are determined by] these different duties and lessons and

extras, and it's a terrible mess. And all [of the different affiliates of the teachers' unions] are together and everyone is trying to struggle for their own. (Local_A.Employer)

Interviewees consistently highlighted the diversity of membership preferences, multiplicity of goals, and the difficulty of establishing a single clear aim at both the central and municipal levels. In order to attempt to integrate these diverse preferences, OAJ's organizational structure features a fairly complex and developed representative democracy through which negotiating goals are established (Figure 5.5).

As discussed in Chapter 4, all of the member organizations are proportionally represented on the council, which produces goals for each negotiation cycle (Figure 5.5, 1). Due to the diversity of members' preferences, these goals are usually quite numerous and general. The OAJ staff—the president serves as the chief negotiator supported by full-time shop stewards—are responsible for conducting negotiations on the basis of the goals generated by the councils (3). The negotiators are relatively free in the negotiating process. After they have the OAJ's goals, they do not have to check in with the boards or councils; they have latitude to negotiate the best possible agreement. After negotiations, the Council decides if they will sign the agreement made by the negotiators, but are not involved throughout the process.

According to Local_B.President, the union's representative system requires that members trust that the councils and executive leadership will do what is

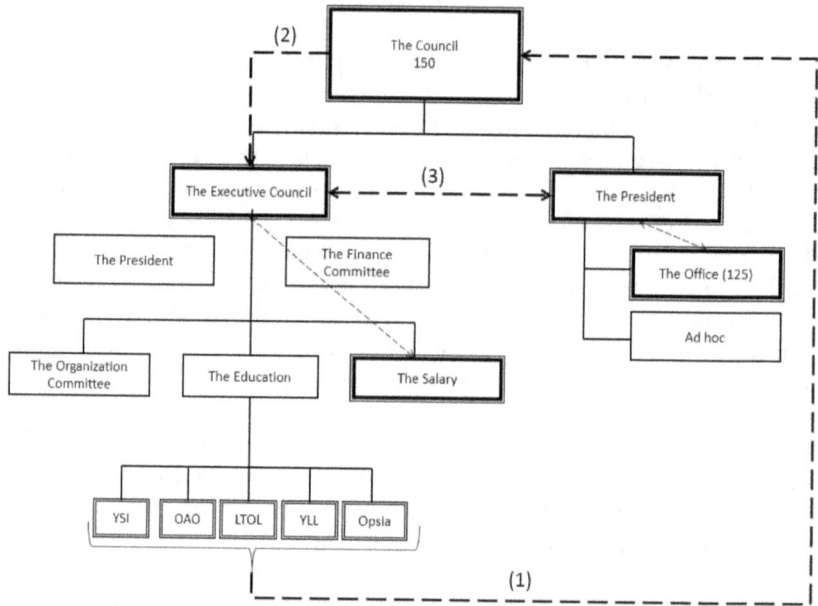

Figure 5.5 OAJ organizational structure

best; it is impossible for the union to function as a direct democracy where everyone can provide their opinion on every issue. This representative system is the primary strategy for aggregating members' preferences—or the union's evaluative capacity (Scharpf, 1997). The system allows the diverse membership to make their preferences and interests heard while entrusting the board to 'see the bigger picture' (Local_B.President).

Ultimately, despite the challenges of representing virtually all of the teachers in Finland and the inevitable diversity of members' preferences, the OAJ has developed a system of interest aggregation, in which this diversity does not pose a major challenge or threat to the union's functioning:

> It is better to struggle internally. It's not very easy to reach agreement, but it's also not very difficult. We must have a long-term plan; [there are] more and more satisfied teachers with a long-term plan. (OAJ.President)

However, there was a universal acknowledgement that representing all teachers 'fairly'—a definition that will likely vary along with members' preferences—is a real challenge. It is a manageable challenge, but one that informs the union's strategies and tactics, as will become increasingly clear. In order to see these strategic implications, a closer examination of OAJ's long-term goals or preferences is required.

OAJ Goals and General Preferences: Multiple, Diverse, and Competing

The OAJ President expressed the broadest conception of his goals as a leader of the organization: "Teachers in Finland want to be members of my organization. What about the future? . . . What [do] we have to do to make them think it is important?" This goal requires a long-term strategy and careful attention to internal questions of fairness. One executive board member stated that "[The goal] is not only to get [the highest percentage raise] to salaries as possible. We also have many things in our salaries that we feel [are] unequal . . . we have both short- and long-term goals." The importance of the long-term view was echoed by all three members of the executive board (OAJ.President; Local_A.Union_Leader; Local_B.President) as well as by the lead negotiator (OAJ.Negotiator.1).

Increasing the amount of money invested in education—in terms of both teachers' salaries as well as local investment in public education—is clearly a significant component of this strategy, but is not the exclusive focus of the union (Table 5.5). In terms of teachers' salaries, union leaders spoke to the importance of addressing the equity and fairness of salary systems (Table 5.5, B) in addition to simply increasing the absolute salary level. Local shop stewards spoke to the importance of school organization, development, and quality, identifying the union as a co-producer with the municipality in the provision of quality public services.

The OAJ's salary strategy sits at the nexus of its salary-specific goals and the diversity and tensions of members' preferences—to increase the amount

Table 5.5 Perceptions of OAJ's goals according to various stakeholders

	INTERVIEWEE	(A) INCREASE MONEY	(B) FAIRNESS	(C) SCHOOL QUALITY	(D) LONG-TERM GOALS
Central	OAJ.President				X
	OAJ.Negotiator.1	X			X
	OAJ.Negotiator.2	X			
Local	Local_A.Union_Leader	X	X		X
	Local_C.Union_Leader	X	X		
	Local_B.Shop_Steward			X	
	Local_B.President	X			X
	Local_A.Shop_Steward	X*	X	X	

*Local_A.Shop_Steward referenced increasing money in the system, but this referred to the development of the education system as a whole, rather than an emphasis on teachers' pay.

of money available while attending to fairness through long-term thinking. In terms of salary negotiations, the OAJ appears to have two major goals—to get as much money to teachers as possible while attending to questions of fairness and equity.[14] Combined with long-term thinking, these three considerations come together in what OAJ.Negotiator.1 referred to as 'tactically clever changes.' Although the descriptive language varied, similar ideas were echoed by several interviewees (Local_A.Shop_Steward; Local_B.President; Local_C.Shop_Steward). The idea of 'tactically clever changes' synthesizes a variety of ideas. First, it is linked to strategies to maximize the total amount of money that comes into the salary system. Second, it provides a way of integrating members' preferences and resolving tensions around fairness. And third, it is premised on the assumption of a long-term strategy.

When OAJ.Negotiator.1 described tactically clever changes, he positioned them as a direct response to the different kinds of teachers and their competing preferences. At the central level, tactically clever changes referred to targeting raises to groups that are growing. If the group of teachers receiving raises is growing—for example, if the national curriculum will require an increase in science teachers—then the total level of salaries over time will continue to rise. Targeting these groups allows negotiators both to accomplish their goal of maximizing the money paid to teachers and also to justify the decision-making between teacher groups.

The idea of salary-maximizing strategies with the highest integrative potential was also expressed by local shop stewards and union leaders. At the local level, these strategies took two main forms. First, with TVA raises, the unions in all three municipalities attempted to identify ways of targeting money that would benefit, or appear to benefit, the most teachers and types of teachers. For example, class-size based TVA is generalizable across class and subject teachers and avoids singling out a particular group or subject. A second strategy—employed in Local A and C—was to devolve decision-making to the school level through school-based TVA. One local shop steward identified this strategy as a way of dealing with the competing preferences of teachers:

> There are so many groups, so interests are not shared. If you ask basic education you will get one answer and high school another. The question is how to make everyone happy. This is why I have suggested that you let schools decide.

According to OAJ's President, in order to implement 'tactically clever changes'—particularly those that target strategic groups—the union must have a long-term plan. The president believes that more teachers will be satisfied with a long-term plan, and that through 'turn-taking'— the idea that some teachers must sacrifice short-term gains for long-term benefits—the union has a greater opportunity to change and improve things for all teachers. But such a system requires "good cooperation so that this time a group will get more and the next time another one," rather than a rigid system which requires that everyone must always receive the same thing.

RELATIONSHIP PATTERNS, INTERACTION ORIENTATIONS, AND SYSTEMIC COMPROMISE

The discussion of OAJ's strategy remains incomplete without addressing the central role of compromise at every level of negotiations. The significance of compromise was highlighted by both union leaders and negotiators as well as employers' representatives at the central and local levels. As OAJ.Negotiator.2 said, "Everything in our agreements is a compromise."

The KUNPAS agreement was certainly a compromise—one in which KT increased teachers' wages in exchange for modernizing the salary system. This compromise was neither an isolated incident, nor the by-product of some ideological commitment to 'getting along.' Compromise is a systemic and strategic component of labor negotiations in Finland. It is ingrained in the relationship patterns and interaction orientations of both the union and the employer association. Understanding this relationship pattern will illuminate the way that compromise interacted with OAJ's orientation to produce the new salary system. Chapter 2 described Walton and McKersie's five relationship patterns—"a set of reciprocal attitudes salient to the parties

Table 5.6 Relationship patterns, Finland

		MOTIVATION ORIENTATION	BELIEFS ABOUT LEGITIMACY	FEELINGS OF TRUST	FEELINGS OF FRIENDLINESS
CENTRAL UNION	AKAVA.Negotiator	Cooperative	N/A	Extended trust	Friendliness
	OAJ.Negotiator.2	Cooperative	N/A	Trust[15]	Friendliness
	OAJ.Social_Scientist[16]	Cooperative	Complete legitimacy	Extended trust	Friendliness
LOCAL UNION	Local_C.Shop_Steward	Cooperative	N/A	Trust	Friendliness
	Local_B.Union_President	Cooperative	Complete legitimacy	Extended trust	Friendliness
	Local_B.Shop_Steward	Cooperative	Complete legitimacy	Extended trust	Friendliness
	Local_A.Shop_Steward	Cooperative	Complete legitimacy	Trust	Friendliness
CENTRAL EMPLOYER	KT.Social_Scientist	Cooperative	N/A	Extended trust	Friendliness
LOCAL EMPLOYER	Local_A.Employer	Cooperative	Complete legitimacy	Extended trust	Friendliness
	Local_B.Employer	Cooperative	Complete legitimacy	N/A	NA

in their interaction" (p. 185)—which were comprised of four attitudinal dimensions (see Table 2.1). Table 5.6 displays classifications of interviewees' descriptions of the relationship pattern between OAJ and employers. Across levels—central and local—as well as both the OAJ and employers, a consistently cooperative relationship pattern emerges.

Despite the nuance and particularity of responses,[17] the general pattern that emerges conforms closely to Walton and McKersie's cooperative pattern. The "complete acceptance of the legitimacy of the other" (Walton & McKersie, 1965/1991, p. 188) was implied throughout discussions, never contradicted, and evident in the working patterns of OAJ and KT. Furthermore, according to Walton and McKersie, this 'full respect' or legitimacy is evidenced by the union accepting "managerial success as being of concern to labor; [and] management recogniz[ing] its stake in stable effective unionism" (p. 185). This view was most comprehensively evidenced and articulated by Local_B. Shop_Steward, who said that the union's job is to work with the employer in:

> providing services for the people of Local B . . . (the union's role is in) trying to take care of employees, that they are heard. If conditions are good, it will provide better services. . . . We may not agree on details . . . as long as there are people doing things there will be disagreements.

The pervasiveness of cooperation between the OAJ and municipal employers in Finland is most evident at the local level. Although the local employer has the final say on all issues, including salaries, there was a consistent affirmation—from both local employers and unions—about the importance of working together.

> We are making good cooperation with the union. Sometimes we disagree and that is ok. Still we want to stay in good cooperation. Because that is the best way for the workers and the pupils . . . [and the pupils are why we are here]. . . . And so we have to . . . to have good cooperation. (Local_A.Employer)
>
> It is not good politics to just be telling . . . we want to discuss and compromise . . . because they are discussing it with their members. (Local_B.Employer)

The views of Local_A.Employer and Local_B.Employer reflect a belief in the legitimacy of the union as a representative of teachers, which is especially striking given that they are legally free to ignore union input if they choose. However, the mutual legitimacy between parties supersedes any differences of opinion.

Table 5.6 displays attitudinal dimensions—individual actors' feelings of trust, friendliness, and legitimacy. But these attitudes, particularly in light of the emerging consensus across both national and local employers and employees, carry both an individual and institutional dimension. The importance of interpersonal relationships in stable and effective employer-employee relationships was acknowledged (Local_B.President), but the consistency of the pattern is also connected to the institutional patterns of relationships and interaction discussed in Chapter 3—the frequency of formal and informal consultation which pervades both the national and local levels.

How does this relationship pattern—as distinct from a one-time effort at cooperation—inform the decision-making and negotiation process, particularly in the case of Finland's salary system? One effect of the cooperative relationship pattern between the OAJ and employers—and the point at which the compromise strategy interacts with the 'tactically clever' strategy—is that both parties enter negotiations with a significant amount of reliable information about both the empirical facts as well as the subjective preferences of the other party.

The OAJ and KT collaborate closely on the collection and monitoring of labor market data. This is relevant to the KUNPAS agreement, as the KUNPAS study is one example of this kind of collaboration. However, rather than an exceptional effort, the KUNPAS study should be viewed as a by-product of systemic and ongoing collaborative efforts. The social scientists for each organization are often in contact in order to monitor labor market trends and calculate the estimated and actual costs of collective agreements.

But beyond statistics and other empirical information, both parties—at both the national and local levels—are very familiar with the subjective preferences of their bargaining opponent due to the nature of their interactions—frequent and ongoing. Local_A.Union_Leader explained that the executive board "know(s) very well the concreteness of financial possibilities to get improvement to our goals" at the central level. And the local shop stewards and employers similarly express a familiarity with the goals of their respective opponents that allows them to understand what is possible.

Thus, union negotiating strategies—'tactically clever' solutions and compromise—sit at the nexus of their complex and competing goals and a systemic cooperative relationship pattern. The quality of objective and subjective information produced by ongoing and frequent interaction allows the union to anticipate 'what is possible' and to attempt to find clever goal-oriented and interest-integrating solutions within a framework of compromise and mutually satisfactory outcomes.

CONCLUSION

Together, the reform process and an understanding of OAJ's capacity and preferences provide the clues required to decipher how the new salary reforms were negotiated and why the OAJ responded the way that it did.

The outcome cannot be explained by OAJ's preferences—the union did not *want* all of the components of the KUNPAS agreement. They were—and to an extent, especially when it comes to the perceived preferences of teachers, continue to be—opposed to paying teachers on the basis of subjective factors, finding these immeasurable, unfair, and biased. Furthermore, they had reservations about local negotiation and opposed the elimination of certain supplements and the decrease in seniority-based pay. However, the OAJ did not block the KUNPAS agreement on the basis of these objectives.

To understand the OAJ's preferences and strategic choices and how they shaped their response, a few contextual factors must be explicitly drawn out in order to understand the reform process and the union's role and response in particular. The calculation of the OAJ's interests in 2002 did not occur in a vacuum, but in response to particular contextual events and factors. In addition to the strategy and tactics of the OAJ and KT, two key contextual observations were identified as significant to the reform process. First, precedence—following or emulating contracts that had been negotiated elsewhere—played a significant role. This can first be seen in VALPAS providing inspiration for KUNPAS. But more significantly, all of the unpopular reforms involved in the OVTES portion of the KUNPAS agreement—HL, the locally negotiated component, and seniority-based reductions—had already occurred in other municipal sector agreements, most notably KVTES. This impacted the union's interest calculations in two ways. First, the OAJ had observed that local negotiation and HL—in both the private and municipal sector—had allowed workers to get more money from employers. But second, the proliferation of these changes throughout the municipal sector may have convinced the union that these changes were inevitable.

The second key contextual factor was the economic circumstances surrounding the reform. Notably, the reform occurred after a recession and coincided with economic recovery. The recession may have created pressures for the reform—incentivizing both the employer and employees to take action. But in spite of the economic pressures, reform would have been unlikely had there not been 'spoils to divide.' The employer knew that modernizing the salary system would 'cost something,' and it seems unlikely that the OAJ would have signed onto the KUNPAS agreement without the promised 3–4% raise.

This leads directly to three critical points about the OAJ's interests. First, the union's opposition to certain aspects of the reform was outweighed by its preferences for other things. It was more important to get more money into the system—in both the short- and long-term—than it was to resist HL and local negotiation. So, part of the compromise can be explained by the fact that the OAJ was motivated to get the additional 3–4% raise provided by KUNPAS. But the OAJ was also aware that "there would be no KUNPAS after KUNPAS" and so they needed to think about other strategies for getting more money into the teachers' salary system (OAJ.Negotiator.2). The OAJ hoped that after municipalities had developed TVA and HL systems, then they would contribute 'their own money' to them (Local_A.Union_Leader; OAJ.Negotiator.1; OAJ.Negotiator.2; Local_B.President). This hope has been largely unrealized; since 2007, municipalities' financial situations have steadily worsened, eliminating any possibility that municipalities would have extra money to contribute toward teachers' salaries.[18]

Some of these long-term strategies to secure additional money, the second point about OAJ's interests, were 'strategic gambles.' Or, put another way, the union may have made some concessions at the central level with the hope that they would be able to negotiate the terms of implementation in ways that were ultimately consistent with their preferences. For example, although the OAJ was ambivalent about HL, they may have hoped to deal with this through successful local negotiations. In fact, it seems that the HL component was an insignificant concern at the time of the original negotiations. And for the first few years of the new system, the majority of the locally negotiated money was allocated to TVA. There was no way of guaranteeing that municipalities would invest additional money in teachers' salaries under the new system.

The acceptance of decentralization relates to the third observation about the OAJ's interests and strategies. Although this strategy was never explicitly articulated in terms of the KUNPAS agreement, contextual evidence supports it. Because of the diversity of teachers' interests that the union is responsible for unifying and representing, decentralizing decision-making may have been a politically palatable strategy despite the fact that local unions had less power. Local union leaders who are now responsible for attempting to satisfy competing interests at the local level have begun to promote school-based TVA as a politically unifying strategy. This strategy of 'kicking the can'—pushing an issue to a lower level and hoping to be able to convince those leaders to deal with it appropriately—is a pattern that connects local negotiation strategies with the KUNPAS negotiations. One negotiator for KT articulated the OAJ's calculation in this way:

> These targets were not too high up on the teachers' union development of wages list, but it was clear that it was beneficial for the union to agree to the contract when the details of the contract would be left to be negotiated during the coming five years . . . money was good and the other matters were left to be negotiated in the future which I am sure OAJ felt like they were on strong ground. (KT.Negotiator.1)

Employers were happy to decentralize decision-making because decentralization was consistent with their management philosophy—to have more control over the money. Union leaders were willing to decentralize because they did not have to make any controversial or divisive decisions and could 'sell' the strategy as moving decision-making closer to the membership.

The three observations about union 'preferences' more aptly describe union strategy as they reflect both what the union prefers as well as what is possible—a calculation of their best possible outcome within their operating environment. The final factor, one that sits at the nexus of the union's preferences and their operating environment, is the cooperative interaction orientation between employers and the OAJ. In Finland, both the union and employer started negotiations from an assumption that the outcome would be a compromise. KT had been looking for opportunities to modernize the teachers' contract—with few changes over the course of 10 years—but 'knew' that they could not restructure without money; they could not get what they wanted without giving something in return. Similarly, the OAJ assumed that in order to get what it wanted—more money for teachers' salaries—it would have to make some concessions.

To understand what happened in Finland, we must first recognize that neither the OAJ's preferences nor its power were fixed or predictable. OAJ's expression of both its interests and power hinged on the nature of the established relationship pattern between the union and KT. The established pattern of cooperation and both actors' desire to maintain it informed all calculations and negotiations.

NOTES

1. However, the teachers who entered the profession before Teacher Education Reforms in 1979 receive relatively lower salaries.
2. However, although seniority-based pay is a consistent feature of both systems, the amount of seniority-based pay was reduced in 2007. Part of the new salary system was a revision of the size of seniority-based raises, which were restructured and diminished. Employers continue to attempt to decrease the size of these raises.
3. For example, if there was a 2% total increase, 1.3% would be negotiated centrally with the remaining 0.7% left to local negotiation.
4. The OAJ hoped that this supplement would be preserved at the local level, but their negotiating success was uneven across municipalities (Local_B.President). Although first class teachers received some 'transitional money' that attempted to 'grandfather in' the changes and close the gap between their new and old salaries, the teachers who 'lost money' were angry about the change (OAJ.Negotiator.1; Local_B.President).
5. Like *tulospalkkio*, school-wide awards based on municipally determined goals, like reducing energy use.
6. These may include *tulospalkkio* (see previous footnote) or other reward schemes like gifts for special achievements or travel reimbursements or meal vouchers.
7. Whether the payment is linked to the municipality or the school/position appears to vary across municipalities.
8. The locally negotiated salary was .30% in 2007 and 2008 and .80% in 2009 and 2011 (Kunnallinen Työmarkkinalaitos, 2008, 2009, 2011).
9. AKAVA-JS (now JUKO), TNJ, TEHY, KVL, KTN, and OAJ collaborated with KT on the study (Heiskanen et al., 2001).
10. Including representatives from the state, AKAVA, STTK, and VTY.
11. These raises were over and above the TUPO raises centrally negotiated in tripartite negotiations; because these raises applied to all sectors, public employees would never catch up on TUPO raises alone (KT.Social_Scientist; OAJ.Negotiator.1; OAJ.Negotiator.2).

12. Almost every interviewee discussed the validity of TVA using either 'fairness,' 'measurability,' or 'objectivity,' and there were no dissenting views expressed.
13. Basic education will be the focus, so 'differences between groups' refer to differences within basic educators.
14. Perceptions of fairness and equity are fundamentally informed by members' interests and the union's evaluative capacity.
15. OAJ.Negotiator.2 acknowledged that there were disagreements and that sometimes it may seem that the other side reads the agreement incorrectly. The comment could not be classified as 'extended trust,' but there seemed to be an undertone of trust in spite of these differences.
16. Classification for this row is based on observed interactions rather than on interview data.
17. There were a few individuals whose responses on trust were difficult to classify. Although there was a general sentiment of trust with both Local_C.Shop_Steward and Local_A.Shop_Steward, their responses were complex. Local_A.Shop_Steward had a personal relationship of extended trust with Local_A.Employer, but described one of her challenges as needing to build teachers' trust in management and leadership in Local_A. Local_C.Shop_Steward expressed different levels of trust in his negotiating partners (higher) versus the administrative staff who oversaw education in Local C.
18. Furthermore, not all municipalities developed systems. An OAJ survey in 2008 revealed that at least 4% of surveyed municipalities had failed to develop a system (Opetusalan Ammattijärjestö, 2008). OAJ.Negotiator.2 suggested that those figures are generous and that far fewer municipalities have good systems.

REFERENCES

Heiskanen, M., Freund, H., Aarnio, A., Hotti, A., Immeli, P., Juutinen, M., . . . Väisänen, M. (2001, November 26). *Kunta-alan palkkatoselvityksen loppuraportti* [The local government sector wage settlement]. Helsinki, Finland: Kunnallinen Työmarkkinalaitos.

Holm, P., Tossavainen, P., Tuomala, J., & Valppu, P. (1999). *Työmarkkinoiden toimintaympäristön muutokset julkisen sektorin palkanmuodostuksen kannalta* [Labor market changes in the operating environment of the public sector wages]. Helsinki, Finland: VATT. Valton taloudellinen tutkimuskeskus, Government Institute for Economic Research. VATT-Keskustelualoitteita (VATT-Discussion papers No. 109). Retrieved from http://www.vatt.fi/file/vatt_publication_pdf/k209.pdf

Kouvonen, S., & Suoperä, A. (2001). *Kuntasektoria koskeva palkkaselvitys KUNPAS*. [Wage settlement for the local government sector]. Helsinki, Finland: Tilastokeskus.

Kunnallinen Työmarkkinalaitos. (2001, April 26). *Henkilöstöstrategia kehittämisen ja johtamisen välineeksi* [Staff strategy as a tool for development and management]. Yleiskirjeen 16/2001 Liite 1. Retrieved April 9, 2013 from http://www.kuntatyonantajat.fi/fi/ajankohtaista/yleiskirjeet/2001/Documents/16-01-liite.pdf

Kunnallinen Työmarkkinalaitos. (2002a, November 13). *Kunnallisen palkkausjärjestelmän kehittämistoimenpiteitä vuosina 2003-2007* [Municipal payroll development system contract]. Yleiskirjeen 1/2003 Liite 1.. Retrieved from http://www.kuntatyonantajat.fi/fi/ajankohtaista/yleiskirjeet/2003/Sivut/0103-Kunnallisen-palkkausjarjestelman-kehittamistoimenpiteita-vuosina-2003-2007.aspx

Kunnallinen Työmarkkinalaitos. (2002b). *Kunnallisen palkkausjärjestelmän kehittämistoimenpiteitä vuosina 2003-2007 koskevan sopimuksen soveltamisohjeet* [2003-2007 Application rules of the municipal salary system]. Yleiskirjeen 1/2003 Liite 2. 10 January 2003. Retrieved from http://www.kuntatyonantajat.fi/fi/ajankohtaista/yleiskirjeet/2003/Sivut/0503.aspx

Kunnallinen Työmarkkinalaitos. (2004, October 26). *Soveltamisohjeet: Joulukuun kertasuoritus* [Application (salary development agreement): December]. Yleiskirjeen 24/2004 Liite 1. Retrieved from http://www.kuntatyonantajat.fi/fi/ajankohtaista/yleiskirjeet/2004/Sivut/2404-Palkkausjarjestelman-kehittaminen-ja-sopimusmuutokset-OVTES.aspx

Kunnallinen Työmarkkinalaitos. (2008). *Paikallisten järjestelyerien käyttö kunta-alalla vuonna 2008* [Arrangement of local salary items in 2008]. Retrieved from http://www.kuntatyonantajat.fi/fi/ajankohtaista/tilastot/tiedustelut-ja-selvitykset/paikalliset-jarjestelyerat/paikallisten-jarjestelyerien-kaytto-2008/Sivut/default.aspx

Kunnallinen Työmarkkinalaitos. (2009, May 1). *Paikallisten järjestelyerin käyttö kunta-alalla* [Municipal payroll system development measures according to the locally negotiated items 1.5.2009]. Retrieved from http://www.kuntatyonantajat.fi/fi/ajankohtaista/tilastot/tiedustelut-ja-selvitykset/paikalliset-jarjestelyerat/paikallisten-jarjestelyerien-kaytto-2009/Sivut/default.aspx

Kunnallinen Työmarkkinalaitos. (2011). *Paikallisten järjestelyerän käyttö vuonna 2011* [Arrangement of local salary items in 2011](online). Retrieved from http://www.kuntatyonantajat.fi/fi/ajankohtaista/tilastot/tiedustelut-ja-selvitykset/paikalliset-jarjestelyerat/paikallisten-jarjestelyerin-kaytto-2011/Sivut/default.aspx

Opetusalan Ammattijärjestö. (2008, March 5). Syksyn 2007 paikallisten opetusalan TVA-neuvottelujen koonti. Luottamusmieskirje [Fall 2007 summary of the local negotiations on evaluating the level of difficulty: Newsletter for the shop stewards]. Liite 6.

Opetusalan Ammattijärjestö. (2012). Uudet sopimukset: lisäävät opettajan ostovoimaa [New contracts: Increasing the purchasing power of teachers].

Scharpf, F. W. (1997). *Games real actors play*. Boulder, CO: Westview Press.

Walton, R. E., & McKersie, R. B. (1965/1991). *A behavioral theory of labor negotiations* (2nd ed.). New York: McGraw Hill.

6 The Canton of Zürich
History and Context

In 1999, the Canton of Zürich implemented a new evaluation system for teachers, *Mitarbeiterbeurteilung für Schulleitende* (MAB),[1] which, in addition to providing feedback to teachers about their performance, also determined whether or not teachers were eligible to receive pay raises. Although the system was implemented in the fall of 1999, its roots can be traced back to the early 1990s and should be understood within the political and economic dynamics of the canton.

Switzerland, like Finland, experienced a recession in the 1990s, which coincided with a wave of NPM reforms that targeted public sector employment and service delivery. Reforms were implemented in 1991 that attempted to bring public sector employment conditions closer to working conditions and contractual arrangements in the private sector, including linking public sector employees' pay to their performance. However, although they technically applied to the whole public sector, the teaching profession was largely unaffected by the changes through the mid-1990s. In 1997, under the leadership of Ernst Buschor, recently elected Director of Education and intellectual architect of Switzerland's NPM movement, the Directorate of Education began developing the evaluation system that was eventually implemented in 2000.

The reforms undertaken in Zürich in the late 1990s provide an excellent complement to the Finnish case. Because of the diverse ways in which teachers' unions can be involved in decision- and policy-making processes, it is important to consider not only teachers' unions' bargaining power, but also the contingent processes through which unions convert their strength resources into political influence. In contrast to the reform of the salary system in Finland, which occurred in the bargaining arena, the reforms in the Canton of Zürich occurred almost exclusively within the political and bureaucratic domains. Although the two cases reflect important differences, the objectives are quite similar—to determine why PRP was possible in Zürich and to determine what role teachers' unions played in that process.

Like Finland, the Zürich case confirms the importance of economic and policy-making contexts: the reforms occurred immediately after a recession and were part of broader civil sector reforms. However, there are distinctions from the Finnish story: a case rooted in the union's competing preferences and collaborative relational preferences, in which teachers' unions' basic opposition to PRP was overcome by compromise. In Zürich, it seems that the teachers' unions' were eventually overpowered: they were 'strong enough' to block the reform through, but not after, 1995. This is a complex and nuanced story, yielding numerous insights.

To facilitate comparability, this case study is similarly structured to the presentation of the Finnish case. Like the Finnish case, the reforms in Switzerland must be understood within their historical context. Nation-building in Switzerland—the unification of previously independent cantons—produced many of institutional features relevant to teachers' unions' influence. This chapter introduces the historical and institutional contexts that inform the general pattern of education policy-making: federalism and subsidiarity, direct democracy, and consociationalism, as well as the character of unions in Switzerland, with particular attention to the *Zürcher Lhererinnen- und Lehrerverband* (ZLV), the largest teachers' union in the Canton of Zürich. Chapter 7 explains the reform process, outlining the MAB system and the dynamic shifts that can explain both the successful delay of implementation through 1995, and its implementation by 2000.

THE CANTON OF ZÜRICH: A BRIEF HISTORY

Switzerland—as a federation of 25[2] previously sovereign cantons[3]—was established when its federal constitution was drafted and ratified in 1848. The federation replaced the previous relationship between the 25 cantons that had been in place since 1816—a confederation of sovereign states that were party to an 'eternal treaty' of collective security by mutual assistance and that participated in the Conference of Delegates. Because delegates were bound by the instructions of their respective cantons, agreement was difficult within the conference. The creation of a common national government was highly contested among the religiously and linguistically diverse Swiss people. In addition to speaking four languages—German, French, Italian, and Romansch—the people of the 25 cantons were divided between largely rural conservative Catholics and predominantly urban radical Protestants. The small cantons whose citizens would be outnumbered in a unified Switzerland—Catholics and non-German speakers—were staunchly opposed to forfeiting their autonomy to a central governing body.

The radical Protestants, who promoted unification, only succeeded after a brief civil war, the Sonderbund War, the last of four religious wars, which began when the Catholics formed a separatist league in 1847 and after several concessions to the Catholic minority (Immergut, 1992; Linder & Vatter, 2001). According to Wolf Linder, the creation of the Swiss federation was "an institutional compromise between the conservatives (Catholics), who were hostile to centralization, and the radicals (liberals/Protestants), who favored a federal government strong enough to make the necessary decisions in the common interest" (1998, p. 39). These dynamics are more than mere context. They are the forces that shaped Switzerland's and the Canton of Zürich's structure of governance—federalism, subsidiarity, and direct democracy (Hega, 2000; Scharpf, 1988).

Early industrialization and neutrality in both world wars facilitated Switzerland's economic prosperity post-World War II. Switzerland experienced consistent growth and full employment, with less than 1% unemployment through the 1970s and 1980s, which may have relieved pressure on labor relations and contributed to the 'industrial peace' for which Switzerland has come to be known. However, the tables turned in the 1990s: GDP decreased for three consecutive years and unemployment increased from 1% in 1990 to 5% in 1994 (Mach & Oesch, 2003). In addition to reversals in GDP trends, a dramatic increase in unemployment—from 0.5% in 1990 to 4.7% in 1996—was also fuelled by tertiarization, feminization, and shifts in the relative size of the foreign labor supply (Mach & Oesch, 2003). Labor market conditions—jobs shifting from manual, unionized jobs, to the service sector—had a significant impact on the labor movement.

At the same time, the recession created new pressures for governments in the provision of public services as they faced the dawn of the age of austerity. Education budgets were not immune to these forces. Particularly germane to this research is the fact that, in the Canton of Zürich through the 1990s, teachers' salaries were frozen because the recession made it economically and politically difficult to give teachers raises. These acute fiscal pressures may have facilitated the emergence and spread of an international trend in Switzerland in the 1990s of NPM, and the MAB reforms must be understood within this context—a deep recession intensifying pressures on government sectors. It is worth reiterating what was developed in Chapter 1: that there is no unifying or consistent doctrine of NPM, but rather a diversity of strategies and reforms that share a common language or orientation but that have been mobilized by different forces and with different goals (Hernes, 2005; Reber, 2006; Schedler, 2003a, b). Switzerland's version of NPM was defined and championed by Ernst Buschor, a professor at the St. Gallen University business school and the head of the Education Directorate when MAB was implemented in public schools.

INSTITUTIONAL CONTEXT: FEDERALISM, DIRECT DEMOCRACY, AND CONSOCIATIONALISM

Due to the predominance of cantons in education policy, a canton—in this case, Zürich—rather than the country, was the appropriate unit of analysis. The Canton of Zürich, a 1,729 km² area with a population of 1,179,044, is divided into 11 administrative and judicial districts and 18 electoral districts and has 171 communities. Its capitol, Zürich, has a population of 365,042

(Vatter, 2000).[4] To reiterate what was outlined in Chapter 3, Zürich was not selected on the basis of its representativeness of Switzerland. Rather, it was selected because it was a case where 'successful reform' had been implemented. However, the particularity of the Canton of Zürich is best understood within the general institutional framework of Switzerland as a whole. Therefore, analysis of the institutional context moves from the general (Switzerland) to the specific (Zürich). Editor: The preceding 5 is also supposed to link to an endnote. Several significant institutional arrangements characterize the Swiss polity and define the general patterns of decision-making relevant to the MAB reforms, and are essential to unpacking what happened and why:

- **Federalism and Subsidiarity:** the non-centralization that creates a multilevel policy environment with shared responsibilities between federal, cantonal, and communal governments. In the case of education, responsibility lies exclusively with cantonal and communal governments.
- **Direct Democracy:** an institutional arrangement designed to protect the rights of cantons and individual citizens in Switzerland's federalist system. A series of referenda allow citizens—and organized interests—to exert significant influence on the Swiss political process.
- **Consociationalism:** the Swiss polity—due to federalism and direct democracy—is characterized by significant and sustained power sharing.

Federalism and Subsidiarity

Switzerland is, along with the United States, Canada, and Australia, a classic federation, featuring non-centralization—as opposed to decentralization—whereby a few competencies are transferred to the central government, while preserving significant autonomy and participation for its cantons (Linder & Vatter, 2001). Policy-making in Switzerland may best be described as multilevel. In some areas this means that policy is shared between federal, cantonal, and communal governments. But other policies—like education—are exclusively within the domain of cantons and communes (2001). This has been attributed to a commitment to subsidiarity, which is closely linked to the principle of federalism and the preservation of cantonal rights and authority (Hega, 2000).

As a result of constitutional non-centralization, Switzerland's education policy is among the most decentralized in the world (Hega, 2000; Linder, 1998). Federalism and subsidiarity are essential for understanding the distribution of policy-making authority in Switzerland, which determined the unit of analysis of investigation—the Canton of Zürich rather than the nation-state. The federation plays virtually no role in education policy (Hega, 2000). Thus, the reform of teachers' evaluation and compensation system in Zürich in 1999 was exclusively in the domain of the cantonal government.

Mirroring institutions at the federal level, the governance of the canton is shared between the Executive Council[5] and the legislature.[6] Each Executive Council member oversees an office of the government. One member serves as the head of the Education Directorate (*Bildungdirektiont*), which oversees primary through university education. One office of the Education Directorate, the *Volksschulamt* (VSA) is responsible for primary schools. Ultimately, municipal governing boards, working with school committees, which are elected by registered voters, implement policies developed at the cantonal level. In terms of human resources, school committees decide teacher appointments. However, cantons retain responsibility for general supervision and management—including budgeting and human resource management. A significant amount of public school finances are provided through taxes levied at the community level. In Zürich, as in the majority of German-speaking Switzerland, communal governments and citizens retain a significant amount of authority over and responsibility for the administration of public education (Hega, 2000).[7] In German-speaking Switzerland, communes typically contribute 50–80% of the funding for compulsory education; the contribution of the canton relative to the community varies as the formulas used to determine funding attempt to provide greater funding to communities with greater financial needs (Hega, 2000). Despite the important role of local community governments in the funding and provision of public education and the fact that communes are responsible for recruiting, evaluating, and retaining teachers, the formal employer of teachers in Zürich is the canton. Salary scales, conditions of employment, and the employment contract are determined at the canton level. It is worth noting that the majority of responsibility for education is divided between the canton and communes—schools have limited decision-making ability.[8]

Direct Democracy

Popular referenda—an institutional arrangement designed to protect the rights of cantons and individual citizens in Switzerland's federalist system—has been called the "linchpin of the Swiss political system" (Immergut, 1992, p. 129). Referenda exert a significant influence on the general pattern of decision-making as well as the particular character of teachers' unions. Referenda and initiatives[9] have a long history in Switzerland: they were established in communities as early as the 15th century, even before they were incorporated in the Montagnard Constitution in 1793 (Ruppen, 2004). Referenda are used at the national and cantonal level, although the institutional openness—the number of signatures required to launch a referendum or initiative and the period of time allowed to gather them—as well as the practice of direct democracy—the uses of direct democracy institutions and the voter turnout—vary across cantons (Barankay, Sciarini, & Trechsel, 2003).

Table 6.1 Instruments of direct democracy in Zürich through 1998

Direct Democracy Mechanism	Signatures	Time Limit	Effective Since
Constitutional Initiative	10,000	6 months	11 June 1969
Statutory Initiative	10,000	6 months	11 June 1969
Mandatory Statutory Referendum	All formal laws ABOLISHED		1869 1 January 1999
Optional Statutory Referendum*	5,000	60 days	1 January 1999
Mandatory Fiscal Referendum	>20 million (>2 million) ABOLISHED		6 June 1971 1 January 1999
Optional Fiscal Referendum	5,000	60 days	1 January 1999

Note: Fisher (2009)

*also introduced the extraordinary mandatory statutory referendum

In Zürich, direct democracy has an established history. However, discussing institutions of direct democracy in Zürich during the period in question (late 1980s–early 2000s) is not a straightforward task. During the period in which the MAB reforms were being finalized and implemented, Zürich changed its laws regarding instruments of direct democracy. The changes were passed in September 1998 and went into effect on New Year's Day of 1999 (Fisher, 2009). Table 6.1 outlines the instruments of direct democracy in the Canton of Zürich before and after these changes. Although the initiatives remained unchanged, both the mandatory statutory referendum and the mandatory fiscal referendum were replaced with an optional referendum.

In addition to these ordinary instruments, extraordinary measures, which allow members of parliament to launch a referendum, are also available (Fisher, 2009; Trechsel & Serdült, 1999). In Zürich, extraordinary mandatory statutory referenda were introduced in 1999 along with the shift from a mandatory (ordinary) statutory referendum to an optional (ordinary) statutory referendum. According to a recent publication by the Canton of Zürich, the votes of 45 members of parliament are required to initiate a referendum (Rintelen, Wyss, Rohrer, & Grutter, 2010).

Referenda can affect legislation both directly and indirectly. When exercised, referenda can be a stumbling block to legislation, as voters may view a policy differently from political parties or interest groups who are likely to be a part of the pre-referendum process. Furthermore, negative votes are more likely, as it is easier to mobilize opponents of a piece of legislation than proponents.[10] The threat of these direct effects also has an indirect influence on the Swiss policy-making process. Due to the tendency for negative votes in a referendum, policy-makers generally attempt to avoid referendum challenges—not wanting to see hard legislative work overturned by a small but vocal block of citizens. As Immergut (1992) argues—the most successful referenda may be those that never occur. Echoing Immergut's view, Armingeon suggests that the use of optional referenda signals a "failure of the Swiss political system to develop compromise solutions through the inclusion of a large number of political actors" (Obinger et al., 2010, p. 193).

As a result, politicians attempt to seek out potential opponents of legislation and try to win over those opponents—often interest groups—early in the policy-making process (Immergut, 1992). One result of dealing with the strategic uncertainty created by the threat of referenda has been an increase in the political influence of organized interest groups, as the Swiss political system has developed approaches to facilitating widespread consensus via compromise solutions (Obinger et al., 2010):

> armed with the membership and financial resources necessary to call for referendum challenges, Swiss interest groups have wrested a niche for themselves as 'gatekeepers' to the referendum process. As intermediaries between political elites and the public, interest groups have exploited their pivotal position in the chain of decision-making to demand extraordinary concessions during the policy process. This gatekeeper role has given a few electorally unimportant interest groups a disproportionate voice in health policy making, and, further, has placed interest groups at the centre of Swiss policy making more generally. (Immergut, 1992)

This suggests that in Switzerland, the influence of a given interest group is not necessarily correlated to its size. The critical threshold may not even be for groups to be large enough to determine the electoral outcome of a referendum, but simply large enough to launch it. Referenda and initiatives may provide a direct avenue for interest group participation and influence, an important consideration regarding the power of teachers' unions in the Canton of Zürich, discussed below. However, direct democracy also exerts an indirect influence on Switzerland's policy style, as politicians are incentivized to develop broad coalitions through extensive consultation and collaboration in an effort to avoid a referendum challenge. This consensus orientation, or what has been called Swiss *konkordanz*, may provide a variety of informal opportunities for interest groups to be involved in, and exert influence upon, decision- and policy-making processes.

Consociationalism, Consensus Orientation, and *Konkordanz*: Approaches to Generating Agreement

The formal institutional features of federalism, subsidiarity, and direct democracy are fundamentally linked to the consensus orientation of the

Swiss political system, another constitutive element of the Swiss polity. Switzerland has been identified as one of Katzenstein's (1985) small corporatist states and Lijphart's (1969) consociational democracies. Based on Lijphart's (1975) study of the Netherlands, the findings of which were elaborated in later work, consociationalism is a broad category whose essential characteristic is a "deliberate joint effort by the elites to stabilize the system" (Lijphart, 2008, p. 29). Swiss consociationalism significantly informs both the general patterns for policy-making, the relevant set of actors involved in reform processes, and the particular character of teachers' unions.

In the Swiss case, many have argued that consensus-seeking orientations and processes are a by-product of direct democracy (Aubert, 1989; Immergut, 1992;[11] Ladner & Brändle, 1999; Wagner, Santiago, Thieme, & Zay, 2004). Although direct democracy represents a formal decision point, or what Immergut (1992) would call a veto point, it is also a process (Frey, 1994; Tsebelis, 2002). In addition to the pre-referendum and post-referendum discussion stages, consensus-oriented processes are also facilitated and incentivized as politicians attempt to avoid a referendum, as discussed in the previous section (Frey, 1994). Ladner and Brändle argue that:

> In a direct democratic system the possibility of blocking any decision by questioning the government's proposals through a referendum makes thorough negotiation between the various interests involved absolutely necessary. It is basically the threat of a referendum that can endanger a carefully arranged compromise after its deliberation in parliament that has fundamentally changed Swiss democracy from a true plebiscitarian democracy *to one characterised by negotiation*. (1999, p. 85, emphasis added)

A consensus orientation can certainly be seen in the design of Swiss political institutions—perhaps most notably in the 'magic formula'[12] that has persisted in both the Canton of Zürich and at the federal level. The permanent institutionalization of a broad-governing coalition creates significant incentive for consensus-based politics and power sharing. However, the groups who are privileged or have the most significant role in the extensive consultation process prompted by the threat of referenda are not the political parties, but the interest groups (Beyme, 1982, p. 228, as cited in Ladner & Brändle, 1999).

The importance of consultation extends across policy-making arenas, including education policy (Wagner et al., 2004). Wagner and colleagues suggest that the widespread consultation used in Switzerland is a direct result of direct democracy, arguing that the threat of referenda encourages public authorities "at all levels to consult widely so as to arrive at decisions that enlist near-consensus support" (2004, p. 26). Thus, unions have at least two avenues to participation in Zürich: formal and informal consultation and using referenda to either initiate or challenge policy.

ZÜRICH TEACHERS' UNIONS

How do these institutional arrangements facilitate or constrain teachers' unions' involvement or influence on the education policy-making process in the Canton of Zürich? What role did teachers' unions play in the implementation of the MAB system? Understanding the position of teachers' organizations in the political landscape—their organizational resources and professional power—is essential. However, a proper understanding of the position of teachers' organizations is best established within the larger context of the history and development of labor relations in Switzerland.

The Trade Union Movement in Switzerland

Swiss labor relations have received limited scholarly attention (Mach & Oesch, 2003). Perhaps this is because through the 1980s, if Swiss industrial relations were referenced, the focus was usually on Switzerland's status as a 'country without strikes,' achieved through its peace obligations (Aubert, 1989). However, it is important to develop a richer picture of the contemporary role and historical development of Switzerland's trade union movement.

Although, with the magic formula of the Federal Executive Council and through proportional representation in the legislature, Christian and Social Democrats gained a seat at the table, historically, Switzerland's politics have been characterized by right-party dominance and relatively weak trade unions (Obinger et al., 2010). Despite the long history of collective agreements as well as the growth of collective agreements after World War II, the strength of unions as indicated by traditional measures like union density is low in a comparative context (Aubert, 1989). In Switzerland, union membership is less than one third of the workforce in any industry; overall, in 2009, 21.3% of the workforce belonged to a union (Ackermann & Moser-Brossy, 2009). Although the trends for the biggest unions—the SGB, FÖV, and VSA[13]—mirror the global secular decline in union membership, membership for teachers and other public sector employees has grown or held steady (Mach & Oesch, 2003).

The process of industrialization did not benefit the labor movement for three primary reasons: there was a lack of urban concentration in Switzerland; unlike the Nordic countries, unions failed to win 'peasants' as allies; and because diversity of religion and language amongst citizens as well as the division between citizens and immigrants inhibited working class solidarity (Oesch, 2011). Thus, unions remained relatively weak, and federally, it seems that cantonal interests and cultural solidarity among minority populations have always exerted a stronger influence at the national level than class action. Linder (1998) argues that the dominance of cultural segmentation rather than class solidarity hampered the development of left political coalitions.

In Switzerland, the union movement generally, as well as teachers' unions in particular, is fragmented, with confessional divisions as well as manual and non-manual divisions. Umbrella organizations—like the SGB (*Schweizerischer Gewerkschaftsbund*) in the private sector, which primarily organizes manual workers, and the LCH (*Dachverband Schweizer Lehrerinnen und Lehrer*), which organizes German-speaking teachers—can make recommendations but cannot enforce these recommendations upon their member organizations (Flückiger, 1998). Despite more frequent industrial disputes in 1945–1947, Swiss unions are not particularly militant. Perhaps because of the weakness of the political left, as early as the 1930s, the trade union movement saw strikes as not the best means of obtaining concessions (Aubert, 1989). Furthermore, the political environment—which encourages consensus and provides unions and other interest groups with opportunities to be involved in political decision-making—as well as cultural values may discourage strikes; a survey conducted in 1972 indicated that the public condemns all violent action and is ambivalent about demonstrations (Sidjanski, 1974).

Unions in Switzerland have been described as "subordinate partners in decentralized and consensual industrial relations" (Oesch, 2010, p. 2). Although unions benefited from economic growth, which fuelled the wage increases and labor market expansion that added to their memberships through the 1980s, employers took a more aggressive stance in the 1990s (Oesch, 2011). If the decision-making domain for this case were the bargaining arena, there would be real questions as to whether Swiss unions could be considered powerful. For example, although teachers' unions in Zürich participate in consultation over wages, the final decision rests in the hands of the government and is ultimately a political question linked to larger budgetary questions. Although wage systems are the responsibility of the Education Directorate (Regierungsrates des Kantons Zürich, 1997), it has limited influence on the amount of money available for teachers' compensation—that decision is made by the Finance Department, under the constraints of political decisions in parliament about tax levels (Bertschi; Wendelspiess; ZLV.Leader).

Although LCH.Leader said that unions 'bargain' with the government about wages, it seems that 'consultation' might be a more apt label. According to ZLV.President, "You have the *bildungsdirektion* and the financial department. . . . They don't negotiate with us. They tell us 'you get this, this, and this.' They tell us one day before they go to the media." However, the response of organized labor to their disadvantaged position in bargaining has been to shift their attention to political influence:

> Unions' position in corporatist policy-making is to some extent secured by Switzerland's direct democratic institutions: by enabling large interest groups to call a referendum on laws they oppose, they give unions a semblance of veto power. (Oesch 2010, p. 5)

Therefore, the focus on unions' strength in Switzerland—and the strength of teachers' unions in Zürich in particular—is on their political influence, as it is the relevant decision-making domain in this case, as well as the primary avenue for union influence in general.

Teachers' Unionism in Switzerland: The ZLV

In light of the broader dynamics of industrial relations in Switzerland, two key dimensions must be considered regarding teachers' unions' strength resources and potential influence. First, one must consider the ways in which teachers, as professionals, may have unique opportunities for influence relative to other organized occupations. Second, it is important to consider the size of teachers' unions' membership and other organizational resources in Zürich in terms of their potential power as an interest group. Although teachers' organizations in Zürich are professionally weaker than teachers in Finland, they are 'strong enough' organizationally.

The Professionalization of Teachers in Switzerland and Zürich

As was the case throughout Switzerland and Europe, the forerunner to state provided and administered public education in the Canton of Zürich was church provided education (Tröhler, 2011). However, the marked shift away from a church-centric model for the provision of education began in 1830 when 10,000 men in the city of Zürich demanded a new constitution, which was established in 1831, and established education as the responsibility of the state (Tröhler, 2011). The new system established a state Education Council who was responsible for overseeing education throughout the canton. The Education Council mandated the establishment of lay school boards (*schulpflege*) in each district or commune, providing an opportunity for civic representation,[14] a tradition still reflected in the contemporary organization and governance of schooling in the Canton of Zürich (Tröhler, 2011). Alongside school boards, throughout the 19th century, school synods—bodies that were primarily composed of teachers and that, in the absence of principals, which were not introduced in Zürich until the 21st century, provided self-governance in the school arena—were active in advocating for changes in schooling and the development of the teaching profession (Tröhler, 2011).

Although up to this point the development of the teaching profession in Switzerland mirrors the history of the profession in Finland, the paths parted ways in the 1970s. In Finland, teacher education was reformed in the 1970s, moving all teacher training to the university and elevating the training and credentials of all teachers. In contrast, in Switzerland, although gymnasium[15] teachers were university trained, primary teachers were still educated at the upper secondary schools until the Teacher Education Act was passed in 1999 (Schneebeli, 1998). Although there have been many recent developments regarding teachers' professional training, these are quite late developments and reflect a lower level, in contrast to Finland, of professional attainment and prestige for the teaching profession as a whole. Because of its absence from the academy, this also means that, according to LCH.Leader, the science of teaching is less well developed in Switzerland, complicating unions' efforts to organize teachers around a common professional ideal.

According to measures of professionalism that are linked to training and credentials, teachers in Switzerland lag behind some of their international peers. This may be significant for understanding the lack of consensus around professional ideals or goals reflected in the views of union leaders, which will be discussed in Chapter 7. However, the late development of university training should not be viewed as an unequivocal sign of low professional standing for teachers in Zürich. Bertschi, designer of the MAB system, explains that public education is important and highly regarded—it is the foundation of Zürich's success—and that teachers are similarly respected—ranked among priests and doctors.

Teachers' Union Organization
In terms of union size and density, nationally, two thirds of Switzerland's 100,000 teachers are members of a union, represented by three independent unions (Wagner et al., 2004). The largest of these is the Association of Swiss Teachers (LCH/ECH), which represents 50,000 teachers across its 20 cantonal organizations; the Swiss public-service union (the *Schweizerischer Verband des Personals öffentleher Dienste/Syndicat Suisse du personnel public*, VPOD/SSP) represents 4,400 teacher members among its ranks, which also include other public service personnel in health, transport, social services, and other industries; and the *Syndicat des Enseignants Romands* (SER) is the regional union in French-speaking Switzerland and represents 10,000 members (Wagner et al., 2004).

The particularities of teachers' unions in Switzerland differ from the broader labor movement in a few important respects. First, although Swiss unions experienced a decline in membership through the 1990s, membership in teachers' organizations and other public sector or 'professional' organizations has held relatively steady (Ackermann & Moser-Brossy, 2009). This is an important reminder that the strength of teachers' organizations can diverge from general trends in a country's labor movement. Second, although linguistic and confessional divisions significantly weaken the national union movement, the impact on teachers' unions is less significant. Because education is almost exclusively within the cantonal domain, linguistic divisions are largely irrelevant; for example, in Zürich, SER has no presence. However, even at the cantonal level, the union movement is fragmented: through 1999, there were two unions in Zürich—the *Zürcher Lhererinnen- und Lehrerverband* (ZLV) and VPOD, which was described as 'left-leaning' and is a broader traditional union that also has some teacher members (Zürich.Union_Leader). However, the ZLV, an affiliate of the

LCH, is the largest teachers' union in Zürich by far—representing between 4,000–5,000 teachers in 1998 ("Eine starke stimme," 1998).

Although through 1999 there were only two teachers' unions in Zürich, tensions developed within the ZLV in the late 1990s and two sub-organizations within the ZLV who represented secondary teachers—OKRZ and SKZ—split from the ZLV in 1999 and formed SekZH (Schneebeli, 2000). The significance of this split is discussed in greater detail in Chapter 7. Because both the VPOD and SekZH organize a relatively small percentage of teachers—relative to the total number of teachers as well as the representation of ZLV—and the SekZH was still a member of the ZLV throughout the majority of the reform process, the ZLV and its actions and influence were the primary focus of investigation.[16] They were the teachers' organization that was the strongest in terms of organizational resources and was therefore best positioned to influence the reform process. VPOD and SekZH were not excluded; they simply were not *central* to the analysis. Therefore, analysis of unions' organizational resources focuses primarily on the ZLV and its umbrella organization, the LCH,[17] as it was the only organization that appeared to have enough members to potentially leverage successful influence on its own.

CONCLUSION: THE ZLV IN CONTEXT

Relative to union density in the Nordic regions, unionization levels confirm the historic weakness of unions in Switzerland. However, this relative weakness—as measured by union density—should not be construed as an absence of union power per se. As a result of the process of direct democracy in Switzerland, any group that is large enough to mount a referendum can gain influence in Swiss politics—a system that is very open to influence by pressure groups (Katzenstein, 1985; Linder & Vatter, 2001). And despite the historic weakness of left parties and labor unions in Switzerland, they did successfully block a number of pieces of legislation through referenda in the 1990s (Oesch, 2011). So the historical numeric weakness of organized labor must be balanced against the unique political and institutional structures—direct democracy and power sharing—that may provide them with influence at times. The key questions regarding the role of teachers' unions in reform processes in Zürich are: When it comes to the political influence of teachers' organizations, at *what times* do they have influence? Why are they able (or not) to exert influence?

The answer to these questions, based on the general pattern of policy-making and its implications for the relevant actors as well as the character of teachers' unions outlined in the previous sections, seems to be that the unions' influence on policy is likely to be indirect. Their success is linked to their ability to present a credible referendum threat and to successfully apply pressure through informal consultation, as "the most important criteria ... to be heard in the pre-parliamentary procedure is the capacity to mount a successful referendum challenge" (Linder & Vatter, 2001, p. 103).

To a large extent, the ability to successfully challenge legislation through a referendum is a numbers game, depending on an organization's ability to unify and mobilize its membership around a given position. Even under the slightly less accessible instruments of direct democracy which came into effect in 1999—requiring 5,000 votes for an optional statutory referendum or 45 parliamentary votes for an extraordinary statutory referendum instead of a mandatory statutory referendum—the ZLV appears to have the "capacity to mount a successful referendum challenge" (Linder & Vatter, 2001, p. 103). The ZLV had approximately 5,000 members in 1998, and according to Bertschi and ZLV.President, over 30 members of parliament were teachers or retired teachers and were considered amenable to 'teachers' interests'—putting the ZLV very close to the threshold of 45 members.

This chapter has outlined why the ZLV *could* have influenced reforms. The ability—or inability—of the union to leverage this influence to effect or alter the reform path is the subject of the analysis of reforms in Chapter 7.

NOTES

1. Previously called the *Qualifikationssystem fuer Volksschullehrer* (LQS). For simplicity, MAB will be used throughout.
2. Now 26.
3. Or half-cantons.
4. Although Zürich can refer to both a canton and a city, in this book, Zürich will refer to the canton unless otherwise specified.
5. The Federal Council is a seven-member executive committee elected by the Federal Assembly. Since 1959, the composition of the Federal Council has been governed by an unspoken rule called the 'magic formula' (Linder, 1998).
6. The only notable difference is that the legislature, the Cantonal Council of Zürich, is unicameral; its 180 seats are elected every four years.
7. I.e., different 'tracks' of education. Although gymnasium is also 'public,' this will focus on compulsory education—1–9 or what is sometimes referred to as 'popular' education. Although much of what is discussed will also be applicable with post-secondary education, there are some differences and specificities.
8. Schools are unable to determine their own curriculum or the breakdown of lessons and subjects, they have limited influence over teacher recruitment or assessment, and they have limited control over budgets.
9. While a popular referendum allows citizens to vote on proposed constitutional amendments, laws, or fiscal issues, popular initiatives allow citizens to submit laws or amendments for consideration.
10. "The propensity of issue-specific referendum votes to be negative can be explained by the problems of collective action. Voters will participate more actively in referenda to the extent that they feel directly affected by the proposed legislation and to the extent that they feel that their individual vote will actually make a difference to the outcome. Because voters respond more strongly to perceived costs than to perceived benefits, those who view the legislation as a cost are more likely to vote than those who view it as a benefit.

148   *International Cases*

    Further, members of smaller groups with relatively homogeneous interests are more likely to evaluate proposed legislation in similar ways and to feel that their individual votes are significant than are members of larger, more diverse groups" (Immergut, 1992, p. 134).

11. "Swiss politicians work hard to prepare legislation that will not be subject to a referendum challenge. To achieve this end, they seek outsources of potential opposition to legislation and try to placate those opponents early on. As the general public has no mechanism for making its wishes entirely clear—the referendum votes are after all limited to 'yes' or 'no' votes—politicians question interest groups closely" (Immergut, 1992, p. 135).
12. In 1959, the seven seats of the executive council were divided between the Free Democratic Party or Liberals (2 seats), the Christian Democratic People's Party (2 seats), the Social Democratic Party (2 seats), and what is now the Swiss People's party (1 seat). In 2003, the formula was modified. The Christian Democrats now only have one seat and the Swiss People's party has two seats.
13. This is the only time when 'VSA' will be used to refer to the union rather than the education department. There are two main trade unions in Switzerland—the Swiss Federation of Trade Unions (SGB) and the Travail Suisse. The Swiss Federation of Trade Unions is historically the socialist/secular union and in 2008 possessed 372,000 members among its 15 umbrella organizations—including its largest, UNIA, which represents 50% of the SGB's membership (Ackermann & Moser-Brossy, 2009). Travail Suisse, formed by the merger of a protestant and Catholic union, is smaller—representing 163,000 members (Ackermann & Moser-Brossy, 2009). There are 213,000 employees represented by independent unions, bringing the total of unionized employees to 748,000 in 2010 (Ackermann & Moser-Brossy, 2009).
14. In rural communes the other six members of school boards were elected; in the city two members were appointed by the church, two by teachers, and three by the public (Tröhler, 2011).
15. Academic secondary school.
16. The views of leaders of the SekZH and VPOD were also gathered.
17. The LCH, as the umbrella organization, supports cantonal organization in achieving goals of professional advancement and improved working conditions.

REFERENCES

Ackermann, E., & Moser-Brossy, D. (2009). Zur mitgliederentwicklung der gewerkschaften im Jahr 2008. [Trade union membership development in 2008]. *SGB*. Retrieved from Schweizerischer Gewerkschaftsbund http://www.sgb.ch/themen/gewerkschaftspolitik/artikel/details/zur-mitgliederentwicklung-der-gewerkschaften-im-jahr-2008/

Aubert, G. (1989). Collective agreements and industrial peace in Switzerland. *International Labour Review, 128*(3), 373–388.

Barankay, I., Sciarini, P., & Trechsel, A. H. (2003). Institutional openness and the use of referendums and popular initiatives: Evidence from Swiss cantons. *Swiss Political Science Review, 9*(1), 169–199.

Eine Starke Stimme [A strong voice]. (1998, October 9). *Tages-Anzeiger*. Retrieved from Nexis UK.

Fisher, J. (2009). *Development of direct democracy in Swiss Cantons between 1997 and 2003* (Working paper No. 16140). Retrieved from Munich Personal RePEc Archive http://mpra.ub.uni-muenchen.de/16140/

Flückiger, Y. (1998). The labour market in Switzerland: The end of a special case? *International Journal of Manpower, 19*(6), 369-405.

Frey, B. S. (1994). Direct democracy: Politico-economic lessons from Swiss Experience. *The American Economic Review, 84*(2), 338–342.

Hega, G. M. (2000). Federalism, subsidiarity, and education policy in Switzerland. *Regional & Federal Studies, 10*(1), 1–35.

Hernes, T. (2005). Four ideal-type organizational responses to New Public Management reforms and some consequences. *International Review of Administrative Sciences, 71*(1), 5–17.

Immergut, E. (1992). *Health politics*. Cambridge: Cambridge University Press.

Katzenstein, P. J. (1985). *Small states in world markets: Industrial policy in Europe*. Ithaca, NY: Cornell University Press.

Ladner, A., & Brändle, M. (1999). Does direct democracy matter for political parties? An empirical test in the Swiss cantons. *Party Politics, 5*(3), 283–302.

Lijphart, A. (1969). Consociational democracy. *World Politics, 21*(2), 207–223.

Lijphart, A. (1975). *The politics of accommodation: Pluralism and democracy in the Netherlands*. Berkeley: University of California Press.

Lijphart, A. (2008). *Thinking about democracy: Power sharing and majority rule in theory and practice*. London: Routledge.

Linder, W. (1998). *Swiss democracy: Possible solutions to conflict in multicultural societies* (2nd ed.). Basingstoke: Macmillan.

Linder, W., & Vatter, A. (2001). Institutions and outcomes of Swiss federalism: The role of the cantons in Swiss politics. *West European Politics, 24*(1), 95–122.

Mach, A., & Oesch, D. (2003). Collective bargaining between decentralization and stability: A sectoral model explaining the Swiss experience during the 1990s. *Industrielle Beziehungen, 10*(1), 160–182.

Obinger, H., Starke, P., Moser, J., Bogedan, C., Obinger-Gindulis, E., & Leibfried, S. (2010). *Transformations of the welfare state: Small states, big lessons*. Oxford: Oxford University Press.

Oesch, D. (2011). Swiss trade unions and industrial relations after 1990: A history of decline and renewal. In C. Trampusch & A. Mach (Eds.), *Switzerland in Europe*. New York: Routledge, 82–102.

Reber, K. (2006, December). *The diffusion of public sector reforms: Empirical evidence from Switzerland on New Public Management*. Paper presented at Hong Kong Economic Association Conference, Hong Kong.

Regierungsrates des Kantons Zürich. (1997, September 3). *1900. Motion: leistungsorientierte Beurteilung der Lehrkräfte der Volksschule* [Performance-oriented evaluation of teachers in primary schools]. KR-Nr. 249/1997.

Rintelen, C., Wyss, T., Rohrer, G., & Grutter, H. (2010). *Canton of Zürich. Zürich, State Chancellery and Economic Development Department (Office for Economy and Labour) on behalf of the Government Council of the Canton of Zürich*.

Ruppen, P. (2004). Switzerland. In B. Kaufmann & M. D. Waters (Eds.), *Direct democracy in Europe: A comprehensive reference guide to the initiative and referendum process in Europe*. Durham: Carolina Academic Press, 118–122.

Scharpf, F. (1988). The joint decision trap: Lessons from German federalism and European integration. *Public Administration, 66*, 239–278.

Schedler, K. (2003a). '. . . And politics?': Public management developments in the light of two rationalities. *Public Management Review, 5*(4), 533–560.

Schedler, K. (2003b). Local and regional public management reforms in Switzerland. *Public Administration, 81*(2), 325–344.

Schneebeli, D. (1998, June 12). Lehrer sind keine mehr erwuenscht [Teachers no longer welcome]. *Tages-Anzeiger*. Retrieved from Nexis database.

Schneebeli, D. (2000, January 20). Eclat unter den lehrern [Argument amongst teachers]. *Tages-Anzeiger*. Retrieved from Nexis database.

Sidjanski, D. (1974). Interest groups in Switzerland. *Annals of the American Academy of Political and Social Science, 413*(1), 101–123.

Trechsel, A. H., & Serdült, S. (1999). *Kaleidoskop Volksrechte: Die Institutionen der direkten Demokratie in den schweizerischen Kantonen 1970-1996*. Basel, Switzerland: Helbing & Lichtenhahn.

Tröhler, D. (2011). Classical republicanism, local democracy, and education: The emergence of the public school of the Republic of Zürich, 1770–1870. In D. Tröhler, T. S. Popkewitz, & D. F. Labaree (Eds.), *Schooling and the making of citizens in the long 19th century: Comparative visions*. New York: Routledge, 153–176.

Tsebelis, G. (2002). *Veto players: How political institutons work*. Princeton, NJ: Princeton University Press.

Vatter, A. (2000). Consensus and direct democracy: Conceptual and empirical linkages. *European Journal of Political Research, 38*(2), 171–192.

Wagner, A., Santiago, P., Thieme, C., & Zay, D. (2004). *Country note: Switzerland*. Retrieved from OECD, Education and Training Policy Division http://www.oecd.org/switzerland/33684152.pdf

7 Eventually Overcoming Resistance
The MAB System

In 1999, the new salary system for teachers (MAB) was implemented in Zürich. It was developed in 1996 and 1997 and approved, with some changes and adjustments, after going through a formal consultation process from 1997–1998. However, the process started much earlier, in the late 1980s. Like Chapter 5, this chapter will explore three questions:

1. What was the MAB and was it a significant change?
2. How or why did the change occur?
3. What was the role of the ZLV in this process?

The story in Zürich was one in which performance evaluation—and consequences for salaries—was *eventually* implemented despite the opposition of teachers (Legler, Sigrist, & Wehner, 2008). Unpacking what happened in the development of the MAB system is complex, as each of several factors provides a partial account of its development. But before attempting to explain the reform process, the major features of the MAB system must be introduced.

THE MAB SYSTEM

Although communities in Zürich bear significant financial responsibility for financing schools, funds to compensate teachers are provided at the canton level. This system helps to ensure that all teachers across the canton receive equitable compensation regardless of whether they teach in a more or less affluent community. The canton also regulates the number of teachers that a school can employ per student population, although the formula is adjusted for student characteristics, such as students with special needs and language learners (Wendelspiess). As outlined above, prior to the implementation of MAB, teachers were compensated based on a standard salary schedule that was linked to their type of school—elementary, lower-secondary, or upper-secondary—and years of experience. However, the ability of teachers to progress through the salary scale was dependent on adequate funds being available at the cantonal level. If there were not adequate revenues to provide salary increases for teachers, salaries were frozen, as occurred in the mid-1990s (Bertschi; Buschor; Schneebeli, 1999b; Wendelspiess).

Rather than automatic step increases, MAB provided a new way to determine which teachers were eligible for raises. Originally, the evaluation was based on up to four components: a report based on observations of lessons (*Beobachtengsbericht*), an interview (*Erkundengsbericht*), a written document from teachers (*Dossier*[1]), and a self-declaration or self-evaluation (*selbst-beurteilung*). After the evaluators observed lessons and conducted their interview, there was an integration meeting (*integrationssitzung*) where the individual evaluators attempted to reach an agreement about what score a teacher should receive. There are four classifications in the MAB:[2] a score of IV is deemed unsatisfactory and could result in a teacher being terminated,[3] a score of III results in some intervention—training and coaching—in the areas deemed in need of improvement, II is a 'good' score and theoretically qualifies early-to-mid-year career teachers for raises,[4] and I is the highest score, required for late-career teachers to reach the maximum salary.

Each year, the canton establishes a quota for promotions and guidelines for determining which teachers are eligible for promotions given an adequate MAB score. For example 3% of the total salary is allocated for promotions and is allocated for teachers with one to four years' experience; then the communities allocate the promotions according to the MAB results. In order to attempt to address the way that the salary freeze of the 1990s had disproportionately affected younger teachers,[5] the MAB was introduced with a sliding scale in terms of earning raises: beginning teachers only needed to be ranked as 'sufficient' (III) to earn a raise, while teachers at steps 4–18 needed to score 'good' (II), and teachers at steps 18+ had to be 'very good' (I).[6]

The debates and tensions regarding MAB that played out over the course of a decade reflect competing visions about the role of the MAB system in both compensation and quality management. Although there is a perception among some teachers and their unions that the MAB is exclusively about compensation, according to the designers of the system, the MAB—as part of a broader Total Quality Management (TQM) framework—is also about monitoring and ensuring quality in schools; it is a framework with individual, school, and system-wide applications that is based on both internal and external evaluations. According to Bertschi, one of the system's designers and a member of parliament, "If we have [a public education system] that costs some billion every year and we want to have a look at how it works, then we have to see the teacher" because he or she is one of the most important influences on student achievement. Bertschi argued that the MAB:

> is a good basis to communicate, to discuss . . . critical points. Because that is one of the problems one never speaks about—'we are only here

to be [good] to the teachers.' No. We have to be [good] to the children as well. If a teacher is not apt for his profession, and he has 20 classes over his life—it's not good . . . we wanted, really, every teacher [to think] from time to time about what he is doing and learn to accept a view from outside.

The MAB system was designed to balance summative assessment and formative development. The assessment function occurs every four years,[7] but should be supplemented by an annual formative evaluation conducted internally (Bildungsdirektion Kanton Zürich, 2011a). Thus, the administration argued that the salary element is only *one* component of the evaluation; the broader emphasis is on personal development and feedback (Regierungsrates des Kantons des Zürich, 2001).

HOW DID MAB REFORM OCCUR?

From the beginning, teachers and their unions voiced significant concerns about the MAB system. In addition to fundamental questions about the nature of evaluating teachers' work—what does effectiveness mean and can it be measured?—and resistance to tying teachers' salaries to evaluations, there were a number of more specific design-related disagreements related to: the role of lay evaluators, the workload, and the number of classifications and their consequences for teachers. How was the system eventually implemented over teachers' and their union's opposition? The answer to that question is not one thing but many. Although this system was implemented in 1999, the story of the MAB system begins earlier—before the development of the system was initiated in 1996, and before Ernst Buschor became the Education Director in 1995. The story of what happened stretches over a decade and sits at the nexus of a variety of factors and events linked to the precedent of past legislation, economic conditions, and shifting political debates. As will become clear, each of these factors *alone* cannot explain the reform process. But, taken together, they tell a compelling story of why reform was resisted for a decade and how that resistance was eventually overcome.

Explanation #1: Delayed Realization of a Legal Mandate

One factor that clearly emerged from all interviewees was the significance of prior legislative action in the eventual development and implementation of the MAB system. Figure 7.1 provides a provisional timeline of key reform events structured around the assumption that the key driver of the MAB reforms from 1996–1999 was the realization of the legal mandate established by SBR 1987/91. Although it provides an incomplete account of the reform process, the role of this legislation is an essential component of what happened in Zürich. SBR 1987/1991 (Figure 7.1, 1b), came into effect in 1991,[8] overhauling civil service salary regulations and incorporating a salary plan that was based on individual salaries linked to a "results-based advancement and promotion concept" (Regierungsrates Des Kantons Zürich, 1996a, n.p.):

> A central element of the new salary scheme is performance-related pay, which is linked to the compulsory performance evaluation. It dictates that officials and employees must have certain qualifications and that they must go through a systematic performance evaluation before they can earn a higher salary or be eligible for promotion to the next salary level. (Regierungsrates Des Kantons Zürich, 1996a, n.p.)

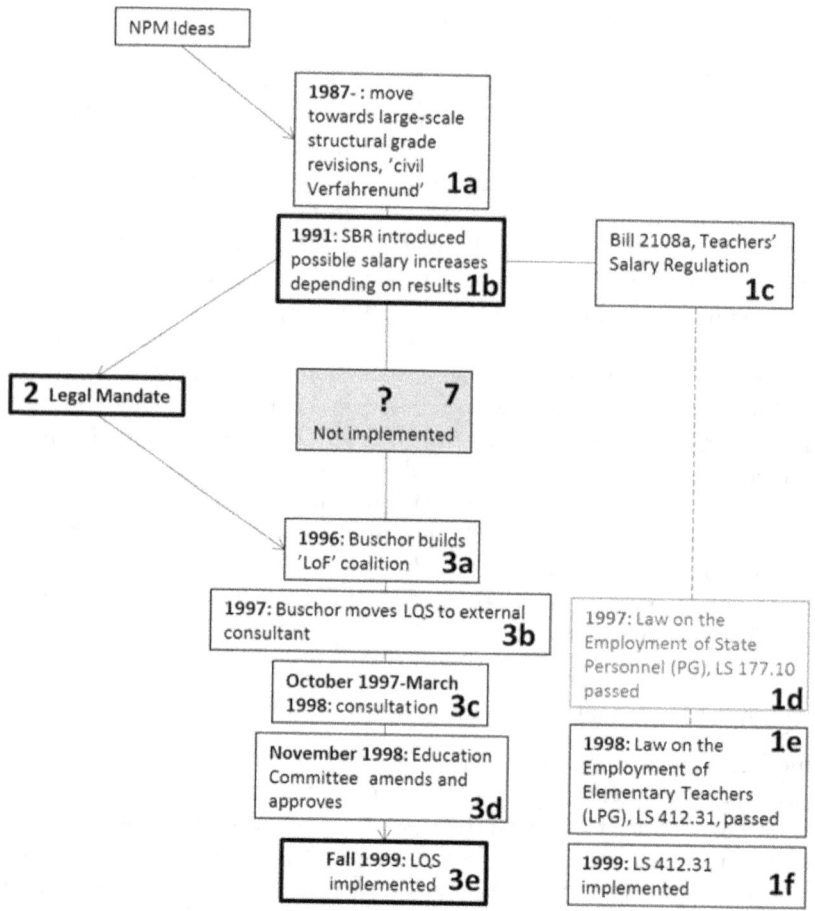

Figure 7.1 Timeline 1: Delayed realization of a legal mandate

Ultimately, SBR 1987/1991—which included a teacher salary regulation (Bill 2108a, 1Regierungsrates Des Kantons Zürich, 1996a)—is the legislation that provided the legal authority and legitimacy (**2**) for the design of the MAB system from 1996 to 1998 (**3a-d**) which was implemented in 1999 (**3e**) (Bertschi; Buschor; Wendelspiess; LCH.Union_Leader). The Personnel Law (**1d**, *Personalgesetz* § 177.10) and related Teacher Personnel Law (**1e**, *Lehrerpersonalgesetz* § 412.31), which were passed in 1997 and 1998, further elaborated the prescriptions of SBR 1987/1991. Specifically, these laws established the right of all government employees, including teachers, to have a regular performance evaluation (Bildungsdirektion Kanton Zürich, n.d.).

However, this account raises an important question: if the legal mandate was created by the legislation in 1991, why was there an eight-year lag between the passage of the legislation and the implementation of the system (**7**)? Although many retrospectively identified SBR 1987/1991 as providing the legal mandate for reforms (Bertschi; Buschor; Wendelspiess; LCH. Union_Leader), the implications of the legislation for teachers were contested and unresolved throughout the mid-1990s. Although it was stated that Bill 2108a (**1c**) allowed the "individualization of teachers' pay based on performance to *a certain extent*" (Regierungsrates Des Kantons Zürich, 1997a, emphasis added), according to a report from the Governing Council in 1996:

> This system [of compulsory performance-evaluation and promotion, used throughout the civil sector] is also set to be widened through the special legislation, to cover teachers in primary schools, middle schools and vocational schools, although this has so far yet to be implemented. (Regierungsrates Des Kantons Zürich, 1996a)

The reference to "special legislation" appears to refer to the Law on the Employment of Elementary Teachers (LPG)[9] which was approved in 1998 (**1e**) and implemented in 1999 (**1f**). It affirms the role of assessment and evaluation (Bildungsdirektion Kanton Zürich Volksschulamt, 2009), gives the Education Directorate responsibility for MAB, and outlines the MAB guidelines, including the consequences of a 'very poor' evaluation (Bildungsdirektion Kanton Zürich Volksschulamt, 2009). Thus, despite the retrospective assessment that SBR 1987/1991 provided the legal mandate for action, its application to the education sector was not a foregone conclusion in 1996. Something shifted or changed in the mid-1990s in order to make the legal mandate a reality. Although 'MAB reforms as fulfillment of the legal demands of SBR' is part of the story of the reforms, as it was a significant component of the administration's argument for and defense of the reforms, it is an incomplete explanation of what happened. It does not explain why the legislation was applied almost immediately throughout the civil sector, but delayed in the education sector. In order to understand the implementation timing in the education sector, other explanations must be considered.

Explanation #2: Implementation Delayed by Economic Factors

Although the significance of the legislative mandate provided by SBR 1987/91 is a critical part of the story, it only provides a partial explanation, leaving many questions unanswered. Changing economic conditions provide one hypothesis to explain the timing of MAB's development and implementation as well as an the period of delay. Figure 7.2 builds on Figure 7.1, adding key economic developments to the importance of the legal mandate.

In the late 1980s, the government recognized the importance of keeping public sector employment competitive with the private sector and perceived that, in the context of the economic boom of the 1980s (Figure 7.2, **4a**), the civil sector lacked 'competitive leverage' (Regierungsrates Des Kantons Zürich, 1996a). Rather than an effort to cut back civil sector pay or employment, SBR 1987/1991 was a response to the demands of occupational groups demanding higher salaries, under the justification of inter-sectoral competitiveness (Regierungsrates Des Kantons Zürich, 1996a).

However, the conditions of growth upon which SBR 1987/1991 was based reversed in the following decade (**4b**) and prevented the promised wage improvements from being realized (Buschor). In light of the recession, parliament passed Bill 3263 in 1992, which gave the Governing Council

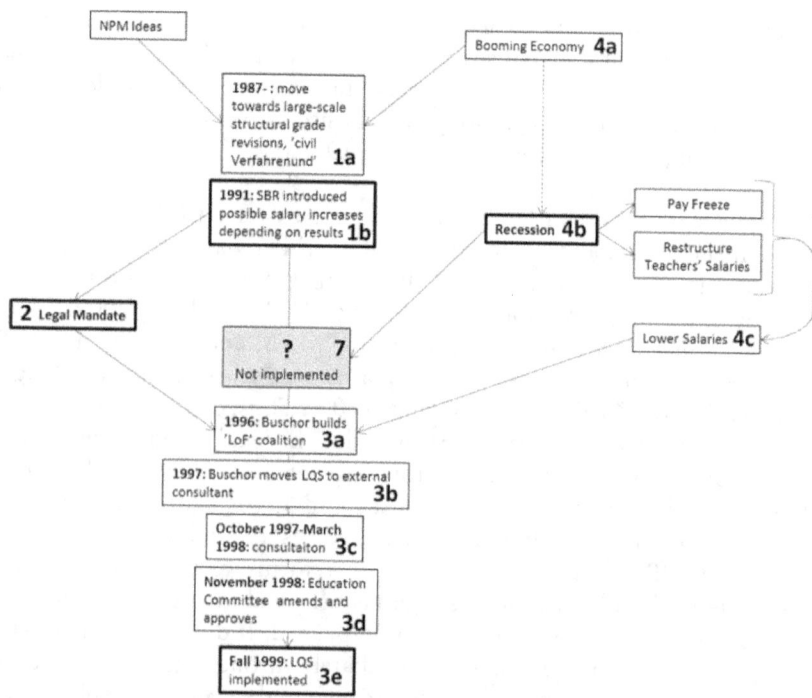

Figure 7.2 Timeline 2: MAB reform in light of economic drivers

the authority to suspend wage increases or promotions when necessary. The Governing Council exercised this authority and, as a result, there were no step-increases in 1993 or 1994, and only limited inflation-related raises (Regierungsrates Des Kantons Zürich, 1996a). Thus, the 9% increases projected by SBR 1987/1991 were never realized, civil sector salaries lagged behind inflation, and the actual wage developments in the mid-1990s were lower than what would have been realized under the old salary system (Regierungsrates Des Kantons Zürich, 1996a). As a result, rather than promised wage improvements, public employees received wage cuts (Wendelspiess, 2000). Teachers' salaries were included in these salary freezes, but were further affected by wage restructuring[10] in 1996, which reduced teachers' starting salary by 8% and extended the period required to achieve the maximum salary, saving the canton 20 million francs (Schneebeli, 1998b; "Lehrer unterlegen," 1998). So perhaps, although it was legally possible, an MAB system was never implemented in the education sector for two reasons: First, because there was no compulsory evaluation system for teachers and second, because salaries were frozen in the mid-1990s (Regierungsrates Des Kantons Zürich, 1997a). If no grade promotions were possible, why develop the system?

In addition to providing an explanation for the lag between legal mandate and implementation, economic forces can also be deployed alongside the legal mandate account to explain the impetus for the development and implementation of the MAB system in the late 1990s. The improvement of economic conditions in the late 1990s, making salary step-increases possible again, was the explanation for pushing for an MAB system in 1996. The administration argued that a compulsory evaluation system had to be developed and implemented in order to be in compliance with the law and in order for teachers to be able to get raises (Regierungsrates Des Kantons Zürich, 2001):

> this [the absence of a compulsory performance evaluation system] is why there has as yet been no opportunity for teachers to be upgraded to a higher salary level. (Regierungsrates Des Kantons Zürich, 1996a)
>
> To allow teachers also to have the opportunity of moving up a salary class, the Education Department is creating an evaluation system for primary schools, which will be applied as soon as possible. (Regierungsrates Des Kantons Zürich, 1997a)

The recession and its effects likely played an important role in the reform process. In combination with the legal mandate argument, it provides a better explanation than the legal mandate argument alone. The government certainly argued that the evaluation system was required by law and was the only way for teachers to earn raises.

In terms of the lag between legal mandate and implementation, the premise of the 'economic conditions' account is that performance evaluation in education was delayed because there was no compulsory evaluation system for teachers and second, because salary freezes removed any incentive to develop or implement a system. In combination with the importance of the legal mandate, economic drivers provide a coherent and plausible account for the timing of changes—including the delayed implementation through the mid-1990s. However, although the account is plausible, it ignores two important facts. First, an evaluation system *had* been developed in the early 1990s—challenging the idea that there was no system and that the economy undermined any motivation to create one. Second, SBR 1987/91 was applied throughout the public sector—virtually everywhere except education—in spite of the *same* economic environment and its challenges.

Explanation #3: The Undeniable Role Of Union Opposition

The adoption of SBR 1987/1991—requiring an evaluation system to be in compliance with cantonal law and for teachers to receive raises—and the improved economic conditions which made raises possible, provides a straightforward explanation of the push to reform in 1995:

> (Buschor) said, now I have problems because in the law it says, if you want to have more money, more salary, you need a qualification, you need an [evaluation] of your performance and for teachers there is no form ... so if we don't have it we can't increase the salaries. (Bertschi)[11]

However, it seems to be an oversimplified account. Although the argument that there was no compulsory evaluation system for teachers through the mid-1990s is *technically* true, it is potentially misleading, though oft-cited reason for delay (Vertschi; Legler, Sigrist & Wehner, 2008). Although no system had been formally implemented, the Wifl/LoF (Figure 7.3, **3a/3b**) committees created in 1997 were not the first to be tasked with the creation of an evaluation system for teachers. The Education Department formed a working group in 1990 (**2a**)[12] to consider the feasibility of a teacher evaluation system, based on the guidelines issued by the Education Council in 1988 (Legler et al., 2008). Even at that time, it was difficult to conceive of equality of teachers' rights and salary increases in relation to other state officials *without* performance evaluation in the long run (Wendelspiess, 2000; Bertschi; Wendelspiess). The working group—which included HR professionals, teacher representatives, psychologists, university faculty, and other representatives (Der Erziehungsrat des Kantons Zürich, 1990; Wendelspiess, 2000)—released its findings in the 'Rose Booklet' (Bildungsdirektion Kanton Zürich Volksschulamt, 2009), which included three concepts for performance appraisal, in 1992 (**2b**).

According to Wendelspiess, the response to the Rose Book was mixed but mostly positive (Wendelspiess, 2000). The group confirmed the feasibility of an MAB system, and the eventual MAB product was built on the foundation provided in the Rose Book (**2b**), when Buschor convened the new task

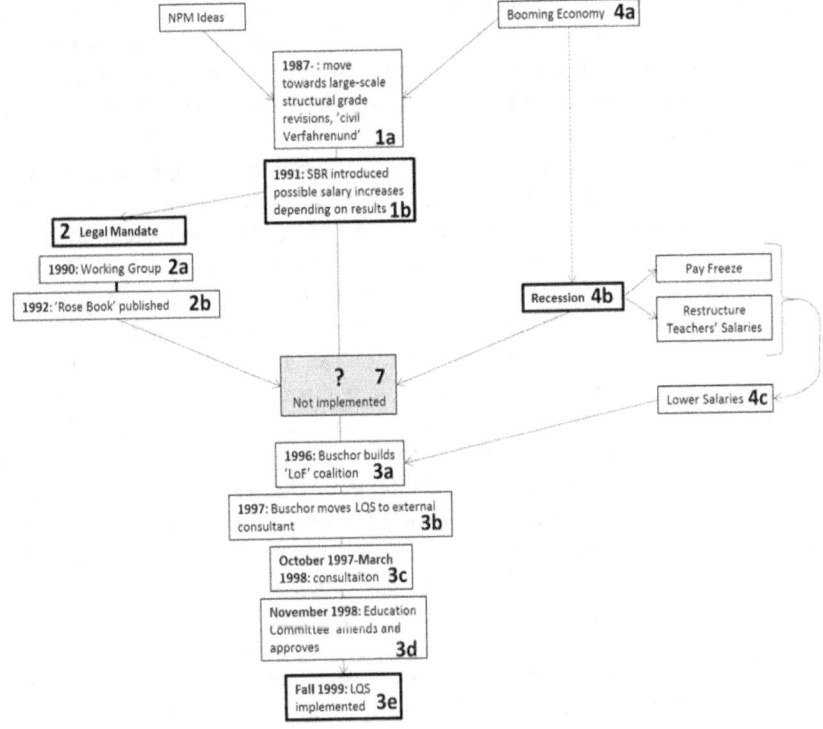

Figure 7.3 Timeline 3: Early evaluation system developments

force in 1996 (Wendelspiess, 2000, Bertschi). Although the task was originally assigned to an internal working group (LoF) in 1996, Buschor subcontracted the task to an external commission in 1997[13] in order to accelerate the process of development (3c) (Wendelspiess, 2000). Bertschi, one of the original members of the 1990 working group, won the contract[14] and, in collaboration with Wendelspiess, produced a draft of the MAB system in four months (Bertschi; Wendelspiess). According to Wendelspiess:

> As a former school leader, an independent HR professional and an active education politician . . . [Bertschi] possessed that knowledge, without which it would not be possible to reconcile the existing knowledge about the evaluation of teachers, the knowledge of Zürich elementary schools and compliance with the possibilities and limitations of the local school board system in the time available. (Wendelspiess, 2000)

The fact that an evaluation system *had* been developed in 1992 makes the explanation that performance evaluation had not been implemented in education, due to the lack of a system and the lack of economic incentives to create one, seem inadequate. Consistent with the legal mandate account, the administration's efforts to develop an evaluation system for teachers were directly linked to SBR 1987/1991. However, the fact that an evaluation system was developed but not implemented raises an important question: why, despite the legal mandate and its implementation throughout the civil sector, was an evaluation system not applied to teachers?

Economic conditions cannot account for the failure to implement an evaluation system for teachers, because the development of performance evaluation systems moved forward in the rest of the public sector in spite of identical economic conditions and resulting salary freezes in the civil sector. The performance evaluation project, which was applied throughout the civil sector, was launched in 1990 and the necessary apparatus was approved by the Governing Council in March 1992 and amended in 1994 (Regierungsrates Des Kantons Zürich, 1996a; Wendelspiess). These efforts were not immune to the impacts of the recession—the system was described as only achieving "limited success because of the constraints of the spending cuts," which resulted in difficulties and diminished enthusiasm (Regierungsrates Des Kantons Zürich, 1996a). However, performance evaluation became "a thoroughly established, indispensable component of the management and administrative framework" throughout the public sector *in spite* of the economic conditions which limited its effects (Regierungsrates Des Kantons Zürich, 1996a).

The resistance and opposition to evaluating teachers and linking their pay to performance appear to be an essential explanation for why the system was not applied to teachers until the late 1990s. The teachers' organization challenged the competence of local authorities to assess teachers and also rejected linking teachers' salaries to these evaluations (Wendelspiess, 2000; Legler et al., 2008). Wendelspiess—in an account that has been confirmed elsewhere (Legler et al., 2008)—refers to a period of debate and conflict over evaluation for teachers[15] throughout the mid-1990s in which teachers' organizations and their allies in parliament staved off the reforms:

> There followed a phase of 'mutual blocking' in the Canton of Zürich which continued for several years: teachers' organizations fought on a broad front, particularly via their closest representatives in parliament, against the introduction of performance-related pay [in] local school authorities. However, the Parliament rejected 15 proposals on this subject and insisted on the principle of legal equality within the civil service. This was taking place during the same period as the transition to a new, progressive personnel law, during which the 'civil servant status' was abolished (carried unopposed by all parties). It was also demonstrated that effective performance appraisal via colleagues was quickly becoming accepted as a normal HR instrument in central government and could be used sensibly. (Wendelspiess, 2000)

Clear consensus emerges across sources—both interviewees and documents—that teachers opposed and successfully blocked the application of the evaluation system to teachers through the mid-1990s. However, this explanation poses one major challenge—what changed? Why were teachers able to block the reforms for a period but not indefinitely? None of the storylines—legal mandates, economic conditions and pressures, or teachers' oppositions—provide a singular account of what happened in the development and implementation of the MAB system that is both parsimonious and adequately complex. Instead, consistent with a diversity-oriented approach to causation that views causal factors as complementary rather than competing, causation sits at the nexus of legislative changes, economic circumstances, and political debate and conflict.

Although the 1999 implementation traces its roots to 1987, the explanation of these events cannot treat the process as a singular development from the passage of SBR 1987/1991 to the implementation of the MAB system in 1999. Instead, it must account for two epochs that pose distinct but interrelated questions: the period of non-implementation that stretched from 1987–1996 and the period of implementation from 1996–1999. Opposition and conflict fuelled by unfavorable economic circumstances overcame the legislative mandate to implement a comprehensive evaluation system for teachers from 1987–1996. But what weakened, eliminated, or marginalized this opposition by 1996 so that the legal mandate could be fulfilled? Both epochs must be explained in ways that are consistent and coherent with the distinct dynamics of each period as well as with one another.

WHY EVENTUAL IMPLEMENTATION: EXPLAINING BOTH DELAY AND ACTION

The previous section provided a detailed account of the events that together tell the story of the MAB reform process—a legal mandate whose delayed realization was shaped by economic forces and teachers' opposition. Although teachers were successful in delaying the application of SBR 1987/91 to the education sector for some time, the landscape shifted in the mid-1990s. Although Ernst Buschor acknowledged that teachers still opposed the reforms in the mid-1990s, the administration was willing to move forward with the reforms in spite of this opposition (Bertschi; Buschor). According to Buschor, although there was opposition, it was "never a complete no."

The lack of a "complete no" is an apt summary of the post-1995 environment, reflecting two potential interpretations of events that together account for the neutralization of teachers' opposition, which had successfully stalled the reforms over the five previous years. One interpretation of the lack of a "complete no" deals with the diversity of the unions' goals and preferences and their capacity for interest aggregation. However, the diverse interests of teachers in Zürich do not appear to provide an adequate explanation for the shift in 1995—nothing changed in the union's interests or capacity to explain the neutralization of teachers' opposition. Instead, there were several shifts, both external and internal, that altered the landscape, tilting the playing field toward the administration and disadvantaging the teachers and their allies.

The external shifts and ZLV's complex preferences provide a compelling explanation of the events outlined in the previous section. They also provide significant insight into the nature and significance of the relationship pattern between the unions and the administration. Like Finland, although the details are different in Zürich, the relationship pattern and interaction orientation is significant. In Zürich, the relationship pattern is best described as accommodative, and is essential to understanding the reform process (Walton & McKersie, 1965/1991). Together, ZLV's orientation, environmental shifts, and the established relationship between the teachers' unions and the administration help to explain why MAB reform eventually occurred in Zürich.

ZLV's Orientation

Unpacking ZLV's orientation regarding MAB is complex. Unlike in Finland, where all interviewees told compatible and coherent stories about the reform process and the nature of interests that produced the policy outcome, accounts of what happened in Zürich were complex and at times apparently contradictory. Ultimately, the complex and divergent understandings of what happened and why it happened are insightful. As in Chapter 5, consistent with the ACI framework, the ZLV's preferences are considered alongside their internal capacity—cognitive and evaluative. Their MAB-specific preferences must be understood through the lens of their general preferences or goals. As the discussion of their preferences makes clear, the ZLV faced significant challenges in terms of their cognitive and evaluative capacity. In contrast to the highly developed representative system of the OAJ, through the 1990s the ZLV relied primarily on direct democracy, which—in light of diverse membership goals—posed challenges to integration and representation. Although these challenges were not the primary cause of the neutralization of teachers' opposition in the late 1990s, the internal dynamics of the union are essential to making sense of complex and competing union preferences.

ZLV's MAB Preferences and Perceptions

Interviewees unanimously confirmed that the ZLV was opposed to the MAB system, but there was no agreement about the root of union opposition. There seem to have been a variety of conflicts over the MAB system. Table 7.1 displays the various descriptions about the nature of union opposition to MAB.

There were three different explanations for the teachers' unions' opposition to MAB. The first explanation, identified by Buschor and ZLV,

Table 7.1 Perceptions and preferences of MAB

	Reasons for Opposition			Additional Concerns		
	Not Possible	Opposed Lay Evaluation	Opposed Link to Salary	Number of Classifications	Too Hard, Too Much Work	Threat to Autonomy/ Individualism
Buschor	Yes.**	Yes.	Yes (but also mixed).		Yes.	Yes.
Wendelspiess	Yes.	Yes.			Yes.	
Bertschi	Yes.	Yes.~	Yes.**			Yes.
ZLV.President	Yes.**		Yes.	Yes.		
LCH.Union_Leader		Yes.**	Yes.			

**Denotes the primary root of union opposition according to each interviewee.

~But even more opposed to peer evaluation.

President, was that the teachers categorically objected to the idea that it was possible to evaluate teachers' work. This was the primary source of opposition, although teachers also opposed linking evaluations to salaries:

> they declared from the beginning onwards that they do not accept . . . this kind of, of evaluation . . . (and) they rejected as well, the consequences of the salaries . . . but the main reason was that it was not possible to judge the quality of the work with this framework, so therefore they reject any consequences of the evaluation. This was the reason, not because of salaries. (Buschor)

The second objection was related to the MAB's reliance on lay evaluators.[16] LCH.Leader did not express an unequivocal opposition to teacher evaluation as an impossible enterprise, but objected vehemently to MAB's approach, arguing that the system of lay evaluation was an affront to teachers' professionalism. The third explanation of teachers' opposition focused on the link to salaries as the primary point of contention, a view voiced by Bertschi. His view is based on his involvement with the 1990 working group. According to Bertschi, the process of developing proposals for teacher evaluation[17] convinced the president of the ZLV,[18] who served on the working group, that it was possible to evaluate teachers—although he maintained his opposition to the salary link. Thus, it seems that all of the factors included in Table 7.1 may have been sources of opposition to MAB for union leaders, union members, and teachers. However, there was a lack of consistency regarding what exactly teachers and their unions opposed or wanted.

This lack of consistency has two likely sources. First, it may reflect disagreement within the union about the MAB system. Second, it likely reflects the union's changing position over time—as certain issues were perceived to be lost, the battle may have moved to new fronts where the union perceived that it had a greater chance of success. A few key shifts that may have changed the union's strategic position are discussed below. But first, the remainder of this section unpacks the union's multiple and competing preferences and how cognitive and evaluative capacity may explain why the union's opposition is hard to precisely identify.

ZLV General Preferences

According to both ZLV.President and LCH.Leader, the union has two main goals: first, to "defend ethical concepts and [the] prestige" of the teaching profession and to promote concepts of pedagogy, and second, to defend pecuniary questions related to working conditions, salaries, and pensions (ZLV.President). Both within and between these two broad goals the union faces challenges in promoting unity across the membership (LCH.Leader; ZLV.President). First, there is tension between members regarding the organization's primary purpose:

> It has been difficult to bring together . . . [there are] always some battles within the teachers' organization between [those who are] more defensive of salaries and time and so on, [and] defending people . . . and then there are the pedagogical dreamers—who would achieve that dream for no pay . . . and we try to manage that. (LCH.Leader)

Then, within the goals, members were divided. Although the ZLV's interests are fairly straightforward in terms of pecuniary questions, uniting teachers around questions of professionalism and pedagogy is more challenging:

> For the conditions . . . in terms of salary we are very united—'we want more money'—more salary less work. Pedagogically, we have more or less every opinion . . . and therefore it is not always easy to get an opinion for this aspect. (ZLV.President)

LCH.Leader also identified the diversity of teachers' opinions as a challenge—particularly when it comes to pedagogical and professional questions. He attributes this division to a lack of a shared vocabulary or mental models among teachers, which he links to the underdevelopment of teachers' professional training:

> If you defend the quality of the profession you will never attain the unity . . . 'broad yes' of all teachers because of the variety of ideas. (LCH.Leader)

ZLV Cognitive and Evaluative Capacity

This diversity of opinion[19] presents challenges for the union leadership, which is tasked with representing the diverse views of their membership. Historically, ZLV's approach to union democracy has been different from OAJ's. While the OAJ's approach to democracy is representative, at the time of the MAB reforms, the ZLV's primary strategy for interest aggregation—consistent with the broader Swiss approach outlined in Chapter 6—was direct democracy. LCH.Leader identifies the historical significance of, and enduring commitment to, a particular version of citizen-democracy in Switzerland as significantly informing union democracy. He identifies this "particular brand of citizen-democracy" as one in which individuals have authority and don't want to be told what to do; in such a system change is slow (LCH.Leader).

The connections to the institutional context of Switzerland are obvious. It seems that the significance of direct rather than representative democracy extends beyond federal or cantonal government. Until recently, the ZLV has relied on surveys to gauge, and attempt to represent, members' interests, but the danger is that often the opinion captured by the survey is split 50/50: "Then we can't do anything . . . because if we do one thing, the others are angry and it is worse" (ZLV.President).

As a result of the limitations of an exclusive reliance on direct democracy, the ZLV is currently in the process of trying to create a representative democracy. They are attempting to create school-based as well as education-level groups where members could talk and reach consensus. Then, "if no one says 'stop' then we just do it" (ZLV.President). However, in 2012, the ZLV was only at the beginning of this process—this representative system did not exist a decade ago. At that time, surveys were still the major tool for measuring, expressing, and representing members' opinions (Bertschi; Girschweiler, 1999; Schneebeli, 1999a). Representative democracy was spawned by the limitations of the old process: "if we try to do this democratic thing, it is hard for it to work" (ZLV.President). The diversity of teachers' interests and the challenges to interest aggregation[20] are important to understanding what happened with MAB. The multiplicity of the ZLV's particular MAB preferences are linked to the nature of their general goals.

ZLV's objections to or support of MAB have clear links to its general goals—to protect and promote professionalism as well as to improve teachers' salaries and working conditions. Professionalism can be further subdivided into two considerations—autonomy or respect for expert practice and the promotion of quality teaching and schools. It seems that the various professional and pecuniary considerations pulled the teachers' association in competing directions. External evaluation—especially by untrained lay evaluators—was a perceived affront to teachers' autonomy. However, on the other hand, LCH.Leader could recognize the importance of ensuring the quality of teaching—and of addressing bad quality rapidly—as a professional responsibility. At the same time, the MAB system was presented as a way for teachers to get more money—which appealed to the organization's efforts to improve teachers' salaries, as the system was presented as the only way for teachers to be eligible for annual increases due to the provisions of SBR 1991 (Regierungsrates des Kantons Zürich, 1996b; Regierungsrates des Kantons Zürich, 1997a; Regierungsrates des Kantons Zürich, 2001).

The lack of unified opposition to MAB was apparent across interviewees. Although the union leaders opposed, in principle, linking teachers' salaries to evaluations, they eventually accepted that it was the best way to improve salaries and then opposed the incentives for being too small. Outsiders also perceived divisions between the unions and their members. Bertschi, Buschor, and Wendelspiess consistently distinguished between the view of 'the organization' and the view of individual teachers:

> Opposition came exclusively through the teachers . . . but it was much more the exception. It was the criticism of the teachers' association, not of individual teachers. . . . And some teachers don't like it, some do like it, but it varies considerably. (Buschor)
>
> In principle, [the] teachers' union is against such a system. And we can live with that very well. But if you speak to individuals, it is always the same: 70–80% say, 'I'm against it, but in my case it was ok. The way I was witnessing and living this in my classroom was ok.' So there really is a double view: 'The system as such, I'm against it.' (Bertschi)
>
> Teachers were more or less unified. But we would also have meetings where teachers would say 'I am very happy with the MAB.' (ZLV. President)

As the previous discussion has made clear, the union's interests were complex and at times unclear—at least to those outside of the union. However, despite the challenging work of attempting to speak with one voice, the teachers' opposition was an important part of the story of MAB, delaying the reform process through the mid-1990s. But to understand why the system was eventually implemented in spite of this opposition—shifting and sometimes fragmented although it may have been—one must move beyond the ZLV's preferences.

Before and After 1995: The Shifting Landscape

What emerged in the previous section is a picture of clear union opposition to the MAB system rooted in multiple objections. The particular nature of the ZLV's opposition was variable: the nature of opposition reads like a moving target, what many of the designers described as a kind of doublespeak (Bertschi; Buschor). However, it is clear, based on the evidence outlined in the first half of this chapter, that the teachers' opposition successfully hampered the implementation of performance evaluation for teachers until the mid-1990s. Until 1995, the teachers and their unions had been listened to; their opposition was a real and legitimate threat to bureaucrats' ability to introduce the new system. What happened in the mid-1990s to overcome this opposition? Like the complex and multifactored reform timeline outlined above, the shift was not one thing but many—a collection of shifts that, together, altered the playing field and neutralized teachers' opposition. Together, these shifts, along with the legislative and economic factors previously discussed, provide a compelling account of the reform process and the role of the teachers' union.

Shift #1: Public Opinion

The entire reform process—from SBR 1987/1991 to the implementation of MAB in 1999—is fundamentally connected to the spread of NPM in Switzerland: Buschor identified the teachers' evaluation system as being linked to the general law (SBR 1987/1991), which was informed by the general framework for NPM—ideas that attempted to bring private sector management styles to the public sector:

> We wanted really to go closer to a normal economy—they are doing a good job, they are fulfilling relevant missions, so why is it not a bit closer in the whole setting? It's [MAB] still a special law, it's not actually the same as [the private sector] . . . but we have made this step. (Bertschi)

Although Buschor's 'effects-oriented public management' (*Wirkungsorientere Verwaltungsführung*) began to form in the 1980s, its spread was particularly notable during the economically challenging 1990s. In Switzerland in the 1990s, NPM reforms were discussed and implemented at every level of government, a process that proceeded in a series of 'phases,' reaching its peak from 1995–1998 (Schedler, 2003[21]). LCH.Leader confirmed that around 1990, "[the union] knew there was a wave of NPM coming" in which politicians would try to apply private sector principles first to the public sector and then to schools. And it seems that in Zürich, the peak of NPM reforms coincided with high levels of public enthusiasm and support. ZLV.President said that the MAB reforms were designed and implemented (1996–1999) under the influence of "NPM euphoria:"

> Most of this thing was very much rooted in NPM. [Buschor] was a very good speaker and gifted in the media . . . so everyone was excited about NPM and we were going to make it better. (ZLV.President)

Public opinion in embracing the NPM ideology had turned against the teachers' union. ZLV.President implied that the NPM euphoria was significant in preventing the ZLV from being able to challenge the reform, but Wendelspiess was more explicit:

> The unions really tried to kill it ... but politically, they knew that parents wanted an MAB ... so they didn't oppose it with 100% conviction. They knew that there could always be a referendum at the end and that public opinion would have settled the matter. (Wendelspiess)

Although measures of public opinion on this issue are unavailable, the available evidence supports the consensus that emerges from interviewees' accounts. Although assessments of the proliferation and extent of NPM reforms in Switzerland have come to varied conclusions,[22] the incidence of NPM reforms lends support to the "NPM euphoria" hypothesis. The incidence of NPM-related education reforms since the 1990s—inspired by reforms initiated at the national level—including changes in the status of teachers and changing approaches to teacher compensation and evaluation, lends further support to the euphoria claims.

In 2000, there were a number of cantons where evaluation systems—either in combination with salary reforms or alone—were being considered. Only seven cantons were classified as 'not considering' any reforms at that time and evaluation and compensation systems were being considered in 14 cantons and had been implemented in two—Zürich and St. Gallen (Ritz & Steiner, 2000, as cited in Müller Kucera & Stauffer, 2003). Thus, the reform of teacher evaluation and compensation was not an isolated event; it should be understood within the context of two related forces—a growing enthusiasm about NPM and the economic recession of the 1990s.[23] The argument for the dominance, proliferation, and popularity of NPM ideas throughout Switzerland is especially salient in the Canton of Zürich. NPM reform was more prominent in German-speaking cantons and municipalities, which may be explained by the fact that the main promoter of NPM in Switzerland, Ernst Buschor, was a German speaker (Reber, 2006). The influence of the intellectual architects of NPM was especially significant in Zürich, as Buschor joined the Canton's Executive Council in 1993 and served as the head of the Directorate of Education from 1995.

Shift #2: Leadership of the Education Directorate

The shift in public opinion, which may have been critical in neutralizing teachers' opposition as it eliminated their most potent weapon, the referendum, was likely not entirely independent of another important shift—a shift in leadership. Although the acceptance of and enthusiasm about NPM among the public may have occurred independently of Buschor's role in the public administration, it is likely that the depth of the 'NPM euphoria' was linked to his leadership, especially given the fact that "he was a very good speaker and gifted in the media" (ZLV.President). But beyond his ability to build support for NPM ideas among the public, Buschor taking the helm of the Education Directorate was a critical shift—one that distinguishes the first epoch (pre-1995) from the second (1995–1999).

Prior to Buschor, the previous Education Director, Alfred Gilgen, had been serving in the role for 20 years (1976–1995). The perception, according to several interviewees, was that he may have been tired and unwilling to touch the 'hot potato' of MAB given his proximity to retirement—especially in light of economic difficulties, salary freezes, and teachers' salary restructuring. So it seems that Gilgen may have avoided MAB development and implementation not because teachers' opposition *couldn't* be overcome, but because doing so was unpalatable. In contrast, Buschor was committed to bringing the principles of NPM to bear; according to the "framework, individual qualifications were key. So we said it is worthwhile to do in schools, even against (the) opposition of teachers" (Buschor). As a result, after "a lot of slowing down" on the evaluation system:

> finally, then, I think it was one act of Buschor. 'Now it's finished, we have discussed it for 8 years. We have to do it or else we cannot raise the salaries.' (Bertschi)

According to one local reporter, there was more change from 1995–1998 than there had been the previous 300 years—reforms that were attributed to a dynamic leader who reformed aggressively, forcing teachers to accept principles that applied almost everywhere else (Inlet, 1998).

Shift #3: Challenges Within the Union

In addition to the general challenges of interest aggregation that always have the potential to complicate union unity and effectiveness, the ZLV was plagued by additional internal tensions and divisions. As early as 1998, tensions between groups of teachers within the ZLV were reported in the *Tages-Anzeiger* (Schneebeli, 1998a). According to reports, the split was between secondary teachers—represented by the OKRZ and SKH—and primary teachers and was primarily over membership dues; the secondary teachers' organizations were accepting members without requiring members of their organizations to pay dues to the ZLV. After attempts to reconcile failed, the ZLV split and the OKRZ and SKZ left the primary teachers to form the SekZH (Schneebeli, 2000).[24]

None of the interviewees discussed this split or linked it explicitly to the MAB reform process. But although it may not have factored explicitly into the reform process, it seems relevant, as it may have impacted inter-organizational unity during the critical period of MAB development or may have served as a significant distraction, keeping the union from channeling all of its energies toward the reform process. Given its absence from the accounts of any of the interviewees, it appears to be a secondary rather than primary factor, but one that provides important context.

Together these shifts—particularly the shift in public opinion and new leadership—explain why the union's influence decreased in the mid-1990s, reversing the effectiveness of their opposition. Although teachers' opposition was a key factor to the delayed implementation of MAB through 1995, the degree of their incorporation in the decision-making process and their

170 *International Cases*

influence on key decision-makers declined. This shift in influence is not an anomaly produced by unique historical circumstances. Rather, it is a function of the established union-management relationship pattern in Zürich.

Relationship Pattern Between the Education Directorate and the ZLV

In Chapter 5, the interaction orientation and related relationship pattern of the OAJ and KT were included in the discussion of the OAJ's preferences. The stable and cooperative relationships between the OAJ and employers were linked with a relational preference—to maintain this cooperative and productive relationship—that informed the union's interests, strategies, and tactics. In Zürich, like in Finland, the relationship pattern between the Education Directorate and the teachers' unions is the key to understanding the MAB reform process. As previously outlined, any causal explanation must be able to explain both epochs of the reform story—the period of delay (1990–1995) and the period of implementation (1996–1999). The relationship pattern provides the key to unlocking that coherent causal account.

The dominant pattern that emerges in Zürich is best characterized as accommodation—defined as an individualistic orientation in which "recognition of the legitimacy of the other's means and ends amounts to an 'acceptance of the *status quo*'" (Walton & McKersie, 1965/1991, p. 187). In this pattern, the parties "have adjusted to each other and have evolved routines for performing functions and settling differences" (Walton & McKersie, 1965/1991, p. 187). The relationship is characterized by moderate respect, limited trust, and limited competition. This pattern is evident in Table 7.2.

On the employer's side, there were pervasive questions about the degree to which the ZLV's views reflected the interests of teachers. So, although there was

Table 7.2 Relationship pattern between ZLV and policy-makers

	MOTIVATION ORIENTATION/ ACTION TENDENCY	BELIEFS ABOUT LEGITIMACY	FEELINGS OF TRUST	FEELINGS OF FRIENDLINESS
Buschor	Individualistic	Acceptance of status quo	Limited trust	Neutralism-courteousness
Bertschi	Individualistic	Acceptance of status quo	Trust	Neutralism-courteousness
ZLV. President	Individualistic	N/A	Varied	Varied
LCH.Union_ Leader	Individualistic	N/A	Varied	Varied

a degree of trust—Bertschi's view accepts that the ZLV is pragmatic and interested in the welfare and well-being of the school—it was limited by questions about the representativeness of the union's views. The employer's characterization of interactions with the teachers' organization—particularly post-1995—was neutral and courteous: they viewed the ZLV as one participant and one voice among many. The union was similarly individualistic—attempting to promote its interests through whatever channels possible. There seemed to be a resigned acceptance that the administration would not listen to them. Their trust and friendliness varied from person to person, demonstrating the personal rather than institutional foundation of these attributes. This is consistent with a relationship pattern of accommodation: "The level of affect among the participants is rather low—not strongly positive or negative. They go about their business, interacting in a courteous but informal manner" (Walton & McKersie, 1965/1991, p. 186).

The salience of the accommodative relationship pattern is strengthened when interviewee responses are considered in light of the institutional context of Zürich. Chapter 5 sketched the contours of Swiss *konkordanz* democracy—a consensus orientation incentivized by the pressures of direct democracy and institutionalized in broad governing coalitions. The relationship pattern or interaction orientations of the ZLV and key members of the Education Directorate must be positioned in this larger structure of interactions. However, the impetus for broad consultation and consensus is closely linked to instruments of direct democracy; it is a strategic response to veto threats. Thus, this approach to consensus has a strong accommodative flavor—parties work together when required.

How does this accommodative interaction orientation inform the MAB reform process and the role of the teachers' union in those reforms? The relationship pattern provides the link that unifies the various causal ingredients—economic and political context, complex union preferences, and the shifting landscape of power—into a coherent explanation of reform. Union opposition—which was complex and multifaceted but relatively constant from 1990–1999—was effective before but not after 1995 because unions lost their 'access pass' to the decision-making process. Because of the individualistic nature of the accommodative relationship between the teachers' union and the Education Directorate, meaningful consultation and incorporation in the decision-making process was inconsistent. Despite an expressed commitment to the importance of consulting the social partners, the evidence suggests that the significance of the consultative procedures, and the amount of influence that various groups actually had, was variable.

In order to understand the 1995 shift, the education reform process must be contrasted with the broader civil sector. For example, in the design of the SBR 1987/1991 reforms:

> From the start, much importance was attached to the participation of the staff associations, who were involved in the project organization.... The findings can ultimately be considered the result of consensual

consultation between the Cantonal Parliament and the staff associations as social partners, although a number of concerns could not be dealt with . . . [as evidenced by] the numerous proposals submitted to the Cantonal Parliament Commission by several interest and professional groups, along with the many hundreds of appeals against the new classification of staff. (Regierungsrates Des Kantons Zürich, 1996a)

Although opposition from social partners was noted, it was not insurmountable, as SBR 1987/91 was implemented and remained in place in spite of opposition and resistance. In contrast, the opposition of teachers and their unions created a real impediment to reform through 1995. However, despite a consistent emphasis on the importance of the union as a partner with whom the Education Director worked closely (Schneebeli, 1998a), the nature of their consultation and incorporation appears to have shifted after 1995.

Prior to 1995, most notably in the 1990–1992 working group, consultation was broad: there were fourteen members in the working group, including two teachers' union representatives, school authorities, and other experts (Der Erziehungsrat des Kantons Zürich, 1990; Bertschi). A wide set of stakeholders, including the union, were involved in the design of a provisional MAB system. In contrast, consultation in the late 1990s took the form of official comment and review *after* the system had already been designed and proposed. The lack of what Bertschi called a 'conventional taskforce' was a key reason why it was feasible to design the system in only four months—it was a simply a 'brainstorm' between Bertschi and Wendelspiess (Bertschi; Wendelspiess). Unlike the working group, the social partners were only engaged *after* the plan had been finalized, during the formal consultation process; they were excluded from the planning process. When the system—its goals and underlying philosophy—was challenged after the planning had been assigned to Bertschi, the government response was that although there were "serious issues which must be properly addressed," the debate should not begin until "the consultation process has had a chance to get underway" (Regierungsrates des Kantons Zürich, 1997a).

The plan was eventually submitted to what Bertschi called 50 "critical people"—including teachers' unions, school commissions, school boards, political parties, and others—in order to get their ideas and criticisms (Bertschi; Bertschi Consulting, n.d.; Bosshardt, 1998). According to Wendelspiess, they received hundreds of written responses throughout this process. However, by this time, significant decisions had already been made. When the Education Committee approved the MAB system in 1998—which was then ratified by parliament—there *were* some modifications as a result of the consultation process (Schneebeli, 1999b). Most notably, the number of levels on the scale of evaluation was reduced—in order to satisfy a criticism advanced by the teachers' union. But the link between salaries and evaluation was not removed, and the role of lay evaluators was not changed (Bosshardt, 1998).

The key to understanding the shift in consultation patterns and the neutralization of teachers' opposition after 1995 lies in the accommodative relationship pattern. Two common themes unite the pre-1995 and post-1995 epochs. First, in both periods, each party was pursuing their individual interests. The administration was attempting to implement an MAB system and the ZLV was attempting to block it. Second, in both periods, the parties only worked together to the extent that collaboration was perceived to be necessary or beneficial to them. The accommodative relationship is constant; what changed is the political landscape—the shift in public opinion weakened the union. When the administration perceived that the union had lost its most significant resource—the ability to challenge legislation and decrees politically—its engagement with the union became much more limited.

Buschor acknowledged that the unions protested their exclusion from the process of developing performance evaluation systems. This was echoed by the President of the SeKZH: "The pay-related MAB was brought in without the cooperation of the teachers. It is therefore to be seen as a failure and has been badly received on this basis." Buschor's response to this objection was that the issue of employee evaluation or assessment is outside of the unions' domain, stating that unions are not involved in these issues anywhere in Switzerland. This shifting landscape of power and the resulting shift in the influence opportunities available to the ZLV may also explain the perceived variability and inconsistency of the union's expressed interests:

> some rejected the system because evaluation couldn't work . . . some (associations) rejected any consequences of the salaries; others accepted incentives, but said they were too low . . . some teachers said that the . . . complexity of teaching is so high, that it cannot be evaluated in an inquiry [that only includes an observation] of lessons and said [that] this complexity needs a much longer period of examination and control and this wasn't possible [and then others said that] there is too much bureaucratization because of NPM. (Buschor)

It seems that the union's strategy had to shift as the playing field shifted to their disadvantage. Given a realistic assessment of their disadvantaged situation, they may have been forced to concede ground that was inconsistent with their underlying preferences and to move the fight to issues that they thought they could win. Teachers' opposition transitioned from opposition to resigned or grudging acceptance, which was rooted in a sense of inevitability combined with a decision to attempt to get the most out of a bad set of circumstances. LCH.Leader talks about this shift:

> The [ZLV] said at the time [1991, SBR], 'no, we don't want a performance salary system because our work isn't . . . fit for the kind of evaluation as you know it with other . . . public sector, or private sectors' . . . but

174 *International Cases*

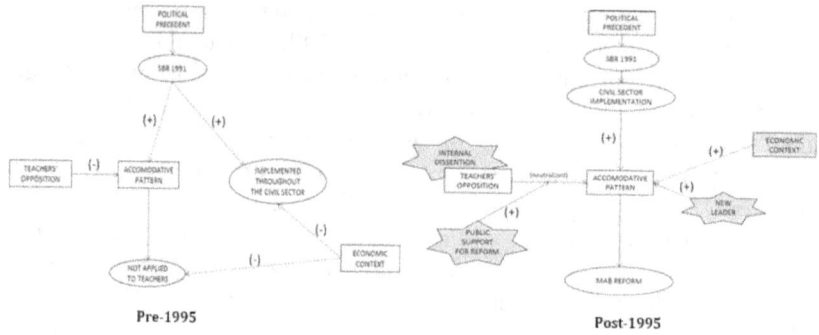

Figure 7.4 Delayed implementation pre- and post-1995

finally they said, 'ok . . . we'll try this system. We already know it won't work, but the damage will be smaller than the damage not to have the improvement of the salary.'

And SekZH.President described their efforts as yielding a "semi-success:" the procedure was simplified, but "we could not prevent the MAB in its current form on its political path. . . . We could not change the basic political decision in support of pay-related MAB—that remained the same as it had always been."

The accommodative union-management relationship pattern in Zürich provides the crucial link around which the ZLV's preferences and the shifts in the policy-making environment in the mid-1990s cohere into a unified causal explanation. Prior to 1995, in spite of the legal precedent provided by SBR 1991, teachers' opposition successfully stalled reforms (see Figure 7.4). The economic context made PRP more difficult, but the economic context did not hamper reform implementation for the rest of public sector employees, suggesting that teachers' opposition was particularly effective.

Shifts in the economic context—improving financial conditions that made raises for teachers possible—and Buschor's leadership and commitment to NPM certainly strengthened the push for reform (Figure 7.4). However, given the accommodative pattern and the consensus orientation of Swiss direct democratic politics, the shift in public support appears to be critical. When the credibility of teachers' blocking power was undermined, so was their influence.

CONCLUSION

Despite a multitude of differences, the reforms in Zürich share a common general attribute with the Finnish case. They are an example of unpopular reforms that linked teachers' compensation to assessments of teachers' performance that were implemented in spite of teachers' and their unions' opposition. In Zürich, the strength of teachers' opposition is evidenced by the five-year period in which they were able to block the application of a performance evaluation from being applied to teachers—in spite of its implementation throughout the public sector and a law that mandated its application in education.

Although both the legislative and economic contexts meaningfully contribute to the reform process in Zürich, they cannot explain the timing of the reforms. Instead, the implementation of the MAB system in Zürich is the story of a changing landscape of union power. Given the central importance of direct democracy in Switzerland, which vests the final veto point in the hands of public opinion and privileges interest groups who can harness this instrument, shifts in public opinion—although they do not appear in the timelines of discrete events and are difficult to substantiate—provide the primary explanation of what happened in Zürich.

The widespread recognition of NPM euphoria—identified by most interviewees and evidenced by the prominence and proliferation of NPM throughout Switzerland, which peaked in the mid-1990s—shifted the balance of power. The union realized that their most valuable resource—the ability to win a referendum to overturn the unpopular legislative and administrative decrees—had disappeared. Despite their ability to launch a referendum—either through an ordinary popular statutory referendum or through an extraordinary referendum initiated in parliament—the enthusiasm for NPM ideas and the belief that these ideas should be applied to teachers in schools would render their efforts to oppose the legislation, ultimately, futile.

The administration also realized this shift. Believing that any legitimate referendum threat was eliminated, they moved swiftly and forcefully to develop and implement the MAB system. Although shifts in public opinion appear to be the dominant cause of the shift in the playing field of power, the introduction of Ernst Buschor as the leader of the Education Directorate was also important. Buschor's commitment to NPM ideas and his willingness to overcome opposition to implement them certainly contributed to the timing of the changes.

The internal challenges facing the ZLV—both in terms of the perpetual challenge of representing members' diverse interests as well as the internal fractures that resulted in a split in 1999—certainly did not make the union opposition any stronger. However, these challenges appear to be secondary to the shift in the external environment. The difference between the impact of teachers' opposition before and after 1995 was ultimately the response of the administration to that opposition. The response is linked to the relational pattern between the administration and the union—an individualistic tendency in which the two parties only worked together when it was perceived to be necessary and useful—and the shifts that made the relationship with the union less important post-1995.

NOTES

1. The dossier was not originally a part of the MAB proposal, but it was added to address teachers' concerns that their work was too complex and couldn't be evaluated in this way and to give teachers the opportunity to "clarif(y) their position on central questions of pedagogy and (to) freely record their intentions, plans and educational goals" (Bertschi; Bildungsdirektion Kanton Zürich, 2011b, n.p.; Wendelspiess)
2. The number of classifications was decreased from six to four in the consultation process due to teachers' opposition.
3. Two MAB scores of IV are required to fire a teacher; but if a teacher receives a IV, he is reevaluated within four months. According to Wendelspiess, this happens with about five teachers per year.
4. In practice, many interviewees reported that there is often enough funding for IIs to receive raises; therefore, evaluators often classify all IIs as Is.
5. Because they were unable, under the salary freeze, to move up the ladder, while senior teachers had already received these increases.
6. An article published in 2003 ("Mehr lohn fuer bestimmte Lehrer," 2003) provides an example of how the system functions: in the previous year (2001–2002), teachers in wage levels 4–10 (with sufficient MAB evaluations) were eligible for promotions; and in the current year (2002–2003), teachers in wage levels 11–15 were eligible. However, one of the major challenges is that the majority of teachers are rated as 'good' and are hypothetically entitled to a wage increase, but there are not enough funds. Through 2003, 98% of teachers were rated as 'good,' but only 30–50% received increases due to lack of funds (Staubli, 2005).
7. Evaluating teachers every four years is in part due to the labor-intensive nature of the evaluations. Beginning teachers do not have an MAB in their first three years. This is part of their 'probationary' period. It is also much easier to fire probationary teachers.
8. The governing council approved the main bill in March 1990 and the commission then developed the system in a series of meetings from 10 July 1990 to 15 January 1991 (Regierungsrates Des Kantons Zürich, 1996a).
9. An application in the education sector of LS 177.10, the Law on Employment of State Personnel (1e).
10. Bill 3460 (Regierungsrates Des Kantons Zürich, 1996a).
11. These views were echoed by Wendelspiess.
12. When it was clear that SBR would be passed and that performance-evaluation would be one component of the comprehensive salary structure.
13. It had been previously tasked to the results-based management (*ausrichtung auf die Wirkungsorientierte Verwaltungsführung (Wif)*) committee (Wendelspiess, 2000).
14. Bertschi described his role in developing the system as controversial because he was a member of parliament and because there were a lot of teachers and members of parliament who opposed the project. The outsourcing of the LoF work—and the logic for choosing Bertschi in particular—was challenged in a parliamentary question (Regierungsrates Des Kantons Zürich, 1997b).
15. Would the evaluation of teachers lead to higher standards of education? (Regierungsrates Des Kantons Zürich, 1997a).
16. School board members.
17. I.e., The Rose Book (1992).
18. The president was not reelected, which Bertschi attributes to the membership expressing its dissatisfaction with his opinions and work on the committee.

This may speak to diverse and competing intra-union preferences and the challenges of interest aggregation.
19. 'Cognitive capacity' (Scharpf, 1997).
20. 'Evaluative capacity' (Scharpf, 1997).
21. A student of Ernst Buschor at the University of St. Gallen who later replaced him when Buschor joined the government of the Canton of Zürich (Noordhoek & Sayner, 2005).
22. At the municipal level, Steiner (2000) found that 25% of municipalities had NPM projects by the end of the 1990s. At the cantonal level, some researchers have concluded that *all* cantons had at least three NPM projects (Widmer & Rieder, 2003, cited Brun & Siegel, 2004), while others have argued that 16 (Rieder & Lehmann, 2002, cited Brun & Siegel, 2004) implemented reforms.
23. The MAB system also occurred in the broader context of reforms related to the civil status of teachers and public workers that was occurring throughout Switzerland. The change occurred in Zürich in the early 1990s, which shifted teachers from civil servant status to that of salaried employee (Wagner, et al., 2004).
24. OKRZ and SKZ later merged into the SekZH.

REFERENCES

Bertschi Consulting. (n.d.). *Task force consultation document*. Zürich: Bertschi Consulting.
Bildungsdirektion Kanton Zürich. (2009). *Das personalrecht der Volksschule im Kanton Zürich: Informationsschrift für Lehrpersonen, Schulleiterinnen, Schulletier und Schulbehörden*. Zürich [The personnel law for primary schools in the Canton Zürich: Information for teachers, principals, and school authorities]. Retrieved from Kanton Zürich Bildungsdirektion Volksschulamt http://www.zh.ch/internet/bildungsdirektion/vsa/de/personelles/anstellungsbedingungen0.html
Bildungsdirektion Kanton Zürich. (2011a). *Mitarbeiterbeurteilung für Lehrpersonen (MAB): Grundlagen und empfehlungen 2011*. [Employee assessment for teachers: Foundations and recommendations 2011]. Zürich.
Bildungsdirektion Kanton Zürich (2011b, July 8). *Richtlinien zur mitarbeiterbeurteilung fur lehrpersonen der volksschule; neuerlass*. [Guidelines for performance evaluation of teachers in primary schools; new draft].
Bildungsdirektion Kanton Zürich. (n.d.). *Rechtliche Grundlagen (MAB)*[Foundations in law (MAB)]. Retrieved from Kanton Zürich Bildungsdirektion Volksschulamt http://www.zh.ch/internet/bildungsdirektion/vsa/de/personelles/personalfuehrung/mitarbeiterbeurteilungmab/rechtliches.html
Bosshardt, W. (1998, November 11). Die lehrer kommen auf den Pruefstand [Teachers put to the test]. *Tages-Anzeiger*. Retrieved from Nexis database
Brun, M. E., & Siegel, J. P. (2004, September 1-4). *What does appropriate performance reporting for political decision-makers require? Empirical evidence from Switzerland*. Paper presented at Conference of the European Group of Public Administration. Ljubljana, Slovenia.
Der Erziehungsrat des Kantons Zürich. (1990). Revision lehrerbesoldungsverordnung, leistungsbeurteilung arbeitsgruppe [Revising the teacher salary regulation, performance evaluation working group]. Zürich.
Girschweiler, H. (1999, October 13). Umstrittene Schulreformen [Controversial school reforms]. *Tages-Anzeiger*. Retrieved from Nexis databse

Inlet, U. (1998, April 28). Bildungsfragen sueffig praesentiert [Education debate presented palatably]. *Tages-Anzeiger*. Retrieved from Nexis database

Legler, A., Sigrist, M., & Wehner, T. (2008). Über die beurteilung von lehrpersonen an Zürcher Voksschulen [On teacher evaluations in Zürich primary schools]. In U. Pekruhl (Ed.), *Performance management an schulen* [Performance management in schools]. Institut für Peronalmanagement und Organisation, 27–48.

Lehrer unterlegen [Teachers defeated]. (1998, August 28). *Tages-Anzeiger*. Retrieved from Nexis database

Mehr lohn fuer bestimmte lehrer [Higher wages for certain teachers]. (2003, July 3). *Tages-Anzeiger*. Retrieved from Nexis database

Müller Kucera, K., & Stauffer, M. (2003). Attracting, developing, and retaining effective teachers, OECD Activity, Swiss country background report. *Attracting, Developing and Retaining Effective Teachers*. OECD, CORECHED. Retrieved from www.oecd.org/edu/teacherpolicy

Noordhoek, P., & Sayner, R. (2005). Beyond new public management: Answering the claims of both politics and society. *A Global Journal, 5*, 204-222.

Reber, K. (2006, December). *The diffusion of public sector reforms: Empirical evidence from Switzerland on New Public Management*. Paper presented at Hong Kong Economic Association Conference, Hong Kong.

Regierungsrates des Kantons Zürich. (1996a, April 17). *1079. Motion: Strukturelle Besoldungsrevision* [1079 Motion: Structural review of salaries]. KR-Nr. 13/1996.

Regierungsrates des Kantons Zürich. (1996b, September 25). *2884. Motion: Betreffend verzicht auf das vorgesehene lohnwirksame Qualifikationssystem (LQS) bei der Lehrerschaft* [Motion concerning abandoning the planned pay-related qualification system for teachers]. KR-Nr. 85/1996.

Regierungsrates des Kantons Zürich. (1997a, September 3). *1900. Motion: leistungsorientierte Beurteilung der Lehrkräfte der Volksschule* [Performance-oriented evaluation of teachers in primary schools]. KR-Nr. 249/1997.

Regierungsrates des Kantons Zürich. (1997b, September 17). *2015. Anfrage: Beschleunigte Einführung des LQS* [2015. Request: the accelerated introduction of the LQS]. KR-Nr. 259/1997.

Regierungsrates des Kantons Zürich. (2001, February 7). *189. Anfrage: Lohnwirksame beurteilung der Zurcher Lehrkräfte* [189. Request: Wage effective assessment of the Zürich teachers]. KR-Nr. 409/2000.

Scharpf, F. W. (1997). *Games real actors play*. Boulder, CO: Westview Press.

Schedler, K. (2003). Local and regional public management reforms in Switzerland. *Public Administration, 81*(2), 325–344.

Schneebeli, D. (1998a, September 20). Die lehrerloehne sind nicht zu tief [Teachers' salaries are not too low]. *Tages-Anzeiger*. Retrieved from Nexis database

Schneebeli, D. (1998b, October 9). Machtkaempfe entzweien die Zuercher Lehrerschaft [Power struggles divide Zürich teachers]. *Tages-Anzeiger*. Retrieved from Nexis database

Schneebeli, D. (1999a, August 28). Die lehrer im Pruefungsstress [Teachers in exam stress]. *Tages-Anzeiger*. Retrieved from Nexis database

Schneebeli, D. (1999b, April 16). Mehr lohn fuer lehrer [Higher salaries for teachers]. *Tages-Anzeiger*. Retrieved from Nexis database

Schneebeli, D. (2000, January 7). Lehrer wollen mehr [Teachers want more]. *Tages-Anzeiger*. Retrieved from Nexis database

Staubli, R. (2005, May 4). PISA: Bestnoten fuer Zürich lehrer [PISA: Top marks for Zürich teachers]. *Tages*-Anzeiger. Retrieved from Nexis database

Steiner, R. (2000). New public management in Swiss municipalities. *International Public Management Journal, 3*, 169–189.

Wagner, A., Santiago, P., Thieme, C., & Zay, D. (2004). *Country Note: Switzerland*. Retrieved from OECD, Education and Training Policy Division http://www.oecd.org/switzerland/33684152.pdf

Walton, R. E., & McKersie, R. B. (1965/1991). *A behavioral theory of labor negotiations* (2nd ed.). New York: McGraw Hill.

Wendelspiess, M. (2000). Mitarbeiterbeurteilung von lehrkräften der Zürcher volksschule: Entstehung und erste erfahrungen mit dem "Zürcher LQS" [Performance evaluation of teachers in Zürich primary schools: the formulation and first experiences of the "Zürich LQS"]. *Schweizer Scule, 6,* 14–22.

8 Finland and Zürich
Multiple Pathways to Reform

The case studies' findings directly challenge any account of teachers' unions that claims that strong unions will always block unpopular reforms (PRP). The cases suggest causal equifinality—that the same outcome can occur in different cases through different sets of independent variables (George & Bennett, 2005). Although both accounts provide examples of reforms that were implemented in spite of their unpopularity with teachers' unions, the accounts are marked by a number of significant differences. Reform in Finland was secured through collective bargaining; in Zürich, the reforms were political—linked to legislation executed by the political bureaucracy. Furthermore, the two cases point to different routes through which union opposition can be overcome—through compromise (Finland) or through power (Zürich).

When considered together, what do these cases suggest about when PRP occurs, when it does not, and the role of teachers' unions in those processes? What implications do these insights—confirmations or revisions—have in terms of theories of teachers' unions' preferences and power? The 'power-through' pathway displayed in Zürich confirms the contingency of power, and both cases provide numerous evidences of the ways in which union power varies over time and space. The 'cooperative compromise' pathway observed in Finland challenges narrow, self-interest-based conceptions of teachers' unions' preferences, suggesting that non-policy considerations, particularly relational preferences, may cause unions to compromise their first-order preferences. Furthermore, both cases illustrate the complexity of unions' preferences, suggesting that union goals are numerous and competing and that these complex and competing goals provide a variety of strategic choices and trade-offs. Together, they suggest what might distinguish Finland and Zürich from contexts in which PRP has not occurred, and they hold insights into the impact of union preferences and influence on policy-making.

The key finding from the case studies, in its most general terms, is that actors' dynamic interactions—not some static input—produce policy outcomes. These interactions occur within institutional and historical contexts that meaningfully impact upon them, but actors' preferences are not exogenously determined and reform processes are not predictable games in which structures and their incentives play out in a black box without human faces. This explanation features two different sets of factors with differing proximity to the policy outcome: the external or contextual factors—leadership, economic context, policy history, etc.—that make reform more likely, and the actors' responses and interactions that determine whether or not reform occurs.

However, significant questions remain. First, do these insights hold predictive power in the US? Or, is the unions-block-reform account an accurate depiction of US teachers' unions? If the US is different, what causal mechanisms or delimiting conditions differ between the cases? In order to answer these questions, and given the emphasis on iterative comparative understanding that guides this research, these emerging hypotheses will be tested within the US context in Chapter 9. However, before the novel causal pathways can be tested, they must be specified or operationalized in a more formal typological theory (George & Bennett, 2005). This chapter concludes with this formal specification. But first, contextual factors and the unions' responses to them are addressed in the following sections. Each section attends to two questions: First, what are the potential implications of these observations for the US context? And second, what transferability questions, if any, might there be?

CONTEXTUAL FACTORS: ORIGINS OF, TIMING OF, AND PRESSURES FOR REFORM

The contextual factors—reform leadership, economic context, and the civil sector and education reform contexts—affect the likelihood of reform in two ways. First, they may be necessary, but not sufficient, conditions for reform, such as the necessity of reform leadership. Second, they may be neither necessary nor sufficient, but instead provide delimiting conditions within and through which causal conditions operate. These conditions—economic contexts and reform histories and discourses, for example—cannot predict the policy outcome, but are significant for understanding the reform process and the response of teachers' unions to reforms. For example, when facing massive public approval of a particular reform, it will be harder for a union—even a strong union—to successfully oppose it. Similarly, economic circumstances may affect the union's ability to resist an unpopular reform. This section outlines the four key contextual factors that emerged from the case studies: the importance of reform leadership, the economic context, broader restructuring of the public sector as a precedent for teachers and schools, and related education reform trends that may affect the resistibility of reforms. However, contextual factors alone cannot explain when and why reform occurs—that is ultimately the product of actors' interactions.

Reform Leadership

Reforms that are unpopular with the union—like PRP—must have a champion. The point is obvious but essential: if the union opposes them and thus is unlikely to initiate them, the only way that these reforms are placed on the agenda and eventually implemented is if someone is committed to realizing them. The process in Zürich provides support for the importance of leadership. Although not the exclusive or primary explanation, the timing of the eventual implementation of the MAB system is at least partly explained by Buschor taking the helm of the Education Directorate. In contrast with the previous Director who, it was speculated, did not want to take on the fight to implement the MAB system, Buschor was an aggressive reformer who was committed to the implementation of MAB as a broader part of the NPM system.

Although the evidence in the Finnish case regarding the importance of reform leadership is less obvious, KT.Social_Scientist was explicit that modernizing the teachers' salary system had been a long-running priority of KT. Given that the changes were not the OAJ's first-order preferences, it is clear that if the employer had not wanted the changes, they never would have occurred. Although the point may seem obvious, it is important. If someone—the employer, government, a policy entrepreneur—does want to implement PRP and does not champion the reform, it will not happen.

The importance of reform leadership has a number of key implications for the US context. The absence of strong reform leadership may provide a key explanation for the low incidence of PRP across the United States. This may be particularly salient given the complex multilayered educational landscape in the US. What may seem obvious and important to the leadership of one state or school district may be doubted in another. PRP may not have been pursued in some states or districts not because the union blocked it, but because the leadership was not convinced it was the best strategy. This may also prove critically important in understanding how relatively decentralized units respond to centralized mandates or proposals.[1]

Economic Context

In both cases, although not the primary or exclusive explanation, the economic context significantly informed the reform process. Reforms in both Finland and Zürich followed a severe recession, which contributed to the reform story in several ways. First, the recession encouraged and enhanced cost-saving and efficiency-enhancing ideas, which had formed in both cases in the late 1980s, just before the recession. Second, the recession, and its impact on public sector wages, may have created additional incentives for teachers' unions to find ways to earn raises for teachers after a period of stagnation and decline.

Economic recessions provided an important influence in the cases of both Zürich and Finland, but, to be more precise, reforms occurred in the *immediate aftermath* of a recession, at the beginning of economic recovery. The reforms in both cases benefited from a relative resource abundance after a period of scarcity. In these cases, the early stages of the post-recession recovery provided a window of time that was 'ripe' for reform. These economic forces certainly cannot be constructed as the cause for reforms; the economic recession of the 1990s was a global force and its impact on reform trajectories is mitigated by a variety of other factors. However, the contribution of the economy should not be ignored and the perception of resource scarcity and abundance may inform the preferences and strategies of teachers' unions.

It will be important to attend to the contribution of economic pressures and incentives to the PRP reforms investigated in the US in Chapter 9. Recessions may create pressures on unions to increase their salaries through whatever means necessary. Alternatively, resource availability or abundance—spoils to divide—may improve the likelihood of reform. In both Finland and Zürich, these conditions were both present in the post-recession recovery phase, but it seems likely that these are neither sufficient nor necessary conditions. However, the researcher must remain open to the ways in which economic conditions impact actors' strategic choices in Chapter 9.

Broader Civil Sector Reform and Restructuring

In both Finland and Zürich, the changes that were applied to teachers were part of a broader effort to reform or restructure the civil sector. In Finland, the compensation components—locally negotiated TVA and HL—had been in use for several years in other municipal sectors. Teaching was simply the last municipal sector where these ideas and strategies were applied. In Zürich, the MAB reforms developed and implemented in the late 1990s were linked to legislation that addressed wages, raises, and evaluation throughout the civil sector in the early 1990s.

In both cases, teachers managed to stave off the changes for a period—longer than any other group of employees—but they were implemented *eventually*. And, in both cases, one of the key arguments mobilized by the government and employers was that teachers were *like everyone else* in the public sector. Notably, this conclusion is both paradigmatic, reflecting beliefs and assumptions, as well as institutional, based on the organization of public sector work. This institutional distinction—and its potential significance—may be most evident in the contrast between these cases and the US context.

In both Finland and Zürich, there is a public/civil sector, characterized by the same employer across various sectors, which includes teachers. In Finland, this is evident in the execution of collective bargaining agreements: teachers, doctors, civil engineers, and the rest of the local public workforce negotiate with the same employer—the municipality. In Zürich, the civil sector wage structure is determined by cantonal legislation and the wage levels—based on economic circumstances and political decisions about tax levels. They are determined by the Finance Department in collaboration with departments, like the Education Directorate, in consultation with social partners—a broad group that includes teachers among other public sector workers and their unions. In contrast, in the United States, teachers are employed by school districts— political and administrative units that are exclusively tasked with the provision of compulsory public education. Often, school districts as governing units are distinct from municipal governments. In many cases, school district boundaries are not the same as municipal boundaries. Thus, in the US, teachers do not have direct public sector counterparts.

Thinking about the ways in which the impact of broader restructuring of the public sector on teachers' work may travel to the US points to a key difference between the contexts. Although Finland and Zürich both feature degrees of decentralization, the decentralization of education decision-making in the United States is unique in important ways. Although other public sector workers are employed by the city, county, or state, teachers are hired and paid by the school district.[2] Although a significant part of the reform story in Finland and Zürich was the transfer to education of practices that had 'already been applied to everyone else;' these teachers' lack of direct peers in the United States may make it easier for teachers to maintain their 'special status.'

Global Reform and the Assault on Teachers?

In addition to the relationship between PRP for teachers and broader civil sector restructuring, it is also necessary to attend to the broader 'education reform shifts' that have characterized the last three decades, as outlined in Chapter 1. These global education reform movements (GERM) both create pressure for PRP reforms, and also undermine teachers' unions' ability to resist them because of the erosion of teachers' professionalism and professionalization produced by GERM (Apple & Teitelbaum, 1986; Burbules & Densmore, 1991; Compton & Weiner, 2008; Maroy, 2009; Robertson, 2008; Sahlberg, 2011). Although global trends are certainly a relevant part of the reform story and its context, these cases—particularly Finland—are not easily explained by significant global education reform pressures and their resulting erosion of teachers' professionalism and professionalization (Hargreaves, 2000).

Chapter 1 outlined the importance of attending to the interplay between global movements and local application and reinterpretation. However, although these global forces are certainly significant in explaining the proliferation of these reform models, global forces alone cannot explain why reforms have been adopted in some countries but not others. This is particularly evident in Finland, as PRP, NPM, and neoliberalism are particularly surprising in the Finnish context. Two factors that were cited as relevant to resisting global reforms are both present in Finland: the ideological context–particularly strong in social-democratic states with commitments to the welfare state (Aasen, 2003)–and the presence of capable veto players motivated to oppose reform (Aasen, 2003; Martens, Nagel, & Windzio, 2010). Furthermore, Finland has largely resisted GERM,[3] avoiding high stakes testing and other performativity trademarks (Sahlberg, 2011). Instead of accountability, Finland is heralded for its trust-based system: the central administration's trust in municipalities, municipalities' trust in schools and principals, and widespread trust in teachers (Niemi, 2012; Sahlberg, 2006; Simola, 2005). Furthermore, Finland's performance in PISA has only further elevated the teaching profession. If there is a context in the world in which neoliberal education reforms are least likely to occur, and where the teachers' union is best equipped to oppose them if they are proposed, it is Finland.

Although global reform pressures, in terms of public sector management and education reform ideology, may help to explain the existence of pressures or motivations for reforms, they cannot explain the union's response to these pressures. The OAJ, by all accounts, was strong enough to resist the reforms. On all measures—ideological compatibility and receptivity, the strength of the teachers' union as a veto player, and teachers' professional resources and credibility—there is no reason to expect to find PRP for teachers in Finland. The explanation for its implementation is incomplete without a consideration of the strategies and actions of the OAJ. Although global reform movements—education reform, NPM, and neoliberalism—are relevant to the Finnish case, attributing explanatory power primarily to dominant global ideological pressures would be misguided. The enthusiasm or public support for reform ideas can, as evidenced in Zürich, certainly constrain the union's strategies and effectiveness in resisting them. But even in contexts in which reform enthusiasm is low—like Finland—reform can still occur. Thus, the salience of reform ideas in particular contexts, and the influence of global ideals—like reform leadership and the economic context—is a delimiting condition rather than a primary cause.

UNION RESPONSE AND TWO PATHS: COLLABORATIVE COMPROMISE OR INDIVIDUALISTIC POWER STRUGGLE

The previous section outlined a number of relevant delimiting conditions that help to explain the timing of reforms and the resources available to unions to resist them. However, these factors alone cannot explain when and why PRP occurs. Finland and Zürich each illuminate a different path to reform—causal recipes that are different but not contradictory, consistent with causal complexity and equifinality (George & Bennett, 2005; Ragin, 1987, 2000, 2008). Without further tests, it is impossible to confirm whether these causal paths are salient beyond the particularities of these cases—that is the task of Chapter 9. However, they provide some provisional answers to the question of when reform occurs and the role of teachers' unions in that process—answers that have significant implications for theorizing about teachers' unions' preferences and power.

The relationship patterns and interaction orientations of the unions and employers in Zürich and Finland appear to be the point of greatest divergence between the two cases. In Finland, there was a clear cooperative relationship pattern—one that both employers and unions were committed to maintaining. In Zürich, the relationship between the unions and employers was more individualistic; it was characterized as an accommodative pattern. There was no evidence of either actor[4] attempting to change the relationship pattern in a cooperative direction. Given these differences, on the surface, it seems difficult to argue that the relationship pattern or the actors' interaction orientations can explain the outcome. Reform occurred in both cases despite different relationship patterns, so neither relationship pattern can be argued to be essential—or in the language of causation, a necessary condition.

However, the influence of relationship patterns must be conceptualized as multiple causal pathways. While a cooperative relationship pattern may not be a necessary condition for PRP, it may provide a new pathway previously not illuminated by existing theories. The contrast between the two cases provides rich ground for hypothesizing about multiple pathways that can be tested in Chapter 9. The cooperative relationship pattern evidenced in Finland provides a potential explanation for why a union might choose to compromise in spite of having the requisite power to challenge or block a reform. The pervasive cooperation of union-employer relationships in Finland created an environment in which compromise was an assumed part of the union's—and employer's—strategic calculations. Both parties assumed that in order to get something that they wanted, they would need to give up something that the 'other side' wanted. Specifically, the union knew that in order to get what they most wanted—more money for teachers—they would have to give up something—compromises on the form of compensation and the locus of negotiation. As a result, the outcome in Finland is not explained primarily by power, but by preferences. Relationally, maintaining the cooperative relationship pattern was a clear aspect of the OAJ's long-term strategy. They knew that if they damaged the relationship for short-term gains, it could compromise their long-term ability to negotiate effectively in the future, as the legitimacy and access the OAJ received from cooperative relationship was significant to their long-term goals. As a result, the relationship provided boundaries and limits to union demands and expectations which directly affected the translation of their multiple and competing preferences into strategies and tactics.

Although the observed relationship pattern—accommodation—in Zürich was different, it does not contradict the hypothesis that a cooperative relationship may define a causal pathway for reform; it simply illuminates a different pathway. In the Zürich case, both parties attempted to pursue their interests individualistically, without regard to the interests of the other party, throughout the reform process. Thus, although the teachers were successful in stalling reform for a period, when public opinion shifted away from the teachers, the Education Directorate was able to fast-track its plans. The development of the system was outsourced to an independent committee, thus eliminating any direct teacher participation. Although teachers' unions were able to comment in the formal consultative process, and the system was tweaked in light of these comments, the major pillars of contestation—the appropriateness of external evaluation and of linking teachers' pay to these evaluations—were finalized without any further consultation of teachers.

Thus, Finland was a case where teachers' opposition was overcome through compromise incentivized by a stable, cooperative relationship pattern whose maintenance promised long-term benefits to both parties. Zürich provides a contrasting case—an example where reform was 'powered through' in spite of union opposition. The relationship pattern is still central to the developments in Zürich, but it *reflects* power dynamics rather than altering or balancing them. In both cases, relationship patterns and interaction orientations are a significant causal factor in explaining why reform occurred, and also provide a key link to the variability of teachers' unions' preferences and power.

IMPLICATIONS FOR THEORIES OF UNION PREFERENCES AND UNION POWER

What are the implications of the findings on the likelihood of successful PRP reform for theories of teachers' unions' preferences and power? Dominant accounts portray union preferences and interests as monolithic. The extent to which these interests are realized is exclusively determined by their power, which is conceptualized as a static resource and a by-product of national institutional arrangements.

Simply put, both teachers' unions' interests and power in Finland and Zürich were far more complicated than this formulation. First, union preferences were complex, with interests, strategies, and tactics reflecting a variety of calculations about how to best achieve multiple and competing goals. Furthermore, union power was not a static concept; it varied over time and over space. These variations were linked to both internal and external factors, but the key point is that even the strongest union does not possess unchecked, unrivalled power—it cannot impose its will all the time. Finally, relationship patterns and actors' interaction orientations may play a significant role in the union's strategic calculations. Finland demonstrates that, other things equal, the union may be more likely to accept a reform than it otherwise would be in order to maintain a good relationship with a collaborative partner. Although this mechanism was only displayed in Finland, the fact that it did not occur in Zürich does not contradict this finding and provides valuable counterfactual evidence regarding delimiting conditions of relationship patterns.

Union Preferences

Both Finland and Zürich challenged monolithic and static portrayals of teachers' unions' preferences. The findings present a more complex picture of union preferences than many existing theories—in terms of the diversity of members' preferences as well as the complexity of their aggregate expression as organizational preferences. Chapters 5 and 7 addressed the variability of unions' preferences in great detail; this section does not repeat those detailed analyses, but draws out a few key analytic generalizations. First, teachers' unions' interests are not clear and straightforward—they are diverse and complex at both the individual (teacher) and collective (union) levels. The interests of individual teachers are as diverse as the particularities of their work[5] as well as their ideas about teaching and the role of the union. The union is tasked with simultaneously representing or reflecting this diversity as well as unifying it. Thus, the union is not driven by a singular goal, but multiple goals.

Second, in both cases, but particularly in the Finnish case, it was clear that the union was driven by multiple, *competing* preferences. The findings from both Finland and Zürich echo Nina Bascia's observation of teachers' and their unions' preferences: "there are several common claims . . . all of them are accurate some of the time" (2008, p. 97). Although the unions' goals may not be contradictory, they may not be able to achieve all their goals all of the time. Instead, when faced with tradeoffs, the union may have to make choices about what it wants most. These choices are based on internal factors—like the relative weights attached to various goals or preferences or conceptions of members' preferences and demands—but they are also strategic or tactical choices based on conceptions of what is possible in both the short- and long-term.

This presents an account that is far more complex than many conventional stories of union interests. As discussed in Chapter 1, the industrial relations literature tends to emphasize unions' monopoly face—their function to protect jobs and increase wages and the potentially deleterious results for firm profit and performance (Bennett & Kaufman, 2004; Booth, 1995; Booth & Kaufman, 2004; Hirsch & Addison, 1986; Kaufman, 2004). Similarly, Moe's (2006, 2011) account relies primarily on the pluralist IGT account of union behavior and a self-interest-based account of teachers' goals and preferences: teachers' union leaders are constrained by members' preferences for higher salaries, benefits, and job protection.[6]

Union leaders may be constrained by members' preferences in line with a pluralist interest group theory account, but this does not produce a clear account of union goals. Because union members are attracted by a range of purposive goals—economic and non-economic—and may have different preferences within a single goal area, the mandate passed from members to leadership is anything but clear (Johnson, Donaldson, Munger, Papay, & Qazilbash, 2007; McDonnell & Pascal, 1988). Leaders are faced with a complex task in choosing how they prioritize goals and the strategies through which they pursue them. These findings lend support to Kaufman's (2002) emphasis on the diversity of union members' interests—that workers are interested in a wide range of economic benefits and that all members do not share equally from all gains.

Ultimately, definitively establishing whether union opposition to PRP was motivated by economic interests or pedagogical or professional objections[7] is impossible, as both explanations are plausible and both were employed as explanations for opposition (Bascia & Rottmann, 2011). But a case for altruism—whether guided by professionalism or some other consideration—does not need to be proven in order to establish the complexity of union preferences. Even focusing on short-term economic self-interest alone, the complexity, diversity, and potential variability of teachers' and unions' preferences are clear. In addition to establishing the empirical complexity of union preferences, these findings also point to the significance of unions' internal capacities or what Walton and McKersie (1965/1991) label intraorganizational bargaining (Scharpf, 1997).

Union Power or Influence on Policy-Making Outcomes

Both cases confirm that union power—the influence that teachers' unions have on policy-making and policy outcomes—is not monolithic. It can vary over space—both within and between countries—and over time, confirming the contingency of power, which is exercised through the influence process (Immergut, 1992; Laswell & Kaplan, 1950). Sometimes these differences in influence may be linked to different strength resources, like membership levels and revenues, available to unions. For example, one would expect a union who represented 75% of all teachers to have more influence than an organization that only represented 13% of teachers.

However, the case studies have confirmed what was outlined in Chapter 1—that the same resources may not translate into equivalent influence over space or over time, confirming the challenges inherent in quantifying or operationalizing teachers' unions' power (McClendon & Cohen-Vogel, 2008; Strunk & Reardon, 2010). Institutions that define the actor constellations who determine policy may imbue identical resources with differential access or influence. This variability, although evident between countries, can also be significant *within* countries. Each source of variability may have significant implications for considering teachers' unions' influence in the United States—providing strong support for the importance of attending to sub-national differences.

Bargaining Power Versus Political Power
When it comes to the institutional arrangements that constrain or enable union influence, the potentially relevant institutions are numerous.

Furthermore, a union's power in one domain may not translate perfectly into another (Streshly & DeMitchell, 1994). Finland and Zürich provide examples of these differences, which carry significant implications for thinking about teachers' unionism in the US context.

First, in terms of differences between Finland and Zürich, the opportunity structure for union participation and influence is markedly different between the two contexts. In Finland, tripartite negotiation between peak associations formalizes a degree of bargaining power for unions. These negotiations are also linked to other avenues of influence through committee participation, consultative processes, and other political channels. In Zürich, by contrast, the union has very little bargaining power. Interviewees and informants disagreed as to whether public sector unions engage in bargaining, but the disagreement seems to be largely semantic; even those who maintain that the unions bargain describe the process as one in which the unions are consulted but have no real veto power over the outcome.

Given the centrality of collective bargaining in conceptions of union strength and power, it would be easy to conclude that the ZLV has no power—especially in comparison to the extensive political and bargaining power of the OAJ. However, due to the particular institutions of Swiss democracy which privilege interest groups—particularly through the role of direct democracy—the ZLV can still exert formidable political power. Although the MAB reform process illuminates some of the challenges to exerting and maintaining this kind of influence, the teachers' ability to stave off the reforms for five years speaks to the significance of this kind of political power.

Before turning to a closer examination of some of the particularities of union influence in Zürich and Finland, a few distinctions about institutional determinants of union power are critical, particularly pertaining to bargaining versus political power. First, bargaining power and political power are not perfectly correlated. Although considerable bargaining power will likely lead to political power (e.g., the OAJ), it is possible for a union to have political power without a commensurate level of bargaining power (e.g., the ZLV). If the uncorrelated nature of bargaining and political power is accepted, then it follows that a union's influence on a particular issue may be issue and context-dependent. For example, the union will have a difficult time influencing anything that is decided exclusively in the bargaining domain in Zürich, like the level of annual raises. Institutionally, the ZLV simply has no levers to influence this outcome. This is an important analytic point and a significant revision to existing conceptions of union strength and power, as they often treat union power as a phenomenon that does not vary over time, space, or issue.

The differences between bargaining power and political power are salient for the US context. First, although bargaining is the bedrock of teachers' unions' organizational power, union influence at the state and national level occurs exclusively through politics. Secondly, and more germane to this inquiry given the emphasis on school districts in Chapter 9, local union influence on a particular issue may involve bargaining, political influence, or both. Furthermore, in districts without collective bargaining, political influence provides the exclusive means for influence. In many ways, Finland and Zürich provide apt analogies for unions across the US, with unions in districts where collective bargaining is legal mirroring Finland, and unions in districts where bargaining is illegal resembling Zürich.

Variation Over Space: Sub-National Differences

Although understanding the institutional domain in which decisions are made—bargaining or political—and the way union participation is constrained or enabled within that arena provides important information about union power in that context, it presents an incomplete picture. Union power is invariant or contingent in numerous other ways.

For example, in Finland, despite the considerable bargaining and political resources available to the OAJ, the power of the national union and that of the locals are marked by considerable differences. As outlined in Chapter 4, due to the laws governing local bargaining, which give employers the right to make the final decision if they cannot reach an agreement with the union, local unions are considerably weaker than their peak associations. This does not explain why the reforms occurred in Finland, as they were negotiated at the national level where the union has considerable influence. However, these differences illustrate the potential for sub-national variation in union influence and confirm the importance of situating definitions and analysis of union strength and power at the appropriate level of decision-making. Hypothetically, if one were interested in understanding the outcomes of local negotiations in Finland—the relative distribution of HL versus TVA compensation—analysis of union influence should focus on the considerable constraints on local union power. The influence of the OAJ nationally would not provide an adequate explanation of the strength or weakness of the local unions.

This is significant when considering the strength and power of teachers' unions in the United States. Given the significance of state and local decision-making in education in the US, the majority of education policy and decision-making does not occur at the national level. In order to understand union influence on these state and local reforms, the particular opportunity structure for union influence at the relevant decision-making level must be taken into account. Given the considerable differences in collective bargaining laws and the resulting variability of union organization and resources, it seems unlikely that all unions, at all levels, in all parts of the US are equally successful at influencing decisions (Johnson & Donaldson, 2006). This should produce caution about generalizations about the power of 'US teachers' unions' that do not attend to the particular processes through which various unions attempt to influence decision-making. Furthermore, the contingency of teachers' unions' power confirms the importance of investigating their influence at the sub-national level in the United States, in order to be able to explain the documented variation of union interest, action, and policy outcomes (Bascia, 1990; Johnson & Donaldson 2006; Johnson & Kardos 2000; Murray, 2004). Although US teachers' unions may have considerable power (Bascia, 1990; Cooper & Sureau, 2008b; Hess & West, 2006; Kahlenberg, 2006; Koppich, 2005; Koppich & Callahan, 2009; Moe, 2006), it is contingent and may vary over space, time, and issue (Malen, 2001; Streshly & DeMitchell, 1994; Urban, 2004).

Variation over Time

The final way that the contingency of union power was observed in Finland and Zürich was in the variability of power over time. This was clear in Zürich, where the reform process was composed of two distinct, but interrelated, epochs. Although union opposition successfully stalled reforms for several years (1991–1995), their influence was diminished in the mid-1990s, confirming the temporal dimension of unions' power.

The difference in Switzerland was rooted in individualistic relationship patterns characterized by opportunism—the union had influence when it could threaten a referendum challenge. Neither the union's interests nor the institutional constraints changed during this period. Instead, the balance of power shifted away from the union in the mid-1990s, as there was a swell of NPM-enthusiasm in Zürich. This observation points toward the final important observation about institutional constraints on union power. Specifically, in addition to determining the resources and opportunity structure for union influence in particular, institutions also determine the other actors who may mitigate union influence. In the case of Zürich, shifts in public opinion as well as an increase in commitment to reform among key leaders provided a countervailing force that offset union opposition. As the research focuses on the US context, it will be important to remain sensitive to the factors that are external to unions that may enhance or detract from their power.

THE SIGNIFICANCE OF RELATIONSHIP PATTERNS: THE PIVOT OF PREFERENCES AND POWER

In addition to providing a more broadly structured framework for approaching actors' preferences than short-term economic self-interest, the theoretical framework and approach of this research also emphasized the potentially significant role of non-policy outcome preferences—especially actors' relational preferences (Walton & McKersie, 1965/1991). Relationship patterns and interactions provide the case studies' most significant problem- and theory-oriented contribution. Theoretically, relationship patterns and actors' interaction orientations speak to both the contingency of teachers' unions' power—explaining its variability in Zürich and its stability in Finland—and mechanisms that may induce actors to compromise.

The two causal pathways represented by Finland and Zürich present significant revisions to widespread assumptions about unions' preferences and also to the variability of union influence. For example, Moe's (2006, 2011) account of teachers' unions is built on the assumption that teachers' unions—if they are powerful enough, which Moe argues, in the case of the US, they are—will block reforms that they oppose. This theoretical articulation ignores the possibility that the union either might not oppose a particular reform or that they might choose, for some reason, not to block a reform that they oppose. The only question, according to Moe's postulate, is whether the union is strong enough to block the reform. In contrast, both international cases confirm the importance of the relationship pattern for explaining the reform pattern.

In Zürich, the relationship pattern was individualistic or accommodative and neither actor seemed to be attempting to alter that pattern. Thus, unions were included when they could threaten the outcome and management took steps to advance their goals with minimal union involvement when they could (1996–1999). In Finland, both the relationship pattern—cooperative—and the actors' interaction orientations—to maintain trust-based cooperative relationships—were clearly evident. These considerations significantly impacted the strategies employed by both the union and management; compromise was viewed as a strategic necessity. Thus, cooperative relationship patterns and a desire to maintain them encouraged compromise in the Finnish case.

These causal pathways further confirm the salience of Walton & McKersie's (1965/1991) theory of labor negotiations. In addition to the importance of intraorganizational bargaining and the causal significance of relationship patterns, the cases also support the relevance of integrative versus distributive bargaining. Integrative bargaining—problem solving approaches that create joint gain, rather than zero-sum distributional conflicts—is closely linked to trust and correlated with cooperative relationship patterns (Bennett & Kaufman, 2004; Walton & McKersie, 1965/1991). Integrative bargaining provides an opportunity for unions to express their voice face rather than their monopoly face, which dominates distributive issues (Freeman & Medoff, 1984).

Furthermore, Finland appears to provide a strong case for examining the theories of professionalism and corporatism outlined in Chapter 1. The OAJ benefits from an extensive corporatist system, which gives unions a seat at the table in significant decisions. Furthermore, teachers' professional standing—a long history of respect for teachers that has only been bolstered by Finland's recent PISA success—appears to give them a special status and credibility in education policy-making (Gunderson, 2005; Williamson 1988). However, neither the advantages of professional standing nor privileged access vis-à-vis corporatist institutions provided the OAJ with a 'blank check' of power. Instead, the desire to preserve their standing—as a cooperative social partner and a defender of quality public education—encouraged the OAJ to compromise.

How do these cases inform teachers' unions' interests and influence in the United States? As this research transitions from the international perspective back toward the US context, some readers may object that these analytic generalizations will not be relevant in the US context because the nature of teachers' unionism or education policy is just too different. Ultimately, that is an empirical, rather than theoretical, question, settled in Chapter 9. But the point may be particularly salient in terms of the cooperative relationship pattern because it mirrors, in many ways, themes of consensus oriented democracies and corporatism.

Does the 'cooperative compromise' pathway depend on the institutional structures and cultural context of small corporatist nations? Katzenstein's (1985) description of the historical and contextual factors that incentivize cooperation are an apt description of the Finnish context, where there was a widespread acknowledgement that "all members of society are in the same small boat, that the waves are high, and that everyone must help pull the oars. Domestic quarrels are a luxury that prudent persons will not tolerate" (p. 35). Although Katzenstein (1985) is careful to argue that the ideology of social partnership should not be equated with an individual predisposition toward compromise, he argues that the 'culture of compromise' is achieved and maintained through institutional arrangements that demand interest intermediation.

If the cooperative relationship pattern observed in Finland is a by-product of its particular consensus oriented and corporatist institutional arrangements, then skepticism about the salience of this causal pathway in the US—a prototypical majoritarian, competitive democracy—is justified. However, the case of Zürich provides a helpful contrast to Finland. Although the details are different—for example, tripartite corporatist negotiation is absent in Switzerland—Switzerland is also classified as a consensus oriented democracy noted for the institutionalization of power sharing arrangements and mechanisms (Lijphart, 1999). However, despite its consensus orientation, Zürich did not feature a cooperative relationship. This counterfactual suggests two things. First, it confirms that power sharing institutions are not a sufficient condition for a cooperative relationship pattern. And second, it suggests that Finnish cooperation, although encouraged by institutions, may also be a relational phenomenon—the product of trust and friendliness between individuals (Scharpf, 1997; Walton & McKersie, 1965/1991).

Although majoritarian political institutions and a competitive political culture and discourse may provide additional obstacles to establishing this kind of relationship pattern, it is certainly possible that individuals, in spite of more aggressive patterns elsewhere, could establish a cooperative relationship based on trust over time. This has been confirmed in studies of local negotiations in the US. Several authors have argued that negotiations may be adversarial in one place and collaborative in another and that some contracts are restrictive while others are flexible (Johnson, 2004; Johnson & Donaldson, 2006; Kerchner & Koppich, 1993; Kerchner, Koppich, & Weeres, 1997; McDonnell & Pascal, 1988; Murray, 2004). A diverse set of causal factors have been identified to explain this variation, from particular bargaining approaches to shifts in beliefs and ideology of bargaining parties, to the history of labor-management relationships, prior contracts, and the personalities of participants (Johnson & Donaldson, 2006; Johnson & Kardos, 2000; Kerchner & Koppich, 1993; Kerchner, Koppich, & Weeres, 1997). All of these studies establish that cooperative and productive union-management relationships are possible in the US.

TURNING TO THE US: DEDUCTIVE CONGRUENCE TESTING TOWARD TYPOLOGICAL THEORIZING

Contradicting the assumption that union preferences are predictable or static, the case studies clearly demonstrate the complexity of union preferences and also point to the significance of the relational context in which strategies and tactics are deployed. Actors' preferences are variable and their power contingent in ways that are constrained but not wholly determined by institutions, history, or other contextual factors. This is a notable departure from approaches that treat actors' preferences as exogenous, like most variants of rational-choice institutionalism (RCI) and sociological institutionalism (SI) (Scharpf, 1997). In RCI, actors' preferences can be imputed from the rules of the game, the set of choices, and assumptions about actors' preference-orderings (Levi & Cook, 1990). In SI, actors' preferences are exogenously determined by broadly defined 'rules of appropriateness' and cultural norms.

Furthermore, the explanation that emerges from the case studies differs from more static forms of institutionalism in important ways. Whereas they emphasize the significance of actors' interacting orientations as the most proximal factor in determining policy outcomes, they also confirm the importance of the historical and institutional policy-making context. However, although institutions inform union strength in some predictable ways—constraining or enabling union participation and also determining union resources—union power is more variable than static portrayals of formal institutions would suggest.

This is not to suggest that formal institutions are irrelevant to the policy-making process—far from it. Formal institutional arrangements—the rules and structures that determine policy and the actors who participate in policy-making—are significant. These institutions determine whether an issue is handled in the bargaining or political sphere and whether it is addressed at the national or sub-national level. They also privilege or disadvantage various actors in their participation in the policy-making process. These institutions help us know where to look: they determine the contours and boundaries of the policy-making arena, but they cannot explain what happens within that arena. What happens is a product of actors' interactions—their interests and relationships.

In order to either confirm the emerging hypotheses outlined in this chapter—to determine the ways in which these hypotheses must be delimited

196 *International Cases*

and reframed in order to account for the US context, or to specify the ways in which US teachers' unionism, either in terms of their preferences or power, is distinct from its international counterparts—further testing is required. Thus, the emerging hypotheses and revisions produced by the Finnish and Swiss cases will be tested in the United States using the congruence method in Chapter 9. The first step in the deductive application of the congruence method is to construct a theory-based map of the property space, which can then be reduced to the most useful types. According to George and Bennett:

> The theory employed in the congruence method may be well-established or it may be formulated or postulated by the investigator for the first time on the bases of a hunch that may turn out to be important. (2005, p. 182)

The greatest challenge is deciding how many variables to include. George and Bennett suggest, "Parsimony and simplicity are always preferable, but they should be sacrificed when complexity is necessary for adequate explanatory theory" (2005, p. 247). The second step is to reduce the property space, and then finally, to construct the research design based on the property space.

Although a variety of factors were found to be relevant to the PRP process, the US test worked, consistent with Ockham's razor, from the center out: it tested the factors that were hypothesized to be most significant or proximal to the reform outcome to see if they can account for the policy outcome. The analysis zoomed out to include increasingly distant causal factors only when required. Through this process, US case studies were used to test whether union preference calculations and interaction orientation can predict reform outcomes.

Figure 8.1 provides a model of the hypothesized relationships that can be applied to out-of-sample cases. It provides a formalization of what George and Bennett call a typological theory, which:

> specifies the independent variables, delineates them into categories for which the researcher will measure the cases and their outcomes, and provides not only hypotheses on how these variables operate individually, but also contingent generalizations on how and under what conditions

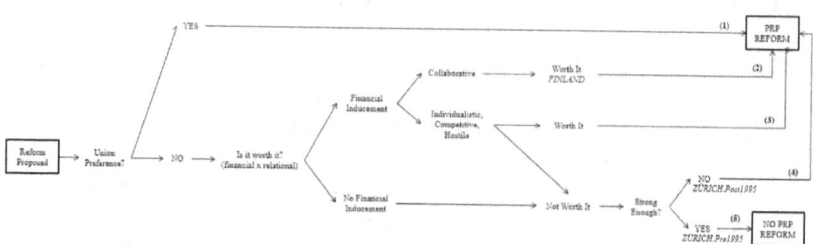

Figure 8.1 A model of reform outcomes

they behave in specified conjunctions or configurations to produce effects on specified dependent variables. (George & Bennett, 2005, p. 235)

Although the formalization of these hypotheses is difficult for the reasons suggested by Immergut (1998) above—complex configurations and many variables relative to few cases—attempting to formalize the hypothesis and apply it to new cases is an attempt to 'put the explanation at risk:'

> Formalization helps put a theory at risk by constraining the logic and clarifying key variables. Formalization promotes rigorous argumentation and structures statistical analysis. It does not improve our capacity to do statistical analysis of questions for which the statistics are not adequate, but it can improve our capacity to identify the factors that must be present, the necessary causal relationships, and the mechanisms that link them. (Levi, 1999, pp. 170–171)

This is the task of Chapter 9—to test the predictions and theoretical generalizations derived from the international cases. If the US cases defy these hypotheses, they may suggest a variety of conclusions, and the final research task will be to determine the delimiting conditions that make these theories and underlying mechanisms operate in these contexts but not in the US cases. However, if confirmatory evidence is discovered, it will considerably strengthen our confidence in these hypotheses.

NOTES

1. District responses to state policy or state responses to federal initiatives.
2. Typically an independent governing unit with its own budget and the ability to levy taxes (see Section 8.3.1).
3. There has been a relative increase in school choice, for example (Seppänen, 2003).
4. Employer or union.
5. Their grade level, subject, and geographic location.
6. This is a typical portrayal of teachers' unions (see McDonnell & Pascal, 1988).
7. Or some combination of the two.

REFERENCES

Aasen, P. (2003). What happened to social democratic progressivism in Scandinavia? Restructuring education in Sweden and Norway in the 1990s. In M. W. Apple & P. Aasen (Eds.), *The state and the politics of knowledge*. London: Routledge, 109–147.

Apple, M. W., & Teitelbaum, K. (1986). Are teachers losing control of their skills and curriculum? *Journal of Curriculum Studies*, 18(2), 177–184.

Bascia, N. (1990). Teachers evaluations of unions. *Journal of Education Policy*, 5(4), 301-312.

Bascia, N. (2008). What teachers want from their unions: What we know from research. In M. Compton & L. Weiner (Eds.), *The global assault on teaching, teachers, and their unions: Stories for resistance*. New York: Palgrave Macmillan, 95–108.

Bascia, N., & Rottmann, C. (2011). What's so important about teachers' working conditions? The fatal flaw in North American education reform. *Journal of Education Policy, 26*(6), 787–802.

Bennett, J. T., & Kaufman, B. E. (2004). What do unions do? A twenty-year perspective. *Journal of Labor Research, 25*(3), 339–349.

Booth, A. L. (1995). *The economics of the trade union*. New York: Cambridge University Press.

Kaufman, B. E. (2002). Models of union wage determination: What have we learned since Dunlop and Ross? *Industrial Relations, 41*(1), 303–316.

Kaufman, B. E. (2004). What unions do: Insights from economic theory. *Journal of Labor Research, 25*(3), 341–372.

Burbules, N. C., & Densmore, K. (1991). The limits of making teaching a profession. *Educational policy, 5*(1), 44–63.

Compton, M., & Weiner, L. (Eds.). (2008). *The global assault on teaching, teachers, and their unions: Stories for resistance*. New York: Palgrave Macmillan.

Cooper, B. S., & Sureau, J. (2008b). The collective politics of teacher unionism. In B. Cooper, J.G. Cibulka, & L. Fusarelli (Eds.), *Handbook of education politics and policy*. New York: Routledge, 263–282.

Freeman, R. B., & Medoff, J. L. (1984). *What do unions do?* New York: Basic Books.

George, A. L., & Bennett, A. (2005). *Case studies and theory development in the social sciences*. Cambridge, MA: MIT Press.

Gunderson, M. (2005). Two faces of union voice in the public sector. *Journal of Labor Research, 26*(3), 3939–3958.

Hargreaves, A. (2000). Four ages of professionalism and professional learning. *Teachers and teaching: Theory and practice, 6*(2), 151–182.

Hess, F. M., & West, M. R. (2006). *A better bargain: Overhauling teacher collective bargaining for the 21st century*. Cambridge, MA: Program on Education Policy and Governance. Retreived from http://www.hks.harvard.edu/pepg/PDF/Papers/BetterBargain.pdf

Hirsch, B. T., & Addison, J. T. (1986). *The economic analysis of unions: New approaches and evidence*. Boston: Allen & Unwin.

Immergut, E. (1992). *Health politics*. Cambridge: Cambridge University Press.

Immergut, E. (1998). The theoretical core of the new institutionalism. *Politics Society, 26*(5), 5–34.

Johnson, S. M. (2004). Paralysis or possibility: What do teacher unions and collective bargaining bring? In Henderson, R. D., Urban, W. J., & Wolman, P. (Eds.), *Teachers unions and education policy: Retrenchment or reform?* Oxford: Elsevier, 33–50.

Johnson, S. M., & Donaldson, M. (2006). The effects of collective bargaining on teacher quality. In J. Hannaway, & A. Rotherman (Eds.), *Collective bargaining in education: Negotiating change in today's schools*. Cambridge, MA: Harvard Education Press, 111–140.

Johnson, S. M., Donaldson, M. L., Munger, M. S., Papay, J. P., & Qazilbash, E. K. (2007). *Leading the local: Teachers union presidents speak on change, challenges*. Retrieved from Education Sector Reports http://www.educationsector.org/sites/default/files/publications/UnionLeaders.pdf

Johnson, S. M., & Kardos, S. (2000). Reform bargaining and its promise for school improvement. In T. Loveless (Ed.), *Conflicting missions? Teachers unions and educational reform*. Washington, DC: The Brookings Institution, 7–46.

Kahlenberg, R. D. (2006). The history of collective bargaining among teachers. In J. Hannaway & A. Rotherman (Eds.), *Collective bargaining in education:*

Negotiating change in today's schools. Cambridge, MA: Harvard Education Press, 7–26.
Katzenstein, P. J. (1985). *Small states in world markets: Industrial policy in Europe*. Ithaca, NY: Cornell University Press.
Kaufman, B. E. (2002). Models of union wage determination: What have we learned since Dunlop and Ross? *Industrial Relations, 41*(1), 303–316.
Kaufman, B. E. (2004). What unions do: Insights from economic theory. *Journal of Labor Research, 25*(3), 341–372.
Kerchner, C. T., & Koppich, J. E. (1993). *A union of professionals: Labor relations and educational reform*. New York: Teachers College Press.
Kerchner, C. T., Koppich, J. E., & Weeres, J. G. (1997). *United mind workers: Unions and teaching in the knowledge society*. San Francisco: Jossey-Bass Inc.
Koppich, J. E. (2005). Addressing teacher quality through induction, professional compensation, and evaluation: Effects on labor-management relations. *Educational Policy, 19*(1), 90–110.
Koppich, J. E., & Callahan, M. (2009). Teacher collective bargaining: What we know and what we need to know. In G. Sykes, B. Schneider, & D. Plank (Eds.), *Handbook of education policy research*. New York: Routledge, 296–306.
Laswell, H., & Kaplan, A. (1950). *Power and Society*. New Haven: Yale.
Levi, M. (1999). Producing an analytic narrative. In J. Bowen & R. Petersen (Eds.), *Critical comparisons in politics and culture*. Cambridge: Cambridge University Press, 152–172.
Levi, M., & Cook, K. S. (1990). *The limits of rationality*. Chicago: University of Chicago Press.
Lijphart, A. (1999). *Patterns of democracy: Government forms and performance in thirty-six countries*. New Haven, CT: Yale University Press.
Malen, B. (2001). Generating interest in interest groups. *Educational Policy, 15*(1), 168–185.
Maroy, C. (2009). Convergences and hybridization of educational policies around "post-bureaucratic" models of regulation. *Compare, 39*(1), 71–84.
Martens, K., Nagel, A. K., & Windzio, M. (Eds.). (2010). *Transformation of education policy*. New York: Palgrave Macmillan.
McClendon, M. K., & Cohen-Vogel, L. (2008). Understanding education policy change in the American states: Lessons from political science. In B. Cooper, J. G. Cibulka, & L. Fusarelli (Eds.), *Handbook of education politics and policy*. New York: Routledge, 30–51.
McDonnell, L. M., & Pascal, A. (1988). *Teacher unions and educational reform*. Santa Monica, CA: The Rand Corporation.
Moe, T. (2006). Union power and the education of children. In J. Hannaway & A. Rotherman (Eds.), *Collective bargaining in education: Negotiating change in today's schools*. Cambridge, MA: Harvard Education Press, 229–256.
Moe, T. (2011). *Special interests: Teachers unions and America's public schools*. Washington, DC: Brookings Institution.
Murray, C. E. (2004). Innovative local teacher unions: What have they accomplished? In R. D. Henderson, W. J. Urban & P. Wolman (Eds.), *Teacher unions and education policy: Retrenchment and reform*. Oxford: Elesevier, 149–166.
Niemi, H. (2012). The societal factors contributing to education and schools in Finland. In H. Niemi, A. Toom, & A. Kallioniemi (Eds.), *Miracle of education*. Rotterdam: Sense Publishers, 19–38.
Ragin, C. C. (1987). *The comparative method: Moving beyond qualitative and quantitative strategies*. Berkeley: University of California Press.
Ragin, C. C. (2000). *Fuzzy-set social science*. Chicago: University of Chicago Press.
Ragin, C. C. (2008). *Redesigning social inquiry: Fuzzy sets and beyond*. Chicago: University of Chicago Press.

Robertson, S. L. (2008). 'Remaking the world': Neoliberalism and the transformation of education and teachers' labor. In M. Compton & L. Weiner (Eds.), *The global assault on teaching, teachers, and their union*. New York: Palgrave Macmillan, 11–30.

Sahlberg, P. (2006). Raising the bar: How Finland responds to the twin challenge of secondary education? *Profesorado. Revista de curriculum y formación del profesorado, 10*(1), 1–26.

Sahlberg, P. (2011). *Finnish lessons: What can the world learn from educational change in Finland?*, New York: Teachers College Press.

Scharpf, F. W. (1997). *Games real actors play*. Boulder, CO: Westview Press.

Seppänen, P. (2003). Patterns of public-school markets in the Finnish comprehensive school from a comparative perspective. *Journal of education policy, 18*(5), 513–531.

Simola, H. (2005). The Finnish miracle of PISA: Historical and sociological remarks on teaching and teacher education. *Comparative Education, 41*(4), 455–470.

Streshly, W. A., & DeMitchell, T. A. (1994). *Teacher unions and TQE: Building quality labor relations*. Thousand Oaks: Corwin Press.

Strunk, K. O., & Reardon, S. F. (2010). Measuring the strength of teachers' unions: An empirical application of the partial independent item response. *Journal of educational Behavioral Statistics, 35*(6), 629–670.

Urban, W. J. (2004). Teacher politics. In R. D. Henderson, W. J. Urban, & P. Wolman (Eds.), *Teachers unions and education policy: Retrenchment or reform?* Amsterdam: Elesevier, 51–80.

Walton, R. E., & McKersie, R. B. (1965/1991). *A behavioral theory of labor negotiations* (2nd ed.). New York: McGraw Hill.

Williamson, P. J. (1988). *Corporatism in perspective*. London: Sage.

Part III
School District Cases

9 Teachers' Unions in the United States
A Sub-National Test

Despite maintaining that teachers' unions tend to block reforms like PRP in the US, even Moe (2011) acknowledges that some anomalies—states or districts that have embraced some version of PRP—exist, confirming that the questions 'when do such results (PRP) occur? And why don't they always?' are salient in the US context. Although Moe argues that many of the "departures from the single salary schedule didn't amount to much" (2011, p. 311), he identifies some innovative PRP programs—like those developed in Texas and Florida in the early 2000s—that appear to be exceptions to his, and many reformers', broader argument about teachers' unions' power and their effect on education policy in the United States.

In 2006, the Texas Legislature passed House Bill 1, which included appropriating $147.5 million for the District Awards for Teacher Excellence (DATE)[1] for the 2008–2009 school year.[2] In the program's first year, 203 districts participated—16% of all districts. The grant was noncompetitive and was awarded to all school districts who complied with the timeline and requirements. The only criteria for awarding bonuses in the DATE program was that teachers positively impact student academic improvement, growth, *or* achievement and that the criteria used by each district to determine this positive impact be quantifiable, reliable, valid, and objective. Plans could be applied to individuals, teams, or entire schools. The amount of each grant was determined by a district's enrollment in the 2006–2007 school year. Districts had to use 60% of funds for incentives for high-performing teachers.[3]

Florida's development of its state PRP program was an ongoing process from 2001, with three iterations introduced over an eight-year period. E-Comp was passed in 2001, replaced by the Special Teachers are Rewarded (STAR) program in 2006, and then by the Merit Award Program (MAP) in 2007. The plans were controversial and unpopular with many teachers, their unions, and district administration (Johnson & Papay, 2009).

MAP preserved many of the goals of the STAR plan but increased the flexibility available to districts as school boards and unions negotiated proposals. Acceptable MAP plans were required to allocate 60% of bonuses to teachers based on learning gains on standardized tests, with the remaining 40% from principal evaluations. However, unlike the STAR program, MAP allowed supplementary bonuses for exemplary work attendance. Also, the percentage of personnel defined as 'top performing' could be defined more flexibly under MAP—in STAR it had to be at least 25%—and bonuses could range from 5–10% of the district's average teacher salary. Perhaps the most significant deviation from the STAR plan was that, under MAP, districts could provide awards to groups of teachers and were not limited to only providing individual bonuses. According to FDOE materials, from 2007–2008 "districts are not legislatively required to do [PRP]; however, to receive an allocation based on the district's proportion of K–12 base funding a performance plan compliant with 1012.225 is required" (Florida Department of Education, 2007). Around 14% of the districts in the state participated in the state's MAP program.

Perhaps these particular instances of reform—whether viewed at the state or district level—are simply aberrations from some general rule that holds all the time, in every other jurisdiction of the United States. However, given the potential diversity of reform experiences across districts and states, "findings reporting [the] average impact offer little [of] use to policy-makers" (Johnson & Donaldson, 2006, p. 113). Furthermore, these 'exceptional cases' have both practical and theoretical value, providing a crucial test of the hypotheses outlined in Chapter 8 in the US context: that there are two causal pathways to overcome union opposition to reform—cooperation or power.

This chapter examines the variable school district participation in these state contexts—instances where the irresistible force of reform appears to have moved the immovable object, as it did in Finland and Zürich. Overall, district participation in state PRP programs was low. Although the low take-up rates could be portrayed as a limitation on states passing voluntary reforms, they provide a unique opportunity to examine the factors that may have led some districts to participate and not others. The decision to focus on school districts has a number of advantages. First, a school district focus is appropriate to the phenomenon being investigated, as the decision of whether to participate in the grants was made at the school district level. Second, examining school district opt-in or opt-out choices to a statewide program provides pseudo-experimental control conditions. This chapter focuses on case selection and other methodological questions as well as introducing the context that is critical to the case analysis in Chapter 10.

METHODOLOGY: CASE SELECTION AND ANALYSIS

Although the research design and methodological choices are consistent with the principles outlined in Chapter 3, a few distinctions regarding case selection and data collection and analysis warrant explanation. The first part of this section outlines the two-step selection process used to identify the six school district cases analyzed in Chapter 10. Then, the second half turns to data collection and analysis.

Case Selection Process

Despite recent increases in its influence, the role of the United States Department of Education (US DOE) and federal legislation remains limited in the United States; significant educational decision-making rests in the hands of states and local school districts (Berkman & Plutzer, 2005). The United States is a federalist political system characterized by a careful balance of power between federal and state governments. The remit of the federal government is constrained to those powers exclusively given it within the Constitution. According to the 10th Amendment of the Bill of Rights, any power not explicitly given to the federal government nor prohibited to the states is reserved to the states (Berkman & Plutzer, 2005). From the founding of the first normal school in the 19th century, public education has been consistently championed as the exclusive domain of the states (Berkman & Plutzer, 2005; Meyer, Scott, & Strang, 1987).

The diversity of interstate and interdistrict policy-making and bargaining contexts is well documented—diversity that defies simple generalizations (Berkman & Plutzer, 2005; Johnson, 2004; Johnson & Donaldson, 2006; Meyer et al., 1987). Although descriptions of US education policy 'averages' may be appropriate in some contexts,[4] they obscure more than they reveal (Johnson, 2004; Johnson & Donaldson, 2006).[5] Generalizing at the national level and ignoring significant sub-national diversity produces flawed theories and descriptions:

> Comparativists too often rely on national-level means and aggregate data when studying countries with high degrees of internal heterogeneity. This tendency to unreflectively gravitate toward national-level data and national units of analysis—what Rokkan (1970) called whole-nation bias—has contributed to a *miscoding* of cases that can distort causal inferences and skew efforts at theory building. (Snyder, 2001, p. 94)

Furthermore, in addition to being the dominant policy-making domains in the United States, focusing on sub-national units presents a number of advantages: it produces more empirically valid descriptions, classifications, and causal inferences; allows (nationally) uneven political processes and changes to be observed; and facilitates the construction of controlled comparisons (Lijphart, 1971; Snyder, 2001).

Although crucial cases where PRP had been implemented—what Moe (2011) labels "small victories for sanity" (p. 215)—existed at both the state and district levels within the United States in 2010, this research focused on district-level decision-making. In *Ten Thousand Democracies*, Michael Berkman and Eric Plutzer (2005) help to put the key role of school districts within US education policy in context:

> No more than 10 percent of public school revenues has ever come from the federal government. Moreover, the US Supreme Court has held that

education is not a fundamental right guaranteed in the federal Constitution.[6] . . . The action in public education, especially in the financing and administration of American schools, is in the more than 14,000 school districts they have created. (p. 20)

Although the role of states—and the federal government—in establishing education policy and mandating reform has expanded since the peak of local control, school districts are particularly significant when exploring teachers' unions in the US, as school districts are the domain of collective bargaining—the bedrock of union organization and a significant mechanism in what Moe calls "the politics of blocking" (Hanson, 1983, 2013; Moe, 2011, p. 275).

However, although there was an identifiable set of districts that had implemented PRP reforms,[7] direct district-level selection presented a series of challenges, particularly because, for the most compelling application of the congruence method, the sample of districts needed to include both districts with and without PRP reforms. Although participating districts could be selected randomly, how could the comparability of selected districts be ensured given the complexity of intergovernmentalization and nested systems (Aggarwal, 2005; Hanson, 2013)? Districts vary in myriad ways, from size and urbanicity to governance and political culture. If differences in union behavior or influence are observed between two districts, how can it be determined that the observed variance is a function of union differences and not some other difference between the districts? Purposive sampling isn't an option because of the lack of substantive a priori theorizing about which variables or combinations of variables matter and how they might constrain or enable teachers' unions' influence on reform outcomes. Random sampling is equally problematic because it provides no systematic account or test of whether observed differences are a function of the variables of interest or of some other factor. In short, selecting cases from within the population of districts that had implemented PRP was complicated by the need to ensure comparability.

However, even if participating districts *could* be selected in a methodologically sophisticated way, identifying comparable non-PRP districts would present a further challenge. Negative cases (non-PRP) needed to be as similar as possible to positive cases (PRP)—ideally with the only difference being the presence of the reform outcome (Ragin, 2000). This selection requirement faces all of the comparability challenges, plus the additional requirement that, beyond descriptive similarities, negative cases needed to be cases where PRP had been considered or attempted but abandoned: cases where reform had 'failed.'

The solution to these challenges was to employ a two-fold selection process, first selecting two states and then selecting a sample of districts from within those states. This twofold selection process had a number of advantages and controlled for many important institutional and contextual variables

(Lijphart, 1971; Snyder, 2001). By first selecting states with state-level merit pay policies or grants to which districts were forced to either opt in or opt out, it was possible to compare participating to non-participating districts under pseudo-experimental control conditions—making the methodologically robust selection of negative cases possible.

State Selection Process
In 2010, there were state-level merit pay policies in fourteen states—Alaska, Arizona, Arkansas, Florida, Georgia, Virginia, Indiana, Iowa, Minnesota, North Carolina, Rhode Island, Tennessee, Texas, and Utah. State selection was based on three criteria: policy design, institutional differences in union strength, and comparability of districts.

In terms of policy design, because the research aimed to isolate the decision- and policy-making process at the local level, the state PRP policies needed to meet a number of criteria. First, the state-level policy could not be mandatory;[8] it needed to allow district choice in terms of participation and non-participation. Second, it needed to allow, as much as possible, local design of the district policy in order to approximate a non-state incentivized reform as closely as possible. Together, these features allowed for a meaningful comparison between a district with and without PRP in terms of how unions shape, influence, or obstruct reforms.

Within the aforementioned states, the policies could be divided into several types. Some of the states simply had state laws that required a certain percentage of salaries to be provided through some form of differentiated compensation policy. These were eliminated from consideration both because they were mandatory—they left no option for non-participation—and because they dictated the exact terms in the legislation leaving no room for local design. A second set of state policies considered for this study included new programs in which the state had selected a few districts to pilot PRP programs. Again, these did not allow for a selection on the basis of participating and non-participating districts, as the program was not open to all districts. After eliminating the states with either pilot programs or legally prescribed requirements four states remained—Florida, Minnesota, Texas, and Utah.

As discussed above, selected cases needed to reflect the 'universe' of cases—strong and weak unions and presence and absence of PRP. So, in addition to policy design, the second criteria guiding state selection was maximizing the diversity of union organization—ensuring that cases included both strong and weak unions.

Executive order 10988, which was signed by President Kennedy in 1962, recognized the appropriateness of unionism in the public sector and gave federal government employees the right to collective bargaining (Kearney, 2010). Along with teacher strikes in New York City in the 1960s that demonstrated the potential for union action in education, executive order 10988 effectively ushered in teachers' unionism (Kahlenberg, 2006). However, as discussed in Chapter 3, collective bargaining laws—whether negotiating is permissible, what can be negotiated—are state-level decisions. These laws significantly impact the teachers' unions' organization across the US: both its sources of union power—membership levels and financial resources—and opportunities for its exercise.

With this in mind, for several reasons, Texas and Florida were selected from among the four remaining states (FL, MN, TX, UT). First, in 2010, when data was collected, Texas was the only state among the four in which collective bargaining is prohibited in the public sector (Type IV), while Florida allowed collective bargaining and prohibited agency fees (Type II). Given the central importance of collective bargaining to union influence, one would expect differences in collective bargaining laws to be correlated with meaningful variation in union membership levels and financial resources across states. And so, the selection of Texas and Florida allowed for a comparison of variation in influence across institutional arrangements.

Finally, the reason why Florida was chosen instead of Minnesota or Utah, which both allow or require collective bargaining, is because it provided a more comparable district sample to Texas. Texas and Florida contain sets of districts that are both comparable to one another and more representative of the nation as a whole—featuring urban, rural, and suburban districts. In contrast Utah and Minnesota each only had one or two urban districts—Salt Lake City, UT and Minneapolis and St. Paul, MN—and none of these districts were among the largest 100 in the United States at the time of research. For a variety of reasons, outlined in the next section, the research focused on large, urban school districts. As a result, the diversity of districts, including numerous large, urban districts in Texas and Florida—Texas had 18 districts among the nation's largest 100 and Florida had 14[9]—allowed for a methodologically robust district case selection process.

District Selection Process

Two considerations guided the district selection process. First, districts were selected to reflect the 'universe' of cases (see Table 3.1). Ensuring both strong and weak unions was addressed primarily through the state selection, and then both participating and non-participating districts were selected in each state. Second, these cases needed to be sufficiently similar in order to isolate the variables of interest. All of the districts were selected from the largest 100 school districts in the United States, in order to control for district size and demographics, which are likely to impact the local reform and policy-making process (Goldhaber, DeArmond, Player, & Choi, 2008; Mintrom, 2009).

In 2008–2009,[10] these districts—1% of the 13,800 districts in the US—educated 22% of the nations' students and had notably high concentrations of non-white and economically disadvantaged students (NCES, 2011).[11] Of the 18 largest Texas districts, 14 participated in the state's PRP program, District Awards for Teacher Excellence (DATE)—77% of the largest districts compared to 16% of the total (Springer et al., 2010), further

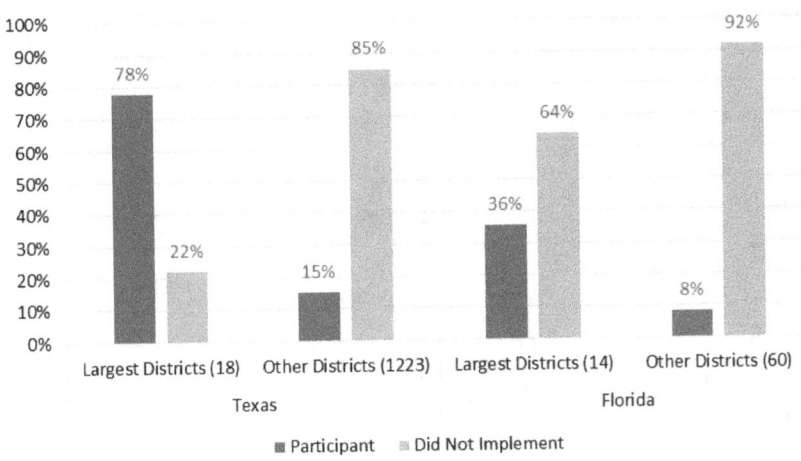

Figure 9.1 Rates of school district participation in Texas and Florida

confirming the need to control for district size and urbanicity. In Florida, participation rates in the state PRP program were even lower than those in Texas. According to correspondence with the Florida Department of Education (FDOE), in the first year of the program, only 10 districts out of 60[12] submitted compliance plans, and only eight of those ten implemented their plans. In 2010–2011, only four districts and over 150 charter schools were participating in the program.

From the 18 districts in Texas and 14 in Florida, a purposive random sampling was used to select both participating and non-participating districts. In Texas, three districts were selected—two from the subset of participating districts and one from the subset of non-participating districts. Of the 14 districts in Florida, five submitted acceptable proposals to the Florida DOE when the program was implemented in 2006–2007. Of these five districts, only two were still participating in the 2010–2011 school year, and one did not implement its plan after submitting its proposal in 2006–2007. The remaining nine districts have never participated. In order to represent the range of participation outcomes, three districts were selected using purposive random sampling—one that was a 'full participant,' one that eventually terminated participation, and one district that never participated. Districts were categorized, numbered, and selected using a random number generator.

Because of the potentially sensitive nature of local politics, the confidentiality of research participants was protected by not disclosing the names of interviewees[13] or their districts. Districts[14] are referenced using the codes outlined in Table 9.1.

Unlike the international cases, which were selected from a sample of 'cell 4' cases for their theoretical significance, the purposive sample of school district cases reflects the 'universe' of types of cases according to the variables identified in Table 3.1—districts with weak (TX) and strong (FL) unions

Table 9.1 School district codes

DISTRICT CODE	STATE	PARTICIPATION STATUS	UNION STRENTH[15]
DISTRICT 1.FL	Florida	Participant	Relatively strong
DISTRICT 2.FL	Florida	Discontinued Participant	
DISTRICT.2FL		*Participant*	
DISTRICT.2FL(2009)		*Non-participant*	
DISTRICT 3.FL	Florida	Non-participant	
DISTRICT 4.TX	Texas	Participant	Weak
DISTRICT 5.TX	Texas	Participant	
DISTRICT 6.TX	Texas	Non-participant	
DISTRICT.6TX		*Non-participant*	
DISTRICT.6TX(2009)		*Opt in Decision (DATE II)*	

and with and without PRP. Although the first phase of research selected on the dependent variable (PRP implementation) in order to focus on crucial cases, in the second phase, including cases from cells 1 and 2 (District.6TX and District.3FL, respectively) was essential in order to apply the congruence method (George & Bennett, 2005). The diversity of these cases allows the researcher to test and probe the theoretical generalizations proposed in Chapter 8 from several angles, subjecting the assumptions to a series of counterfactuals.

First, District.1FL and District.2FL most closely resemble the crucial cases investigated in the first phase of research, providing a test of the hypotheses of why PRP reform occurs in cases with strong unions. They could strengthen existing theories or, if they cannot be explained by existing theories, they may point to new causal pathways, uncovered through inductive process tracing. This would contribute to a more fine-grained contingent generalization, suggesting that although the causal pathways identified in Chapter 8 might be sufficient conditions for reform, they are not necessary. Second, District.3FL provides an opportunity to consider 'why PRP *does not* occur' and to test the necessity and sufficiency of the causal pathways. If either of the causal pathways are evident in District.3FL and do not produce reform, the causal sufficiency of these pathways would be undermined. Finally 'cell 1' (District.6TX) and 'cell 2' (District.4TX, District.5TX) cases provide an opportunity to explore the incidence of reform in contexts in which unions—according to all interviewees—were largely irrelevant to the outcome. These cases illustrate the non-union factors that may influence reform.

The comparative analysis proceeded through a series of stages. First, the typological theory was applied to the participating districts in Florida. Then, it was expanded to include the non-participating Florida case. The final stage of comparative analysis was to examine the weak union cases. Throughout the analysis, the focus was on the degree to which actors' preferences, power, and relationship patterns could explain the reform outcome. In order to maximize comparability between all of the case studies, the tables and figures employed in the analysis are modeled off of those used in Chapters 5 and 7 as much as possible.

CONTEXTUAL CONDITIONS

The analysis in the next chapter focuses on testing the hypotheses developed in Chapter 8—that actors' interactions and their complex and competing preferences are the proximate causes of policy outcomes. However, although actors' preferences and interactions are hypothesized as the most significant causal factor, other factors and conditions, including institutions, economic context, and shifts in popular opinion and beliefs, are not irrelevant. On the contrary, the understanding of the interrelationship between these causal forces, articulated in Chapter 8, confirms the relevance of these other factors. Their importance is expressed and reflected *through* actors' preferences and interactions; the economic context, dominant reform ideas, and institutional context constrain and enable both policy-makers' ability to advance reform and unions' ability to resist it.

Before turning to the analysis in Chapter 10, the remainder of this chapter does four things: it provides an overview of the relevant institutional context of school district governance in the United States, it delves more deeply into union organization in Texas and Florida, it summarizes the policy context—the growing momentum behind PRP reform in the US—within which the investigated reforms occurred, and, finally, it highlights salient dimensions of the economic environment. These conditions and contexts should not and cannot be ignored, as they inform actors' preferences and strategies. However, these factors are largely controlled by case selection and research design.

Institutional Context: The School District

US school districts are notably different from what might be assumed to be functional equivalents in both "centralized national educational systems, where districts and schools often function as simple subordinate units in sovereign national bureaucracy" (Meyer et al., 1987, p. 186), and other relatively decentralized systems, like Switzerland. US school districts are responsible for managing the growth of schools through the administration of funds, a significant portion of which are raised at the local level through local property taxes (Berkman & Plutzer, 2005; Ehrensal & First, 2008). They are also involved in policy, either through the initiation of policy or the interpretation and implementation of state-mandated policy (Ehrensal & First, 2008; Sykes, O'Day, & Ford, 2009).

The governing authority of the local policy-making process within these school districts is an elected[22] school board working with a board-appointed superintendent. According to Ehrensal and First (2008), these school boards have the delegated authority of all three branches of government, authority that legally is state power. Thus, school board members are said to be state representatives and are charged with ensuring that state policies are carried out at the local level. However, the local boards *do* have real powers, within state and federal statutes—like hiring, firing, and decisions about curriculum. And, because they are elected by their local constituencies and are thus accountable to voters, school boards are often responding to the directives of higher governmental authority *and* the demands of the local electorate. As a result, the degree to which they comply with state policies completely and within the spirit of said policies is variable (Ehrensal & First, 2008). A final distinguishing feature—particularly in international context—is that school boards are usually an independent governing body, distinct from any other elected city governments. This is a salient distinction relative to Finland and Switzerland, where regional and local governments also have considerable authority. However, in those cases, local authority over schools ultimately rests in the elected cantonal (Switzerland) and municipal (Finland) governments, which are tasked with the provision of *all* public services in their domain. In contrast, in the US, school districts and school board politics are usually[23] one-issue political domains.

In general, across the US, although the superintendent and her central office staff are responsible for producing research, making recommendations, and shaping the agenda, the power of the superintendent relative to the board varies (Wirt & Kirst, 1997). The degree to which the superintendent is able to affect or determine the board's decisions and the amount of oversight of the superintendent's activity varies across school boards (Wirt & Kirst, 1997). The school board functions as "a pivot between community demands and school operations" (1997, p. 100), and the superintendent is constrained by public demands and resulting board opinions:

> They must anticipate reactions of board members to their actions because the board does have the basic power to fire them. . . . The superintendent operates within considerable latitude as long as he or she stays within the board's ideological zone of tolerance. (Wirt & Kirst, 1997, pp. 151–152)

Thus, the division of responsibilities between boards and superintendents is a constantly constructed, rather than self-evident, arrangement. The relationship between the superintendent and the school board can—as

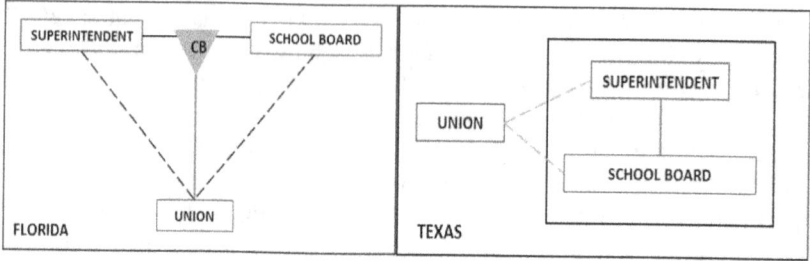

Figure 9.2 School district governance in Florida and Texas

evidenced by several of the cases that experienced superintendent or board turnover during the period in question—vary over time within a district. However, Figure 9.2 provides a picture of the general patterns observed in each state.

The different visual displays of the Superintendent-School Board relationship between the two states in Figure 9.2 are not accidental. Across districts, many interviewees talked about the importance of effective school board governance—of a board that was appropriately engaged without being "managerial." Although interviewees in Texas occasionally referenced board-superintendent dynamics, they were typically positive references. The picture that consistently emerged from Texas school districts was captured by the Superintendent of District.5TX, who referred to a corporate governance model with a strong executive and a hands-off board. All three Texas superintendents had significant decision-making authority; their (non-) participation in the DATE grant was an executive decision that was merely presented to the board for approval (Central_Office.5TX,; School_Board1.5TX; School_Board2.5TX; Superintendent.4TX).

In contrast, based on interviewees' descriptions, school boards in selected Florida districts appeared to have relatively greater power, influence, and involvement in decision-making. At times, superintendents felt that they could not pursue their objectives or preferences due to school board opposition (Superintendent.3FL; Superintendent.1FL). This was particularly important in terms of union participation and influence, as the governance triangle depicted in Figure 9.2 provides a variety of possible relational alliances. Florida and Texas, given their marked differences, provide fertile soil for testing theories about union power and impact on reforms through a series of congruence tests.

Union Strength and Power in Texas and Florida

In terms of defining key institutional differences, one of the most notable differences across school districts, controlling for the impact of size and available resources, is the degree of inclusion of teachers' unions in local negotiations and decision-making. In the discussion of case selection, the basic institutional differences between Texas and Florida—one state where collective bargaining is illegal and another where it is required—were outlined. However, the picture of union strength and power in the two states is a bit more complex and warrants further discussion. Curiously, despite the different institutional contexts in the two states, statewide union membership was similar between the states in 2010—61% in Florida and 65% in Texas. However, it was clear that unions in selected Florida districts were much stronger than their Texas counterparts both quantitatively and qualitatively.

Quantitatively, the state-level trends do not reflect the particularities of local unionism in the selected cases. Unions in the selected Texas districts had membership rolls numbering in the 100s—750 in District.4TX and approximately 350 in District.6TX—compared to 8,000[24] union members in District.3FL and 5,500[25] members in District.1FL.[26] A likely hypothesis for the divergence between state-level representation and the district-level figures may be provided by significant regional differences in union organization: a union leader in District.6TX suggested that unions in southern Texas have experienced significant growth, which has not occurred in the north where District.6TX is located. Similarly, there may be important differences between large cities in Florida and other districts. However, providing an explanation for these disparities is beyond the scope of this research. The key point is that there are clear differences in union strength resources between the selected districts in Florida and their counterparts in Texas. This also reinforces the importance of considering union activity and influence at the district level.

Qualitatively, the difference in union influence, although suggested by membership levels, extends beyond these figures. School district officials and school board members across all three Texas districts unanimously confirmed the relative weakness of teachers' unions:

> They are really supportive. They are very vocal . . . but they're, you know, this is Texas. And we're a right to work state and so they really have no . . . um . . . strength when it comes to negotiating contracts or anything. They're not involved in that. But, um, they talk to us all time. (School_Board1.4TX)
>
> It is not a, it is not a union state; it's a right to work state . . . they do try to influence policy decisions . . . especially in areas of compensation or HR . . . they are usually not [successful]. (School_Board1.5TX)
>
> No, no, we don't fear them at all. They cause us a little heartburn from time to time, but they certainly don't have enough leverage, at least my decisions. (Superintendent.6TX)

The characterization of the unions' weakness in all three districts referred to both a general weakness as well as their particular inability to impact the

DATE reform process. Institutionally, the union did not have the right to negotiate or bargain about salaries, which meant that, in contrast to Florida where negotiations with the union were the first step, the district decided to participate—or not—in DATE without any conversation or negotiation with the union. It seems that the Texas unions' best chance for influence was indirect—by influencing the constitution of the school board. However, even that did not appear to be a very successful avenue of influence. The superintendent in District.5TX contrasts the union's resources and success in elections with his experience of unions in Virginia and Michigan:

> They [VA] had political action committees where they raised money and funded campaigns and they voted in school board members ... and the union here would probably do that if they were strong enough—which they aren't—and if they were wealthy enough—which they aren't. They, they do their best to be contrarians but they just don't have the political clout that they did in Virginia. (Superintendent.5TX)
>
> They have a forum for political or school board candidates and they endorse certain ones. And of course, you can imagine, only the ones that curry favor do they endorse. But they have not been very successful in electing candidates. (Superintendent.5TX)

In summary, there was consensus from district leaders and school board members that unions in the selected Texas districts were weak—organizations that were trying, largely unsuccessfully, to influence policy outcomes in an institutional environment that stacked the deck against them. This perspective was only confirmed by union leaders in each district:

> In District.5TX we have a very entrenched anti-union political establishment that has only reinforced here the tendency of most school districts to attempt to control the educational environment with little collegial participation of the educators themselves. Therefore, even on issues of utmost importance like lay-offs, bond referendums, or wages the district refuses to talk, let alone negotiate with the unions. (Union_Leader.5TX)
>
> The school board ... appears afraid to rock the boat, but they have usually been friendly enough. I wish they would seek our input more, but they appear to be "afraid" to talk to me too much. We have supported three of the elected Board members, and they do appreciate us, but they certainly don't want us to have much power. After all, Texas is not a collective bargaining state. They like the "at will" designation. (Union_Leader2.4TX)

Policy Context: Compensation Reform

The widespread use of the single-salary schedule throughout the US, like the compensation structures in Finland and Zürich, is rooted in the historical development of the teaching profession, a history that preceded teachers' unionism. Although now widely criticized as inefficient, the single-salary schedule was a reform in the 1920s that targeted inequity and discrimination—lower salaries for women and black teachers (Johnson & Donaldson, 2006; Odden & Kelley, 2002). Although PRP reforms are certainly not new,[27] there was a resurgence of political enthusiasm for teachers' compensation reform in the United States in the first decade of the 21st century.

Despite widespread criticism of previous 'merit pay' reforms, PRP reemerged in the first decade of the 21st century (Murnane & Cohen, 1986; Odden & Kelly, 2002; Podgursky & Springer, 2007). The Denver Public School District's ProComp program, which teachers voted to support by a three to two margin and the public voted to finance in a referendum in 2005, has been identified as "opening the flood-gates" for compensation reform (Outside_Agency.1FL[28]). Although unique for its comprehensiveness, ProComp is only one example of the proliferation of PRP across the country (Johnson & Papay, 2009). In 2006, the Department of Education announced a new grant, the Teacher Incentive Fund (TIF), which committed millions of federal dollars to supporting "performance-based teacher and principal compensation systems in high-need schools" (U.S. Department of Education, 2009, n.p.). It identifies the traditional 'lock-step' salary schedules as a problem:

> Under the compensation systems in place in virtually all school districts, teacher salaries increase based on teachers collecting graduate credit for additional study, increasing number of years on the job, or moving out of the classroom into an administrative position. Such pay systems fail to take into account classroom effectiveness, the challenges that teachers face to accelerate student learning in high-poverty schools, and the shortages in those schools of instructors who teach hard-to-staff subjects like math, science, special education, and English as a second language. (U.S. Department of Education, 2009, n.p.)

The solution to this problem, according to the TIF, was to develop differentiated approaches to compensation that are based on "student achievement gains" and classroom evaluations (U.S. Department of Education, 2009, n.p.). By the time MAP had been implemented in Florida and DATE in Texas in 2007 and 2008 respectively, the Department of Education had already distributed $99 million in 34 TIF grants. The American Recovery and Reinvestment Act of 2009 gave Obama and the Department of Education the opportunity to realize their commitment to PRP (see Figure 9.3), expanding the TIF to provide $437 million to 62 grantees (U.S. Department of Education, 2010).

These developments are significant for two reasons. First, even though the reforms investigated in this research focus on state and local policy in Texas

218 *School District Cases*

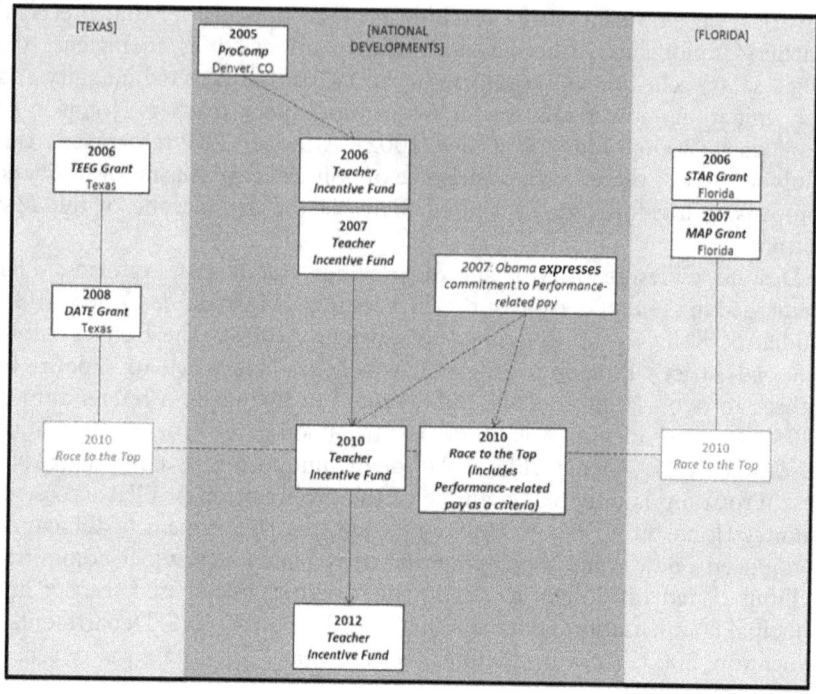

Figure 9.3 Multiple timelines of PRP reform

and Florida from 2006–2008, the national developments that preceded and followed these reforms played into how decision-makers thought about the reforms in 2010–2011 and how they retrospectively explained—and justified—their responses. Figure 9.3 provides a timeline of national developments presented alongside the key events investigated in Texas and Florida. Many interviewees across districts referenced reforms that were occurring in neighboring districts and on the national stage. Their knowledge and perception of those reforms shaped the way they thought about the process in their district. In both Texas and Florida, there were large urban districts who received TIF grants in the 2007 cycles and the experience of these districts—including public controversies that played out in the media—shaped the perceptions and preferences of local decision-makers in the selected districts (Central_Office.5TX). Furthermore, because interviews were conducted from 2010–2011, the interviewees' experiences with the Race to the Top process provided a lens from which they talked about the experiences of attempting to negotiate and develop DATE or MAP programs.

The second reason why these national developments—including the post-DATE/MAP developments—are relevant is because they are indicative of the broader momentum that was building and has built around PRP efforts and reforms. According to Outside_Agency.1FL:

as a unit. In a few cases, however, this was not feasible; for example, the poems in MS. 41 of Corpus Christi College, Cambridge, have been dealt with at three different places in the book. The Bibliography, which follows the Introduction, is presented in a more compact form than in the earlier volumes; to save unnecessary repetition, editions and periodicals frequently cited are abbreviated according to the list of abbreviations on pp. cxlix–cl. The texts and notes are printed in the usual way. A list of the accent marks in the manuscripts is given on pp. cxxxix–cxlv, immediately after the Introduction. The contents of the folios in the manuscripts are listed in the footnotes to the Introduction, instead of being placed together at the end; the list of small capitals, a feature of the earlier volumes, is omitted here, as impracticable for so many different manuscripts. Attention is called to the analytical Table of Contents on pp. ix–x, which will facilitate the finding of material on any desired poem.

No special virtue is claimed for the order in which the poems are printed in this volume. All that can be said is that the order adopted seemed a natural one from the beginning, and that no better order suggested itself. The texts, except those of the LEIDEN RIDDLE and the Hague manuscript of BEDE'S DEATH SONG, are based on photostats, supplemented in each case by a first-hand examination of the manuscript. For reasons stated in the introduction to the LEIDEN RIDDLE, it seemed best to base the text of that poem on the readings of earlier editors. As in *The Exeter Book*, words or letters which are illegible or lost from the manuscript are indicated by points within brackets; no attempt has been made to restore such losses in the text, but the suggested restorations are recorded in the notes.

It is a pleasure to acknowledge my gratitude to Professor Robert J. Menner, of Yale University, for his generous help on the introduction and text of SOLOMON AND SATURN; to Professor Francis P. Magoun, Jr., of Harvard University, for the loan of some materials illustrative of the RUNE POEM; to Professor Philip W. Souers, of Newcomb College, Tulane University, for lending me the photographs of the Franks Casket which are reproduced in this volume, and for criticizing my introduction to the Franks Casket; to Professor Harry Morgan Ayres of Columbia University, for reading the

PREFACE

THIS VOLUME, numbered Volume VI of the *Anglo-Saxon Poetic Records*, contains the many verse texts, most of them short, which are scattered here and there in manuscripts not primarily devoted to Anglo-Saxon poetry. The title, *The Anglo-Saxon Minor Poems*, seems the most convenient one available, although a number of the poems, notably the BATTLE OF MALDON and SOLOMON AND SATURN, are not "minor" in the ordinary sense of that word. As a general rule, only those poems have been admitted which are written in the regular alliterative verse; but the DEATH OF ALFRED, which has rime instead of alliteration, is included with the five other Chronicle poems, following the practice of earlier editors, and the metrical charms are printed in their entirety, though most of them are only partly in verse and their metrical structure is often far from regular. The only poem included here which has not previously been published is the SEASONS FOR FASTING, discovered not many years ago in a British Museum manuscript. With the publication of this volume only the two poems in MS. Cotton Vitellius A.xv, BEOWULF and JUDITH, remain to be edited; they will appear together in Volume IV, now in preparation.

In its general arrangement, this volume is intended to conform as closely as possible to the earlier volumes of the series. But with fifty-three poems to be edited, from seventy-two separate manuscripts and several other sources, it was necessary to modify the plan to some extent. The Introduction has become a series of introductions to the several poems, with descriptions of the manuscripts; these, though placed together, are more or less independent of each other. These introductions are necessarily much compressed, and problems of selection of material have been difficult; but it is hoped that nothing of importance has been omitted. Wherever possible, poems from the same manuscript are discussed

> From the, the first time that the issue [arose in District.1FL around 2005] to today, what's really changed is the national discourse around, one, teacher compensation, and two, teacher evaluation. You now have compensation reform, particularly performance-based compensation has long been a classic case of "it's amazing the conclusions you draw if you don't bother to let the facts get in the way." So, some people support it for the wrong reasons, because it's a way to beat up teachers and get rid of bad teachers, and some people don't support it for the wrong reasons, because they don't want to see any link between compensation and the mission of the organization—which is student learning. But I think that the nation has grown a great deal and this is now a part of the lexicon of the school reform discussion [as evidenced by the bipartisan support for performance-related pay and the TIF].

He contrasted the rapid change that occurred between 2005 and 2010, saying that:

> Five years ago, if a superintendent were to say . . . I think we may need to make changes in how we're compensating teachers. There are very few superintendents who were willing to be out front on that issue because they would have been punished for taking a stance like that. . . . [*Researcher: By the unions?*] By the unions, likely by the school board, maybe even by the broader community. In other words, you didn't have a large constituency organized in support of that kind of direction. (Outside_Agency.1FL)

So, the state-level reforms that occurred between 2005 and 2010 occurred in the midst of this shift and transition. This state of change and transition, which was playing out nationally as well as at state and local levels, is certainly a part of the story of reform. It helps to explain why these policies emerged at this time and why they were politically feasible.

Economic Context

If a financial dimension were added to Figure 9.3, there would be one key event—the 2008 subprime mortgage crisis and the unfolding financial crisis. At the time of interviews (2010–2011), both states and all of the selected districts were in a state of financial crisis—a theme echoed by almost every interviewee. Although financial difficulties were leading to widespread concern that the state grants would disappear in the face of growing budget deficits and pressures to cut at the state level in 2010, both grants had been implemented in a time of relative prosperity. According to Superintendent.1FL, from 2005–2007 the "economy wasn't a problem and budget dollars weren't a problem." Similarly, the Human Resources Director of District.2FL identified the period through 2006 as one of rapid growth—followed by a period of incredible decline.

So, although analysis must remain sensitive to the fact that the dire post-2008 economic conditions likely inform the thinking of interviewees, the financial conditions during the reform periods were fairly typical—or at least not particularly dire. Thus, although financial considerations play an important role in the policy-making process, as teachers and their unions will always be invested in improving their salaries and working conditions and districts will attempt to maximize the efficiency of the spending of limited resources, the economic conditions at the time the reforms were implemented differed markedly from those post-recession.

CONCLUSION

Ultimately, all selected districts operated under similar policy contexts—environments in which PRP reforms were gaining momentum and popularity. All districts were also responding to state legislation, which some would characterize as activist or overstepping state authority, that incentivized without mandating PRP. And all districts were operating in similar prerecession financial environments. Although the particularities of their financial management, tax bases, and budgetary priorities varied, due to the pseudo-experimental design, there was no systematic variation in districts' economic prospects. Thus, all districts were acting under fairly similar sets of conditions: they were all faced with similar economic contexts and activist state legislation that was attempting to steer local decision-making. Although these conditions were relevant to the policy story in each district and were a part of the unions' calculation of their preferences and strategies, these conditions cannot explain different outcomes across cases. Analyzing these outcomes, and the forces that produced them, is the task of Chapter 10.

NOTES

1. It was the last in a long line of compensation reform programs in Texas beginning with career ladder programs in the 1980s. The forerunner to DATE was the Teacher Educator Excellence Grant (TEEG), which targeted awards to low-income schools.
2. In 2009, the Texas legislature renewed the DATE grant (referred to as 'DATE II' by District.6TX), providing $397 million for the 2009–2010 and 2010–2011 school years (Texas Education Agency, 2011).
3. Initially, it appeared that districts had to contribute a 15% match to the grant in the first year, although this was revised.
4. For example, in international comparisons.
5. For example, national averages of teachers' salaries conceal important differences in teachers' salary structures between states and school districts.
6. This is not to suggest that education is not a 'right of citizenship' in the United States, but simply that it is not explicitly addressed in the federal constitution, but is devolved to the state level.

7. Teacher Incentive Fund grantees, among others.
8. There was some disagreement about the degree to which the Florida MAP/STAR plans were optional, but despite it being labeled a state 'mandate,' the vast majority of districts did not participate and there were no consequences for non-participation. So, effectively, the policy was optional.
9. Based on the 2006–2007 school year, the most recent year for which data was available at the time of selection (National Center for Education Statistics, 2011). This year was selected because the state PRP policies investigated in Texas and Florida were passed during the 2006–2007 school year.
10. The year of the reforms investigated.
11. A result of the high level of reliance on local property taxes for funding.
12. And a group of charter schools.
13. For a code of interviewees by district and role, see Appendix VII.
14. For more information about districts, see Appendix VI.
15. Discussed below.
16. Newspapers and websites are not cited in order to protect district and interviewee confidentiality. However, any information gained through a secondary source and used in this book was confirmed through interviews.
17. The goal was to talk with two school board members in order to attempt to capture the potential diversity of the board. In one district, District.2FL, it was only possible to interview one board member (see Appendix 7.1VII.i), and in District.6TX, the researcher was asked to not interview board members. In all other districts, the two board members were selected in an attempt to maximize the diversity of the interviewees.
18. For example, although the union leader may have been unavailable, a senior staff member may have been interviewed. Or, if the superintendent was unavailable or unwilling to be interviewed, a key—and often referred—central office staff member with relevant experience and insight was interviewed.
19. For a detailed description of interviewees by district, see Appendix 7VII.
20. The interview schedule for US cases is provided in Appendix 8VIII.
21. All interviews had been recorded and transcribed.
22. More specifically, the majority of school boards are elected. There are some school boards that are appointed, and some districts that are under mayoral control. But even appointed school board members are viewed as "responsible to their communities or section of the city" (Ehrensal & First, 2008, p. 73).
23. Examples include cities with mayoral control or significant municipal involvement in school board politics.
24. Confirmed by an online news source (2008).
25. Confirmed by an online news source (2009).
26. Information on District.2FL was unavailable.
27. There were three waves of PRP reforms preceding the 21st century iteration—in the early 1900s, in the 1960s, and in the 1980s (Johnson & Papay, 2009).
28. Outside_Agency.1FL was the technical assistance provider to Denver in the design of ProComp and also helped Barack Obama with his speech supporting PRP in 2007. For complete interviewee codes, see Appendix VII.

REFERENCES

Aggarwal, V.K. (2005). *Reconciling institutions: Nested, horizontal, overlapping, and independent institutions.* Princeton: Princeton University.

Berkman, M.B., & Plutzer, E. (2005). *Ten thousand democracies: Politics and public opinion in America's school districts.* Washington, DC: Georgetown University Press.

Ehrensal, P. A., & First, P. F. (2008). Understanding school board politics: Balancing public voice and professional power. In B. Cooper, J. G. Cibulka, & L. Fusarelli (Eds.), *Handbook of education politics and policy*. New York: Routledge, 73–88.

Florida Department of Education. (2007). *Florida performance pay guidance: 2007–2008 and beyond*. Retrieved from the Florida Department of Education website: http://www.fldoe.org/news/2007/2007_04_18-2/Performance_Pay_Guidance2007-2008.pdf

George, A. L., & Bennett, A. (2005). *Case studies and theory development in the social sciences*. Cambridge, MA: MIT Press.

Goldhaber, D., DeArmond, M., Player, D., & Choi, H. (2008). Why do so few public scool districts use merit pay? *Journal of Education Finance, 33*(3), 262–278.

Hanson, R. L. (1983). The intergovernmental setting of state politics. In V. Gray, H. Jacob, & K. N. Vines (Eds.). *Politics in the American states: A comparative analysis*. Boston: Little, Brown, 27–56.

Hanson, R. L. (2013). Intergovernmental relations. In V. Gray, R. L. Hanson, & T. Kousser (Eds.), *Politics in the American states: A comparative analysis*. London: CQ Publishers, 30–62.

Johnson, S. M. (2004). Paralysis or possibility: What do teacher unions and collective bargaining bring? In R. D. Henderson, W. J. Urban, & P. Wolman (Eds.), *Teachers unions and education policy: Retrenchment or reform?* Oxford: Elsevier, 33–50.

Johnson, S. M., & Donaldson, M. (2006). The effects of collective bargaining on teacher quality. In J. Hannaway & A. Rotherman (Eds.), *Collective bargaining in education: Negotiating change in today's schools*. Cambridge, MA: Harvard Education Press, 111–140.

Johnson, S. M., & Papay, J. P. (2009). *Redesigning teacher pay: A system for the next generation of educators*. Washington, DC: Economic Policy Institute.

Kahlenberg, R. D. (2006). The history of collective bargaining among teachers. In J. Hannaway & A. Rotherman (Eds.), *Collective bargaining in education: Negotiating change in today's schools*. Cambridge, MA: Harvard Education Press, 7–26.

Kearney, R. C. (2010). Public sector labor-management relations: Change or status quo? *Review of Public Personnel Administration, 30*(1), 89–111.

Lijphart, A. (1971). Comparative politics and the comparative method. *The American Political Science Review, 65*(3), 682–692.

Meyer, J., Scott, W. R., & Strang, D. (1987). Centralization, fragmentation, and school district complexity. *Administrative Science Quarterly, 32*(2), 186–201.

Mintrom, M. (2009). Local democracy in education. In G. Sykes, B. Schneider, & D. Plank (Eds.), *Handbook of education policy research*. New York: Routledge, 793–804.

Moe, T. (2011). *Special interests: teachers unions and America's public schools*. Washington, DC: Brookings Institution.

Murnane, R. J., & Cohen, D. K. (1986). Merit pay and the evaluation problem: Why most merit pay plans fail and few survive. *Harvard Educational Review, 56*(1), 1–17.

National Center for Education Statistics. (2011). *Characteristics of the 100 largest public elementary and secondary school districts in the United States: 2008–2009*. Washington, DC: U.S. Department of Education Institute of Education Sciences. Retrieved on May 15, 2011, from http://nces.ed.gov/pubs2011/2011301.pdf

Odden, A., & Kelley, C. (2002). *Paying teachers for what they know and do: New and smarter compensation strategies to improve schools*. Thousand Oaks, CA: Corwin Press.

Podgursky, M., & Springer, M. G. (2007). Teacher performance pay: A review. *Journal of Policy Analysis and Management, 26*(4), 909–948.

Ragin, C. (2000). *Fuzzy-set social science*. Chicago: University of Chicago Press.

Rokkan, S. (1970). *Citizens, elections, parties: Approaches to the comparative study of the processes of development*. New York: David McKay Company.

Snyder, R. (2001). Scaling down: The subnational comparative method. *Studies in Comparative International Development, 36*(1), 93–107.

Springer, M. G., Lewis, J. L., Ehlert, M. W., Podgursky, M. J., Crader, G. D., Taylor, L. I., . . . Stuit, D. A. (2010). *District awards for teacher excellence program: Final evaluation report*. Retrieved from the National Center on Performance Incentives website: http://www.performanceincentives.org/data/files/news/BooksNews/FINAL_DATE_REPORT_FOR_NCPI_SITE.pdf

Sykes, G., O'Day, J., & Ford, T. (2009). The district role in instructional improvement. In G. Sykes, B. Schneider, & D. Plank (Eds.), *Handbook of education policy research*. New York: Routledge, 767–784.

Texas Education Agency. (2011). *District awards for teacher excellence (D.A.T.E.)*. Retrieved from http://www.tea.state.tx.us/date.aspx

U.S. Department of Education. (2009). *Teacher incentive fund: Fact sheet*. Retrieved September 1, 2013, from http://www2.ed.gov/programs/teacherincentive/factsheet.pdf

U.S. Department of Education. (2010). *Teacher incentive fund: Frequently asked questions for the 2010 competition and grant awards*. Retrieved from http://www2.ed.gov/programs/teacherincentive/faq.html

Wirt, F. M., & Kirst, M. W. (1997). *The political dynamics of American education*. Berkeley: McCutchan Publishing.

10 School District Analysis
A Series of Congruence Tests

The analysis in this chapter is organized around a series of tests. First, the findings outlined in Chapter 8 are tested in District.1FL and District.2FL—the two cases with strong unions where PRP was adopted. In both cases, unions' acceptance of reform can be explained by their complex preferences and by relational patterns. In particular, the cooperative compromise pathway is evident in both cases.

Then, District 3.FL, where conditions were similar to the other two Florida districts, but where PRP was not adopted, provides a valuable counterfactual case to test the correlations observed between District.1FL, District.2FL, Finland, and Zürich. If similar preferences and relationship patterns were evident in these cases but did *not* result in reform, such findings would cast doubt on the emerging hypothesis. However, District.3FL does not contradict the findings—it strengthens them. Relationships in District.3FL were fraught with conflict—between the union and the superintendent as well as between the superintendent and the school board. The conflict with the union removed the superintendent's ability to forge an agreement based on trust and a desire to preserve a collaborative relationship. In addition to exacerbating the conflict between the superintendent and union, the internal conflict between the school board and superintendent eliminated both paths for reform—winning over the opposition or overpowering them.

In the third and final phase, the Texas cases provide an opportunity to explore the incidence of reform in contexts in which unions, according to all interviewees, were largely irrelevant. Notably, despite union weakness in Texas, there were many districts that did not participate in the state's PRP program. This suggests that there are non-union reasons why reform may not occur. Although the questions—when do such results (PRP) occur? And why don't they always?—are particularly focused on the union's role in those outcomes, the Texas cases provide an opportunity to consider other factors that influence the reform process.

TEST #1: 'CELL FOUR' CASES: STRONG UNIONS WITH PRP

District.1FL and District.2FL provide opportunities for testing the emerging hypotheses about why PRP reform occurs in spite of strong unions.

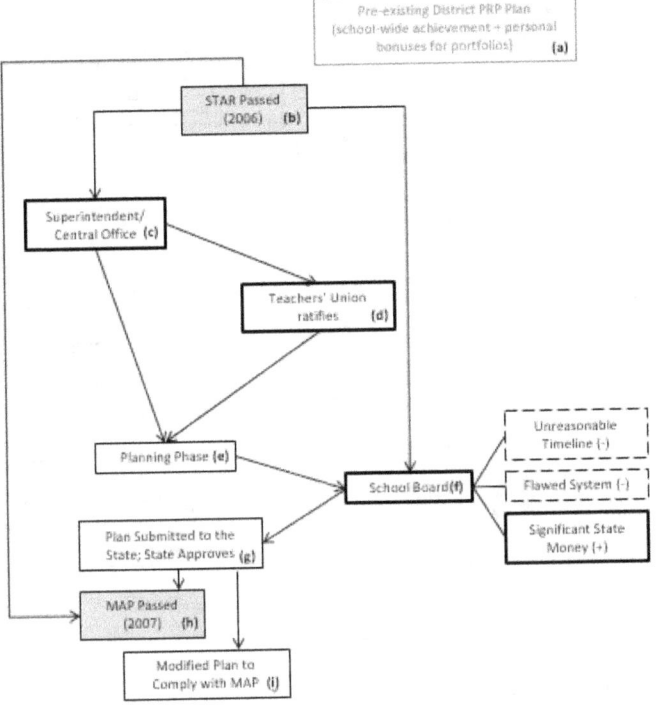

Figure 10.1 District.1FL timeline

Although the union in both districts opposed PRP in concept, a stable and trust-based relationship with the district made participation possible. Figures 10.1 and 10.2 present the reform timelines in District.1FL and District.2FL. Both districts opted to participate in the STAR program in 2006, and both districts had some experience with PRP prior to STAR. However, both district-initiated programs that preceded STAR were based primarily on a portfolio of teachers' work and neither program was compliant with the state requirements. So, both had to develop a new plan.

In District.1FL, although the administration, school board, and teachers' union eventually agreed to participate in the STAR program, both had reservations about the program. The school board filed a formal complaint about the timeline and requirements of the program, but grudgingly decided to participate in order to obtain the significant monies attached to the grant. When STAR was replaced with MAP in 2007, District.1FL updated its system to comply with the new requirements.

Similarly, in District.2FL, the administration and local union had already negotiated a provision whereby the district could design a PRP plan prior to STAR's passage in 2006. As a result, participation did not have to be negotiated, and the responsibility for designing a plan that would comply

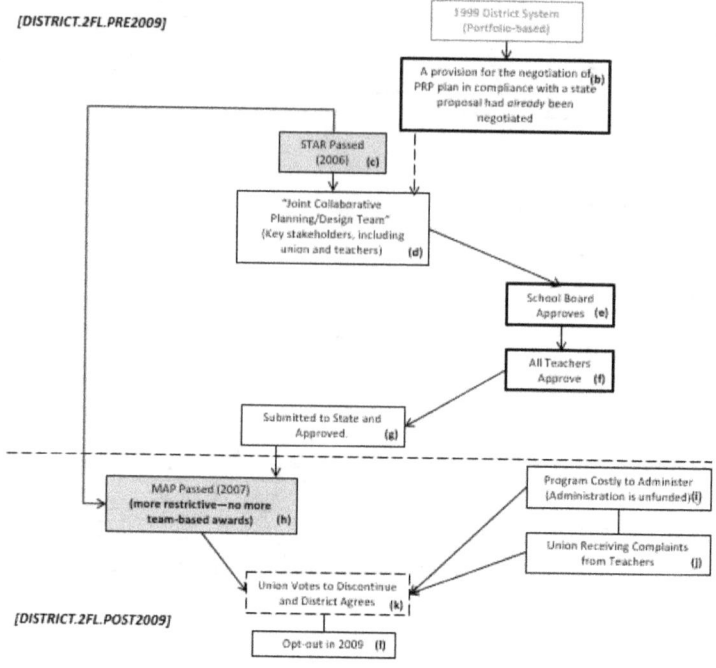

Figure 10.2 District.2FL timeline

with state requirements was passed to a joint collaborative team of key stakeholders, including union representatives. Like District.1FL, when MAP replaced STAR in 2007, District.2FL updated its plan. This section only focuses on District.2FL's decision to participate in STAR and MAP (District.2FL.PRE2009); its decision to opt out of the MAP program in 2009 is addressed later in this chapter.

Although Figures 10.1 and 10.2 display the key decisions and processes that led to District.1FL's and District.2FL's participation in PRP, they obscure the complex calculations that led to those decisions. Although teachers' unions in both districts agreed to participate in the state grants, both unions were initially opposed to PRP. Thus, it is essential to better understand the teachers' unions' opposition and the relational patterns that made compromise possible. In terms of the preferences of teachers' unions, both District.1FL and District.2FL appear to mirror the preferences of unions in Finland and Zürich. First, unions were generally opposed to PRP. According to an outside consultant who had worked with District.1FL on developing PRP as well as a variety of other reforms:

> The teachers' union in District.1FL has very strong leadership. And, it didn't want to do anything that was close to [PRP] in the past. (Outside_Agency.1FL)

The teachers' unions' opposition to PRP was rooted in a set of concerns about producing competitiveness instead of collaboration, the perceived ineffectiveness of 'incentives' on teachers' motivation, and challenges of measurability and fairness.

> Bottom line is that well, it's ineffectual. [The assumption is] that merit pay will somehow motivate teachers to work harder and do more for their students and that's just not what we've ever seen. . . . I think the key flaw was the misconception that teachers would be motivated to work harder because of merit pay in order to receive [additional compensation]. . . . I've seen enough incarnations of bonus pay systems that I've yet to see one system or even conceive of a system that would really be effective. (Union_Leader.2FL)

Table 10.1 displays the teachers' unions' reported perceptions of PRP, and reasons for opposing it. If unions in Florida are as strong and influential as interviewees suggested, how can the implementation of these reforms be explained given the teachers' unions' opposition to PRP? In particular, can the complexity of teachers' unions' interests and their relationship pattern explain the reforms?

Both District.1FL and District.2FL are cases where the union accepted something that it did not prefer in order to get something that it wanted more—additional compensation. Union_Leader.2FL makes the interest calculation explicit. In spite of the union's strong opposition to PRP on the basis of its effectiveness, measurability, and fairness:

> Our logic was simple. If they are going to give us $4 million, and it is kind of going in the pockets of teachers, we are going to go ahead and accept it. And we did. (Union_Leader.2FL)

It is clear that money was relevant to the decision to participate in both District.1FL and District.2FL.[1] However, although the financial inducement was part of their calculation, money alone cannot explain reform outcomes. The same financial opportunity did not convince District.3FL—or the 64 other non-participating districts in Florida—to participate. Clearly, money alone cannot buy reform. At best, it provides a necessary but insufficient condition for PRP reform. So what made reform possible in these districts? How were they able to overcome union opposition?

The international cases suggested two possible causal pathways through which unions' opposition may be overcome. First, the case of Zürich suggested that the union may 'accept' a trade-off when it has been outmaneuvered or overpowered: when it can no longer block the policy, it may accept it in order to maximize pay-offs or to save face. On the other hand, the Finnish case suggests that trade-offs or compromise may be encouraged by a cooperative relationship pattern. Given the potential long-term

Table 10.1 District.1FL and District.2FL union perceptions and preferences

		CONCERNS				AIMS		
		Competitive	Incentive	Measurability	Fairness	Recruit/ Retain	Reward Performance	Increase Pay
DISTRICT.1FL	Superintendent.1FL	X	X	X	—	"could be used as a valuable tool"	—	—
	Central_Office.1FL	—	—	X	X	—	—	—
DISTRICT.2FL	Superintendent.2FL	X	X	—	X	—	—	Y
	Union_Leader.2FL	X	X	X	X	—	—	Y

benefits to maintaining cooperation, the union's preference calculations and resulting strategies and tactics may be influenced by their desire to preserve the cooperative pattern. Were the unions overpowered in District.1FL and District.2FL, or did they cooperate?

Both districts express a clear cooperative relationship pattern. The responses of each interviewee in District.1FL and District.2FL, coded according to Walton and McKersie's (1991) relationship patterns, are displayed in Table 10.2.

In both districts, unions were collaborative partners in the decision to participate in the MAP program as well as the design of the district plan. In District.2FL, interviewees traced the collaborative relationship back ten years to the establishment of interest-based bargaining in the late 1990s (Central_Office.2FL; Union_Leader.2FL). The trust and cooperation that is now standard operating practice in the district emerged from a complete breakdown of trust—a conflict-ridden negotiating impasse in 1999—which forced the district and union to develop a new strategy for working together. The district implemented what Fisher and Ury (1981) labeled the interest-based bargaining (IBB) process, which was established as a response to the 1999 impasse and identified as an improvement over traditional adversarial approaches and essential to the district's ability to participate in programs like MAP:

> You have some people who say 'well, you're gonna give away the farm in interest-based bargaining.' No, you don't. It's the same. But you end up with really better agreements, longer-lasting agreements, agreements less likely to break down. And, you know, it's a more creative solution is what we found in ten years. It just gets, it typically just got better and better because you wind up, you get a lot of trust that develops between parties, so if you're going to do something crazy like, you know MAP (laugh), they are more likely to go along with you. Or if you say something about it, it's more likely to trust that what you're telling them is the truth because you've been transparent, the relationship is built on trust. (Central_Office.2FL)

Figure 10.3 provides a visualization of the relationships in District.2FL. Relationships identified as good, strong, or collaborative are solid lines; strained relationships or those characterized by conflict will be dashed in subsequent diagrams. Heavier lines reflect stronger or more important ties in terms of influencing decision-making processes, and black lines show direct or formal engagement while grey lines reflect the union's indirect attempts at influence—through lobbying or persuasion of other stakeholders. The Superintendent in District.2FL was the key decision-maker, as indicated by the double-lined box, and the importance of interest-based bargaining (IBB) was also highlighted by interviewees. District.2FL appears to be a district where all stakeholders are working relatively harmoniously together.

Table 10.2 Cooperative relationship patterns in District.1FL and District.2FL.

		MOTIVATION ORIENTATION/ ACTION TENDENCY	BELIEFS ABOUT LEGITIMACY	FEELINGS OF TRUST	FEELINGS OF FRIENDLINESS
District.1FL	Superintendent1.1FL	Cooperative	Legitimacy	Complete Trust	Friendliness
	Central_Office.1FL	Cooperative	N/A	Trust	N/A
	School_Board1.1FL	Cooperative	Legitimacy	Trust	Friendliness
	School_Board2.1FL	Cooperative	Legitimacy	Limited Trust*	Friendliness
District.2FL	Central_Office.2FL	Cooperative	Complete Legitimacy	Trust	Friendliness
	School_Board1.2FL	Cooperative	Complete Legitimacy	Trust	N/A
	Union_Leader.2FL	Cooperative	Complete Legitimacy	Extended Trust	N/A

*varies from issue to issue

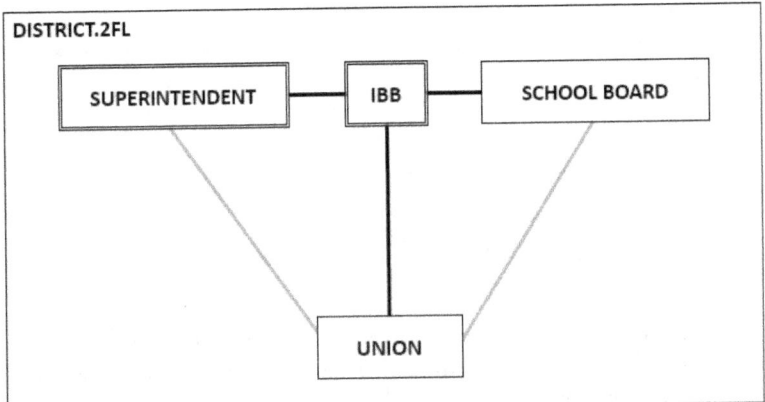

Figure 10.3 Relationships in the governance triangle in District.2FL

It might be easy to identify IBB as the essential characteristic that describes the harmonious relationships in District.2FL. However, an emergent theme across interviewees in District.2FL is the interplay between institutionalized structures (IBB) and personal relationships. The reinforcing nature of institutions and relationships is evident in one administrator's statement, and echoed across interviews—the repeated practice of IBB builds interpersonal resources that sustain it (Central_Office.2FL). The importance of the personal relationships was particularly clear with the union leader in District.2FL, who expressed some uncertainty about how things might change with a leadership transition:

> We still have the same type of process and we feel like we have a good relationship with the people that are here right now, but with a new superintendent coming in and a new school board members taking over, we don't know where we are going to end up a year from now, you know? (Union_Leader.2FL)

This confirms—consistent with the international cases studies—that although institutions inform and influence interpersonal relationships, they are independent phenomena and interpersonal relationships matter. Their importance is further confirmed by District.1FL, where the MAP program—and its predecessor, STAR—coincided with a period of tumultuous leadership. Due to political controversies and clashes between the superintendent and the school board, the superintendent's leadership was short-lived; he left the district around 2007.

In many ways, despite leadership instability and a period of conflict between Superintendent1.1FL and the school board, the union leader in District.1FL appears to have been the stable factor in the otherwise unstable relationship triangle between the superintendent, school board, and union (Figure 10.4).

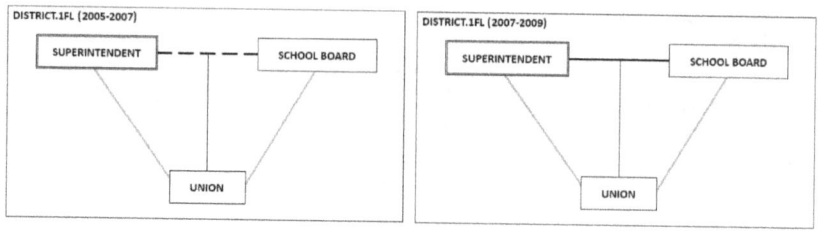

Figure 10.4 Relationships in the governance triangle in District.1FL

In District.1FL, the union leader was identified as a key reason why the district was able to participate in the STAR program in 2006 and then the MAP program in 2007. One school board member said that the union leader has "gone out on a limb" (School_Board2.1FL), taking positions and making agreements in spite of opposition from the state teachers' union. Although school district leaders and school board members acknowledged the potential for disagreement with the union, they consistently confirmed their confidence in its leader:

> Unions are [exist to] for adults. And, you know, the, the school district serves children. So, you automatically have the potential for conflict. Sometimes it does conflict. But a lot of times, when we align on, you know a topic, that . . . that we can agree on . . . we, you know our union boss, she's the same boss that's been there for years . . . she trusts that we have the best interests of students and teachers in mind. She does. And vice versa . . . I mean we've had some knock-down, drag-out sort of arguments where we didn't agree on the approach, but, we did have on this topic, a . . . you know, full trust in each other. And when you have that, you can work together. (School_Board2.1FL)
>
> I can't think of a conflict where we didn't always resolve it and always resolve it with kids and their education top of mind . . . and I think that has to do more with the character of the leadership of the union. And they're not all . . . poised with that kind of leadership, but this particular union was terrific in that regard. And I found them a great reform partner. (Superintendent1.1FL)

Furthermore, School_Board2.1FL argues for the importance of choosing the collaborative path even when the 'power-through' path may be available—for example, under the auspices of a state mandate:

> It would have been easy and I think a lot of districts did push a (Race to the Top) plan through against the union's will. Um, it would have been easy because we had the state mandate, just do it and you know collective bargaining . . . but we weren't willing to do that because we felt that the long-term relationship and ability to work together trumped

you know, sort of the temporary power granted by the state mandate. (School_Board2.1FL)

The consistency of relationship patterns and union preferences across District.1FL and District.2FL provide compelling support for the cooperative compromise pathway outlined in Chapter 8. But can the reform outcome of District.3FL be explained?

TEST #2: 'CELL TWO' COUNTERFACTUAL: STRONG UNION, NO PRP

District.3FL provides an excellent counterexample to District.1FL and District.2FL, as it is a negative case that is very similar to positive cases (Ragin, 2000). Like Districts.1FL and 2FL, the union in District.3FL was opposed to STAR and MAP. However, unlike these other districts, the opposition to state PRP plans could not be overcome—even though participation carried significant financial inducements. What can explain this different outcome?

Figure 10.5 provides an overview of the process in District.3FL. Although the district submitted a few proposals in response to both STAR and MAP, according to district officials, none of these submissions were serious

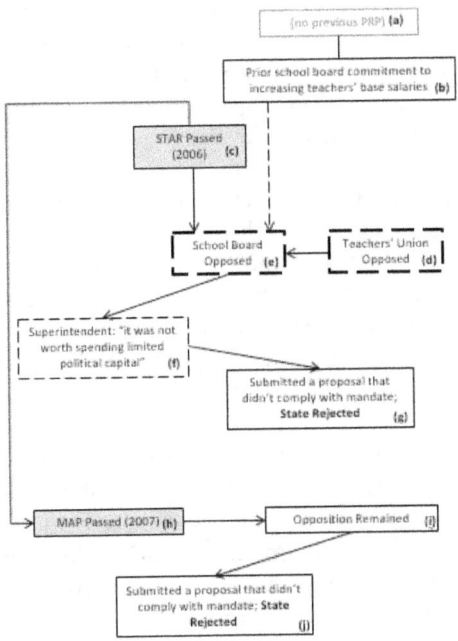

Figure 10.5 District.3FL timeline

attempts to participate. The plans did not comply with state requirements and were rejected by the state. Can this outcome be explained by union opposition? Although the superintendent of District.3FL described "no *open* opposition to performance-related pay," other actors identified union resistance (Central_Office.3FL; School_Board1.3FL; School_Board2.3FL). According to one school board member, "They didn't want anything to do with it" (School_Board1.3FL).[2] Although these union preferences are similar to those of District.1FL and District.2FL, unlike those districts, union opposition in District.3FL could not be overcome—why?

Several differences from Districts.1FL and 2FL are immediately evident in Figure 10.5. First, District.3FL did not have any previous experience with PRP. Second, the sequence of decisions is reversed, with school board opposition driving the superintendent's resigned decision to not seriously pursue PRP. The third difference is the location of the teachers' union in Figure 10.5. The latter two differences are by-products of the relationship patterns in District.3FL and the deep power struggles between the stakeholders.

Constructing a relationship pattern table, like those displayed for District.1FL and District.2FL (Table 10.2), was virtually impossible in the case of District.3FL. It would have obscured more than it illuminated due to the complex relational dynamics of District.3FL. First, there were a number of time-specific relational cleavages that defied any kind of pattern analysis; even if relationships were stable before and after the time in question, they were fraught with conflict and tensions during this period. Second, it was not possible to speak about a relational pattern between 'the district'—the superintendent, the administration, and the school board—and the union, as intra-district relationships were splintered and defined by a power struggle between the school board and the superintendent. This power struggle (Figure 10.6) is crucial to understanding the most notable difference between District.3FL and participating districts.

Unlike District.2FL and District.1FL, where the superintendent emerged as the key decision-maker in the district, the superintendent's leadership in District.3FL—both generally and on the particular issue of PRP—was rendered ineffective by internal dynamics and divisions. The comments of one school board member are insightful into the board-superintendent relationship and are echoed by other board members (School_Board1.3FL; School_Board3.3FL):

> He had some difficulties getting things done in the district. . . . And the board . . . there were a couple board members who really opposed him, and I don't know why . . . the board did divide and there was, one or two that really made life miserable for him and probably for them too. I don't know. The personalities did not work well together . . . a lot of the personalities played into board dynamics at the time I think. (School_Board2.3FL)

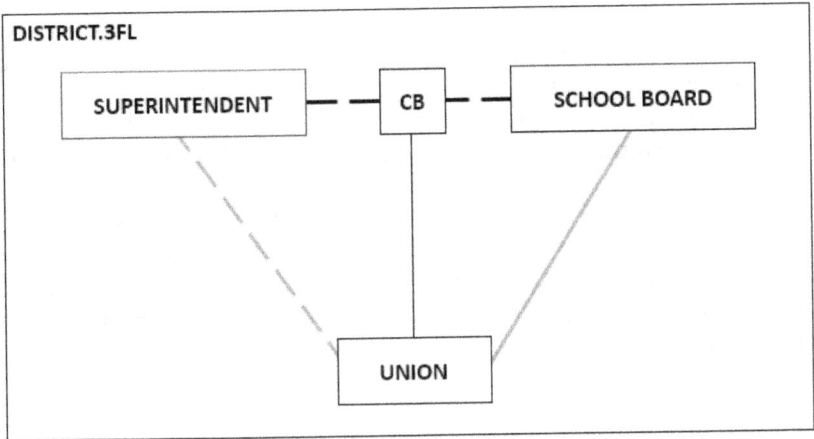

Figure 10.6 Division in District.3FL (2006–2008)

The superintendent also had a fraught relationship with the local union. He attests that the relationship got off to a rocky start because of some of the reforms he promoted early in his tenure:

> I probably wasn't the most popular person with the teachers' union. And … for a number of reasons, but primarily because I pushed the button often on teacher termination for what I viewed as conduct that wasn't becoming of the profession. . . . So, early in my tenure, I had a number of . . . tough moments with the teachers' union. (Superintendent.3FL)

The difficulty of the union-superintendent relationship was further exacerbated by a controversial contract negotiation in which he attempted to change the number of hours in teachers' contracts. When a satisfactory agreement could not be reached, the superintendent imposed the contract—a significant breakdown of the collaborative bargaining process in District.3FL (Central_Office.3FL). Based on the reports of school board members as well as the human resources officer, it seems that the superintendent attempted to power through reforms against opposition, which resulted in strained relationships and the perception of disrespect:

> [Due to board antagonism] Superintendent.3FL decided that he was just going to work around in spite of us . . . and I kept telling him, you know . . . I get what you're doing but you're killing me here. I understand why you don't want us in your face, but at the same time, you know, you accepted the job. We're gonna be in your face. And . . . so the relationship was, was much different . . . I don't think he had much respect for the board. (School_Board1.3FL)

> Superintendent.3FL was very bright and hard working, but . . . how can I put it . . . showed a lack of respect for people in the district including board members and I guess the union. He was, in my opinion, somewhat difficult to work with in general . . . the union at that time might have felt that their input was not valued enough. (School_Board3.3FL)

What is notable about the dynamics that emerged from District.3FL is that there appears to be a significant intra-district battle for influence. The superintendent perceived the school board to be working to advance their own agenda—often allying themselves with the union in opposition to the superintendent:

> I will tell you, I am very convinced that several of my board members spent more time with members of the collaborative bargaining team than I ever did. So . . . the board was pretty sophisticated in terms of knowing their responsibilities for policy but they also didn't hesitate to um, when it served them either politically or in terms of moving a policy that maybe the administration didn't favor. (Superintendent.3FL)
>
> The district probably did have a better reputation with the union. . . . There was more trust with [the leader of collaborative bargaining] and that group than there was, than in me. (Superintendent.3FL)

These complex relational dynamics are the key to unpacking District.3FL's non-participation in the PRP grants. Ultimately, participation was vetoed in the collaborative bargaining group. The school board had committed to increasing teachers' base salaries (Figure 10.5, b) and perceived bonuses to be inappropriate until those commitments had been realized. Ultimately, then, the union and school board were allied—bonded by a common goal to increase teachers' salaries as well as a common distrust of the superintendent (e, d). Although participating in STAR or MAP was *not* ultimately in conflict with raising salaries, as the funding for PRP was totally independent from the district's general budget, politically, the distinction was impossible. The school board would not consider any reforms until they had fulfilled their commitment to improve the base salaries, and the superintendent was convinced that teachers would begrudge incentives in the face of the perceived 'unfulfilled promise' of base raises. Thus, although Superintendent.3FL expressed an interest in participating—in spite of some reservations—he did not feel like he could make any progress against the opposition of the school board and the teachers' union:

> So, I thought if we took off on this other process people would say, 'Wait, you're taking money away from a board priority to advance the merit pay issue,' and they never would have been satisfied. People might have said, 'You can do it if you get to the average like you promised, but you have to get there first.' So the pragmatic side of me said, 'until we

get there, I'm not going to use the little political capital that a superintendent has on that because it's a no win for me.' (Superintendent.3FL)

In summary, the picture that emerges from District.3FL confirms the findings of Chapter 8. The superintendent would have wanted—despite his reservations about PRP, a complication discussed later in this chapter—to participate in the PRP program. However, although he technically may have been powerful enough to do so against school board and union opposition—he could have imposed contract and acted unilaterally to attempt to force the reform through—the dynamics of District.3FL caused him to decide that it 'wasn't worth it' (f).

Furthermore, his options to maneuver or persuade were severely limited by the relational dynamics of the district. His relationship with the union as well as the school board was characterized by distrust and lack of cooperation. It is impossible to know whether a cooperative relationship could have secured the union's agreement to participate, but it is certain that the broken relationship *ensured* that Superintendent.3FL had virtually no chance to change the union's mind—to convince them that participating in STAR or MAP could provide additional pay for teachers in the short-term and was not in conflict with the shared goal of increasing teachers' pay in the long-term.

Ultimately, this was the strategic compromise that unions in District.1FL and District.2FL both chose to make. Together, the three Florida districts confirm that cooperative relationships are a significant explanation for why PRP occurs. However, given assumptions of causal asymmetry, multiple pathways to non-reform are possible, and these pathways are not simply the inverse of reform pathways. A closer examination of the variable incidence of PRP reform in districts where unions were relatively weak provides an opportunity to explore some of the non-union factors that may explain PRP reform outcomes.

TEST #3: 'WEAK UNION' COUNTERFACTUALS

Although it is widely accepted that unions matter, this research has aimed to revise existing theories and develop new hypotheses for *the ways* in which they matter. The reform experiences of Texas school districts provide an opportunity to peel back some of the fundamental assumptions about the impact of unions on reform.

Many union critics suggest—both explicitly and implicitly—that education reforms are clear policy solutions that should and would be implemented *if not for unions*. However, even where unions are weak, compensation reform has been historically uncommon (Hess & West, 2006). These cases, such as the non-participating districts in Texas (District.6TX), provide examples of non-reform that *cannot* be attributed to unions, and directly confront any causal explanations that blame unions for non-reform. By focusing on contexts where unions are weak, this analysis and discussion shed light on relevant non-union drivers of (non-)reform—factors that may also be relevant in strong union contexts. Furthermore, it challenges and complicates some of the fundamental ideological and theoretical assumptions underlying existing theories of teachers' unions, which, as these cases demonstrate, are ultimately untenable.

Figure 10.7 displays the timeline of District.6TX's non-participation. It illustrates that the decision to not participate was exclusively driven by the superintendent. Although the union was opposed to PRP, this did not factor into the superintendent's decision. The main driver of District.6TX's non-participation was its inaccurate initial conception of the financial requirements of the DATE grant. Ultimately, the district opted to not participate because of the perceived requirements for a local contribution or match (Superintendent.6TX). The causal significance of this false assumption in explaining the district's non-participation is demonstrated by the fact that they later reversed their position—participating in what they call

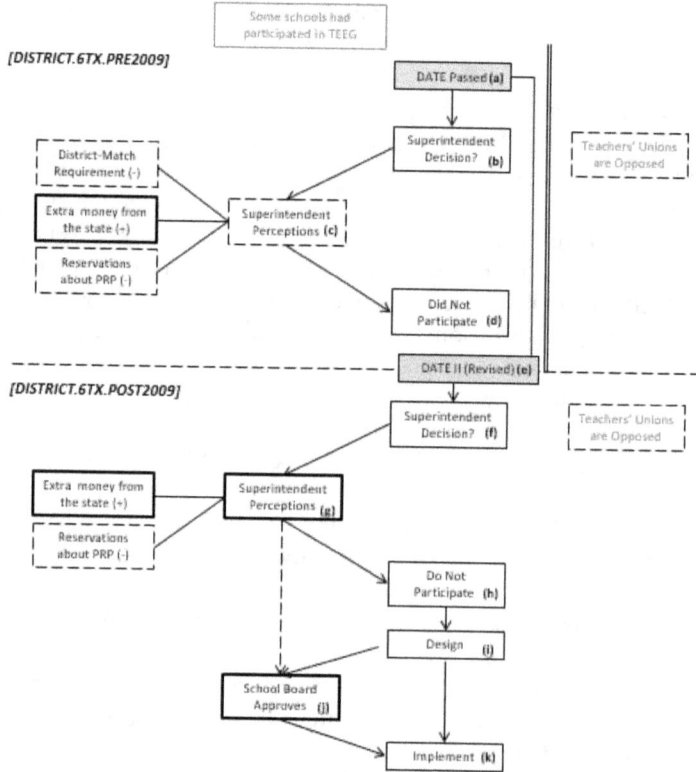

Figure 10.7 Timeline for District.6TX's decision to participate in 'DATE II'

'DATE II'—when they realized that the perceived "district match" requirement "no longer applied."[3]

Although the point is somewhat obvious and banal, it is essential: reforms—or their absence—may be explained by the preferences, strategies, and tactics of school managers and decision-makers, and the perceptions, both accurate and erroneous, on which they are based. In the case of District.6TX, the superintendent's decision to not pursue participation in DATE in 2008 was related to his perception of financial demands. However, the financial reservations were a kind of final straw that confirmed District.6TX's non-participation in the context of the superintendent's broader ambivalence about PRP:

> I didn't really see any basis for it, you know? ... I just don't know that ... when you've provided that additional pay ... what we're saying that's for ... my thinking is that it oughta be, that we can clearly identify that there was value-added, that there was something that this particular person brought to the table that resulted in achievement gains for kids. And I just have not seen methodology that you can clearly attribute that to a single teacher over that small period of time. (Superintendent.6TX)
>
> I think I'm an advocate [of PRP] if somebody could show me, you know, and I could be absolutely convinced, that we could identify merit. (Superintendent.6TX)

Although the financial questions appear to be the cause of the superintendent's decision to not participate in DATE in 2008, his broader reservations about PRP—particularly linking teachers' pay to student test scores—were not unique to District.6TX. Table 10.3 presents the perceptions of PRP of superintendents and key central office staff members in the three Texas districts. The majority of interviewees expressed concerns about the measurability of teachers' performance and the fairness of PRP systems. Interviewees in both District.4TX and District.6TX also expressed concerns about the impact of PRP on collaboration between teachers (Table 10.3, (1)) or expressed doubt about whether financial rewards motivated teachers. The superintendent of District.5TX is the only district leader in Texas who did not express doubt or ambivalence about PRP.

Questions about the effectiveness and desirability of PRP were not unique to Texas districts. Table 10.3 shows that the confidence of the superintendent in District.5TX—*not* the ambivalence of the superintendent in District.6TX—is the exception. In every district except District.5TX, the district expressed reservations or concerns about some aspect of PRP—its effect on collaboration, its ability to motivate, or its measurability or fairness. These concerns were consistent across both participating (District.1FL, District.2FL, and District.4TX) and non-participating districts (District.3FL and District.6TX).

Table 10.3 School district administration preferences and perceptions

		(1) Competitive vs. Collaborative	(2) Motivate/ incentivize	(3) measurability	(4) fairness	(5) Recruit/retain	(6) reward performance	(7) Pay teachers More	(8) Perception of Local Match
DISTRICT.1FL	Superintendent1.1FL	X	—	Y*	—	—	Y	Y	N/A
DISTRICT.2FL	Central_Office.2FL	—	Y	X	X	Y	Y	Y	N/A
DISTRICT.3FL	Superintendent.3FL	X	X	Y*	X	—	Y	N°	N/A
DISTRICT.4TX	Superintendent.4TX	X	—	X	X	Y	—	Y	N[1]
	Central_Office.4TX	X	Y	X	X	Y	Y	—	
DISTRICT.5TX	Superintendent.5TX	U	Y	Y	Y	—	—	Y	N
	Central_Office.5TX	Y	Y	X	X	—	Y	Y	
DISTRICT.6TX	Superintendent.6TX	—	—	X	—	Y	—	Y	Y
	Central_Office2.6TX	X	X	—	—	—	—	—	
	Central_office1.6TX	X	X	Y*	X	—	—	Y	

*: Yes, possible, but with caveats.
—: missing data
U: unsure
°: Although they wanted to raise teachers' salaries, they wanted to raise the base salary.

Although the strategic calculations and their conclusions varied—some decided it was 'worth it' while others did not—the reservations about PRP were almost universal. Even in participating districts, decision-makers expressed significant ambivalence. In District.1FL, concerns about measurability and its preferences for group- rather than individual-based compensation were only overcome by the benefit of receiving additional funds for teachers' compensation:

> You know in our district when it initially started it was 7 million dollars and that's, that's quite a bit of money so that you can, we found that we could reward more teachers for performance under the state system than we could on our own. (Central_Office.1FL)
>
> [After creating a record of opposition] . . . we were forced to pass it, um . . . even with all the flaws because if we didn't, we were going to not be eligible for the $7 million. And it was a really awful vote to have to take. None of us felt good about it—in the sense that, we thought that it was seriously flawed, but it was just one of those moments where you have to decide the lesser of two evils. And . . . uh, the greater evil so to speak would have been to lose $7 million of pay for teachers [despite being totally unfair to 75% of teachers]. (School_Board2.1FL)

The pervasiveness of superintendents' reservations is both theoretically and practically significant. Theoretically, they are important because they directly challenge one of the underlying assumptions of many union critics—that the explanation for certain policy outcomes, like the absence of PRP, can be attributed to union opposition. The implicit argument is that these reforms would have been implemented 'if not for unionism.' It suggests that someone—vaguely termed 'reformers,' presumably government leaders and their allies—knows what the optimal policy solution is and wants to implement it, but is prevented from doing so by strong countervailing forces with opposing interests—unions. Based on these assumptions, the absence of these optimal policy solutions must be attributed to the countervailing forces' success in thwarting them. This research has already presented considerable evidence that the interests and impact of these countervailing forces is far more complex than this account would suggest. However, the widespread ambivalence of school district leaders suggests that preferences—and resulting strategies and tactics—of key decision-makers may be as variable and complex as the interests of teachers' unions.

Although this book has largely avoided the question as to whether PRP is the *right* policy solution, regardless of who is correct in the debate about PRP, the salient point is that teachers' unions are *not* the only actors who have questions, doubts, or concerns about certain tenants of PRP. A depiction of PRP reform as a two-sided drama, in which one side (policy-makers and school leaders) unequivocally supports PRP and the other (unions) unequivocally opposes it, is inconsistent with the evidence. Instead, all decision-makers are asking themselves the same question: Is this worth it? The answer to that question depends on whether the perceived benefits of a reform outweigh the perceived cost of participation. Even in the absence of strong unions, this is not a straightforward question for decision-makers, as the Texas cases demonstrate.

District.4TX ultimately decided that it was 'worth it,' but only because they had the freedom and flexibility to design a plan that addressed their key concerns about fairness, measurability, and not eliminating cooperation (Figure 10.8). According to the superintendent of District.4TX, if they had been forced to provide rewards to individual teachers based on student test scores—as was the case in Florida—the district would not have participated. Their non-participation would not have been driven by teachers' opposition, but by the superintendent's opposition:

> One of the biggest problems that I have with [PRP] is that it eliminates the sharing of best practices . . . you have a collaborative environment. If that had not been allowed, that was our plan, that was the only plan that we were going to submit, and had it not been approved, we were out. (Superintendent.4TX)

Even in District.5TX—the district that demonstrated the greatest enthusiasm and confidence in PRP—the superintendent's calculation about whether PRP was 'worth it' was tipped by the DATE grant (Figure 10.9). Although he had always been a proponent of the reform:

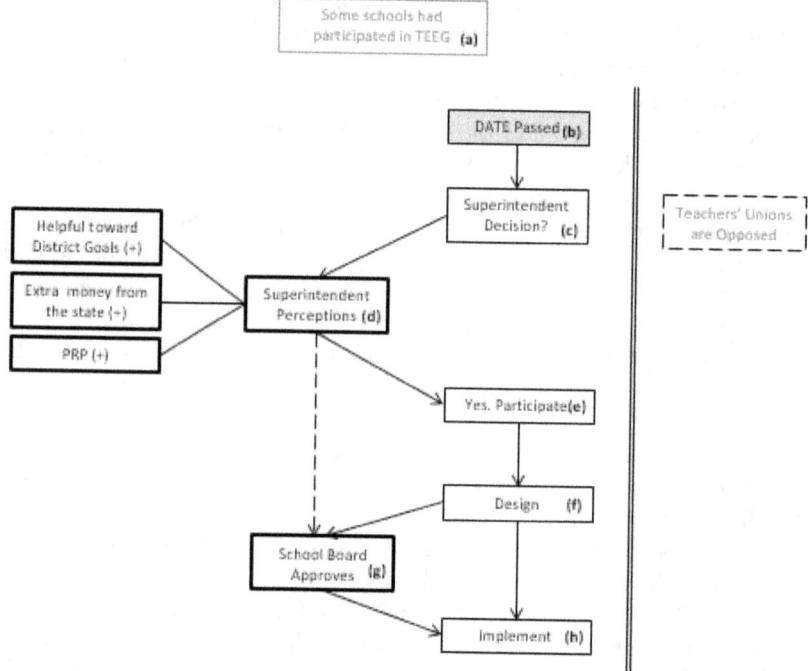

Figure 10.8 District.4TX timeline

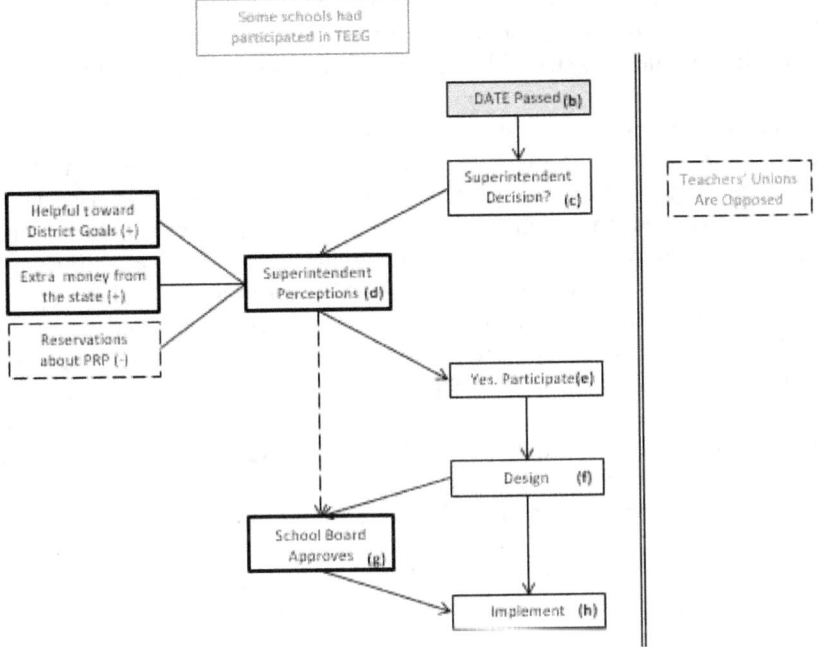

Figure 10.9 District.5TX timeline

> It takes an incredible, incredible amount of time, and um, and uses up a huge amount of political capitol with the teaching rank and file in pursuing, uh, something that, I [did not] believe has um, enough of a return on that investment to pursue it. (Superintendent.5TX)

His statement confirms that even in the absence of teachers' unions there may be perceived costs that outweigh the perceived benefits even for reform proponents. These perspectives strongly challenge any suggestions that unions are exclusively, or even primarily, responsible for the absence of PRP in the United States. This is not to suggest that strong unions are irrelevant to the policy-making process. However, policy-making outcomes—and the relevant contribution of teachers' unions to those outcomes—must be understood within a framework in which all actors are making decisions and calculations as to whether a particular reform is 'worth it.'

TEST #4: EXPLAINING THE REVERSAL OF DISTRICT.2FL

This section has examined the reform process in each district and confirmed the salience of relationship patterns and the viability of the cooperative pathway in the US context. It has also accumulated further evidence of the fundamental complexity of actors' preferences when it comes to PRP—including the preferences and perceptions of policy-makers. The only remaining puzzle is District.2FL's eventual decision to opt out of the MAP program (Figure 10.2).

The conclusion of the first test was that a cooperative relationship pattern between the teachers' union and the school district was critical to understanding District.2FL's participation. State legislation and associated funding provided an incentive, but the relationships secured the union's cooperation in spite of their concerns. What changed between 2006 and 2009 to cause the district to opt out of the MAP program? Did the cooperative relationship disintegrate, or how can the shift be understood?

The relationship between the union and the district did not change during this period. However, the perceptions and preferences of both the union and the district changed overtime. As represented in Table 10.1, there were always concerns about the measurability and fairness of PRP. Initially, everyone in the district was able to agree that the availability of state monies made participation in the district's best interest in spite of these reservations:

> But again, one of the things we did is we looked at it this way. You know, first of all, it's $4 million that's not going to come to the district [otherwise]. So it's an advantage for us to put together a system that will allow us to . . . put this in the pockets of our best teachers. (Central_Office.2FL)

However, several factors led to different calculations and, by 2009, the conclusion that participation was not 'worth it.' The union had received a number of complaints from disgruntled members during their two-year participation in the MAP program (Union_Leader.2FL; Central_Office.2FL). At the same time, the district was finding the MAP program increasingly costly—in terms of both time and money—to administer. The financial and administrative burden was becoming more difficult to sustain in the face of other competing priorities. So, in 2009, both parties agreed that it was no longer worth it to continue to participate in the program (Union_Leader.2FL; Central_Office.2FL).

CONCLUSION

How does the typological theory, outlined in Chapter 8, hold up to the US tests? In general, the US cases provide support for the two causal pathways identified in Chapter 8. The support for relationship patterns was particularly strong. The US cases also suggest a few additional insights and further revisions to existing assumptions and descriptions of teachers' unions. Figure 10.10 displays a modified version of Figure 8.1.

One significant addition to the model based on the US cases—particularly the weak union cases—is required. Specifically, it was clear that reform may not occur in a district *not* because of union opposition, but because the leader,

School District Analysis 245

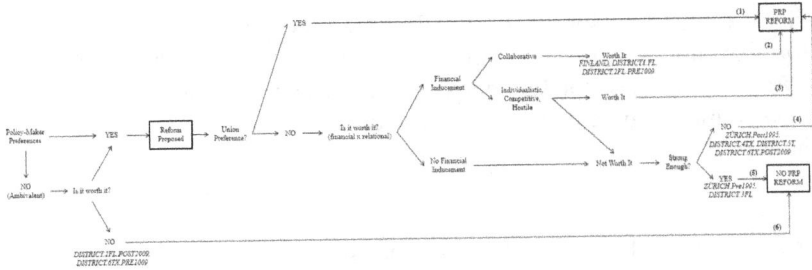

Figure 10.10 Revised typological theory of PRP reform

key decision-maker, or reformer did not want to pursue PRP (Figure 10.10, path 6). In fact, a surprising finding—for those who assume that there are a set of obvious and commonly held policy solutions that are blocked by obstinate unions—was that the majority of school district leaders were at least somewhat ambivalent about PRP. The only district whose leader expressed a virtually unwavering confidence in PRP was District.5TX. Every other leader had at least some reservations about the measurability and fairness of PRP, its impact on collaboration, or its effectiveness as a motivator.

In terms of policy-maker preferences, the majority of superintendents would have been classified as ambivalent. The majority of school district leaders decided that it was worth it to pursue reforms, because it was a way to get more money to the district and to teachers and because they believed that they could design systems that would achieve district goals in spite of their reservations. However, District.6TX initially chose not to participate in DATE—not because of union opposition, but because the superintendent was not interested in pursuing a reform about which he was ambivalent in light of a perceived district match requirement.

When the potential for leadership ambivalence or opposition was applied to districts with strong unions (Florida), those pictures—which had been brought into focus through an examination of interaction orientations and union preferences—only became clearer. District.2FL's eventual decision to opt out was a mutual decision, according to all interviewees, on the part of the union and the district. Both parties had decided that reform was not worth it: the union because of perceived unfairness and complaints from members, and the district because of the financial and administrative costs of overseeing the program. To attribute this outcome to union opposition overcoming a popular reform would be to grossly mischaracterize what actually happened and the complex interests of both teachers' unions and district leaders.

The classification of District.3FL in Figure 10.10 also deserves comment and speaks to the inherent complexity of formalizing the model. The superintendent in District.3FL expressed some ambivalence about PRP, but also expressed an interest in pursuing the reform *if* he had not perceived it to be impossible, or, at the very least, 'not worth' the expenditure of his limited political capital as a superintendent. Did the union in District.3FL block the reform? Although it seems that the reform died before it ever began, that was, in large part, because the superintendent knew that attempting reform would be too politically difficult due to union opposition—and their close links to the school board.

WHEN DO SUCH RESULTS (PRP) OCCUR?

Together, the US and international cases contribute to a revised typological theory that suggests three possible pathways for PRP reform: the power-through explanation, the cooperative compromise explanation, and the union preferences explanation.

First, in the power-through pathway, teachers' unions oppose the reform, but motivated reformers are able to overcome union opposition (Figure 10.10, 4). If the teachers' union decides that PRP reform is not worth it, reform may still occur if the union is not strong enough to block it *at that time*. Unions in selected Texas districts were described as weak: a weakness that was consistent and fairly invariant, linked to the institutional arrangements that constrained unions in the state. Thus unions in District.4TX, District.5TX, and District.6TX post-2009 were unable to block reforms that they opposed. In addition to cases like those researched in Texas where unions are consistently weak, Zürich provides an example of a case where union power varied over time; union opposition successfully blocked reform until 1995, but was neutralized post-1995. Thus, Zürich post-1995 provides an example of the power-through pathway. This explanation speaks to the contingency of teachers' unions' power.

Second, in the cooperative compromise explanation (Figure 10.10, 2), unions are opposed to the reform[4] but are convinced, through a cooperative or collaborative relationship with reformers, to support it. In this scenario, compromise is in the unions' short- and long-term best interest. This path was exemplified in Finland, where the new salary system was implemented in 2007 as a compromise between OAJ and KT. The union conceded on PRP (HL) in order to get raises for teachers. This interest calculation was linked to the complexity of union preferences and goals, but it was also linked to the OAJ's relationship pattern with their negotiating partners. The cooperative relationship pattern was well established—evident at both the central and local levels—and impacted both parties' strategic calculations. Both started from the assumption that the result of negotiation *would* be a compromise, and the union attempted to find tactically clever solutions within this framework.

It would be easy to write this off as a particularity of Finnish institutions, culture, and history. After all, it is a small nation with trademark corporatist institutions and a power sharing and consensus oriented political culture (Katzenstein, 1985). However, there were marked differences between and variable relationship patterns across US school district cases with strong unions (Florida), and these differences were highly correlated with reform outcomes. While both District.1FL and District.2FL displayed cooperative relationship patterns between the school district and unions, District.3FL—where PRP was not implemented—was marked by relational strife between the superintendent and the union.

The third potential pathway to reform—one that was not observed in the cases studied, but remains possible—is labeled the 'union preferences pathway.' In this hypothetical path, the union either prefers PRP reform (i.e., first-order preference), or calculates that it is in its best interest (strategic-calculation of interest), and opts to support reform independently of the relational incentives to do so. There are two versions of this pathway in Figure 10.10 (1 and 3), but the basic premise of this pathway is that the union prefers PRP (1) or decides that accepting or pursuing PRP is 'worth it' (3) independently of either the power or the persuasion of key leaders or policy-makers. Although neither version of the union preferences pathway was empirically observed, there is no reason to assume that they are impossible, given variable, complex, and competing union preferences. Thus, they remain important theoretical possibilities that should not be eliminated in future research.

Given the three explanations for reform, it would be straightforward to posit that non-reform is simply the inverse of these causal conditions. PRP is unlikely to be possible in cases where neither pathway exists—either if relationship patterns do not facilitate compromise or, in the absence of these conditions, if reformers are not powerful enough to overcome union opposition (Figure 10.10, 5). However, one of the central tenets of this research is its emphasis on causal asymmetry, complexity and equifinality (George & Bennett, 2005; Ragin, 1987, 2000, 2008). Because causality is often asymmetrical, the causal pathway for non-reform is unlikely to be the exact inverse of the pathways for reform.

Chapter 10 made a key contribution to the factors that drive non-reform, highlighting the significant role of non-union causes, namely the complex preferences and ambivalence to PRP among key decision-makers and stakeholders. The explanations for when PRP is likely to occur all assume that policy-makers *want* to reform. However, District.6TX proves that reform may not occur even when a union is too weak to block it. It exemplifies the third potential cause of non-reform most clearly: lack of motivation or reform commitment in leadership (Figure 10.10, 6). Regardless of the union's preferences related to PRP and its relative strength to oppose reform, PRP will not occur if key leaders or policy-makers do not prefer PRP, or do not think it is worth the costs. Although demonstrated most clearly in District.6TX, this explanation was also evident in District.2FL's decision to eventually opt out of Florida's PRP system. Both District.6TX and District.2FL (post-2009) illustrate that unions are not the only actors who may be ambivalent about reform.

So, if we were to look at the universe of cases where reform has not occurred, there are two major pathways to non-reform. First, PRP efforts may be opposed and thwarted by union opposition, as evidenced by Zürich pre-1995 and District.3FL (Figure 10.10, 5). However, non-reform may also be explained entirely by non-union factors. PRP may not have occurred in some cases because no one—including leaders and policy-makers—*wanted* to pursue PRP reform.

What are the implications of these findings for theory and practice? Chapter 11 consolidates the evidence regarding both the problem-oriented and theory-oriented questions driving this research. It consolidates the theoretical implications of these findings for theories of union preferences and power, revisions that have significant implications for policy-making as well as future research.

NOTES

1. And also in the Texas districts, as explored later.
2. They wanted to increase salaries, but only wanted overall raises.
3. This misconception is believable; there was a period where District.4TX also believed that there would be matching requirements. However, their perception was corrected and they participated.
4. In terms of their first-order preferences.

REFERENCES

Fisher, R., & Ury, W. (1981). *Getting to yes: Negotiating agreement without giving in*. New York: Penguin Group.

George, A. L., & Bennett, A. (2005). *Case studies and theory development in the social sciences*. Cambridge, MA: MIT Press.

Hess, F. M., & West, M. R. (2006). *A better bargain: Overhauling teacher collective bargaining for the 21st century*. Cambridge, MA: Program on Education Policy and Governance. Retreived from http://www.hks.harvard.edu/pepg/PDF/Papers/BetterBargain.pdf

Katzenstein, P. J. (1985). *Small states in world markets: Industrial policy in Europe*. Ithaca, NY: Cornell University Press.

Ragin, C. C. (1987). *The comparative method: Moving beyond qualitative and quantitative strategies*. Berkeley: University of California Press.

Ragin, C. C. (2000). *Fuzzy-set social science*. Chicago: University of Chicago Press.

Ragin, C. C. (2008). *Redesigning social inquiry: Fuzzy sets and beyond*. Chicago: University of Chicago Press.

Walton, R. E., & McKersie, R. B. (1965/1991). *A behavioral theory of labor negotiations* (2nd ed.). New York: McGraw Hill.

Part IV
Conclusion

11 Useful Conflict?
Finding the Path to Progress

Over the past decade, fiery anti-union rhetoric has turned to action as teachers' unions are portrayed as defenders of a 'failing' education system and immovable obstacles impeding essential reforms. The solution often presented to this constructed problem is to remove the obstacle—weaken teachers' unions and limit their influence and voice. Such a view is premised on the assumption that the interests of teachers' unions are fundamentally incompatible with the public interest and 'what's best for kids.'

This book has presented research suggesting that this account of teachers' unions—their preferences, strategies, and impact on policy—is reductive. Narrowly, in terms of where and why PRP occurs, the evidence has demonstrated that overpowering is not the only pathway to implementing a controversial reform like PRP: cooperative relationships may make productive compromise possible. PRP reform has occurred in Finland, Zürich, and parts of the United States where unions are strong and can be attributed to a number of potential causal pathways—rooted in power, relationships, and preferences. Although non-reform may be partly due to union opposition, the case studies also highlight a number of non-union factors that are significant to understanding the low take-up rate of PRP reform across the US. Most notably, policy-makers are not confident about the inherent value of PRP. These findings are both theoretically and practically significant.

THEORETICAL IMPLICATIONS

The evidence accumulated throughout this book points toward the need for more complex and nuanced theories about teachers' unions and their impact on education policy. First, both teachers' unions' and policy-makers' preferences and interest calculations are complex and dynamic—not invariant and predictable. Second, teachers' unions' power—particularly in the complex, multilayered US education policy-making landscape—is contingent: varying over space, time, and issue. And finally, union-management relationships provide a significant mechanism through which interest revision may occur.

Complex Reform Preferences

Turning first to preferences, it is clear—particularly from the detailed exposition of teachers' unions' preferences in Zürich and Finland—that, confirming previous research (Poole, 2000; Vallaint, 2005), the interests of teachers' unions are complex and multifaceted. This complexity can be approached from a number of angles. First, the preferences of individual teachers are complex. The Swiss teachers' union (LCH) leaders' juxtaposition of those concerned with defending salaries with "pedagogical dreamers" who would "achieve that dream for no pay" and the perceived tension and interplay between professional aims and economic interests provides an apt characterization of teachers' diverse interests. Unions' goals reflect many purposes, emphasizing both system maintenance objectives to improve teachers' and the unions' financial position as well as goal attainment preferences related to teachers' professionalism and effectiveness, and both types of goals have short- and long-term dimensions and strategies. And even *within* the category of economic interests, teachers' preferences are unlikely to be monolithic or straightforward. As evident in both Finland and Zürich, secondary teachers may have different preferences than elementary teachers, or math teachers might have different preferences than language teachers, due to the fact that policies presenting gains for one group may promise losses for another.

Although the findings about teachers' unions' preferences are significant vis-à-vis dominant theories, an equally significant and surprising finding, in terms of particular PRP preferences, was the complex preferences of key leaders and decision-makers regarding PRP reform. The unions-block-reform account is premised on two unarticulated assumptions: first, that policy-makers *know* how to design schools, including teachers' pay, effectively, and second, that they *want* to structure schools in this way (Wilber, 1998). This logic—that teachers' unions are the only obstacle to the realization of policy-makers' perfectly designed reforms—is evident in Moe's (2011) discussion of the Denver ProComp plan:

> This pay-for-performance plan is widely hailed as a national model and an example of what can be achieved when districts and their unions work together on reform. It is also indicative of the limitations that come along with union buy-in. . . . The Denver plan is probably better than the single salary schedule. But it is still a pale version of what a serious, well-designed pay-for-performance plan might look like if the sole concern were to make the schools as effective as possible. *The reason is simply that, with the unions heavily involved in its design, it is built to protect the occupational interests of teachers.* (p. 253, emphasis added)

According to Moe, the ProComp plan is watered down because student test scores play a limited role among a variety of other factors, including professional development, performance evaluation, and school-wide bonuses—all factors that have some research base. Furthermore, the district "bought off the union" by increasing teachers' base salaries in addition to providing incentives (Moe, 2011, p. 253). These compromises are portrayed as the unfortunate consequences of concessions to a powerful union.

However, the consistent theme that emerged from the US case studies was that superintendents and school district officials are often not fully convinced that PRP—at least the particular versions promoted by many reformers—is a good idea. Chapter 10 documented the hesitation, ambivalence, and concern of superintendents across the US cases. Even those who were generally supportive of PRP expressed concerns about measurability, fairness, or competitiveness, fundamentally calling the logic—that teachers' unions are inevitably the source of the 'watering down of reform'—into question. PRP reform may be influenced by teachers' unions' opposition, but it may also be a product of the preferences, strategies, and decisions of leaders (Hess & Kelly, 2006; Wirt & Kirst, 1997). Furthermore, as Kerchner and colleagues argue, "To criticize unions for opposing a particular reform assumes that reforms themselves don't deserve a vigorous debate" (1997, p. 4). It seems that overlooking the vigor and pervasiveness of the debate about PRP (see Adams, Heywood, & Rothstein, 2009; Johnson, 1986) has produced an oversimplified view of the preferences of both teachers and policy-makers.

Contingency of Power

In terms of unions' power, there is not a clear, direct relationship between static measures of union resources and their influence on reform (McClendon & Cohen-Vogel, 2008; Strunk & Reardon, 2010; Urban, 2004). This finding confirms Immergut's description of the contingency of power, which is "not an essential or invariant characteristic of particular interest groups" (1992, p. 8). Teachers' unions' power—both within and beyond US borders—is contingent in at least three ways: across issues, time, and space.

First, different "strategic opportunities [stem] from the logic of political decision processes" (Immergut, 1992, p. 8). These are evident between countries—the opportunity structure for union influence differs considerably between Finland, Zürich, and the US—and between issues. Zürich provides the best example of this type of contingency: although the ZLV was relatively weak in terms of traditional collective bargaining, it had the potential to exert considerable political influence—as evidenced by its success at delaying MAB implementation for almost five years.

The case of Zürich also points to the second key way in which teachers' unions' power is contingent—over time. The union saw its influence decline considerably in the mid-1990s, undermining its ability to stave off PRP reform. So even within a particular political decision-making process, union power is not invariant over time.

Finally, union power can vary significantly over space, within a given polity. Although differences between the opportunity structure for union influence *between* Finland, Zürich, and the United States are easily identified, a closer examination of the sub-national contexts confirms the considerable diversity in union power *within* each country. In Finland, this was notable in the differences between opportunities for union influence at the national and local level, and in the United States, sub-national variability is especially significant.

The sub-national variability of teachers' union behavior and influence—due to both institutional variance as well as the independence of local associations vis-à-vis state and national unions—in the United States is well documented (Bascia, 1990; Johnson & Donaldson 2006; Johnson & Kardos 2000; McDonnell & Pascal, 1988; Murray, 2004). Teachers' unions' strength resources are highly variable at the state and local level, as evident in both their measurable resources—such as density, financial power, and others—and the qualitative differences that were clear between the Florida and Texas districts. These differences *must* have implications on various state and local unions' relative influence. However, although acknowledging that laws and other institutions can vary across states, many accounts treat union power across this variable landscape as a largely invariant phenomenon.

Given the contingency of union power in general, and the complexities of the decentralized US education policy landscape, any analysis that attempts to describe education politics or the role of teachers' unions in the United States as a whole should proceed with extreme caution, leery of whole-nation bias (Lijphart, 1975a; Snyder, 2001). Although federal politics of education are attractive because of their singularity, the number of issues which are exclusively federal are incredibly limited, and even these issues must attend to the complex inter-dynamics of multilevel compliance and implementation (Sroufe, 1994). Very rarely can the complex and messy reality of state and local variation be entirely avoided or ignored. It is difficult to summarize this diversity into one coherent, monolithic, or invariant picture of what education policy is like on average; it is also undesirable, as these differences may hold extremely valuable insights (Murillo, 2012).

As evidenced by the case studies in Chapter 10, even if unions *usually* behave or influence policy in a particular way, they don't always, and exploring these 'exceptional' cases illuminates alternatives. In most cases, there is no American system of education policy: there are 50 systems, or 14,000 systems, operating in more or less similar ways. Similarly, this research confirms that teachers' unions in the United States should not be approached as one invariant entity, as there are important differences across districts and states. Generalizing at the national level obscures more than it illuminates. Dominant theories' oversimplified assumptions about teachers' unions' preferences and neglect of relationship patterns and their potential interest-intermediating effects are two accumulating errors that produce incorrect conclusions regarding power.

Relationships Matter

In addition to their contributions to theorizing about unions' preferences and power, the case studies present overwhelming evidence that relationship patterns and actors' interaction orientations have significant implications for understanding both actors' preferences and the variability of union influence. Stable, trust-based relationships provide an avenue for cooperation and compromise that can be precluded by power struggles. Furthermore, relationship patterns provide a mechanism for interest intermediation—changes and shifts between first-order preferences, interests, and strategies.

Although relationship patterns and the beliefs and personalities of the individuals within those relationships are critical to understanding the behavior and influence of unions and the resulting policy outcomes, they are certainly not a panacea. They are only one factor that informs strategic interactions that are rooted in complex and competing perceptions and preference calculations between actors. However, relationship patterns are frequently overlooked, and when this occurs, the preferences, strategies, and impact of teachers' unions are misunderstood.

The fact that the cooperative relationship pattern evidenced in Finland is generalizable to the United States is, in some ways, theoretically surprising. There would be a variety of ways to explain why cooperation is possible and even likely in Finland, but unlikely, if not impossible, in the United States. First, one could look to the literature on types of democracy. While Finland is a consensus oriented or consociational democracy, the US is a prototypical majoritarian or competitive democracy (Lijphart, 1999). While the former is characterized by institutions that would encourage stable and cooperative relationships and broad coalitions, the latter is not. Second, in terms of labor relations in particular, Finland employs a corporatist model that has embraced trade unions as legitimate social partners via concertation, while labor relations in the US are often characterized by mistrust, suspicion, and antagonism (Bacarro, 2003; Compston, 2003; Lehmbruch, 1977; Molina & Rhodes, 2002; Schmitter, 1982; Richardson, 1982; Rhodes, 2001; Visser & Himerijck, 1997). Finally, Finland's inclusive democracy is further distinguished by its small state status—a particular brand of consociational explanations that are premised on the necessity of cooperation for the survival of small states in an uncertain global environment (Katzenstein, 1985).

These theories all imply that cooperation and compromise in Finland are by-products of the particularities of Finnish institutions. None of these institutional conditions 'travel well' to the US context. However, cooperative relationships that produced compromise were observed in US school districts. How can this puzzle be explained and what are the theoretical implications of the explanation?

The generalizability of cooperative relationship patterns to the United States confirms that particular formal institutions—i.e., consociationalism or corporatism—are not necessary conditions for cooperation (Compston,

2003; Culpepper, 2002; Schmitter, 1982). Although Finland's historical, cultural, and institutional development have produced a particular consensus orientation that may help to explain the presence or stability of cooperative relationships, the absence of these institutions does not preclude cooperation in the US. Furthermore, although cooperative relationships may be encouraged by consensus orientations, they are also not an inevitable by-product of these institutions—they are not *sufficient* conditions.

Because relationship patterns are not entirely institution dependent—institutions provide neither necessary nor sufficient conditions—they can be altered, as evidenced by the US cases.[1] This is not to suggest that relationship patterns are unpredictable products of idiosyncratic personality differences and preferences. The existing relationship pattern—the relevant relationship history and established modus operandi—as well as actors' desire to *change* this pattern, impacts actors' interest-formation, strategies, and willingness to compromise. Contexts with developed institutions that support cooperative relationships and their maintenance are likely to demonstrate more stable relationship patterns—i.e., Finland. However, contexts that lack these institutional supports can still establish cooperative relationships through informal norms and procedures as well as established histories that build trust between participants; relationship patterns may simply be more volatile in these contexts (Johnson, 2004; Johnson & Donaldson, 2006; Johnson & Kardos, 2000; Kerchner & Koppich, 1993).

This provides the best account for cooperation in the US context: it is possible, but it is less predictable and may be more volatile. This volatility is where the majoritarian institutions and more competitive union-management ideologies may come into play. Majoritarian institutions produce greater turnover in states and school districts—in the election of school board members as well as in the tenure of superintendents. Because individuals' beliefs about union-management legitimacy and productivity are relevant to relationship patterns, this frequent turnover introduces a high number of opportunities for disruption to an established relationship pattern (Johnson & Donaldson, 2006).

Together, the evidence accumulated through this research—that teachers aren't the only actors who may oppose PRP, that teachers' unions' preferences are significantly complex, and that relationship patterns may further complicate simple pictures of union interests or strategy—leaves the unions-block-reform argument with little ground on which to stand.

FROM THEORY TO PRACTICE: LESSONS FOR PRACTITIONERS

What lessons do the case studies contain for practitioners? How can they be employed to develop better strategies for productively engaging teachers' unions to maximize the effectiveness of education policy-making? In the context of mounting economic pressures and fiscal consolidation plans, how can governments overcome union opposition to 'essential' reforms in education? What role can and should teachers' unions play in these difficult choices? Should they be eliminated? Can they contribute to more productive solutions—those that preserve the effectiveness of public service provision and ensure that the public sector can attract qualified employees?

George and Bennett (2005) argue that what practitioners need is a generic knowledge of the conditions that favor the success of a specific strategy and a correct image of their opponent. This research suggests policy-makers who are operating as if teachers' unions are unequivocally powerful organizations whose interests are fundamentally antithetical to the public good likely have an inaccurate image of their 'opponent.' Furthermore, when policy-makers, researchers, and the media treat reform as a two-sided battle, they make a deeply flawed assumption, as the consistency and depth of union opposition and policy-maker support is far from uniform. A more successful strategy for finding the "starting point on the path to progress" (Duncan, 2014, n.p.) would involve two things: investing in more productive relationships and abandoning reductive assumptions and stories about reform.

Willingness to Consider Compromise

The dominant view of union-management relationships in the United States is characterized by inherent conflict. A history of anti-union sentiments provides the groundwork for a distrust and suspicion of unions. Although a pluralist approach to unions—with its emphasis on conflict and distributive bargaining—is ideologically dominant in the United States, it is not the only available framework. European labor relations—particularly Germany, Northern Europe, and Scandinavia—approach unions quite differently, guided by an emphasis on social partnership and codetermination that is rooted in a history of corporatism (Jurgens, Berthon, Papania, & Shabbir, 2010). In contrast to the pluralist conception, in Northern Europe, corporations include employees in decision-making and are "a coalition of various participants . . . striving for continuity of the firm as a whole" (Lenssen & Verobey, 2005, as cited in Jurgens et al., 2010, p. 771). These cases provide a more optimistic picture of the potential for compromise. In the social partnership model, compromise appears to neither sacrifice the public interest, nor to manipulate or control unions. But the emphasis on the potential for compromise prompts two questions. First, is compromise really a good thing? And second, is it possible in the US context?

Many union critics argue that compromising with teachers' unions is inherently objectionable. If unions' interests are inherently and fundamentally selfish and inconsistent with the public interest, if every gain for teachers' unions is a loss for what is best for students, then weakening unions is justified. Moe (1995) recognizes the value of union-management compromise in the private sector because "the system of rules to come out of all of this is advantageous to everyone and people are always free to leave if they have better opportunities elsewhere" (1995, p. 125). However, he takes a different view of compromise in the public sector, arguing that rather than creating mutual advantage, it is coercive (Moe, 1995). The differing assessment of the value of compromise in politics or the public sector is rooted in Moe's assumptions about preferences and power. The government and administration is responsible for representing the public interest and unions are exclusively concerned with promoting their self-interests. Thus, there is no mutual benefit to achieve through negotiations: any gain for unions is a loss for the public—a collusive spoil-sharing agreement.

Compromise may also be viewed skeptically by teachers' unions who view any agreements with governments to be concessions to ill-conceived reforms that harm public education and weaken teachers' unions (Compton & Weiner, 2008). Within this view, although compromising with government may appear pragmatic in the short-term by securing least-bad alternatives, it is an unacceptable compromise of the essential principles that the union should defend (Compton & Weiner, 2008).

Part of the disagreement over the value of compromise—is it right or wrong, good or bad, fair or unfair—lies in confusion about its meaning, as a wide range of actions and outcomes have been labeled compromise. Day (1989) defines compromise as "an agreement between A and B to make mutual concessions in order to resolve a conflict between them" (p. 472). Implicit in Day's definition is the idea that concessions must be mutual, eliminating one of the common uses of the term in reference to unilateral concessions. According to Day, this latter term is not compromise but appeasement—"to pacify, propitiate, or satisfy demands" (*The Shorter Oxford Dictionary*, as cited in Day, 1989, p. 473).

Compromise—as distinct from exchange, punishment, compensation, or appeasement—involves both sides gaining something and both sides losing something (Day, 1989). According to Day, compromises are good—instrumentally or prudentially—when they provide an enduring resolution to conflict, and they are wrong if they violate moral rights—i.e., fairness—or have bad consequences (Day, 1989). Perhaps compromising with unions—gaining something and losing something—can be good *if* information is exchanged and learning occurs throughout the negotiation process. M. P. Follett identifies the difference between distributive compromises, which split the difference between two positions, and integrative compromises, which are creative (as cited in Day, 1989). The latter form of compromise requires imagination and is only possible if compromise is approached in a cooperative rather than adversarial spirit. These ideas resonate with Walton and McKersie's (1965/1991) framework and are further developed below, but in terms of the inherent value of compromise, the key idea is that compromises can be efficiency enhancing if both sides are learning through the process and producing new, previously unknown, solutions. If it is *possible* that compromise can be good—resolving conflicts and producing fair and effective policy solutions—the second question is if compromise is possible in the US context. Is the widespread distrust of compromise and entrenched conflict-oriented approach toward unions empirically grounded or ideological?

The case studies in the US, consistent with previous research, demonstrate that cooperative relationships and collaborative agreements between teachers' unions and school districts *are* possible in the US. Although there is diversity across local unions, school districts, and the policies produced (Johnson, 2004; Johnson & Donaldson, 2006; Johnson & Kardos, 2000; Kerchner & Koppich, 1993; Koppich, 2006; McDonnell & Pascal, 1988), the link to relationship patterns and Walton and McKersie's (1965/1991) negotiation theory carries a number of significant implications beyond the narrow implications for the likelihood of PRP reform.

In confirming the salience of concertation and cooperation in the US context, this research demonstrates that the conflict-ridden relationships of teachers' unions and policy-makers are not solely a product of the US pluralist system in contrast to corporatist approaches (Visser & Himerijck, 1997). If cooperation were institutionally determined, it would be impossible in the US. However, its presence in some school districts confirms the salience of distinctions between *structures* of interest intermediation and *practices* of concertation (Schmitter, 1982). Several studies have confirmed the possibility of structurally undetermined cooperative agreements which depend on the exchange of information and the nature of strategies, dialogue, and debate (Bacarro, 2003; Culpepper, 2002).

Thus, in addition to challenging dominant assumptions of teachers' unions' preferences, power, and resulting pathways to reform, this research suggests that policy-makers and union leaders in the US have a choice in how they approach the union-management relationship. Antagonism is not inevitable and the ideology of conflict is escapable. Furthermore, beyond being possible, cooperative approaches may be preferable to antagonism, and embracing the antagonistic, power-oriented path may have significant consequences that undermine long-term capacities for systemic change and improvement.

These findings are significant for both teachers' unions and policy-makers. If unions want to be able to inform the perspective of decision-makers, to persuade them to see education problems and potential solutions differently, a commitment to an adversarial relationship may be counterproductive. Similarly, policy-makers may find cooperative engagement around seemingly intractable problems aided by a foundation of trust. For those who would label teachers' unions "terrorist organizations,"[2] these conclusions will be difficult to entertain, let alone accept. However, Walton and McKersie's (1965/1991) framework of labor negotiations provides a foundation through which the potentially costly implications of unnecessarily conflict-oriented and aggressive engagement with teachers' unions can be traced. Walton and McKersie's framework suggests that cooperative, trust-based relationships may enable more effective problem solving than individualistic or competitive approaches.

Although distributive bargaining, which is premised on zero-sum conflict, is the dominant conception of bargaining interactions, integrative bargaining provides an alternative. In integrative bargaining, parties can increase their joint gain through mutual problem solving. Distributive bargaining is unavoidable in any situation in which the interests of the two parties are fundamentally opposed—completely non-overlapping. However, the degree to which bargaining problems are integrative or distributive is both empirical and ideological. Yes, in some situations, the two parties, by definition, want different things. And in these situations, distributive conflict is inevitable. However, the degree to which problems are identified as integrative or distributive can also be ideological. If one party *assumes* that the issue is distributive, then it will be handled distributively. This is particularly important because integrative potential may not be immediately apparent: "the task of the negotiators is to *discover* the high payoff possibilities. That is, the various alternatives and their potential benefits are not known to the parties before they engage in integrative bargaining" (Walton & McKersie 1965/1991, p. 17).

Because both parties operate with incomplete information in the bargaining process and because distributive bargaining tactics are "designed to obscure, not clarify, resistance points" (Walton & McKersie, 1965/1991, p. 54), these joint-gain maximizing solutions are impossible to discover within a distributive process. Thus, an errant assumption that joint benefits are impossible will preclude them from being realized:

> Either party can increase the payoffs by individual problem solving, but maximum results are available through joint problem solving. If the parties correctly assume that there are such potential benefits, they will proceed deliberately to discover the alternatives that increase the joint gain available to them. (Walton & McKersie, 1965/1991, p. 17)

Walton and McKersie argue that the effectiveness of problem solving (integrative bargaining) depends on a variety of factors: motivation, transparency and information, and trust (1965/1991, p. 139). Trust, in particular, is essential; absent trust, integrative problem solving is unlikely to occur (Walton & McKersie, 1965/1991, p. 159). Distrust is a distraction to the problem-solving process, producing defensive behavior, and can lead to deliberate miscommunication, which directly hampers problem solving. In contrast, trust encourages more transparent communication and supports experimentation (Walton & McKersie, 1965/1991). This is where the relationship pattern (attitudinal bargaining) is incredibly significant. Walton and McKersie propose, as a general rule, that in cooperative relationships, integrative bargaining is utilized to solve more problems (1965/1991, p. 203).

Furthermore, Culpepper (2002) emphasizes the potential for unions to generate policy innovations—rather than merely assenting to reforms—in what he labels pacting, which "combines elements of powering and puzzling[3] in a context in which states do not have access to the information they need to enable their reforms to succeed" (p. 776). Furthermore, beyond being simply a means of generating conflict-resolving compromises, Culpepper (2002) argues that negotiated reforms can provide an avenue for developing new and better solutions. He argues that unions have valuable information about their members' preferences and how to create policies that satisfy reform goals and can engender members' support:

> While opposition to reform is relatively easy to generate (since there are potential losers from welfare reform who are very aware of the consequences), only an organization with dialogic capacity of the nature discussed here will be able to develop a cognitive frame capable of changing the nature of debate and mobilizing a majority of its members. (Culpepper, 2002, p. 778)

Thus, in addition to making compromises possible, collaborative or cooperative relationships provide two additional benefits. First, they provide opportunities for teachers to contribute their knowledge and experience to the decision-making process. Well-intentioned policy-makers may not have all of the information that they need to make good decisions, and teachers may have this information. Collaborative relationship may provide an avenue for teachers' professional knowledge to be expressed in productive, outcome-enhancing, and integrative ways. And second, more cooperative negotiation processes can improve implementation (Streshly & DeMitchell, 1994). The OECD argued in their "Teachers Matter" report that, although stakeholder groups should not have unchecked veto authority, their participation and buy-in is critical to successful reform implementation: "unless teachers are actively involved in policy formulation, and feel a sense of 'ownership' of reform, it is unlikely that substantial changes will be successfully implemented" (OECD, 2005, p. 15). Cooperative relationships, which enable and encourage problem solving through informal social relations, may provide a mechanism to avoid or diminish longer, more detailed, and more cumbersome contracts that often result in tedious and expensive legal arbitration—a process that is often a by-product of competitive, low-trust, patterns (Walton & McKersie, 1965/1991, pp. 202–204).

In *Special Interests* (2011), Moe provides the evidence that confirms the significance of Culpepper's argument for education reform in the United States. According to Moe, his survey data demonstrates that when teachers' unions oppose PRP[4] and preserve seniority-based protections and tenure, they are simply reflecting teachers' preferences. Walking down Wisconsin's path—eliminating or weakening unions—is not going to change the fact that teachers oppose many education reforms. Teachers will continue to dislike PRP, they will continue to object to the growing emphasis on punitive accountability, and they will oppose what many perceive as rampant over-testing. Eliminating unions may leave policy-makers with an even more intractable problem. In contrast with common economics assumptions, reformers (management) do not have perfect information (Wilber, 1998) and could benefit from teachers' perspectives. If unions are eliminated, integrative problem solving will suffer from an absence of an organized voice for teachers. Because policy-makers depend on teachers to implement their reforms, widespread teacher dissatisfaction and lack of buy-in will undermine reform capacity. And if frustration with working conditions and accumulating reform mandates drives good teachers from the profession and deters future teachers from entering it, student learning opportunities will suffer.

Abandon Reductive Reform Stories

It is too early to pronounce that teachers' unions in the United States always oppose particular reforms and use their power to block them. This may accurately describe some cases of reform, but ignores many 'exceptions.' Rather than being aberrations, these cases provide insights into how union-management relationships could be structured to avoid the politics of blocking and gridlock. If the research findings and their implications could be summarized into one key application, it would be this: there has been a growing trend among policy-makers and education reformers in the US context to pursue opportunities to limit teachers' unions' power and to undermine their legitimacy. These efforts have been rooted in particular assumptions about teachers' unions, covering laws that lack empirical grounding. However, this research demonstrates that alternatives to these antagonistic approaches exist and that cooperative approaches may have advantages over power-centric alternatives. Furthermore, current efforts to weaken and delegitimize teachers' unions—both in discourse and in practice—may be doing long-term damage, eliminating the opportunity for trust-based, collaborative relationships to be established.

The hostility toward teachers' unions seems to be a conflict that has outgrown and outlived its usefulness. Aggressive stances toward unions that threaten their existence and rhetoric that corrodes any potential for collaboration or trust are unwise. Eliminating or overpowering unions is not the only path to securing reforms. Although neither universal nor even common, collaboration and cooperation, which could lead to creative, integrative solutions, are possible in the United States. Anti-teachers' union strategies have been driven by assumptions and theories that are untenable and the widespread dismissal of unions' potential to be productive reform partners appears to be grounded in ideology rather than evidence. Furthermore, by creating a false binary between pro-union and anti-union, reformers eliminate the opportunity for the policies and principles of America's unions to be probed, questioned, and justly criticized. Teachers' unions in the United States may be a part of America's public education problems, but they are only one part of a system that is too busy locking horns over intractable, ideological conflict to critically listen and engage in creative and integrative problem solving. Reformers may be winning 'victories' to weaken unions, but their chosen strategy is losing the war for real, meaningful changes that will provide better educational opportunities for all students.

NOTES

1. District.2FL, in particular, is a notable example of shifts in relationship patterns. The stable and cooperative relationship that was in place during the period of reform replaced an incredibly hostile relationship present through the late 1990s.
2. Secretary of Education, Rod Paige, called the National Education Association a "terrorist organization" in 20004.
3. Heclo (1974).
4. Moe's research mirrors previous findings of teachers' opposition to PRP both in the US and internationally (Farrell & Morris, 2004; Ingvarson, Kleinhanz, & Wilkinson, 2007).

REFERENCES

Adams, S. J., & Heywood, J. S. (2009). The perils of quantitative accountability. In S. J. Adams, J. S. Heywood, & R. Rothstein (Eds.), *Teachers, performance pay, and accountability: What education should learn from other sectors*. Washington, DC: Economic Policy Institute, 13–64.
Bacarro, L. (2003). What is alive and what is dead in the theory of corporatism. *British Journal of Industrial Relations, 41*(4), 683–706.
Bascia, N. (1990). Teachers' evaluations of unions. *Journal of Education Policy, 5*(4), 301–312.
Compston, H. (2003). Beyond corporatism: A configurational theory of policy concertation. *European Journal of Political Research, 42*(6), 787–809.
Compton, M., & Weiner, L. (Eds.). (2008). *The global assault on teaching, teachers, and their unions: Stories for resistance*. New York: Palgrave Macmillan.
Culpepper, P. D. (2002). Powering, puzzling, and 'pacting': The informational logic of negotiated reforms. *Journal of European Public Policy, 9*(5), 774–790.
Day, J. P. (1989). Compromise. *Philosophy, 64*(250), 471–485.
Duncan, A. (2014, June 16). *Drawing the right lessons from Vergara* [Web log post]. Retrieved from http://www.ed.gov/blog/2014/06/drawing-the-right-lessons-from-vergara/
Farrell, C., & Morris, J. (2004). Resigned compliance: Teacher attitudes towards performance-related pay in schools. *Educational Management Administration & Leadership, 32*(1), 81–104.
George, A. L., & Bennett, A. (2005). *Case studies and theory development in the social sciences*. Cambridge, MA: MIT Press.
Heclo, H. (1974). *Modern social policy in Britain and Sweden: From relief to income maintenance*. New Haven, CT: Yale University Press.
Hess, F., & Kelly, A. (2006). Scapegoat, albatross, or what? The status quo in teacher collective bargaining. In J. Hannaway & A. Rotherman (Eds.), *Collective bargaining in education: Negotiating change in today's schools*. Cambridge, MA: Harvard Education Press, 53–89.

Immergut, E. (1992). *Health politics*. Cambridge: Cambridge University Press.
Ingvarson, L., Kleinhanz, E., & Wilkinson, J. (2007). *Research on performance pay for teachers*. Camberwell, Victoria, Australia: Australian Council for Educational Research. Retrieved from http://research.acer.edu.au/workforce
Johnson, S. M. (1986). Incentive for teachers: What motivates, what matters. *Educational Administration Quarterly, 22*(3), 54–78.
Johnson, S. M. (2004). Paralysis or possibility: What do teacher unions and collective bargaining bring? In R. D. Henderson, W. J. Urban, & P. Wolman (Eds.), *Teacher unions and education policy: Retrenchment or reform?* Oxford: Elsevier, 33–50.
Johnson, S. M., & Donaldson, M. (2006). The effects of collective bargaining on teacher quality. In J. Hannaway, & A. Rotherman (Eds.), *Collective bargaining in education: Negotiating change in today's schools*. Cambridge, MA: Harvard Education Press, 111–140.
Johnson, S. M., & Kardos, S. (2000). Reform bargaining and its promise for school improvement. In T. Loveless (Ed.), *Conflicting missions? Teachers unions and educational reform*. Washington, DC: Brookings Institution, 7–46.
Jurgens, M., Berthon, P., Papania, L., & Shabbir, H. A. (2010). Stakeholder theory and practice in Europe and North America: The key to success lies in the marketing approach. *Industrial Marketing Management, 39*, 769–775.
Katzenstein, P. J. (1985). *Small states in world markets: Industrial policy in Europe*. Ithaca, NY: Cornell University Press.
Kerchner, C. T., & Koppich, J. E. (1993). *A union of professionals: Labor relations and educational reform*. New York: Teachers College Press.
Kerchner, C. T., Koppich, J. E., & Weeres, J. G. (1997). *United mind workers: Unions and teaching in the knowledge society*. San Francisco: Jossey-Bass.
Koppich, J. E. (2006). The as-yet-unfulfilled promise of reform bargaining. In J. Hannaway & A. Rotherman (Eds.), *Collective bargaining in education: Negotiating change in today's schools*. Cambridge, MA: Harvard Education Press, 203-228.
Lehmbruch, G. (1977). Liberal corporatism and party government. *Comparative Political Studies, 10*(1), 91–126.
Lijphart, A. (1975). The comparable-cases strategy in comparative research. *Comparative Political Studies, 8*(2), 158–177.
Lijphart, A. (1999). *Patterns of democracy: Government forms and performance in thirty-six countries*. New Haven, CT: Yale University Press.
McClendon, M. K., & Cohen-Vogel, L. (2008). Understanding education policy change in the American states: Lessons from political science. In B. Cooper, J. G. Cibulka, & L. Fusarelli (Eds.), *Handbook of education politics and policy*. New York: Routledge, 30–51.
McDonnell, L. M., & Pascal, A. (1988). *Teacher unions and educational reform*. Santa Monica, CA: The Rand Corporation.
Moe, T. (1995). The politics of structural choice: Toward a theory of public bureaucracy. In O. E. Williamson (Ed.), *Organizational theory from Chester Barnard to the present and beyond*. Oxford: Oxford University Press.
Moe, T. (2011). *Special interests: Teachers unions and America's public schools*. Washington, DC: Brookings Institution.
Molina, O., & Rhodes, M. (2002). Corporatism: The past, present, and future of a concept. *Annual Review of Political Science, 5*(1), 305–331.
Murillo, M. V. (2012). A discussion of Terry Moe's special interest: Teachers unions and America's public schools. *Perspectives on Politics, 10*(1), 134–136.
Murray, C. E. (2004). Innovative local teacher unions: What have they accomplished? In R. D. Henderson, W. J. Urban, & P. Wolman (Eds.), *Teacher unions and education policy: Retrenchment and reform*. Oxford: Elesevier, 149–166.

Organization for Economic Co-operation and Development. (2005). *Teachers matter: Attracting, developing and retaining effective teachers*. Paris: OECD.

Poole, W. (2000). The construction of teachers' paradoxical interests by teacher union leaders. *American Educational Research Journal, 37*(1), 93–108.

Rhodes, M. (2001). The political economy of social pacts: Competitive corporatism and European welfare reform. In P. Pierson (Ed.), *The new politics of the welfare state*. Oxford: Oxford University Press, 165–196.

Richardson, J. (1982). *Policy styles in Western Europe*. London: Allen & Unwin.

Schmitter, P. (1982). Reflections on where the theory of neo-corporatism has gone and where the praxis of neo-corporatism may be going. In G. Lehmbruch & P. Schmitter (Eds.), *Patterns of corporatist policy making*. London: Sage, 259–279.

Snyder, R. (2001). Scaling down: The subnational comparative method. *Studies in Comparative International Development, 36*(1), 93–107.

Sroufe, G. E. (1994). Politics of education at the federal level. In J. D. Scribner & D. H. Layton (Eds.), *The study of educational politics: The 1994 commemorative yeabook of the politics of education association 1969–1994*. London: Routledge, 75–88.

Streshly, W. A., & DeMitchell, T. A. (1994). *Teacher unions and TQE: Building quality labor relations*. A Thousand Oaks: Corwin Press.

Strunk, K. O., & Reardon, S. F. (2010). Measuring the strength of teachers' unions: An empirical application of the partial independent item response. *Journal of educational Behavioral Statistics, 35*(6), 629–670.

Vaillant, D. (2005). Education reforms and teachers' unions: Avenues for action. *Fundamentals of educational planning*. Paris: UNESCO International Institute for Educational Planning.

Visser, J., & Hemericjk, A. (1997). *A Dutch miracle*. Amsterdam: Amsterdam University Press.

Urban, W. J. (2004). Teacher politics. In R. D. Henderson, W. J. Urban, & P. Wolman (Eds.), *Teacher unions and education policy: Retrenchment or reform?* Amsterdam: Elesevier, 51–80.

Walton, R. E., & McKersie, R. B. (1965/1991). *A behavioral theory of labor negotiations* (2nd ed.). New York: McGraw Hill.

Wilber, C. K. (1998). Trust, moral hazards, and social economics: Incentives and the organization of work. In C. K. Wilber (Ed.), *Economics, ethics, and public policy*. Lanham, MD: Rowman & Littlefield Publishers, 93–107.

Wirt, F. M., & Kirst, M. W. (1997). *The political dynamics of American education*. Berkeley: McCutchan Publishing.

Glossary

ABBREVIATIONS, ACRONYMS, AND TERMS

ACI	Actor-centered institutionalism
AKAVA	Confederation of Unions for Academic Professionals in Finland
Bildungsdirektion	Education Directorate (Zürich)
DATE	District Awards for Teacher Excellence (TX)
FQS	Formative Evaluation system developed by LCH. Union_Leader
GERM	Global Education Reform Movement
Hallitus	OAJ's 21-member Executive Board
HL	Supplemental pay for professional performance
HI	Historical institutionalism
HRM	Human resource management
Järjestelyerä (JAR)	Locally negotiated salary component
JUKO	Public Sector Negotiators (AKAVA)
KT	The Municipal Employers, Finland
KUNPAS	The statistical study of wage differences in the municipal sector
KVTES	General collective bargaining agreement for municipal employees
LCH	Swiss Federation of Teachers
	Lehrerpersonalgesetz Teacher personnel law (Zürich)
LQS	Qualification system for elementary school teachers (later re-named MAB)
MAP	Merit Award Programme (FL)
Määrävuosilisä	Seniority-based supplemental compensation
MAB	Employee assessment system, implemented in Zürich in 1999
NPM	New Public Management
OAJ	The Trade Union of Education, Finland
OECD	Organization of Economic Co-ordination and Development

268 Glossary

OKRZ	The Association of High School and Junior High Teachers (Zürich)
OVTES	National agreement covering all teachers in Finland
Personalgesetz	Personnel Law
Peruspalkka	Base salary
PRP	Performance-related pay
Regierungsrates	Executive council or 'government'
RCI	Rational choice institutionalism (or 'RC' for rational choice)
SAK	The Confederation of Finnish Trade Unions
Schulpflegen	School boards (Zürich)
SER	Regional teachers' union in French-speaking Switzerland
SekZH	Association of Secondary Teachers of the Canton of Zürich
SI	Sociological institutionalism
Sisu	A Finnish word with no direct translation, popularized in the Winter War, which has been described as kind of sustained culture, perseverance, or grit
SKZ	Secondary Teacher Conference (Zürich)
STAR	Special Teachers are Rewarded (FL)
STTK	The Finnish Confederation of Salaried Employees
TEEG	Teacher Educator Excellence Grant (TX)
TIF	Teacher Incentive Fund
Tilastokeskus	Statistics Finland
TNJ	The Negotiating Organization of Salaried Employees (represents health careworkers in the municipal sector, including TEHY and SuPer)
TS	Collective agreement for technical employees in the municipal sector
TUPA	School-wide awards based on the fulfillment of municipal goals
TUPO	Finland's system of central incomes policy agreements via tripartite negotiations
TVA	Supplemental pay based on task-complexity
Työkokemus	Seniority-based supplemental compensation
U.S. DOE	United States Department of Education
Valtuusto	OAJ's 150-member council
VALPAS	Study of state sector wages, published in 1999
VPOD/SSP	The Swiss public-service union
VSA	Department within the directorate of education that is responsible for primary schools in Zürich
Ylituntipalkkio	Additional lessons
YSI	Association of basic education teachers, Finland
Zürcher Kantonsrat	Cantonal Council of Zürich
ZLV	Zürich teachers' union, an affiliate of the LCH

Appendix I
Data Collection and Analysis

The information listed in parentheses refers to the (primary; secondary) resources of data for each component of the framework. Secondary resources refer to those used for confirmation or validation of primary resources.

Policy Process

1. What was the reform/policy outcome? *(Interviews; Documents)*
2. What was the reform or decision-making process? *(Interviews; Documents)*

Institutions

3. What are the general patterns for education decision-/policy-making? *(Secondary Sources/Informants; Interviews)*
4. Which set of actors* were involved in this particular decision-/policy-making process? *(Interviews; Documents)*
5. What institutional arrangements define the particular character of unionization (particularly teachers) in this case? *(Secondary Sources/Informants/Interviews)*

Actors[1]

6. PERCEPTIONS: What were the actors' perceptions of the policy problem or proposed policy?[2] *(Interviews; Documents)*
7. PREFERENCES: What were the actors' preferences regarding the proposed policy? *(Interviews; Documents)*
8. INTERACTION ORIENTATIONS: What were the actors' interaction orientations? *(Interviews)*
9. CAPACITY: How did the teachers' unions approach interest aggregation and representation? *(Interviews/Informants)*

Appendix II

Finland Interview Schedule[3]

Background
- How long have you been in your current position?
- What are your major responsibilities?
- What are the biggest challenges you face (have faced) in your current position?
- What are the biggest challenges in terms of teachers' compensation (present and future)?
- How would you describe your (organization's) goals?
- What are the most significant challenges to achieving your goals?

Reform Overview
- Describe the reform.

Process of Development
- Can you talk about the evolution of the teachers' salary system?
  - What would you describe as the key 'driver'/cause of the new components of the salary system?
  - What impact have these changes had? How have they evolved over time?

Actors
- Who was involved in the negotiation/development process?

Typical Negotiation Process
- From your perspective (in your particular role), describe the negotiation process.
- What happens when there is a disagreement at the negotiating table (generally)?

Relationships

- What are the relationships like between (your organization) and (other organization(s))?

Perceptions and Preferences

- Why were these components needed?
- Or what 'problem' did they propose to solve?
  o What evidence or models did (proponents) of (various components) point to as support for these policies?
  o How did (opponents) respond to this evidence?

- What did you want when it came to these developments?
  o When the changes were first proposed, what was (your/your organization's) initial reaction?
  o Is/was your organization/your members happy with these changes?

Conflict and Compromise

- What was your/their response at the negotiating table?
- How were the differences eventually resolved?

Intraorganizational Dynamics

- How do you communicate with your members (union members/municipalities) to ensure that you are representing their interests well?
  o *I can imagine that given the differences/diversity, municipalities/teachers may want very different things. How do you identify common goals in OVTES negotiations?*
  o *Who do you work with (at your organization) to develop (your organization's) goals and strategies regarding negotiations?*
- Many have said that the OAJ is a very strong influence in education and if they oppose something it will not happen. Would you agree with this?
- What would you identify as the key to overcoming OAJ opposition in this instance?

Appendix III

Zürich Interview Schedule

Background
- How long have you been in your current position?
- What are your major responsibilities?
- What are the biggest challenges you face (have faced) in your current position?
- What are the biggest challenges in terms of teachers' compensation (present and future)?
- How would you describe your (organization's) goals?
- What are the most significant challenges to achieving your goals?

Reform Overview
- Describe the MAB system/reform.

Process of Development
- Can you talk about the evolution of the MAB system?
  - *What would you describe as the key 'driver'/cause of the MAB system?*
  - *What impact have these changes had? How have they evolved over time?*

Actors
- Who was involved in the negotiation/development process?

Typical Negotiation Process
- From your perspective (in your particular role), describe the negotiation process?
- What happens when there is a disagreement at the negotiating table (generally)?

Relationships

- What are the relationships like between (your organization) and (other organization(s))?

Perceptions and Preferences

- Why were these components needed?
- Or what 'problem' did they propose to solve?
  o *What evidence or models did (proponents) of (various components) point to as support for these policies?*
  o *How did (opponents) respond to this evidence?*
- What did you want when it came to these developments?
  o *When the changes were first proposed, what was (your/your organization's) initial reaction?*
  o *Is/was your organization/your members happy with these changes?*

Conflict and Compromise

- What was your/their response at the negotiating table?
- How were the differences eventually resolved?

Intraorganizational Dynamics

- How do you communicate with your members (union members/municipalities) to ensure that you are representing their interests well?
  o *I can imagine that given the differences/diversity, municipalities/teachers may want very different things. How do you identify common goals for the ZLV?*
  o *Who do you work with (at your organization) to develop (your organization's) goals and strategies regarding negotiations?*
- Is the ZLV strong? How or why are they influential?
- What would you identify as the key to overcoming ZLV opposition in this instance?

Appendix IV
Finland Interviews and Informant Contacts

Interviewees are listed by code and their relevant experience and key involvements are described. Collectively, the experiences of the 16 interviewees ranged from national negotiations (TUPO) to individual municipality negotiations, and union representatives were involved in all levels of union governance. In addition to these interviewees, 15 informants provided background and contextual knowledge of the Finnish case. Informants included:

- academic researchers (7),
- National Board of Education members (2),
- a representative of the employers' association (1),
- national-level OAJ employees (2),
- local participants (3—principal, shop steward, employer).
- The researcher also conducted four school visits.

Interviewees

AKAVA.Negotiator: Worked as a lawyer at AKAVA for 28 years; chief negotiator for AKAVA from 2000–2009.

KT.Social_Scientist: Worked at KT from 2000 and was involved in the design and implementation of the KUNPAS study as well as negotiations from 2000–present.

KT.Negotiator.1: Retired from KT in 2002; served as one of the lead negotiators in the education sector. *(in writing)*

KT.Negotiator.2: Negotiator in the education sector 2002–present. *(in writing)*

Local_A.Employer: Responsible for Basic Education in Local A. No longer conducts negotiations with the union (that function has been moved to Human Resources) but conducted negotiations in 2007 when reforms were implemented.

Local_A.Shop_Steward: Chief negotiator for Local A union.

Local_A.Union_Leader: Serves on Valtuusto and the Executive Council as a representative of Local A.

Local_B.Employer: Negotiator for Local B. (Human Resources Department)

Local_B.President: Local B President, but also serves on Valtuusto, the Executive Council, and holds a number of other leadership positions.

Local_B.Shop_Steward: One of two negotiators for Local B union since 2009; served as shop steward previously.

Local_C.Shop_Steward: Negotiator for Local C union; has served as shop steward from 2011.

Local_C.Union_Leader: Has been involved in the local union for twenty years; serves on Valtuusto; is a principal.

OAJ.President: Union president since 2010; worked as a manager at the union since 2007.

OAJ.Negotiator.1: Has worked as a negotiator at OAJ since 2002; chief shop steward (*Neuvottelupäällikkö*) since 2010.

OAJ.Negotiator.2: Works at the central organization; supports local shop stewards in decentralized negotiations.

OAJ.Social_Scientist: Worked at the OAJ since 2000; counterpart to KT.Social_Scientist.

Appendix V
Zürich Interviews and Informant Contacts

Interviewees are listed by code and their relevant experience and key involvements are described. In addition to these interviewees, 13 informants provided background and contextual knowledge of the Swiss case. Informants included: academic researchers (12) and one teacher. The researcher also conducted a school visit.

Interviewees

Ernst Buschor: Member of the Executive Council from 1993; Education Director from 1995 through the early 2000's.

Jean-Jacques Bertschi: Member of Parliament; member of the 1990 working group that produced the Rose Book; expert designer of the MAB system.

Martin Wendelspiess: Head of the VSA, early 1990s–present; collaborator on 1990 and 1997 developments; responsible for implementation.

LCH.Leader: One of the founders of LCH in 1989; head of the Pedagogical Institute through the 1990s; developer of the FQS system.

ZLV.Leader: Current President; member of the union since 1990s.

SekZH.Leader: Leader 1994–present. (*provided written responses in German*)

Appendix VI
School District Selection

The set of districts from which the sample districts were selected was the 18 districts in the state of Texas and 14 districts in Florida that were among the 100 largest districts in the United States for the 2006–2007 school year (National Center for Education Statistics, 2008).[4] The characteristics—enrollment, percentage of students economically disadvantaged,[5] and percentage of non-white students[6]—of population samples is represented in Table VI.i.

Table VI.i Population sample statistics, Texas and Florida districts

	INTERVIEWEE CODE	ROLE	STATUS
DISTRICT.1FL	SUPER1.1FL	Superintendent (2005–2007)	Interviewed
	SUPER2.1FL	Superintendent (2007–present)	Unavailable for Interview
	CO.1FL	Human Resources Officer	Written Correspondence
	OA.1FL	Outside Consultant	Interviewed
	SB1.1FL	School Board Member	Interviewed
	SB2.1FL	School Board Member	Interviewed
	Union_Leader.1FL	Union President	Refused Interview (multiple people contacted—organizational refusal)
DISTRICT.2FL	Superintendent.2FL	Superintendent	Declined Interview
	Central_Office.2FL	Human Resources Director	Interviewed
	School_Board1.2FL	School Board Member	Interviewed
	School_Board2.2FL	School Board Member	Unable to Secure Interview
	Union_Leader.2FL	Union Leader	Interviewed

(*Continued*)

Table VI.i (Continued)

	INTERVIEWEE CODE	ROLE	STATUS
DISTRICT.3FL	Superintendent.3FL	Superintendent	Interviewed
	Central_Office.3FL	Human Resources Officer	Interviewed
	School_Board1.3FL	School Board Member	Interviewed
	School_Board2.3FL	School Board Member	Interviewed
	School_Board3.3FL	School Board Member	Interviewed
	Union_Leader.3FL	Union Leader	Unable to Interview
DISTRICT.4TX	Superintendent.4TX	Superintendent	Interviewed
	Central_Office.4TX	Central Office Staffer	Interviewed
	School_Board1.4TX	School Board Member	Interviewed
	School_Board2.4TX	School Board Member	Interviewed
	Union_Leader1.4TX	Union Leader	Unavailable/Refused
	Union_Leader2.4TX	Union Leader	Written Correspondence
DISTRICT.5TX	Superintendent.5TX	Superintendent	Interviewed
	Central_Office.5TX	Associate Superintendent	Interviewed
	School_Board1.5TX	School Board Member	Interviewed
	School_Board2.5TX	School Board Member	Interviewed
	Union_Leader.5TX	Union Leader	Written Correspondence
DISTRICT.6TX	Superintendent.6TX	Superintendent	Interviewed
	Central_Office1.6TX	Administrator	Interviewed
	Central_Office2.6TX	Administrator	Interviewed
	School_Board1.6TX	School Board Member	Not Interviewed
	School_Board2.6TX	School Board Member	Not Interviewed
	Union_Leader.6TX	Union Leader	Interviewed

Source: Enrollment data comes from the National Center for Education Statistics (2008). The percentage of the student population that is non-white (PerMin) and the percentage of students economically disadvantaged (PerFRL) comes from the Florida Department of Education (2007b). All data is based on the 2006–2007 school year.

As outlined in Table VI.i, the smallest district in the Texas sample population enrolls 48,334 students, the largest enrolls 203,000, and the mean of the 18 districts is 76,402 students. Sixteen of the eighteen districts enroll fewer than 100,000 students, with two districts that are almost twice as large as the third largest. The adjusted mean for the cluster of sixteen districts below 100,000 students is 63,695.

In Florida, the smallest district enrolls 52,012 students, the largest enrolls 354,000, and the mean of the 14 districts is 134,810. Twelve of the fourteen districts enroll fewer than 200,000 students, with two districts that are twice or three times as large as the mean, and three to four times as large as the median.

In Texas, the percentage of economically disadvantaged students ranges from 19.6–94.5% with a mean of 55.7% and a standard deviation of 24.5%. The percentage of minority students ranges from 27.3–99.4% with a mean of 73.8% and a standard deviation of 20.5%. In Florida, the percentage of economically disadvantaged students ranges from 29.7–59% with a mean of 44.2% and a standard deviation of 9.6%. The percentage of minority students ranges from 29–90.6% with a mean of 52.6% and a standard deviation of 17.3%. Within the population samples in both Texas and Florida, there is not a simple or direct relationship between the enrollment in the district and the percentage of economically disadvantaged or minority students.

Appendix VII

Interviews for US Cases

INTERVIEW SELECTION AND EXECUTION

Table VII.i School district interviewees

		TEXAS DISTRICTS			FLORIDA DISTRICTS		
		Enrollment	PerMin	PerFRL	Enrollment	PerMin	PerFRL
N	Valid	18	18	18	14	14	14
	Missing	0	0	0	0	0	0
Mean		76402	73.7944	55.7111	134810	52.5071	44.2286
Median		62056	74.1500	56.1500	101360	52.6000	42.3000
Std. Deviation		4.08833E4	2.04593E1	2.44909E1	88217	1.72807E1	9.63057
Variance		1.671E9	419.582	599.802	7.782E9	299.624	74.487
Range		155000	71.10	75.90	302000	61.60	29.30
Minimum		48334	27.30	19.60	52012	29.00	29.70
Maximum		203000	99.40	94.50	354000	90.60	59.00
Percentiles	25	52548	59.8250	33.4000	66230	35.8500	41.1750
	50	62056	74.1500	56.1500	101360	52.6000	42.3000
	75	82252	92.5000	79.7750	179810	65.8250	50.1750

District.1FL Interview Summary

Two stakeholders were unavailable to be interviewed—Superintendent2.1FL and Union_Leader.1FL. Although Superintendent2.1FL was unavailable to be interviewed, Central_Office.1FL was interviewed in order to supplement the other interviews and provide more insight into the operations, strategies, and processes surrounding the implementation of PRP in District.1FL. Additionally, both board members' tenure spanned both superintendents and so they were able to provide insight into the leadership styles and strategies of both superintendents.

Union_Leader.1FL never responded to any attempts to arrange an interview—even referrals from other district stakeholders were unsuccessful. Other union personnel and staffers were then contacted and a few responded and implied that they would participate. In the end, they said that they could not speak to the interviewer until they received organizational clearance—which they apparently never received. Although it would have been ideal to speak with someone at the union, it is very clear that they were an important collaborative partner based on the other interviews conducted. Because of the degree of collaboration, many of the stakeholders appeared to know Union_Leader.1FL well and spoke very highly of her and her leadership of the union. The consistency of these accounts suggests their reliability.

District.2FL Interview Summary

The superintendent was unavailable to be interviewed. He had recently left the district for a new job and his new employer would not allow him be interviewed. Central_Office.2FL was interviewed as a 'functional equivalent' in order to gain insight into the district's practices and strategies.

At the time of interviewing, there had recently been a school board election in District.2FL. Several of the board members retired, leaving only two board members on the board who had served during the period (2006–2009) in question. The second board member was unavailable for an interview. However, the consistency of responses across all stakeholders suggests that the information gained from the school board member interviewed—as well as other stakeholders—is reliable.

District.3FL Interview Summary

Union_Leader.3FL—the executive director of the local union, who had served in the position for 37 years—died in 2008. He presided throughout the reform process in question and was a stable leader: he was described as politically astute, with a long history of working in the county, including a very cordial working relationship with the superintendent (Central_Office.3FL). However, the picture that emerges is one in which the union worked more closely with the school board than the superintendent.

The union experienced a period of significant transition after Union_Leader.3FL's death. Before a new official executive director was hired, there were two interim executive directors who served for short stints—each with his own style (School_Board2.3FL). In contrast to the collaborative work that was described by School_Board1.3FL as standard for the district, the interim executive directors came in with their own styles and a "much more demanding posture," which was described as a huge setback (School_Board2.3FL). Because of these events, a 'functional equivalent' for Union_Leader.3FL was not available. A third school board member was interviewed because of complex dynamics between the school board and superintendent.

District.4TX Interview Summary

Of the two large unions in District.4TX, one leader—despite saying that she would be willing to provide information—was unwilling to participate in this research. However, Union_Leader2.4TX described the union's role in the district as being fairly limited—which appears to be true of the state as a whole, as confirmed by Union_Leader.5TX and Union_Leader.6TX. So while interviewing Union_Leader1.4TX would have been preferred, concern over incomplete information is minimal.

District.5TX Interview Summary

All identified key stakeholders were available and willing to participate in this research. Union_Leader.5TX was hesitant to commit time to an interview but provided a written statement outlining the union's limited role in the district policy-making process.

District.6TX Interview Summary

Superintendent.6TX requested that school board members not be interviewed. Because the decision to not participate in the DATE grant was a fairly centralized process—and appears to not have involved the board—this situation, although not preferable, does not call the information provided by the interviewed stakeholders into question.

Appendix VIII

General School District Interview Guide

Background
- How long have you been in your current position?
- What are your major responsibilities?
- How long have you been [in the capacity that you are currently in] OR for what time period did you serve in [x capacity]?

Reform Overview
- Describe the plan that you developed.

Process of Development
- Describe the process through which PRP became a point of discussion.
- Who would you say was most instrumental in moving discussion of PRP forward?
- Can you describe the process through which consensus was reached about the plan's design and potential implementation?
- What impact have these changes had? How have they evolved over time?

Actors
- Who were the major actors involved in designing the plan? (Or the decision to not design a plan.)
- Were there any (other) groups who you would identify as key players in the decision to implement/not implement PRP?
    - *Did parents participate in or influence the decision to (not) attempt PRP?*
    - *On the whole, would you say that your district has actively engaged parents?*
    - *So was their (un)involvement in the decision for/against PRP higher/lower than or about on par with typical parent engagement?*
    - *Was there a general sense of support, opposition, or neutrality in terms of public opinion?*

Typical Negotiation Process

- From your perspective (in your role), describe the negotiation process.
  - *(TX) Since you don't have collective bargaining, in what, if any, ways are unions involved in discussions about policy?*
  - *(FL) Outside of the collective bargaining process, how are unions included in policy discussions?*
  - *(FL) How often does the collective bargaining stall or require arbitration?*

Relationships

- Describe the working relationship between the union and district.
  - *How would you describe/characterize the union president?*
  - *How would you describe the superintendent?*
  - *How would you describe the school board?*
  - *How often do you meet/collaborate with them?*

Perceptions and Preferences

- What actors or groups of actors were interested in potentially implementing PRP? Why?
- What actors or groups of actors were opposed to PRP or had significant reservations? What were these reservations?
- When it comes to PRP, how would you describe your position?
  - *What are your major goals? (Or, in an ideal world, how would a discussion about implementing PRP end?)*
  - *What are your major reservations?*
  - *Did you have any goals or requirements that were absolutely non-negotiable? (Did you perceive that 'they' had any goals or requirements that were absolutely non-negotiable?)*
  - *What did you perceive to be 'their' major goals/reservations?*
  - *When the changes were first proposed, what was [your/your organization's] initial reaction?*
  - *How satisfied were you with the final plan?*

Conflict and Compromise

- What, if any, challenges/conflicts arose during the decision-making/planning/implementation process?
  - *How were any challenges/conflicts resolved?*
  - *What compromises, if any, were made between these groups' original goals and the final plan?*
- What would you identify as the key to overcoming opposition in this instance?

Financial Context

- What role did financial considerations play in the decisions to participate/not participate in the state's PRP program? (incentive to participate/disincentive/no effect)
  - *If you had not been experiencing financial strain, do you think that you would have made the same decision?*
  - *If not for [whatever reason was given for financial disincentives], do you think that the district would have opted to participate?*
- Over the course of your time working with the school district, how limiting were/have financial considerations (been)?
- Based on your experiences and your knowledge of other districts, would you say that your district has more, fewer, or about the same amount of resources as other districts in your state?

If the District Opted Not to Participate

- In your opinion, what factors were the most influential in the decision to not pursue a PRP plan/policy?

NOTES

1. Emphasis was initially on two groups of actors—teachers' organizations and policy-makers. However, the inquiry remained open to the presence of other significant actors.
2. Hypotheses, known facts, idiosyncrasies
3. The questions would be tailored to the role/knowledge of the interview and evolved over time.
4. This year was selected because the first state PRP policies investigated in this thesis (MAP, which was preceded by STAR and DATE) were passed during the 2006–2007 school year.
5. Represented by those students eligible for Free or Reduced Price Lunch (FRL) a federal meal subsidy program.
6. Or 'minority students'—even though in some districts, a non-white subgroup is *not* the mathematical minority.

Index

accountability 15–16, 27, 31, 261
actor-centered 5, 47
AKAVA 97–8
A Nation at Risk 14, 16
Arter, D. 32, 96
attitudinal bargaining 52–4, 260; *see also* interaction orientation; modes of interaction; relational pattern
Armstrong, M. 20
autonomy: of teachers 16, 165; of municipalities/regions: 89, 99, 137

Bacarro, L. 31, 255
Ball, S. J. 15, 17, 19
Bascia, N. 23, 67, 188–9
Bascia, N. & Rottmann, C. 189
Basic Education Act 90
Berkman, M. B. & Plutzer, E. 65, 205
Bertschi, Jean-Jacques 145, 147, 152, 159
Buschor, Ernst 134–6, 153, 158–61

case study 60–1
causality 64, 69, 196–7; causal equifinality 180, 185; causal mechanisms 4, 48, 67, 181; causal pathways 64, 186, 193
Cawson, A. 31–3
Chubb, J. E. & Moe, T. M. 24–5
codetermination 30, 257; *see also* social partnership
cognitive capacity *see* internal capacity
collective bargaining 24, 28–9, 56, 190–1; in Finland 85, 98–9, 109–110; in the US: 65–6, 191, 207–8
Collier, D. 60

comparison 68, 70, 78; international 68–9; iterative: 69; subnational 67–8, 205
compromise 29, 32, 180, 186–7, 192–4, 246, 257–9, 261
Compston, H. 32, 52, 255
Compton, M. & Weiner, L. 16, 184, 258
concertation 31–3, 255, 259
consensus 56, 87, 109, 256; democracy 95–7; orientation 140–3, 256
consociationalism 137, 140–1
consultation 66, 85–6, 96–7, 140–3, 170–3
contingent generalizations 65, 69
convergence 18–19
cooperation 29, 35, 54–5, 97, 125–8, 186, 194, 255–6, 259, 262
corporatism 30–1, 193–4, 246–7, 255–9; *see also* codetermination; social partnership
crucial cases 6, 47, 61; selection of 63–4, 65–9, 205–10
Culpepper, P. D. 32, 256

decentralization 17, 18; of collective bargaining: 98, 143; in Finland 87, 89–91, 98–9, 110, 130–1; in Switzerland 137; in the United States 184 (*see also* school districts)
direct democracy 137–41, 146–7, 171; within the ZLV 165
distributive bargaining 28–30, 257–8, 260
distrust 236, 257, 260; of compromise 259
Duncan, Arne 3, 257

elite interviews 72–5
evaluative capacity *see* internal capacity

federalism 135–8, 205
Fisher, R. & Ury, W. L. 56
Freeman, R. B. & Medoff, J. L. 25, 28–9, 193; monopoly face 25; voice face 28–9, 33

George, A. L. & Bennett, A. 6–7, 47–8, 60–5, 70–77
Gerring, J. 61
global education reform movement (GERM) 15, 19, 185
Goldhaber, D. 3, 37
Gunderson, M. 30, 57, 193

Hall, P. A. & Soskice, D. 32
Hanushek, E. 25
Harvey, D. 5, 17
Hoxby, C. 4, 23

Immergut, E. 35, 138–41, 189, 197, 253
incentives 15, 20, 112–13, 227, 236, 253
individualism 24, 28, 33
industrialization 17, 87–8, 97, 136
integrative bargaining 29, 52, 124–5, 193, 260–1
interaction orientation 54, 113–14, 121–3; *see also* modes of interaction; relational preference
interest groups 35, 70, 95–6, 139–43; Interest Group Theory 26–8, 53, 188
internal capacity 52–3, 122–3, 162–5
intraorganizational bargaining 52–3

järjestelyerä 86, 107–8
Johnson, S. M. & Donaldson, M. 67
Johnson, S. M. & Kardos, S. 67, 191
Johnson, S. M. & Papay, J. 21

Kahlenberg, R. 23, 192, 207
Katzenstein, P. J. 32–3, 52, 69–70, 141
Kaufman, B. E. 25, 28–9, 189
Kerchner, C. & Koppich, J. E. 23, 32, 194, 256
Kerchner, C., Koppich, J. E. & Weeres, J. G. 253
Kerchner, C. & Mitchell, D. E. 50
King, G., Keohane, R. & Verba, S. 64

Koppich, J. E. 4, 23, 259
Konkordanz 140, 171
Kunnallinen Työmarkkinalaitos (KT) 86, 98, 103, 112–13
KUNPAS 103–8, 112–13; local money 117–18; role of compromise 125; significance of collaboration 128–9
Kussi, P. 88
KVTES 98–9, 109, 129

Layder, D. 57, 72, 75
Lazear, E. P. 21, 22
LCH 143, 145–6, 252
Levin, B. 14, 17
Lijphart, A. 69, 95, 141, 194
local negotiations 110, 119, 130, 191

MAB 6, 134–6, 151–3
magic formula 141–2
merit pay 74, 207, 217
modes of interaction 56
Moe, T. 188, 193, 203; *Special Interests* 3; on compromise 257–8; the politics of blocking 24–6, 206, 252–3
Moravcsik, A. 50
Murnane, R. J. & Cohen, D. K. 22, 217

Niemi, H. 89, 92–3, 185
neoliberalism 13, 16–9, 184–5
New Public Management 16–19, 134–6, 165–9, 175

OAJ 85–6, 91–2; collaboration and compromise 125–8; preferences 114–121; strategy 123–5; structure of 93–7, 121–3
OECD 15
Olson, Mancur 26–7, 31
OVTES 99, 109, 113

Parsons, T. 30, 35
Pawlenty, Tim 1
peak associations 97–8
perceptions 51–2, 57, 114–20, 162–3, 227, 239, 244, 255
performance-related pay 14, 19, 61–3, 218–19
performativity *see* GERM
Pesonen, P. & Riihinen, O. 88–9
Pierson, P. 17
Podgursky, M. J. & Springer, M. G. 20–1, 217

policy entrepreneur 15, 182
policy epidemic 17
Poole, W. L. 33, 50, 252
power 5; consensus-based 35; contingency of 6, 35, 191, 195, 253–4
preferences: change over time 120; complex and competing 28, 51, 114, 123–5, 212, 247, 252–5; differences across members 6, 53, 120–3; short/long-term 114, 125, 129, 186, 237, 252
Prentice, Graham, Burgess, Simon, & Popper, Carol 20
professionalism 15–16, 22–3, 30–3, 50–2, 165, 184, 252; in Finland 91–3, 193; in Switzerland 144–5
public sector reform 14, 110

Ragin, C. C. 6, 61, 64, 247
raises 86, 95, 103–7
rational choice theory 27, 47–9, 57, 195
Reber, K. 136, 168
recession 129–30, 219–20
referenda 137–41, 146
reform leadership 181–2, 185
relational pattern 54, 192–5, 255–6; see also interaction orientation; modes of interaction
relational preferences 33, 180, 186–7
retrenchment 18
Rhee, Michelle 2–3
Rhodes, M. 31

Sahlberg, P. 89, 91, 93–4, 185
salary freeze 152, 157, 169
salary structure 86, 104, 216–17

Scharpf, F. W. 33, 136, 189, 194–5; actor-centered 5, 47
Schedler, K. 136, 167
school districts 205–6, 212–14
Simola, H. 17, 185
Simola, H., Rinne, R. & Kivirauma, J. 17, 90–1
social partnership 30, 51, 194, 257
subsidiarity see federalism

tactically clever solutions 95, 114, 123–5, 246
teacher evaluations 21, 152–3, 160, 187
teachers' unions: interests 1, 24–33, 227, 241; power 23–4, 35–6, 253; preferences 33, 47, 49–54, 57, 123–4, 164, 188–9, 189–92, 252; strength 24, 34–5, 70
trade unions in Switzerland 142–4
tripartite agreements (TUPO) 85, 96–8, 112
trust 53, 171, 185, 193; 260; culture of 90; in school districts 225, 229, 232; within the union 122
Tucker, M. 31
TVA 86, 106

Urban, W. J. 36, 192, 253

VALPAS 111, 129

wage cuts 91, 157, 160
Walton, R. E. & McKersie, R. B. 5, 28–9, 52–5, 127, 193, 229, 258–61
welfare state 13, 17–18, 86–9, 96–8

ZLV 135, 144–6

For Product Safety Concerns and Information please contact our EU representative GPSR@taylorandfrancis.com
Taylor & Francis Verlag GmbH, Kaufingerstraße 24, 80331 München, Germany

www.ingramcontent.com/pod-product-compliance
Lightning Source LLC
Chambersburg PA
CBHW052213300426
44115CB00011B/1671